European Foreign
Policies

Europe Today
Series Editor: Ronald Tiersky

European Foreign Policies

Does Europe Still Matter?

Edited by
Ronald Tiersky and
John Van Oudenaren

ROWMAN & LITTLEFIELD PUBLISHERS, INC.
Lanham • Boulder • New York • Toronto • Plymouth, UK

Published by Rowman & Littlefield Publishers, Inc.
A wholly owned subsidiary of The Rowman & Littlefield Publishing Group, Inc.
4501 Forbes Boulevard, Suite 200, Lanham, Maryland 20706
http://www.rowmanlittlefield.com

Estover Road, Plymouth PL6 7PY, United Kingdom

British Library Cataloguing in Publication Information Available

Library of Congress Cataloging-in-Publication Data

European foreign policies : does Europe still matter? / edited by Ronald Tiersky
and John Van Oudenaren.
    p. cm. — (Europe today)
  Includes bibliographical references and index.
  ISBN 978-0-7425-5778-9 (cloth : alk. paper) — ISBN 978-0-7425-5779-6
(pbk. : alk. paper) — ISBN 978-0-7425-5780-2 (electronic : alk. paper)
  1. Europe—Foreign relations—21st century. 2. European Union countries—
Foreign relations—21st century. I. Tiersky, Ronald, 1944- II. Van Oudenaren,
John.
  D2025.E895 2010
  327.4—dc22
                            2010009087

∞ ™ The paper used in this publication meets the minimum requirements of
American National Standard for Information Sciences—Permanence of Paper
for Printed Library Materials, ANSI/NISO Z39.48-1992

Printed in the United States of America

Contents

Preface

At the core of this book are persistent questions about the future of Europe. Europe could be more of a powerhouse in the world order. Why isn't it? Europe ought to shoulder more of the responsibility for world peace and security. Why doesn't it? Europeans ought to see that their own interest is to seek greater international influence and stronger global commitments. Why don't they?

The purpose of this book is to provide the geopolitical and historical background necessary to understand Europe's international influence in the twenty-first century. For teachers, the book is suitable as a stand-alone textbook for a course in European or comparative foreign policy. It can also be combined with our more general *Europe Today* textbook as the basis of a yearlong course in two semesters. We hope that our academic colleagues and general readers as well will also find the book useful.

The book takes a long view and a wide perspective. It combines chapters on the most foreign policy–active European countries and on the European Union's foreign policy with broader chapters on Europe's relations with the United States, Russia, China, and the Middle East and a chapter on Europe and globalization.

Europe's nation-states and peoples live today in a world order much different from the eighteenth and nineteenth centuries, when Europe was the core of world geopolitical power and international economic and financial relations. One reason for the decline was the Old Continent's self-destruction in the unprecedented bloody wars of the twentieth century. A second reason was the simultaneous emergence of new great powers, first the United States and the Soviet Union, more recently China, and, increasingly, countries such as India and Brazil. Europe today is in some respects a regional power in the global international system. But if that is true, primarily in geostrategic terms, it's also the case that Europe's geographic reach and geopolitical weight on the Eurasian continent have increased with the European Union's massive enlargement from its original six member states in 1958 to twenty-seven in 2009. (Russia, the rump state of the collapsed Soviet Union, has been most affected by the European Union's expansion.) And in a globalized economic and financial system, the European Union area, with the largest nominal gross domestic product in the world and many of the world's most important financial markets and business corporations, is led back, like it or not, into a competitive international order in which the pursuit of economic self-interest has new foreign policy and geostrategic implications. Geopolitics and geoeconomics are increasingly intertwined aspects of a broader competitive struggle across the globe in which wars between states have become rare but in which trade balances, exchange rates, and even corporate competition have considerable significance in balances of political power.

How the Europeans will do in these intertwined competitions is not at all clear. The historical pendulum of the rise and decline of empires and states is real. The capacity for renewal of old states and for the creation of new political configurations is less so. Europe is the most fascinating case study in this respect. The process of European integration is vitally important to the development of global political civilization because it is a voluntary, that is, democratic, association of countries that realize that theirs has become a common fate. The European Union is not an empire. It might be described as a semistate or, better, a hybrid federation/confederation of nation-states in which national interest and national sovereignty are simultaneously the glue that holds the structure together and the force that pushes back.

The glue holding the European Union together is mainly economic and financial: the single market and the economic and monetary system. Economics is easy, at least compared to politics. National interest in the making of foreign policy is the most powerful force pushing back against integration, partly because national interests are harder to reconcile but ultimately because foreign policy is a matter of strategic ambition and political will in which the psychological desire to take responsibility struggles constantly with the benefits of avoiding effort and sacrifice.

* * *

The editors want to thank—once again—Susan McEachern of Rowman & Littlefield Publishers, who has been such a crucial friend of the entire Europe Today series, including this volume; Alden Perkins, senior production editor at Rowman & Littlefield; and Lilia Kilburn and Nicol Zhou, who prepared the index.

Ronald Tiersky and John Van Oudenaren
Amherst, Massachusetts, and Bethesda, Maryland

1

Introduction

Europe and the Geopolitical Order

Ronald Tiersky

Historically, a country's geography was always the beginning point of its international relations. Geography created a nation's borders, many of its strategic dilemmas, and essential elements of foreign policy national interests. Deceptively simple, this principle does describe much of international affairs in most times and places through the centuries. And in many respects, geopolitics is still the basis of the international system.

Nowhere more than in historical Europe did geography define foreign relations. Where any particular country was found on the map tended to predict its allies, enemies, and friends as well as its patterns of trade and cultural exchange. In Europe, it could be said, geography was destiny.[1]

THE SUBSTANCE OF EUROPEAN GEOPOLITICS

The Historical Legacy

In the nineteenth-century European balance of power, the most powerful countries each had a particular place or role based on geography and economic power from which a national foreign policy strategy was derived. Britain, situated across the English Channel from France, became the offshore balancing power, whose role was to play a game of alternating alliance with the big continental governments so as to preclude any one of them from achieving geopolitical hegemony. Britain, like the other powers in this amoral geopolitical balance, had no permanent friends or enemies. It had only national interests.

1

During much of the nineteenth century, France, even though a declining power after Napoleon's defeat in 1814, appeared very large to its neighbor Germany because the latter was still a disunited congeries of hundreds of principalities. Prussia was the most powerful of these. Guided by the strategic genius of Chancellor Otto von Bismarck, it created, through several wars, the modern German nation-state in the form of the Second Empire in 1871.

Thereafter, the rise of German power was a persistent threat to its geographical neighbors, France first of all. "In a single man's lifetime," the great French leader Charles de Gaulle wrote in his *War Memoirs*, France and Germany had gone to war three times—1870, 1914, and 1940. To the east, Russia's strategic view also had to focus on the threat of German expansionism. Thus, in World War I, Russia allied itself with France and Britain to Germany's west. And once President Woodrow Wilson brought the country into the conflict in 1917, Russia and the United States were allies as well. In World War II, in spite of the Bolshevik Revolution and the advent of Stalinist communism, the Soviet Union joined with Britain and the United States (and also de Gaulle's French Resistance movement) to defeat Germany again, this time the Third Reich.

"The German problem" was at the center of Europe's disasters. In addition to extremist politics, an essential element in the German problem was borders. The Germans themselves spoke of Germany as "the country in the middle" because it had—and still has today—more international borders than any other European country. Borders invite conflict, especially those not the result of clear geographical dividing lines, such as the Pyrenees separating France and Spain. Poland's geopolitical situation was particularly anguishing given that it was caught between fanatically expansionist Germany and expansionist Russia. Not surprisingly, Poland's fate, from the three partitions (1772, 1793, and 1795) to the twentieth century's two world wars, was catastrophic.

Beginning with the first use of the combat airplane in World War I, several centuries of European "continental-domestic" wars were, in the space of only a few decades, engulfed in the emergence of a new era of international relations, the contemporary geostrategic world. Geopolitically based international relations persist, but the recognizable patterns of war and peace, trade and finance, and terrorism and narcotrafficking have been globalized. And in this world of global strategic calculations, patterns of economic strength and weakness, the realm of geoeconomics, have merged with foreign policy in the traditional meaning of the term.

It is in many ways difficult to separate the geostrategic and geoeconomic worlds. A strong national economy was always the basis of an effective foreign policy. Today, a strong national economy of global reach, a geoeconomy, is necessary to any big country's overall success.

During the Cold War that succeeded World War II, rivalry between the United States and the Soviet Union constructed the principal fault lines in international relations. Each was a superpower with global reach.

In World War II, the United States fought separate naval and air wars across the planet against Japan and Nazi Germany. In the following decades, the United States became engaged literally around the world, acting from the Western to the Eastern Hemisphere and from the global North to the global South. The Soviet Union, theoretically a superpower with global reach based on nuclear weapons, was in fact a giant conventional geopolitical power supported by an economy whose fragility was camouflaged by its huge military.

The Soviets in the late 1940s manufactured a Stalinist empire in contiguous Eastern Europe. These Soviet bloc countries formed a strategic buffer between the Soviet Union and Western Europe. Across the Atlantic Ocean, the United States and Western Europe joined in the North Atlantic Treaty Organization (NATO), which was a military and political deterrent that simultaneously protected Western Europe from Moscow and, at least implicitly, threatened the latter. The Soviet bloc regimes were "fraternal" countries, part of an expanding communist bloc (then including China, Vietnam, and other countries) whose ultimate goal, in the communist ideology, was world revolution.

Postwar European Integration and Eurasian Geopolitics

The process of European integration that has gone on now for fifty years represents a major geopolitical achievement. The geographical expansion of the European Union (EU, used here to include all its predecessor institutions as well) has remade the political composition of the European continent and in some ways altered the geopolitics of the broader Eurasian continent through the Russia/Black Sea/Caucasus region heading toward Central Asia.

European integration proper began with the conclusion by six countries of the 1957 Treaty of Rome establishing the European Economic Community (EEC). These countries—France, Germany, Italy, and the three Benelux countries—had previously established the European Coal and Steel Community, which became operational in 1952. Successive enlargements of the EEC produced today's EU in 1992, with the signing of the Treaty on European Union, called the Maastricht treaty. Following the collapse of communism in 1989–1991, the EU took in the liberated Soviet bloc countries, unifying the geographical European continent. This was Europe "whole and free" as then-president George H. W. Bush put it.

Integrating the European countries made sense for four reasons. First, economic recovery and prosperity was needed. The Coal and Steel Community

following on the Marshall Plan launched thirty uninterrupted years of economic growth in Western Europe. Second, the new West Germany, initially
mistrusted because it was the successor (with East Germany) to the Third
Reich, became firmly anchored in democratic Western Europe, and its own
new democratic system was guaranteed against extremist forces. Third, the
integration of Western Europe and American military protection deterred
the Soviet Union from expansion. Fourth, development of the EU's internal
economic market in the 1990s increased Europe's economic and financial
competitiveness in the age of globalization.

Just as it was during the Cold War, Europe's most significant international
security problem today is Russia. For one thing, the durability of Europe's
"Russia problem" is the paradoxical result of the success of EU enlargement,
which has put the EU's eastern frontier directly on Russia's western border.
From Moscow's point of view, not only is Russia's Cold War security buffer
gone, but the former Soviet bloc countries are naturally hostile and worried about Russia's geopolitical intentions at a time when Russian domestic
politics revolves around the goal of remaking the country as a great power.
For another thing, the EU-Russia border is also an economic dividing line.
With the exception of Russia's few wealthy cities such as Moscow and St.
Petersburg, Russian per capita gross domestic product lags behind the living
standards even in most of the relatively poor postcommunist EU countries.
For Russians—not only its leaders but also many of the Russian people—this
situation is felt as a constant humiliation of the former superpower.

Nevertheless, unlike the Soviet period, EU-Russia problems today do not
involve military threats. For example, despite Moscow's protests, even the
U.S. plan to install an antimissile system in the Czech Republic and Poland
against the vague future threat of an Iranian missile attack, proposed by
the George W. Bush administration and subsequently abandoned by the
Obama administration, represented no military danger to Russia. Russian
leaders rejected the implicit geopolitical intimidation involved ("you can't
stop us") that was reminiscent of Russia's own attempt at intimidating
Western Europeans through missile deployments in the so-called European
missile crisis of 1979–1983.

For EU countries, there is also a threat of intimidation that is political,
not military. Russia's brief and in Europe unexpected war with Georgia in
2008 was a military operation to be sure, but Moscow could hardly con-
template a war against the EU area—if only because the EU area is also the
NATO area. What EU governments worry about is Russian exploitation of
its position as a major supplier of natural gas. Moscow assures Europe that
Russia will always be a reliable energy supplier. Yet deliveries of natural gas
have been interrupted several times in the past few years because of conflicts between Russia and Ukraine, which is the major transit country for

gas pipelines. The larger issue is that Moscow wants to discipline Ukraine because it is the last bulwark in Russia's former sphere of geopolitical influence. If Ukraine could completely get out from under Moscow's influence, perhaps by joining NATO, the Russian obsession with great-power status would suffer a mortal blow.

In the long run, Russia's position is weaker than the EU's. Europe is its major export market. Russia must sell its oil and gas because energy exports are, unfortunately for the Russians, the main success of the entire economy. Thus, a weakened Russia must operate a delicate foreign policy balancing act in which it might lose either by an excess of cleverness or by not enough cleverness and subtlety in its dealings with Western Europe. On the EU side, major importing countries, above all Germany, which is the EU's largest economy, must avoid fighting among each other over policy toward Russia if Moscow attempts to divide and conquer by trying to reward those who cooperate and punish the others.

Caught in its relations with the EU, in a larger framework Moscow wants to avoid being completely encircled and politically isolated by a semihostile EU and NATO in the West and by its incompatibilities with Iran, India, and above all China in the East. During the Cold War, it was rightly said that Russia "had no friends." Moscow could conceivably end up in the same situation in the twenty-first century.

The EU and the Union for the Mediterranean

In July 2008, following a French initiative, a so-called Union for the Mediterranean (UM) was created, one of the EU's many partnership arrangements beyond its borders. The UM is an economic, commercial, and political treaty that encompasses the EU with North African and Middle Eastern countries in a kind of circle around the Mediterranean coast.

While not much more than a sketch at the present time, a European geopolitical intent is evident. The EU and UM are overlapping circles that bring poorer and less stable countries inside a framework designed to stimulate economic development and democratic evolution in North Africa and the Middle East. There is basically no prospect of EU membership for these countries, but the fact of a privileged relationship with the EU that brings economic benefits and political inclusion may incite some illiberal governments to evolve. The strategy, in other words, is much the same as the EU's eastern enlargement of 2004 minus actual EU membership. In the long term, a geopolitical imagination could envision an overlapping of the EU, the UM, and the African Union as one regional network in an emerging global governance system. As attractive as this might look on a map, however, any resemblance to reality is a long way off.

The EU and NATO

The post–Cold War EU enlargement was related to the similar expansion in NATO's membership. This so-called double enlargement increased NATO's membership from nineteen to twenty-eight and the EU's membership from fifteen to twenty-seven. NATO's eastern enlargements, beginning in 1999, preceded the EU's "big bang" eastern enlargement in 2004 that brought in the post–Soviet bloc Central and Eastern European countries (CEE). Bringing those countries inside NATO, which meant that the United States was their ultimate security guarantee, was a simple matter compared to all the domestic political and economic changes the much less developed CEE countries had to make in order to meet EU membership requirements.

EU membership can complement NATO membership, anchoring a particular state more fully in the West and out of Russia's reach, or in certain cases can be an alternative to it. As of 2009, twenty-one countries belong to both the EU and NATO, and several others are members of one or the other. (The case of Turkey, a longstanding bulwark of NATO that has long sought EU membership, is the most important and difficult case of this category.)

Whenever NATO or EU membership is a dangerous proposition for a particular country, membership of one plus a special association with the other can be a politically workable solution, with concern for Moscow's reaction being an obvious issue. For example, Russia might be willing to concede Ukraine's and Georgia's joining the EU because Russia's economic and political interest is to see that EU governments do not regard Russia as a permanent adversary. On the other hand, Russia would consider NATO membership for Ukraine, the most important remaining non-NATO country in Russia's "near abroad," as a strategically aggressive action by the West.

Europe and the United States

The influence of the United States in European affairs has been a perennial combination of advantages and disadvantages for the Europeans. During the Cold War, there were several episodes of semi-independent European foreign policy, such as the de Gaulle presidency in France in 1958–1969 and the *Ostpolitik* period in West German foreign policy under Chancellor Willy Brandt in 1969–1972. But on the whole, U.S. protection against Soviet influence limited and at times smothered European attempts at diplomatic autonomy. The Cuban missile crisis of October 1962 was the most telling example. Khrushchev's high-stakes gamble at installing nuclear missiles in Cuba forced even de Gaulle to show his hand: when the chips were down, France stood with the United States. In de Gaulle's view, the

Cuban missile crisis was particularly frustrating because it obliged a choice between East and West, the very choice that de Gaulle's separate détente with Russia had to avoid. For de Gaulle, the missile crisis forced a "return to Yalta," that is, to a stalemated, dependent Europe divided into two blocs each dominated by a superpower.

In the twenty years since the Cold War ended, the old European need for U.S. military protection is gone. Nevertheless, a new European strategic view has been slow to crystallize. A once-necessary dependence all too easily became a kind of addiction. The reality of independence becomes hard to fathom.

Relations between the EU and the United States have evolved somewhat in recent years. Washington used to downplay the EU's foreign policy importance as opposed to bilateral relations with the most important European allies, such as Britain, France, and Germany. Today the United States deals with the EU at the official level but without much pretense that the EU itself is a relevant actor in foreign policy and strategic affairs. Attempts to build an EU Common Foreign and Security Policy have been consistently disappointing. On trips to Brussels, Presidents George W. Bush and Barack Obama made sure to visit EU as well as NATO headquarters, but these are basically courtesy calls.

EUROPEAN FOREIGN POLICY AND EUROPEAN FOREIGN POLICIES

Three Types of Power

In discussing the EU's influence in international politics three types of power can be distinguished: hard power, soft power, and transformative power. The distinction between hard power and soft power is now a staple of international relations thinking.[2] Hard power is coercion, the decision for war or peace or heavy sanctions in the face of international conflict. Hard power, as the Prussian military theorist Carl von Clausewitz said, is the continuation of foreign policy by means other than diplomacy and negotiation. Soft power means influencing other countries to do what you want rather than leaving them no alternative in the face of hostile action. Soft power wins cooperation through the force of attraction and the benefits of co-optation, through the offer of political inclusion and the provision of economic advantages.

In the exercise of hard power, the Europeans have been less ambitious and successful than advocates of European integration have hoped. EU military forces are present, some in combat but most in peacekeeping, policing, and training operations, in several conflicts around the world, such as with NATO in the International Security Assistance Force in Afghanistan and independently on the basis of a UN mandate as in Kosovo. Nevertheless, the EU has failed to emerge as a force to be reckoned with on its own, and by general agreement, European governments have not done enough on their own to build their military capabilities.

Iraq and Afghanistan are the most important cases in point. European governments disagreed violently about supporting the Bush administration's 2003 invasion of Iraq to overthrow Saddam Hussein. Whether or not the Iraq War was justified, the important fact here is that France and Germany rejected the war, as did European public opinion. With the partial exception of Britain, the adequacy of European military participation in stabilizing and rebuilding postwar Iraq has been a constant controversy. European support for the war in Afghanistan to destroy al-Qaeda and to keep the Taliban from regaining power has been similarly controversial, all the more striking in that the Europeans thought that this was a necessary war. The psychological background to Europe's attitude toward the use of military force was suggested in one critic's famous 2003 commentary:

> Europeans insist they approach problems with greater nuance and sophistication. They try to influence others through subtlety and indirection. They are more tolerant of failure, more patient when solutions don't come quickly. They generally favor peaceful responses to problems, preferring negotiation, diplomacy, and persuasion to coercion. They are quicker to appeal to international law, international conventions, and international opinion to adjudicate disputes. . . . They often emphasize process over result, believing that ultimately process can become substance.[3]

However this may be, the EU wields a third type of power that is its particular, more or less unique contribution to international political evolution. This is the power of enlargement and special relationships, a "transformative power" that has produced dramatic political and economic reforms in those countries whose governments want to join the EU and are willing to meet certain hard-to-reach benchmarks necessary to qualify and some reforms also in countries whose governments want the benefits of preferential access to the EU economy and other economic advantages. For membership candidate countries, the benchmarks are stable political institutions guaranteeing democracy, the rule of law, human rights, and protection of minorities; a functioning market economy able to face the competitiveness and standards of the EU single market; and the administrative capacity to implement the entire existing body of EU laws and administrative rules. For countries that want special EU relationships, the pressure to conform is much less strong, but the possibilities of what might be called "positive contamination" are significant over time. "European power," writes the originator of the term "transformative power," "continues to be confused with weakness. . . . The US may have changed the regime in Afghanistan, but Europe is changing all of Polish society, from its economic policies and property laws to its treatment of minorities and what gets served on the nation's tables. . . . Europe doesn't change countries by threatening to invade them: its biggest threat is to cut off contact with them." Europe's transformative power "is the most important development in international relations since the creation of the nation-state."[4]

This is certainly an overstatement, but the fact is that the EU encompasses 500 million people today, with another 150 million people in countries (e.g., Turkey and Ukraine) looking for membership. It is a club of countries that other countries ask to join knowing that the requirements for membership involve difficult reforms at home.

Foreign Policy and Foreign Policies

As the EU developed, the complexities of merging nation-states blurred traditional distinctions between foreign and domestic policies. The case of the EU, where foreign policy begins and domestic policy ends, is even less clear than the case of a traditional sovereign nation-state. The EU's structures also change the traditional connection between foreign policy and domestic structure, as discussed by the realist and liberal internationalist approaches to foreign policy and international relations.

Realist international relations thinking long conceptualized the world order as something like a collection of billiard balls. In the realist view, states are basically hermetic, their integrity guaranteed by national sovereignty. States encounter and bounce off each other in the pursuit of national interests. Normally, the relations between states take the form of diplomacy and negotiation. From time to time, the clash of national interests is serious enough to result in war.

But foreign policy also can be conceived as the projection of domestic society. In this case, at least over the medium and long term, a state's foreign policy is the international expression of the nature of its domestic society.[5] Thus, the liberal internationalist conception of international relations asserts that because of the expansion of democratic government throughout the world, the world order is characterized increasingly by multiple layers of convergent national interests, institutions, and informal networks of "governance" as opposed to the more or less hermetic nation-state.

Europe's role in international affairs today is located at the intersection of realist and liberal internationalist conceptions of how the world order works. The issue is what we mean when we refer to "Europe." On the one hand, Europe today means the EU; on the other hand, Europe means, as it always has, Europe's various nation-states. A third kind of Europe refers to the play of law, bureaucratic administration, and informal political alliance that links nation-states and the EU, that is, the Europe that is implied in the term "European integration." In some ways, Europe remains a hermetic collection of states; in other respects, it is a framework of merged national sovereignties; and in yet another meaning Europe today is actually the interplay of the two. In such a political construction, traditional distinctions between what is domestic and what is foreign are harder than ever to make.

Europe and America

It is obvious that the special influence of U.S. foreign policy on Europe and European foreign policy on the United States needs to be emphasized. Russia may be Europe's greatest security problem, but the United States is Europe's omnipresent political and cultural complication.

For decades, indeed perhaps for a century, the United States has been deeply part of the European psyche. Since World War II, one could even say World War I, the United States has been a European power. Whereas during the Cold War many Europeans felt stifled by the United States, today increasing numbers of Europeans are concerned that Europe is falling off the radar screen in Washington. They worry that the United States is becoming fixated on China and the U.S. role as a Pacific power.

As before, the very existence of the United States complicates European identity and too often confuses the European sense of purpose. The superpower foreign policy of the United States is sometimes the object of justified European criticism, but at the same time U.S. activism intensifies European self-doubt and unquestionably reinforces a certain European lack of ambition. What the United States wants and does (or does not want and does not do) is a constant point of reference for European governments. Leaders in London, Paris, and Berlin do not wake up asking themselves what the others are thinking. They all think first about what Washington is thinking.[6]

Europe today, as was implied previously, counts in the world order more because of what it is—the expanding EU—than what it does in meeting Europe's geostrategic responsibilities. In other words, the very existence of an integrated, prosperous, democratic geopolitical Europe is a more important influence in the world order than is the lack of a more substantial European diplomatic-military activism. Europeans instinctively feel that they can rely on the United States to take the strategic initiative, even if the United States sometimes makes big mistakes. This is a satisfactory bargain with history, many Europeans will say.

A telling moment arrived when the "miniconstitution" Lisbon treaty went into effect at the end of 2009 and European governments had to choose a permanent EU president and a foreign policy "high representative" with potentially significant authority. For months, the prominent if controversial former British prime minister, Tony Blair, had been favored for the president's job. With someone such as Blair as president and perhaps another internationally experienced leader as foreign policy representative, the EU would suddenly exude international relations gravitas, become a significant international player in its own right. In the event—and after typical EU internal complexities—a nondescript Belgian prime minister and a hardly known British EU commissioner were selected for these positions.

This outcome seemed to have two meanings. Choosing less prominent personalities for potentially important international positions meant reasserting the primacy of national governments as the center of gravity in EU relations with the rest of the world. At the same time, European leaders revealed again why European integration is a kind of self-limiting enterprise, one that brings countries together with the result, all too often, of reaffirming their incompatibilities. As far as most of the big and medium-size countries are concerned, for some time to come there seems to be enough Europe in terms of foreign policy; most European governments prefer the bedrock structures of nation-states and national interests to pursuing a chimerical "idea of Europe."

In terms of practical strategic affairs, simultaneous developments in the war in Afghanistan reaffirmed the limits of European efforts to share military burdens even when their governments repeatedly commit to the importance of the fight against global terrorist networks and also the significance of the effort in Afghanistan for the future of NATO. In November 2009, President Obama asked the partners of the United States in the Afghan War (some forty-two of them) to send additional troops to support the "surge" strategy he had decided on, similar to the one that had worked in the Iraq War. He hoped to get commitments for 10,000 soldiers to combine with the 30,000 the United States would add to the 68,000 Americans already there. Only 7,000 were pledged, however, and, remarkably, only 5,000 of these would be NATO (i.e., European) soldiers. As usual, Britain pledged the most, planning to field nearly 10,000 soldiers in all. Italy (4,000) and Poland (2,800) would also increase their forces. But the Dutch force, about 2,200, was scheduled to leave in 2010 and the Canadians (about 2,800) in 2011. France and Germany did not commit to providing additional troops, although they did not rule out doing so in the future.

In these countries, especially France and Germany, government decisions were understandably affected by public opinion, which all over Europe now opposed or had lost interest in the war. Yet the future of Afghanistan and, more important, the repercussions for its nuclear-armed neighbor Pakistan present dangers of global terrorist networks and nuclear proliferation that concern Europe. Strategic leadership in such cases means taking a case to the country as well as paying attention to popular worries.

Europe and Globalization

At the same time, 2009 conceivably marked the start of growing European influence as an unexpected result of the world financial crisis that began in late 2007 and the climate change negotiations for the Copenhagen summit conference of December 2009. Here, as in strategic affairs, the quality of leadership matters greatly.

Paris and London have taken a lead. Britain's Gordon Brown and France's Nicolas Sarkozy denounced the heedlessness of big investment banks in creating the financial collapse and were in the forefront of negotiations for structural reform of the international financial system. The two presidents also instituted a one-time 50 percent surtax on bankers' bonuses with an invitation to other governments to join it.

In negotiating the December 2009 Copenhagen summit on climate change, Sarkozy was particularly active. The Europeans arrived with more concrete proposals than other governments, but they faced a new shuffle of global leadership in which the United States and China constituted a "group of two" at the top, but India and Brazil also were now in the front rank, raising again the question of how much the Europeans still counted. France and Britain may have acted in tandem at these meetings, but clearly the EU itself was not a player. Germany's deliberately low profile was particularly noticeable from this point of view.

Globalization is now an aspect of geopolitics because, as always, a strong economy is the necessary foundation of a durably strong foreign policy. And because financial and economic globalization affects European interests as much or more than security dangers, the new geoeconomic challenges may impel European governments toward a more assertive international policy. To the extent that the United States becomes an increasingly beleaguered superpower, Washington may find new reasons to encourage European assertiveness.

Ultimately the choice facing the Europeans, as a former French foreign minister puts it, is "whether [Europe] will be one center of power in an unstable and competitive multi-polar world, i.e., whether it will be a genuine world power; or whether [Europe] will become a kind of branch office of the western world, a passive space on the map, a Switzerland writ large where life is good but which has no influence on the course of events. This is an enormous issue," he adds, "that depends not on the [EU] treaties but on what goes on inside peoples' heads."[7] The authors of this book tend to agree that world peace and stability would benefit from a more ambitious, assertive Europe, just as Europeans themselves would benefit from a renewal of the continent's historic dynamism.

A rapidly changing international order with rising new great powers in the global East and South would be better balanced and more resilient if there were a more resolute Europe in the West. A complacent, marginalized Europe, satisfied with prosperous irrelevance, is possible but far from inevitable.

SUGGESTIONS FOR FURTHER READING

de Gaulle, Charles. *Memoirs of Hope: Renewal and Endeavor.* New York: Simon and Schuster, 1971.

DePorte, Anton. *Europe between the Superpowers: The Enduring Balance.* 2nd ed. New Haven, CT: Yale University Press, 1986.

Ferguson, Niall. *The War of the World: Twentieth-Century Conflict and the Descent of the West.* New York: Penguin, 2006.

Fritsch-Bournazel, Renata. *Europe and German Unification.* New York: Berg, 1992.

Ginsberg, Roy J. *The European Union in International Politics: Baptism by Fire.* Lanham, MD: Rowman & Littlefield, 2001.

Hill, Christopher, and Karen E. Smith. *European Foreign Policy: Key Documents.* London: Routledge, 2000.

Hoffmann, Stanley. *The European Sisyphus: Essays on Europe, 1964–1994.* Boulder, CO: Westview Press, 1995.

Howorth, Jolyon. *Security and Defense Policy in the European Union.* New York: Palgrave Macmillan, 2007.

Judt, Tony. *Postwar: A History of Europe since 1945.* New York: Penguin, 2005.

Kagan, Robert. *Of Paradise and Power: America and Europe in the New World Order.* New York: Alfred A. Knopf, 2003.

Lieven, Anatol, and Dmitri Trenin, eds. *Ambivalent Neighbors: The EU, NATO and the Price of Membership.* Washington, DC: Carnegie Endowment for International Peace, 2003.

Macridis, Roy C., ed. *Foreign Policy in World Politics.* Eds. 1–8. New York: Prentice Hall, 1958–1989.

Smith, Michael E. *Europe's Foreign and Security Policy: The Institutionalization of Cooperation.* Cambridge: Cambridge University Press, 2004.

Thatcher, Margaret. *The Downing Street Years.* New York: HarperCollins, 1993.

Tiersky, Ronald. *François Mitterrand: A Very French President.* 2nd ed. Lanham, MD: Rowman & Littlefield, 2000.

Tiersky, Ronald, and Erik Jones, eds. *Europe Today: A Twenty-First Century Introduction.* Lanham, MD: Rowman & Littlefield, 2007.

Van Oudenaren, John. *Uniting Europe: An Introduction to the European Union.* 2nd ed. Lanham, MD: Rowman & Littlefield, 2005.

2

The European Union as a Foreign Policy Actor

Toward a New Realism

John Van Oudenaren

The entry into force, on December 1, 2009, of the Treaty of Lisbon ended an almost five-year period of political uncertainty and turmoil in the European Union (EU), in which the EU's member state governments had debated among themselves and with their own electorates reforms intended to make the EU "a more active, capable, and coherent actor on the international stage."[1] This period had begun in May and June 2005, when voters in two of the EU's founding member states, France and the Netherlands, rejected a European Constitution that had been drafted by a special constitutional convention in 2002–2003 that would have introduced important reforms aimed at strengthening the EU. Government leaders scrambled to overcome the electoral debacle by concluding the Lisbon treaty, which contained many of the same reforms but was downgraded from a constitution to a mere treaty. But this plan went awry in June 2008, when voters in Ireland rejected Lisbon. The treaty finally went into effect as Irish voters approved the treaty in a second referendum in the fall of 2009, and the parliaments of the other EU member states all approved the document.

The treaty established two new positions intended to improve the coordination of EU policies and give the EU a higher international profile: a European Council president who would serve a two-and-a-half-year term, and a de facto EU foreign minister, officially called the High Representative of the Union for Foreign Affairs and Security Policy. The treaty also created a 7,000-person EU diplomatic corps that would report to the high representative and endowed the EU with "legal personality" that would enable it to conclude international agreements in its own name. At a summit meeting in December 2009, the member states selected Prime Minister Herman van Rompuy of Belgium to be the first European Council president under the new treaty and British politician Catherine Ashton to be the new high representative.

EU FOREIGN POLICY THROUGH THE END
OF THE COLD WAR

The entry into effect of the Lisbon treaty marked the culmination of a long process going back to 1951, when six Western European countries (Belgium, France, the Federal Republic of Germany, Italy, Luxembourg, and the Netherlands) concluded the Treaty of Paris establishing the European Coal and Steel Community. This was followed by the conclusion, in 1957, of the Treaty of Rome establishing the European Economic Community, which created a common market for goods (and, in principle, services, capital, and labor) among the same six countries. In addition to the common market, which was based on the removal of all tariff barriers among the six and the establishment of the common external tariff, the distinguishing feature of the European Community (or EC, as the organization was often called) was the set of institutions established to administer the EC.

They included the European Commission (hereafter "Commission"), the EC executive empowered to propose EC legislation and to exercise regulatory functions in areas covered by the Treaty of Rome; the Council of Ministers, composed of foreign (or, in different formations, finance, industry, transport, or other) ministers from the six member states, whose function was to pass EC legislation; the European Court of Justice (ECJ), which was empowered to rule on disputes involving the Treaty of Rome and legislation passed under the treaty; and the Common Assembly (later renamed the European Parliament), whose members (chosen from national parliaments) consulted on legislation and helped to provide greater democratic legitimacy to the EC.

These institutions were all, to one degree or another, "supranational" in character, by which is meant that they were supposed to take decisions for the EC as a whole and which would be binding on the individual member states. The members of the Commission were nominated and chosen by the member states, but once in office, they were not to take instructions from national governments but rather to function as a "college" that would take decisions for the EC as a collective entity and make proposals intended to develop EC policies in areas such as trade, agriculture, and transport. The ministers on the Council of Ministers *were* supposed to represent their national governments, but the passage of legislation in the council was by majority voting (using a system in which the larger member states received more votes than the smaller member states). Once an EC law passed, the member states were obliged to respect and implement the law, even if they had voted against it in the council. In the event of an actual or alleged breach of EC legislation or of the Treaty of Rome, the ECJ could rule against a member state, and force its government to bring its laws and policies into compliance with EC norms. The parliament was initially a weak body, with only a consultative role, but over time it gained increased legislative powers, especially after 1979, when direct elections to the European Parliament were instituted.

The supranationality of these institutions was what distinguished the EC from other international organizations such as the United Nations and the North Atlantic Treaty Organization (NATO), where governments retained all of their sovereignty and could not be compelled to take decisions or pass laws with which they disagreed. The powers and responsibilities assigned to the EC by the member states were strictly limited, however, and did not extend to foreign and defense policy. In these areas, the member states were free to pursue purely national policies. To the extent that they cooperated with each other, they did so bilaterally or within other organizations, most importantly NATO, of which the United States, Canada, and non-EC European states were also members. The institutions of the EC thus began life without a mandate to conduct or even participate in the formulation of European foreign and defense policy.

In the absence of such a mandate, the EC concentrated on its internal development. There was no such thing as an EC foreign policy, although by virtue of its role as an economic entity, the EC did begin to act on the international stage. To implement the common external tariff, for example, the EC negotiated as a unit in the General Agreement on Tariffs and Trade (GATT) in order to set the tariffs that the EC would levy on imports from the rest of the world and to determine the tariffs that other countries in turn could impose on EC exports. The EC also concluded association agreements with other countries, especially the former European colonies of France, Belgium, and the Netherlands, that involved preferential market access, foreign aid, and political cooperation of various kinds. These activities, which were mandated by the Treaty of Rome, provided an opening wedge that enabled the Brussels institutions—the Commission in particular—to begin to pursue a de facto foreign policy. Matters of "high politics," however, and security and defense policy in particular remained off limits to the EC, as the member states had no interest in diluting their sovereignty in this politically sensitive area or in weakening NATO, which was seen as Western Europe's ultimate guarantee against the Soviet threat.

The EC began to develop a true foreign policy profile in the 1970s under the rubric of European Political Cooperation (EPC). At the December 1969 Hague summit, the leaders of the six called on their foreign ministers to prepare a report on political union, meaning foreign policy cooperation. The foreign ministers' report led to the launch, in December 1970, of EPC.

The member states agreed to consult on questions of foreign policy and, where possible, take common actions with regard to international issues. The launch of EPC was tacitly linked to the first enlargement—the admission to the EC on January 1, 1973, of Denmark, Ireland, and the United Kingdom—as the existing member states led by France insisted that the widening of the EC had to be accompanied by a "deepening" intended to reinforce its internal cohesion and define a more distinctive international profile. Another important development in this period was the establishment, by decision of the member states at the Paris summit of 1974, of the European Council: a new EC decision-making body that consisted of the heads of state and governments of the member states who would meet several times a year to take decisions on internal and external issues of interest to the EC.

Unlike in areas such as international trade and competition policy where the Treaty of Rome endowed the EC with supranational powers, foreign policy cooperation was to be conducted on a strictly intergovernmental basis. Member states could not be outvoted in the Council of Ministers, made subject to regulations promulgated by the Commission, or subjected to rulings by the ECJ. They had to agree unanimously on foreign policy actions and to coordinate these actions as a matter of negotiation among foreign ministers or heads of government, much as they did in other international bodies such as NATO or the United Nations. As a consequence of these procedural limitations, foreign policy cooperation remained quite weak. Member states could and did go their own way on such issues as relations with the Soviet Union or policy toward the Middle East. In the 1973 Arab-Israeli War, for example, France and Italy adopted a pro-Arab position, while West Germany and the Netherlands tilted more toward Israel.

The 1980s saw an upturn in EC foreign policy cooperation, one that helped set the stage for a stronger, more unified Europe that was to emerge after 1989. Enlargement emerged as a visible and in many ways the most successful expression of the EC's international profile. The first enlargement, in 1973, was a matter of unfinished business: of reversing the original decision by the United Kingdom not to join the EC after taking part in the preliminary negotiations. The next enlargements—to Greece in 1981 and Portugal and Spain in 1986—were more expansive and outward looking. They entailed a decision on the part of European leaders, strongly backed in Washington, to use the EC as an instrument to project stability and prosperity on the European periphery. In this sense, the Mediterranean enlargement of the 1980s set the pattern for the eastern enlargements of the post–Cold War period, when Western Europe extended the benefits of membership to the former communist countries of Central and Eastern Europe as a way of cementing their futures as stable democracies and market economies.

At the Fontainebleau summit in 1984, EC leaders endorsed a proposal by French president François Mitterrand to establish a committee to explore ways to improve the functioning of the EC. This action ultimately led, in 1986, to adoption of the Single European Act (SEA), the first significant revision of the EC's founding treaties since 1957. Although the primary focus of the SEA was completion of the single market for goods, services, people, and capital, it also strengthened the legal basis for EPC, making foreign policy cooperation a treaty obligation rather than a voluntary political act. The implications of the ambitious single market program were primarily European and domestic: the program was intended to speed growth and job creation and make Europe a more dynamic economic actor. But the "1992 program" (so named after the target year by which all remaining barriers to the free flow of goods and services was to be completed) also had important international implications. It made the EC a more important market for other countries, particularly for those on the eastern and southern periphery of the EC, and set the stage for enlargement (in 1995) to three additional countries—Austria, Sweden, and Finland—and to the formation of the European Economic Area (EEA)—basically an extension of the single market—with Iceland, Liechtenstein, and Norway.

The other major development of the 1980s was the beginning of EC involvement in security and defense policy. In addition to the "relaunch" represented by the SEA, the member states, reacting to another Mitterrand proposal, took the significant step of reactivating the Western European Union (WEU), a European security organization whose origins went back to the Brussels Treaty of 1948 but that had lapsed into irrelevance after NATO assumed responsibility for the defense of the continent. In October 1984, the seven members of the WEU agreed to hold meetings of foreign and defense ministers every six months and to work to harmonize member state views on defense, arms control, East–West and transatlantic relations, and European armaments cooperation. By 1987, the WEU had developed to the point where it helped to coordinate an actual military operation, namely, the participation of European navies in minesweeping operations in the Persian Gulf in the late stages of the Iraq-Iran War.

Reactivation of the WEU, promoted by the French but accepted to some degree by the other WEU members, was to give Europe greater weight and more of a voice in the world at a time when U.S.–European relations were strained over policy toward the Soviet Union. The United States under President Ronald Reagan had increased spending on defense, pulled back from arms control negotiations with Moscow, and tried to block construction of a natural gas pipeline linking Siberia and Europe on the grounds that it would increase European dependence on the Soviet Union and funnel large amounts of hard currency to Moscow. These were all policies that raised concerns among European governments, all of which, to varying degrees, preferred a softer approach to dealing with the communist bloc.

It is noteworthy that as the EC developed a foreign policy profile, "multilateralism," which was to figure so prominently in European thinking from the late 1990s on, did not play much of a substantive or symbolic role. The member states engaged in a kind of internal multilateralism as they built the institutions and policies of the EC, but EC policy toward the international system as a whole was characterized by a sort of collective unilateralism in which the EC resisted having its internal trading arrangements, which effectively discriminated against the outside world, subject to the global norms embodied in the GATT.

In the political sphere, the EC countries were not nearly as enthusiastic about the United Nations as they later were to become. West Germany was not even a member of the United Nations until 1973 (due to East–West differences over the legal status of East Germany), and France, Belgium, and the Netherlands all resented the way in which the UN General Assembly had turned into a forum in which they were constantly under attack for their residual colonialism. Powers such as Germany and Italy resented how the United States had teamed up with the Soviet Union in the Nuclear Nonproliferation Treaty (NPT) of 1968 to use UN structures to impose a permanent nonnuclear status on them and did not ratify the treaty until 1975. France in fact showed its extreme dislike for nuclear disarmament by refusing to adhere to the NPT or any of the treaties limiting nuclear testing. All this was to change, however, in the 1990s, when the EU redefined itself as the world's chief defender and interpreter of multilateralism in economics and foreign policy.

POST–COLD WAR EUPHORIA

By the end of the 1980s, the EC appeared well positioned to increase its international influence and develop a stronger foreign policy profile. The single-market program was on track, and the southern enlargement was widely regarded as a success for both European internal and external policy. The WEU had been revived, and discussions were under way about economic and monetary union and the creation of the single currency.

The EC was not prepared, however, for the sudden and dramatic changes that took place in Central and Eastern Europe in 1989, culminating in the collapse of the Berlin Wall on November 9 of that year. Change in the communist world had been under way since 1985, when the reform-minded Mikhail Gorbachev took power in the Soviet Union and began to press for economic and social reforms in his own country and, by implication, in the other countries of the Warsaw Pact. Gorbachev's goal was to reform rather than destroy communism, and few in the West saw the collapse of the communist system as imminent. Western governments debated how they might help Gorbachev introduce more democratic rights and elements of free market capitalism into the Soviet system, but they also feared the possibility of a violent backlash, such as that by the Chinese communists against the Chinese student movement in 1989.

The changes in Central and Eastern Europe only accelerated, however, as communist leaders lost control of the forces Gorbachev had unleashed. Hungary and Poland, the leaders in the reform process, moved toward partially free elections and the legalization of opposition political parties. Hungary also precipitated the final crisis of East Germany when, in the summer of 1989, it opened its border with Austria, allowing thousands of East Germans (prevented by the Berlin Wall and the fortified inner-German border from emigrating directly to West Germany) to flee to the West by the indirect route through Hungary. Desperate to prop up the legitimacy of their crumbling state, the East German authorities threw open the Wall, a move that only hastened the decline of the state's authority.

In March 1990, East Germany held free elections in which the voters opted overwhelmingly for parties that favored rapid reunification with West Germany. The Soviet Union, which had lost millions of people during World War II and saw the destruction of a strong Germany as its chief gain from the war, initially rejected proposals for unification but within a period of months relented, allowing the two German states to negotiate what was in effect a takeover of the east by the west. The culmination of these fast-moving diplomatic developments was the formal reunification of Germany on October 9, 1990, and the withdrawal of all Soviet military forces from German soil.

One of the rationales for European integration after World War II had been to promote reconciliation between France and Germany and keep West Germany anchored in the West. With Germany suddenly unified, questions arose as to whether it would retain its post-1945 westward orientation or reorient itself, economically and politically, toward the east. Having absorbed the five states and 16 million people of the former East Germany, the Federal Republic was larger than it had been before 1990 but also considerably poorer in relative terms and less able to play its traditional role of "paymaster of Europe" by underwriting generous subsidies to poorer member states, such as Greece, Portugal, and Spain.

Reacting to these concerns, the most important European political leaders of the day—Mitterrand, Commission president Jacques Delors, and above all German chancellor Helmut Kohl—sought to reaffirm the centrality of integration in what suddenly had become post–Cold War Europe. Kohl had alarmed and irritated his European neighbors with his unilateral moves to accelerate the unification process, but he now sought to reassure, insisting that with its new internal and external challenges, Germany had more reason than ever to want a strong and united Europe. Kohl found a willing partner in Mitterrand. In April 1990, the two leaders issued a joint letter in which they called for new steps toward European political union. This proposal led to the convening, in December 1990, of an intergovernmental conference (IGC) at which the member states pledged to negotiate major revisions of the founding treaties that would set up new institutions and define agreed policy directions to meet the new domestic and international challenges—all of which went under the rubric of "political union." This conference was to run in parallel with a second IGC, already scheduled, that was charged with negotiating the establishment of the single currency.

If European governments could agree that the collapse of communism and German unification called for renewed efforts at integration, they were less aligned when it came to defining the substance of a new push for European unity and the goals the proposed EU should pursue. France and Germany agreed on the importance of monetary union, while Britain was determined to keep its own currency. In traditional Gaullist fashion, France concluded that with the Soviet threat a relic of the past, the NATO alliance was less important than it had been in the Cold War and that Europe's priority should be to reduce U.S. influence on the continent and reassert its own identity. Britain, on the other hand, was committed to preserving a strong NATO and the U.S. presence in Europe, based on the long-standing "special relationship" between the Anglo-Saxon powers. Germany tended to straddle the French and British positions, wanting retention of NATO and the U.S. presence as a sort of guarantee of last resort for a country located in the heart of Europe but in line with France in thinking that the post–Cold War world called for a stronger, more autonomous Europe with its own foreign policy and defense capability.

These conflicting visions were thrashed out—and only partly resolved—at the IGCs that took place in the course of 1991 and that concluded in a frantic round of all-night bargaining in the Dutch city of Maastricht in December. The result was the Treaty of Maastricht, formally known as the Treaty on European Union, which extensively revised the EC's founding treaties. The EU was formally established. The EC did not disappear, but it became just the part of the EU that dealt with economic and regulatory issues, including the new common currency.

The new union was a complicated structure based on three "pillars." The first pillar was the original EC but with expanded powers and new institutional structures designed to make it function more like the future central government of an emerging European federation. The changes included greater use of majority voting in many decision-making areas, increased powers for the European Parliament, and, most important, the new European Central Bank (ECB), which was to exercise sweeping powers in the monetary area.

The second pillar was the old EPC but institutionally and legally strengthened. The treaty formally established the Common Foreign and Security Policy (CFSP), which stipulated that the EU and its member states would pursue certain objectives, which included safeguarding the fundamental values and interests of the EU, strengthening the security of the EU and its member states, and promoting international cooperation and democracy and human rights. These objectives were to be pursued by consultation leading to the defining of common positions and by the implementation of selected "joint actions."

As in the EPC, the EU was to take CFSP decisions by consensus, with none of the majority voting that characterized the first pillar. There was no central budget and very limited roles for the European Parliament and the European Commission. Above all, there was a certain studied ambiguity about the ultimate ambitions of the EU in the international arena, especially as they related to defense. The treaty specified that the CFSP "shall include all questions related to the security of the Union, including the eventual framing of a common defense policy, which might in time lead to a common defense."[2] This wording left unresolved exactly what such terms as "eventual" and "might in time" meant. Britain was content to defer any real action in this area to an indefinite future and to continue relying on NATO, whereas France was eager to get started on building up a European defense capability as an alternative to NATO for at least some aspects of defense.

The third pillar of the EU was reserved for what were called "justice and home affairs." These were challenges such as illegal immigration, terrorism, drug trafficking, and organized crime that were mainly matters of national responsibility but that national governments recognized called for more coordinated, Europe-wide policy responses. This was especially the case after the single-market program largely eliminated border controls within the EU, allowing illegal activities in one EU country to spill over into others. To deal with these issues, the member states established new intergovernmental mechanisms—committees of ministers and other high officials, for example—charged with improving cooperation through the exchange of information and by taking joint actions. As in the second pillar, the role of the central EU institutions was limited, and cooperation among the member states was still largely voluntary, subject to being blocked by veto in the Council of Ministers and not subject to rulings in the ECJ.

With the negotiations over economic and political union behind it, the EU turned to another pressing issue: enlargement to the east. In the immediate aftermath of the collapse of communism, there was some talk in

Europe of a possible Europe of "concentric circles" in which the EU would form a tightly integrated inner core; countries such as Poland, Hungary, and the Czech Republic might form a trade and economic area linked to but not actually in the EU; and Russia and the other countries that had been part of the Soviet Union would form the outermost circle. However, political leaders and public opinion in Central and Eastern Europe were unhappy with suggestions that they accept what they regarded as permanent second-tier status in Europe and pressed for nothing less than full membership in NATO and the EU.

Germany was an early backer of eastern enlargement. It traditionally had close economic ties with the countries to its east and southeast and had an interest in using the EU to project stability so as to contain problems—environmental degradation, unsafe nuclear power plants, ethnic conflicts, increased organized crime—that otherwise would spill over into Germany. France and many other countries were less enthusiastic. While not opposed to enlargement as such, they were likely to derive fewer benefits from it than Germany and were concerned about its costs. Many in Europe also worried that the rapid influx of ten or more new members would dilute the EU's cohesion and slow its decision-making capacity and thus endanger the ambitious projects formulated in the 1980s for a single currency and a common foreign policy.

To buy time while these questions were sorted out and to provide immediate help to newly democratic countries still reeling from the collapse of their economic systems, the EU undertook a number of interim steps, including the establishment of a special London-based bank—the European Bank for Reconstruction and Development—to provide loans to the ex-communist countries, bilateral technical assistance programs that involved pairing Western European institutions and experts with their Central and Eastern European counterparts to tackle such matters as legal and financial sector reform and environmental cleanup, and, most important, the conclusion of "Europe Agreements" with ten countries of the region: Bulgaria, the Czech Republic, Estonia, Hungary, Latvia, Lithuania, Poland, Romania, Slovakia, and Slovenia.

The EU member states reached a consensus of sorts on enlargement in the run-up to the June 1993 session of the European Council in Copenhagen, at which they invited all those countries with which the EU had concluded Europe Agreements to become members of the EU, but only after they had met certain criteria with regard to economic viability and the establishment of democratic institutions and free market economic systems. Meeting these conditions, which became known as the Copenhagen criteria, became the chief preoccupation of the Central and Eastern European states for the next decade and one of the main tasks of the European Commission and other EU institutions, which ramped up financial and technical assistance to these countries to help them prepare to meet European standards across the entire spectrum of EU laws and regulations.

Complementing the push toward enlargement, the European Council decided that the main focus of CFSP should be relations between the EU and its periphery. This was comprised of the enormous and complex arc of countries that would border the EU after its expected enlargement: to the southeast, Albania and the former Yugoslavia; to the east, Russia, Ukraine, Belarus, and the other countries of the former Soviet Union; and to the south, North Africa and the Middle East. None of these countries were near-term candidates for EU membership, but their prosperity and stability were seen as important for the EU.

The former Yugoslavia was an especially difficult challenge. Unlike Czechoslovakia and the Soviet Union, both of which dissolved peacefully after the collapse of communism, Yugoslavia, a federation of six ethnically and religiously diverse republics that had been created after World War I, broke apart to the accompaniment of much violence and bloodshed. Trouble began in June 1991, when two of the republics, Slovenia and Croatia, declared their independence. The Yugoslav federal army, dominated by ethnic Serbs, intervened in both countries, ostensibly to preserve the federation or, failing that, to protect the rights of ethnic Serbs living in Croatia. The EU seized the chance to mediate the crisis, with one European foreign minister famously declaring, "This is the hour of Europe, not the hour of the United States."

Notwithstanding the EU effort to lead, the situation in the Balkans deteriorated. In March 1992, Bosnia-Herzegovina declared its independence from Yugoslavia, which in turn provoked the Serb minority region in Bosnia to declare its independence from Bosnia, creating a minirepublic that was not internationally recognized but was supported, politically and militarily, from neighboring Serbia. In the ensuing battles between the forces of the three ethnic and religious groups that made up the population of Bosnia—the predominantly Muslim Bosnians, the Orthodox Serbs, and the Roman Catholic Croats—more than a million people fled their homes to escape the "ethnic cleansing" carried out primarily (although not exclusively) by the Serbs. Europeans watched the fighting on their televisions, while EU and UN efforts at mediation and peacekeeping failed to stem the violence.

In the end, the Clinton administration, which had been reluctant to get involved in the conflict, intervened and helped to restore peace. After several especially egregious attacks in the summer of 1995 on civilians by the Serbs, U.S. and allied warplanes, acting through NATO, flew some 800 combat missions against Serb targets. The military action was followed by a peace conference, convened by the United States in Dayton, Ohio, at which the presidents of Serbia, Croatia, and Bosnia agreed on a peace settlement for Bosnia, based on the establishment of a loose federation of Serb and Bosnian-Croat political entities and to be enforced by NATO peacekeepers.

Chastened by its weak performance in the former Yugoslavia, the EU began to look for ways to strengthen CFSP. In March 1996, the Italian government, in its capacity as holder of the rotating EU presidency, presided over the opening of an intergovernmental conference charged with reviewing the Maastricht treaty. The review conference was required under the terms of the treaty itself and was one of the compromises reached by the member states in 1991 regarding the CFSP. Those countries such as France that favored a strong European policy looked to the review as a way to amend and strengthen the foreign policy and defense provisions of the Maastricht treaty, while those such as Britain that were less enthusiastic about CFSP were only too happy to kick final resolution of this issue another few years down the road.

The Treaty of Amsterdam, which resulted from the IGC and entered into force in May 1999, produced several reforms intended to strengthen the second pillar. Recognizing that not all member states would want to participate in all EU military actions and that insistence on unanimity could prove a recipe for paralysis, the EU agreed to establish a procedure whereby "coalitions of the willing" could take part in such actions under the EU flag. The treaty tightened links between the EU and the WEU as the operational arm of a nascent EU defense policy. Most important, to give a voice to the EU's foreign policy, the treaty established the post of high representative for CFSP, who would be charged with articulating EU positions on the international stage and representing the EU in important international forums.

While the member states were putting the finishing touches on the Amsterdam treaty, trouble again broke out in the Balkans and threatened to outrun any improvements that the EU was making in its capacity to influence developments on its periphery. Only temporarily chastened by the NATO actions in Bosnia, the Serbian dictator Slobodan Milosevic again began stirring up ethnic hatreds in the region. In early 1998, military and police units from Serbia began attacking villages and driving out their inhabitants in Kosovo, a province of Serbia populated mainly by ethnic Albanians who long had struggled to achieve autonomy and recognition of their civil and political rights. Europe again was presented with the spectacle of ethnic cleansing on its doorstep. After various international diplomatic efforts failed to get Milosevic to desist from his actions, in March 1999 NATO again launched attacks on Serb targets. After a seventy-eight-day bombing campaign, Serbia eventually capitulated and accepted an internationally backed arrangement under which Kosovo became a de facto UN protectorate, policed by NATO forces.

In both the Bosnia and the Kosovo crises, the EU played an important—indeed by far the most important—role in postwar reconstruction and assistance. This was in line with the EU's long-established role as a civilian power and drew on the same capacities that the EU had developed to assist the Central and Eastern European countries to prepare for EU membership by helping them rebuild their economies and political systems. European leaders were not happy, however, with simply cleaning up after conflicts and wanted to make Europe a more proactive player on the international scene, capable of intervening militarily in peacekeeping or peace enforcement missions without relying exclusively on NATO and the United States for usable military power.

An important factor at this time was a change of thinking in Britain, where in 1997 the Labour Party under Tony Blair took power after years of Conservative rule. Blair was a strong supporter of NATO and a close friend of the United States—indeed, he later was to pay a heavy political price for his association with President George W. Bush and his support for the 2003 Iraq War—but in the context of the late 1990s he moved Britain toward what long had been the French position, embracing the idea that Europe needed an autonomous military capacity. At their meeting in St. Malo, France, in December 1998, Blair and French president Jacques Chirac issued a pathbreaking "Declaration on European Defense," in which they stated that the EU "must have the capacity for autonomous action, backed up by credible military forces, the means to decide to use them and a readiness to do so in order to respond to international crises."[3] The EU as a whole backed this general proposition, and, by way of implementation, in December 1999 the European Council called for the establishment of an EU force, consisting of units contributed by the member states, capable of deploying within sixty days 50,000 to 60,000 troops to remote regions for peacekeeping, humanitarian intervention, and other missions.

Meanwhile, the EU had begun a new round in its seemingly permanent quest for institutional reform. In June 1999, one month after the Treaty of Amsterdam went into effect, the European Council called for the convening of yet another IGC to consider changes in the composition and responsibilities of the Council of Ministers, the Commission, and the European Parliament, all of which had to be reconfigured to make room for the countries of Central and Eastern Europe (plus two small Mediterranean countries, Cyprus and Malta), which were expected to accede to the EU sometime in the early 2000s. The admission of twelve or more member states would mean some dilution in the relative power of the existing members, and the 1999–2000 IGC was in some respects an attempt by the latter to rewrite the "rules of the game" before new members joined and would have a full say in any future reforms.

As it happened, the IGC fell short of expectations. It produced, in December 2000, a new agreement, the Treaty of Nice, that specified how many seats in parliament, votes in the Council of Ministers, and so forth each member would have and made certain other reforms, such as the adoption of a Charter of Fundamental Rights of the European Union. But the negotiations leading to the treaty were marked by bitter squabbles among the member states about their relative power and a reluctance to streamline the EU by turning more power over to the central institutions in Brussels. The treaty went into effect in late 2002 and served as the main legal framework for the EU for the remainder of the first decade of the new century and the key document containing the ground rules for the admission of new member states into the EU. This was only after some last-minute drama involving the voters of Ireland who, in a referendum required by the Irish constitution (the constitutions of the other member states did not require referenda), voted in June 2001 to reject the treaty but then reversed themselves in a second referendum in October 2002.

The vote in Ireland, traditionally a very pro-EU country, reflected a growing skepticism within the European electorate about the course of European integration. Although it could be argued that the constant haggling by European governments over the basic treaties in the name of reform was a factor contributing to this skepticism, the quest for reform was not yet played out. In December 2001, the European Council decided to convene a European Convention that would be charged with drafting a constitution for the EU. For advocates of a stronger, more cohesive Europe, the constitution was to settle, once and for all, the institutional structure of the EU, much as the Constitutional Convention held in Philadelphia in 1787 established the basic framework under which the United States was to function for the next two centuries and beyond. Chaired by former French president Valery Giscard d'Estaing and composed of representatives of member state governments and parliaments and representatives from the Commission and the European Parliament, the convention produced a draft constitutional treaty that it forwarded to the member state governments in June 2003.

The draft constitution proposed sweeping changes in the structure of the EU, in some respects comparable to those of Maastricht a decade earlier. The treaty abolished the three-pillar structure, creating in its place a single union with "legal personality" and the competence to sign international treaties with sovereign states. It established the post of an EU president, to be elected by the European Parliament; cut back the size of the European Commission to make it a more effective decision-making body; and set up a new system of majority voting by the member states designed to speed the adoption of legislation in an enlarged union. In the area of foreign policy, the most notable change was the creation of the post of EU foreign minister, which was intended to provide the EU with a single, high-profile voice that would carry greater weight on the world stage.

Giscard's ambitions for a European constitution were never realized because of the verdicts of the French and Dutch electorates. However, after a period of internal debate about how best to proceed, in December 2007 the member states finalized the Lisbon treaty, which contained, albeit with less fanfare, most of the foreign policy reforms contained in the constitutional treaty. The new high representative post was created by combining the posts of the old high representative and the member of the European Commission responsible for external affairs. In deference to British sensibilities, the term "EU foreign minister" was dropped, but the new position was intended to create the "single telephone number" that foreign leaders were to contact to communicate with the EU. The treaty also created the new diplomatic service and established new guidelines for EU interactions with the outside world.

POLICY INITIATIVES

Amid the seemingly endless discussion of how to organize EU foreign policy and improve the EU's institutional structures, the EU has made headway in upgrading EU relations with key countries and regions and in raising the EU's international profile. Even prior to the creation of the EU and the establishment of the CFSP, the EC was a formidable international actor, albeit chiefly in economic and trade policies and closely related areas such as health, safety, and environmental regulation. Along with the United States, the EC traditionally had been the most influential actor in international trade negotiations. The EC already negotiated as a unit within the GATT, and the EU continued to do so within the World Trade Organization, which was established in 1995 as the successor to the GATT. EU policies relating to trade, foreign aid, competition (antitrust), and many other areas of regulation are not part of CFSP. They are handled within the first pillar, where the Commission and the European Parliament have greater say over policy and the member states act collectively under binding laws and regulations. But the role that the EU plays in these areas clearly underpins the EU's influence as an international actor and is seen by advocates of a stronger European foreign policy as a model for what CFSP should become.

The introduction of the euro in January 1999, although driven primarily by factors internal to the EU (e.g., the need to bolster the single market and to improve economic efficiency), also had important international ramifications, as the ECB took its place beside the U.S. Federal Reserve as one of the world's two most influential central banks. Some European commentators called for the consolidation of the multiple European representation in bodies such as the Group of Seven industrial nations and the governing boards of the International Monetary Fund and the World Bank, a move that would decrease Europe's numerical strength in such bodies but, it was argued, increase Europe's effective weight by creating a single powerful voice that would equal or surpass that of the United States and the emerging developing world powers such as China.

In regulatory affairs, the EU became an increasingly influential actor, in many respects supplanting the United States in its traditional role as the global regulatory trendsetter. In 1997, the European Commission demonstrated its power to regulate international business by setting strict conditions for the merger of two American companies, Boeing and McDonnell Douglas, on the grounds that the combined company would have adverse implications for the European markets. This move foreshadowed increasingly aggressive European moves against successful U.S. firms, including the blocking, in 2001, of the planned merger of General Electric and Honeywell and the levying of large fines against Microsoft and Intel for alleged antitrust violations.

Even as the EU flexed its muscles as a global economic power, the emphasis in the fledgling CFSP remained on the European periphery. In November 1995, the EU and the countries of North Africa and the eastern Mediterranean launched the Barcelona process, which called for expanded economic, political, cultural, and human ties across the Mediterranean and the eventual creation of a free trade area. This initiative was promoted by Spain, France, and the other Mediterranean countries of the EU and was intended to balance the eastward tilt of EU policy that came with the enlargement imperative. Paralleling these policies aimed at stabilizing the EU's southern periphery was an active policy toward Russia, Ukraine, and the other former Soviet republics, with which the EU concluded postcommunist Partnership and Cooperation Agreements and extended substantial grant aid to help these countries restructure their economies.

While the focus of CFSP was primarily regional, the EU also attempted to wield greater influence at the global level. In the UN General Assembly and in the specialized agencies of the United Nations, the member and candidate countries of the EU (often joined by the EEA countries and some of the aspirant countries of southeastern Europe and the former Soviet Union) generally harmonized their votes, resulting in a powerful bloc of more than thirty countries that lent an aura of instant multilateral legitimacy to any proposal initiated in or backed by Brussels. Of the five permanent members of the UN Security Council, two—Britain and France—are EU member states, bound by the terms of the Maastricht and subsequent treaties (including Lisbon) to concert with and keep the other member states informed about their activities on the Security Council and to "ensure the defence of the positions and the interests of the Union."[4] Collectively, the

EU and its member states were also the largest providers of foreign aid to developing countries.

Global issues of concern to the EU included climate change, the proliferation of weapons of mass destruction, and terrorism. Following the September 11, 2001, terror attacks on New York and Washington, the EU stepped up antiterrorism cooperation with the United States (and many other countries), in so doing upgrading the level of intra-EU coordination within the third pillar in order to make the EU a more effective international actor in this area. In October 2003, the foreign ministers of Europe's "big three" (France, Germany, and the United Kingdom) visited Tehran in a diplomatic bid to convince Iran to desist from pursuing a nuclear weapons capability. The three pressed the Iranian leadership to suspend uranium enrichment and to allow intrusive inspections by the International Atomic Energy Agency. In return, they offered to resist U.S. pressures for economic and political sanctions on Iran for its nuclear activities and pledged a large package of economic incentives. With this visit, which led to an ongoing dialogue with Iran, Europe was seen as having seized the initiative on a key international policy issue. There was some grumbling in the smaller countries of the EU that the three had acted outside formal CFSP structures, but the big-three initiative was adopted as an EU initiative and endorsed by all the member states and the CFSP high representative.

Closer to home, the EU continued to look for ways to stabilize its southern and eastern peripheries, a task that became more urgent in the post-9/11 world, with its focus on terrorism from the Islamic world, and as the date of enlargement to the countries of Central and Eastern Europe—May 1, 2004—approached. In late 2003, the EU folded both the Barcelona process and its policies toward Ukraine, Moldova, and other Soviet successor states into what was called the New Neighborhood Policy (NNP), a new initiative aimed at stabilizing and promoting prosperity on both the southern and the eastern peripheries of an enlarged EU. Russia, which wanted a separate "strategic partnership" with the EU more befitting its status as a great power, declined to take part in the NNP, but Russia and the EU declared in 2001 that together they would create a "common economic space" involving the EU and Russian markets and later expanded this initiative to call for "common spaces" in the areas of justice and home affairs, foreign and security policy, and research and education.

In addition to the focus on the European periphery and an increasingly active policy with regard to global issues such as the environment and terrorism, the third leg of EU foreign policy from the 1990s on was the cultivation of a series of partnerships—often dubbed "strategic partnerships"—with key powers and regional groupings around the world. In December 1995, the EU and the United States significantly upgraded their relations by launching the New Transatlantic Agenda, which called for cooperation in a wide range of areas and twice-yearly summits. The first Euro-Asian summit took place in 1996 and brought together the EU member states, the Commission, and the Association of Southeast Asian Nations as well as China, Japan, and South Korea. Regular summits and institutionalized cooperation also began with the Latin American trade grouping Mercosur and with Russia, South Africa, and other countries and regional groupings. In all these areas, the EU, newly empowered by the CFSP provisions of the Maastricht treaty, pursued a mixed policy that combined both traditional economic diplomacy with upgraded political relations based on regular consultations.

The combination of economic and regulatory power and the new tools of CFSP resulted in the EU's being able to wield significant amounts of what political scientists began to call "soft power" (as distinguished from the "hard power" embodied in military forces, where the United States was clearly still dominant). After 2001, many critics of the Bush administration in both Europe and the United States held up the EU as a kind of successful countermodel to the United States, which was said to be too wedded to hard power and neglectful of the softer aspects of state power and foreign policy influence. Conversely, where Europe was said to lack influence was in the area of hard power—usable military force. EU efforts to meet the ambitious Helsinki goals lagged because of unwillingness on the part of member state governments to increase defense spending or to reform military establishments still organized along outdated Cold War lines. European militaries lacked the transport and intelligence capabilities to undertake large and sustained missions on the periphery of Europe or even farther afield and still relied on conscript soldiers who were forbidden by law to be deployed overseas or to combat situations. Nonetheless, even in this area, the EU began making some progress. After providing the bulk of the national peacekeeping forces earmarked to the NATO-led missions in the Balkans in the late 1990s, in the early 2000s the EU began to test its capacity for autonomous overseas military deployments, as called for by Blair and Chirac in the St. Malo declaration.

The EU undertook its first peacekeeping operation in 2003, when it took over from NATO a modest mission in the Former Yugoslav Republic of Macedonia. Later that year, the EU undertook its first fully autonomous military operation—without assistance of any kind from NATO. This was a peacekeeping mission in the Democratic Republic of the Congo, initiated by the French precisely in order to show, many observers believed, that the EU could act independently on the world stage. Over the course of the next five years, the EU engaged in twenty crisis management operations, many quite small but the largest (a refugee protection mission in Chad) involving 3,500 troops.

"EFFECTIVE MULTILATERALISM"

In addition to carrying out particular actions and policies such as aid programs and peacekeeping operations, the EU and its member states increasingly have developed a common European outlook on international politics. The formation of a "European reflex" had been envisioned from the beginnings of EPC in the 1970s but had long appeared difficult to achieve. In the 1990s and early 2000s, it was becoming a reality. No single term or phrase can adequately sum up this worldview, but "effective multilateralism," codified in the European Security Strategy of 2003, best encapsulates the emerging European worldview.

European views on multilateralism cannot be understood apart from the differences between the United States and Europe over foreign policy that, despite the persistence of differences of outlook *within* Europe, increasingly came to define a common European perspective on the world. Relations between the United States and Western Europe went through a difficult phase in the early 1990s, as the two sides squabbled over the crisis in the Balkans. American officials criticized Europe for failing to deal with a massive humanitarian disaster in its own backyard, while Europeans resented the Clinton administration for its posture of carping from the sidelines while refusing to commit American troops to help deal with the crisis. Other issues also exacerbated relations, including trade disputes and the pace of NATO and EU enlargement, which the United States wanted to accelerate from the more measured approach favored by the Europeans.

By the mid-1990s, U.S.–European relations had stabilized, as the two sides cooperated in implementing the Dayton peace agreement, dampened down trade disputes, and settled on a timetable for the admission of three countries—Poland, Hungary, and the Czech Republic—to NATO. Nonetheless, an undercurrent of tension persisted in transatlantic relations even in the late Clinton years, as Europeans resented what they regarded as American boasting about U.S. power (Secretary of State Madeleine Albright called the United States the "indispensable nation," implying that without its involvement, nothing important could be accomplished), bragging about the strength of the U.S. economy, and U.S. reluctance to apply to itself the same standards that it sought to apply to others on issues such as trade.

"Multilateralism" became the weapon of choice by which European politicians, often prodded by nongovernmental organizations, struck back at U.S. power. In case after case, this was done by promoting a treaty that ostensibly addressed some international problem and that the United States itself in principle supported but making certain provisions of the treaty in question so onerous—either to overall U.S. national interests as defined by the administration or to key domestic interest groups and the Congress—so as to leave the United States with an unpalatable choice between accepting an agreement on highly unfavorable terms or rejecting the agreement and being branded as a "unilateralist."

The land mine ban of 1998 was the first notable case of this pattern of interaction. Canada and Norway initially led the international campaign to ban antipersonnel land mines that were scattered across Third World conflict zones and were killing and maiming many people every year. The United States was not responsible for these mines (most of which were of Soviet origin) and generally had a positive record on helping to clean up these mines, but it was unwilling to sign a land mine ban unless it obtained a five-year exception allowing it to keep such mines along the demilitarized zone in Korea so as to help guard against a possible attack from the north. The European and other powers refused, and the United States under Clinton chose not to sign the treaty.

A second such case concerned the 1999 agreement to establish the International Criminal Court (ICC). The United States had been an early backer of a UN court to try war criminals, which it saw as a logical outgrowth of the ad hoc tribunals set up to try such criminals from the former Yugoslavia, Rwanda, and elsewhere. But the United States wanted ironclad protections against the court's ever being used to prosecute U.S. soldiers deployed overseas and wanted to preserve a special oversight role for the UN Security Council. Europeans—some of whom were themselves initially quite skeptical about the court and also wanted to preserve a Security Council role—went some way to meet U.S. concerns but were unwilling to yield on the central issues in dispute. Failing to secure the changes that it sought in the treaty establishing the ICC, the United States voted against it, and Clinton only reluctantly signed the treaty on the last day it was possible to do so, with the recommendation that the Senate not take steps toward ratification.

A third case in which the United States and Europe tussled over multilateralism concerned the Kyoto Protocol on limiting greenhouse gas emissions. Under pressure from the domestic environmental lobby, the Clinton administration signed the treaty, but it took no steps to secure its ratification or to implement policies that actually would have cut greenhouse gas emissions during the economic boom years of the 1990s. Instead, the administration looked to an elaborate set of counting rules and arrangements whereby the United States could comply with the treaty by purchasing offsets in developing countries that cut their emissions output and by certain other measures, such as the planting of trees on idle farmland. European negotiators balked, insisting, as one environmental minister phrased it, that the United States had to suffer real economic "pain" in order to comply with Kyoto.

With the election of George W. Bush to the presidency in November 2000, the undercurrent of tension in EU–U.S. relations that had been simmering during the Clinton years turned into a full-blown crisis. European elites had a strong cultural dislike for Bush (much as they had once mocked the "cowboy" Reagan) and objected to Bush's record as governor of Texas, where he was perceived as responsible for numerous executions of convicted criminals. For his part, Bush took a more nationalist approach to defending U.S. interests as he perceived them and, unlike Clinton, saw no need to pay lip service to international agreements that failed to accord with U.S. interests and that had no chance of being ratified by the Senate. Bush officials declared the Kyoto Protocol dead; "unsigned" the Rome Statute, which committed the United States to the ICC; and undertook other actions, such as imposing limits on steel imports from Europe to protect U.S. industry, to which European officials and industry objected.

Europeans rallied to support the United States following the September 11, 2001, terror attacks on New York and Washington, but relations soon deteriorated again over the Bush administration's conduct of the "war on terror," its continuing refusal to return to what Europeans insisted was the true multilateral path by ratifying Kyoto and other international agreements, and, most important, the run-up to the 2003 U.S.-led invasion of Iraq. Britain, backed by Italy and Spain, supported the war, while France and Germany, backed by Russia, were adamantly opposed. European public opinion was strongly against the war, and large antiwar demonstrations in European cities in the weeks before the conflict put Blair, Prime Minister Silvio Berlusconi of Italy, and Prime Minister José Maria Aznar of Spain under intense political pressure.

Chirac in particular seized on the political turmoil generated by the Iraq War and its aftermath to push for a stronger Europe that not only would be independent of the United States but also would act, in concert with other powers such as China, Russia, and India, as a counterweight to U.S. power in a multipolar world. France and Germany endorsed a Belgian proposal to establish an independent EU military planning cell in apparent disregard of a 2002 understanding within NATO that assigned the alliance the primary role in planning military operations. Many in Europe—and especially Chirac—were furious at what they perceived as attempts by the Bush administration to divide Europe over the issue of Iraq, seen most vividly, they believed, in Secretary of Defense Donald Rumsfeld's famous distinction between the "old Europe" of the fifteen countries and the "new Europe" of the Central and Eastern European countries about to join the EU.

The European Security Strategy, which was issued in draft form by CFSP high representative Javier Solana in June 2003 and formally adopted by the European Council in December of that year, was in large part the EU's response to the internal split over Iraq. *A Secure Europe in a Better World,* as the strategy was called, was a middle-of-the-road document intended to restore a consensus around certain basic principles. The document identified five emerging threats—terrorism, proliferation of weapons of mass destruction, regional conflicts, state failure, and organized crime—and called on the EU to deploy military and especially nonmilitary means to address these threats. Along with building security in its own neighborhood, the EU's key policy objective was defined as promoting a new international order based on "effective multilateralism," a term that was associated with the development of international law, a stronger United Nations, and a network of global and regional institutions.

Among the elites who staff the think tanks, bureaucracies, and the major media in Europe, most of whom share an overwhelmingly prointegration ideology, effective multilateralism took on almost religious significance and was constantly invoked and intoned to explain the EU's special role in the world. This fervid embrace of multilateralism was all the more remarkable for being a relatively new development in European approaches to the international system—one that reflected a growing confidence that the EU could define the nature of multilateralism and use it to its own advantage as well as the sharp differentiation from the United States, which invariably was portrayed as "unilateralist," that the embrace of multilateralism entailed.

The strategy called for a union that was more active, more coherent, and more capable and emphasized the building of partnerships. The EU was to develop "strategic" partnerships with Canada, China, India, Japan, and Russia and an "effective and balanced partnership" with the United States. Building on bilateral relationships going back to the 1970s, the Commission and the high representative set about institutionalizing the major strategic partnerships through such mechanisms as annual summits and various action plans and other documents aimed at intensifying cooperation in support of ostensibly shared values and objectives, the most important of which, it was implied, was support for multilateralism.

In addition to its strategic partnerships with these major powers, the EU had developed special bilateral relationships with a large number of small and medium-sized countries, including the candidate countries of the EU, the EEA countries, countries covered by the New Neighborhood policy, and the Africa-Caribbean-Pacific countries, a grouping linked to the EU by preferential trade deals and special institutional arrangements going back to the 1960s. Together with the EU member states, these countries—some 109 in total—constituted what one author dubbed the "Eurosphere," a large grouping of states that increasingly took their lead from Brussels rather than Washington or some other power center on political, economic, and regulatory issues. The sheer size of this group ensured that Europe rather than the United States would, as this author put it, "run the 21st century."[5]

A NEW REALITY SETS IN: 2004 AND BEYOND

In retrospect, 2004 can be seen as the high-water mark of post–Cold War European optimism about the international order. In March of that year, terrorist bombings in Madrid killed 190 people, but they also brought about the electoral defeat of the pro-U.S. Aznar government, bringing to power José Luis Zapatero, who promised to align Spain with France and Germany and to refocus Spain's foreign policy on the EU. In May, ten countries—eight in Central and Eastern Europe along with Cyprus and Malta—entered the EU, bringing total membership to twenty-five. (Two other candidates—Bulgaria and Romania—were judged not yet ready for membership, but were slated to join in 2007 and subsequently did so.) One month later, the June 2004 session of the European Council reached agreement on a new constitutional treaty.

There seemed to be few limits to what European soft power could accomplish. Leaders such as Chirac, who long had been skeptical about Turkish membership in the EU, began warming to the idea, in part because Turkey, a traditional U.S. ally, had so visibly fallen out with the United States over Iraq. The argument was made that the large Turkish army would give the EU weight as a military power and that Turkey's location, while a possible source of instability, also could project EU influence into the Middle East and Central Asia. The year ended on the high note of the Orange Revolution in Ukraine, a spontaneous turn toward democracy by the people of that country in reaction to a fraudulent election for which the EU, by virtue of its force of example and its democracy-promoting programs, claimed a large share of the credit. As if to reinforce the point about Europe's growing influence, "hard-power" America was increasingly bogged down in an Iraq War gone bad.

By 2005, however, a more sobering reality began to set in. The rejection of the constitutional treaty by the voters in France and the Netherlands came as a shock to integration-minded European elites and had profound implications for foreign policy. The votes put on hold any near-term plans to create a stronger EU foreign policy apparatus and ended talk of an early round of further expansion to the east. They were particularly damaging to Turkey's prospects for membership. Polls indicated that voters in both countries were influenced by fears of globalization and immigration. In November 2005, Angela Merkel was sworn in as chancellor of Germany after a hard-fought electoral victory over Gerhard Schröder. This was followed some eighteen months later by Chirac's departure from the French political scene and the inauguration of the centrist Nicolas Sarkozy as president. Merkel and Sarkozy were described as "Atlanticists," and both moved to improve relations with the United States—without, however, abandoning the commitment to make the EU the more active, capable, and coherent power called for in the 2003 strategy document.

Against the backdrop of these developments in Europe, the international situation was changing in ways that challenged EU thinking about the global order. EU relations with China, while still basically friendly, began to deteriorate over trade and Chinese policies that encouraged ever-increasing surpluses with Europe. Beijing was unresponsive to European expressions of concern about its role in Africa and human rights in Tibet and was unwilling to consider mandatory restrictions on its emissions of greenhouse gases. In Russia, the Putin regime's steady turn toward nationalist authoritarianism clashed with EU aspirations to promote democracy, while Russian exploitation of the supply of energy for political purposes made a mockery of the joint calls for a "common economic space." Even India, a friendly, democratic country, complained about the lack of substance in its relations with the EU. Increasingly, it appeared that the EU's "strategic partnerships" with key actors were self-serving intellectual constructs rather than the stuff of a new international order.

Relations between the EU and the United States improved markedly during Bush's second term, even though the scars of the previous years set limits to what could be accomplished in transatlantic relations. In March 2005, the United States announced that it was backing the E3 initiative toward Iran. The U.S. refusal either to talk directly with Iran or to back European efforts had been a source of frustration in Europe, raising concern that the United States was contemplating what many believed would be a disastrous military strike against Tehran and its nuclear facilities. Cooperation in the Middle East peace process took place through a quartet, comprised of the United States, the EU, Russia, and the United Nations, that replaced the old U.S.–Russian cosponsorship that had marginalized and irritated the European powers. Other steps that gave substance to what Bush called "a new era of transatlantic unity" included cooperation with France in Lebanon and continued close cooperation against terrorist groups. Tensions nonetheless persisted—over Iraq, Kyoto, counterterrorism tactics, some trade issues, and, in a new area of dispute, a Franco–German proposal (subsequently abandoned) to lift the EU embargo on sales of arms to China that had been imposed after the Tiananmen massacre of 1989.

As Bush's term limped to a close, the reality of multipolarity was beginning to permeate European perceptions of the international order and Europe's place within it. As used by Schröder, Chirac, and the European Commission earlier in the decade, multipolarity implied the rise of a loose coalition of major powers, tacitly deferring to one degree or another to EU conceptions of global governance and committed to checking overweening U.S. power, which was portrayed as the major problem facing the international community. With U.S. power in relative decline and Russia, China, and midlevel powers such as Iran and Venezuela striking out in new directions, this conception of the international system was difficult to sustain.

These changes in the international system led to a flurry of interest in a revitalization of the U.S.–Europe relationship and a new "Atlantic" order. A growing number of European (and U.S.) commentators began to argue that with the rise of India and China, the United States and Europe had only a limited time to join in using their influence to strengthen international norms and institutions in ways that would shape the behavior of the Asian giants into the future. In a book that attracted considerable attention in European press and political circles, for example, former French prime minister Edouard Balladur called for a new union between Europe and the United States aimed at strengthening the West.[6] Such ideas gained little traction, however, as the realities of the multipolar distribution of power—and of U.S.–European divisions over many issues—were already such as to render impractical any return to the old Cold War verities of Atlantic solidarity.

OUTLOOK AND CONCLUSIONS

Of the many factors likely to shape the development of the EU as a foreign policy actor over the next several years, four stand out. First, global political, economic, and eventually military multipolarity will affect how Europe defines its interests and thinks about relations with other powers. The redistribution of global power under way in the past decade is likely to continue. If anything, change has been accelerated by the recent economic crisis, in which China and India seem to have fared relatively better than either the United States or the EU. In the context of true multipolarity, the EU will need to fashion policies based neither on the crude containment of U.S. power championed by Chirac and Schröder nor on the simple reaffirmation of Atlantic or Western solidarity advocated by some of their critics.

Second, like other international actors, the EU will be forced to live with straitened economic circumstances. While the economic crisis began in United States and at first seemed to bypass Europe, by 2009 it was clear that in some respects it was hitting Europe harder than the United States, as Spain, Greece, Ireland, and the new member states of Central and Eastern Europe proved vulnerable to rising debts and their own asset bubbles and as German exports suffered heavily from global economic woes. Under difficult economic and fiscal conditions, it will be hard for the EU to sustain the high levels of spending on international assistance and other policy mechanisms that underpin European soft power and even harder for it to make the large investments required to bolster the EU as an effective wielder of military power.

Third, the EU's future as a foreign policy actor will be influenced by how the Lisbon reforms function in practice. Many European advocates of a stronger and more assertive EU saw the appointment of two relatively unknown politicians, van Rompuy and Ashton, to the two new posts created by the Lisbon treaty as a bad sign—an indication that the member states intended to continue asserting their national prerogatives at the expense of EU unity. Despite the creation of the new post of European Council president (occupied by van Rompuy), individual member states continued to preside over, on a six-month, rotating basis, the Council of Ministers. Spain, the first presidency country in the Lisbon era, played an active role in the first six months of 2010, scheduling meetings and setting forth an ambitious policy agenda for the EU that some saw as in competition with the prerogatives of van Rompuy and Ashton. Some observers worried that, notwithstanding all the effort put into reform, the Lisbon treaty had not gone far enough in creating the single European voice and that powers such as the United States, China, and Russia might be confronted by an even greater cacophony of voices speaking for and in the name of the EU. Such fears seemed to be confirmed in early 2010, when the Obama administration announced that President Barack Obama would not attend a U.S.–EU summit that the Spanish government had hoped to host in Madrid in the late spring, giving as one reason the continued lack of clarity about how Europe's new constitutional arrangements would function and what they meant for partners such as the United States.[7]

Finally, change in the United States, in particular the election of Obama in November 2008, created a new situation for the EU. European commentators were enraptured by the new president, who was seen as embracing European foreign policy values and even, in the view of some, committed to transforming the United States into a European-style social democracy. But the change was not without its challenges. Pundits worried that Obama, as a political leader perceived as legitimate in Europe, would be in a position to demand greater sacrifices from Europe in places such as Afghanistan. While hopes for a revitalized U.S.–EU relationship ran high as many of Bush's bitterest critics assumed policy positions in the State and Defense departments and elsewhere in the new administration, it was unclear whether the president himself was as enamored of Europe as many of his advisers. With his roots in Hawaii and his associations with Africa and Asia, and with his understandable focus on domestic challenges, Obama did not gravitate toward a "Europe-first" policy. Many of his early meetings with European leaders were described as perfunctory and lacking the kind of enthusiasm he brought to his encounters with leaders in Russia or the Muslim world. Like other presidents who have faced daunting domestic and international challenges, Obama was certain to develop his own personal calculus of how helpful or unhelpful, relevant or irrelevant, Europe was to the broad array of challenges he faced.

Indeed, while Obama remained enormously popular in Europe (as witnessed by his being selected for the 2009 Nobel Peace Prize by the Norwegian Nobel committee), already by the end of 2009 the bloom had come off the rose of European–U.S. relations. European governments largely turned a deaf ear to Obama's request that they send large numbers of additional combat troops to Afghanistan, where Obama himself was sending an additional 30,000 troops to deal with the deteriorating security situation. The December 2009 Copenhagen summit on climate change was a disappointment to Europe both for its substantive outcome (no new binding commitments on cuts in greenhouse gas emissions) and in how the summit decisions were made. The Copenhagen outcomes hinged on tough bargaining between the United States on the one hand and China and several other developing countries on the other, while the EU, which had long regarded itself as a leader in the area of climate change, was elbowed aside. While Europe welcomed Obama's willingness to engage with Iran and try to revitalize the Arab–Israeli peace process that they believed Bush had neglected, Obama had little to show for his efforts in his first year in office.

Along with these four major areas, other challenges are certain to arise to complicate the EU's efforts to become a more effective foreign policy actor, to defend European interests, and to make a positive difference on the world scene. With its very great if, in relative terms, somewhat diminished political, economic, and human resources, Europe has the ability to cope with these challenges. But doing so will be far more difficult than was assumed in the early years of post–Cold War optimism and will require both intellectual vision and political leadership—both in Brussels and in the national capitals.

SUGGESTIONS FOR FURTHER READING

Dinan, Desmond. *Europe Recast: A History of European Union.* Boulder, CO: Lynne Rienner, 2004.

European Union, Institute for Security Studies (Paris). Chaillot Papers series. Available at http://www.iss.europa.eu.

Gnesotto, Nicole, ed. *EU Security and Defence Policy: The First Five Years (1999–2004).* Paris: EU Institute for Security Studies, 2004.

Nuttall, Simon. *European Foreign Policy.* Oxford: Clarendon Press, 2000.

Serfaty, Simon. *Architects of Delusion: Europe, America, and the Iraq War.* Philadelphia: University of Pennsylvania Press, 1998.

3

Europe and the United States

The Obama Era and the Weight of History

Philip Stephens

The sun shone on the transatlantic alliance when, in the spring of 2009, U.S. President Barack Obama joined European leaders in Strasbourg to mark the sixtieth anniversary of the North Atlantic Treaty Organization (NATO). After the wrenching arguments of George W. Bush's presidency, the United States had chosen in Obama a leader every bit as popular in Europe as he was at home. With their opinion poll ratings sinking under the weight of economic recession and social discontent, Europe's leaders hoped to catch a little of Obama's stardust. The competition to get along-side the U.S. president was intense. Obama, for his part, was generous in his praise for his hosts and reassuring about the future of the Euro-Atlantic community.

France had chosen the summit as the moment to underscore the new Atlanticism in its foreign policy. Defying—his critics would say defiling—the memory of General Charles de Gaulle, Nicolas Sarkozy formally ended his country's forty years of self-imposed exile from NATO's military command. There was as much symbolism as substance in this decision, but it added to the sense of a fresh start. Obama told a cheering audience in Strasbourg that he saw an opportunity for the United States and Europe to renew "the strongest alliance that the world has ever known."[1]

The president's view was one widely endorsed by his hosts. The British politician and diplomat Chris Patten had once called the alliance the "indispensable partnership"—a conscious echo of America's self-description as the indispensable nation. NATO, all attending the Strasbourg summit still agreed, had served as the essential bulwark against Soviet communism.[2] It now served as the guarantor of the spread of liberal democracy in Europe from the Atlantic to the Urals. It was an alliance rooted in the

43

shared values of individual freedom, pluralism, and market economics as well as in mutual security.

Yet for all the hopes that Obama's presidency would open a new, more soothing chapter in the partnership, the Strasbourg gathering raised as many questions as it offered answers. It had been easy enough to define the purpose of NATO when Soviet forces had gathered menacingly on the borders of the West. The territorial defense of Western Europe was an imperative that needed little explanation. Twenty years after the fall of the Berlin Wall, the role of the alliance was less certain. This new world was one in which the enemy was at a distance and the threats were diverse. NATO had not been configured to confront al-Qaeda terrorism, failed and failing states, piracy in the Indian Ocean, and nuclear weapons proliferation. The alliance—or parts of it—was fighting in Afghanistan but without great enthusiasm among its European members. Obama had crossed the Atlantic with hopes that partners of the United States would see the summit as the occasion to substantially increase their military commitment to the alliance. The president was largely disappointed.

The story of Europe's relationship with the United States during the period since 1945 must begin with a caution. To refer to "Europe" or even "Western Europe" in this context is to assume a coherence in the continent's view of the world that frequently was missing. Europe seen from the U.S. side of the Atlantic often looked a lot more united than it did when viewed from close up. The partnership with the United States was as much a series of alliances as a single arrangement. Many of the strands were interlocking; others diverged.

The explanation lay in the nature of European integration. Governments created in the European Union (EU) a unique vehicle for economic integration and political cooperation. Yet in the realm of foreign and security policy, decisions remained the province of national governments. On matters of war and peace, the EU had largely remained, in de Gaulle's famous phrase, a "Europe des patries," a Europe of the nation-states. During the decades following the close of World War II, there were as many tensions within Europe—most obviously the enduring rivalry between Britain and France—as there were differences with successive administrations in Washington.

That is not to say that there were not strong binding threads. Until the collapse of the Soviet Union, confrontation with Moscow provided the vital glue of partnership within Europe as well as the central pillar of the alliance with the United States. The passing of communism would subsequently provide a big part of the explanation for the doubts that would later be raised about the future purpose of the alliance.

Europe's governments shared some distinct impulses. To be European during the second half of the twentieth century by and large was to be a multilateralist: to show a reverence for the international rules and institutions that were the basis of the West's postwar bargain. Many of these institutions, of course, were of largely American design. The United Nations, an open trading system, the Bretton Woods institutions, and NATO provided the global framework in which European integration would flourish. Europe's attitude was rooted in the experiences of the first half of the twentieth century and in the geopolitical reality of the second: competition had been the source of devastating war; cooperation would brake the pace of relative decline.

On the eve of war with Iraq in early 2003, a senior official in George W. Bush's administration was heard to complain bitterly about Europe's preference for diplomacy and engagement over action. The only thing Europeans were really good at, he said, was convening meetings. In one important respect, this official was right. With the exception of Britain and occasionally France, the Europe of the second half of the twentieth century had indeed preferred talk to action.

The president's adviser, though, was too careless of history to understand why. Meetings were a big part of the explanation for the absence of war between the continent's major powers. The nations that had emerged broken and exhausted after 1945 decided that the major conflagrations that had left their continent in ruins were enough. Henceforth, they would settle their disputes in the conference rooms of Brussels rather than on fields of Flanders. What the French like to call the "construction of Europe" was a substitute for the continent's periodic destruction.

There were other reasons why Europe did not punch its weight in foreign policy. Most obviously, the generous military guarantee provided by the United States through and beyond the Cold War absolved Europe's governments of the need to make their own hard military choices. Until the collapse of the Soviet Union, the balance of nuclear terror on the continent was a powerful force for stability. It seemed strange to say subsequently, but the threat of mutually assured destruction bestowed a curious sense of security.

Insofar as European nations had to look to the world beyond during this period, their focus was as often on the legacy of empire than on the struggle with communism. National stories, not least in the unraveling of a colonial past, were more important in the framing of domestic politics than in the endeavor to forge a common European position. Thus, the European commitment to the common front against communism did not prevent Britain and France from taking robustly different views of their national interests—or about the role in European security that should properly be allotted to the United States. In broad terms, France was on the side of more Europe and less America, and Britain was on the side of more America and less Europe. But the character of the U.S. president also mattered. European leaders sometimes competed for the attention of the occupant of the White House. On other occasions, they preferred to keep their distance.

For all that, it suited and reassured Europe's politicians that the United States had become their continent's leading power. Europe during the second half of the twentieth century faced the reality of decline. In such circumstances, the only thing more irritating than U.S. primacy was U.S. indifference. The arrogance of the White House could be humiliating, but the outcome that European governments most feared was one in which the United States lost interest and left them to their own devices. For its part, Washington found itself conducting several different sets of relationships—with the EU over economic, trade, and, latterly, climate change policy; with governments in London, Paris, and Bonn/Berlin over "harder" foreign policy and security issues; and with the plethora of small as well as larger nations in NATO over collective security. It was little wonder that Secretary of State Henry A. Kissinger once famously lamented Europe's lack of a single telephone number.

This opening chapter in this alliance was written in the rubble of 1945: at the end of a conflict that had left most of the European continent broken and exhausted. For Americans and Europeans alike, the relationship was framed by the unfolding realization that Stalin's Soviet Union was determined first to divide Europe and then expand communism's influence westward.

The Europe that emerged in the immediate aftermath of the war reflected in large part the genius of Franklin Delano Roosevelt, the resolve of Harry Truman, and the generosity and insight of George Marshall. The new global institutions—the United Nations, the International Monetary Fund, and the rest—held up a mirror to the new geopolitical realities. Most had been shaped in collaboration with Washington's European allies. Britain and France had been consulted, in the case of the former closely so. But the rule book depended above all on U.S. power.

The Europeans took time to adjust to the world as it was becoming. Britain had been left exhausted in victory, France still bore the physical and psychological scars of German occupation, Italy teetered toward communism, and Germany was devastated and divided. Poland, Czechoslovakia, Hungary, and the rest were under Stalin's control.

Winston Churchill was convinced that Britain would remain one of the great powers. While he backed U.S. efforts to promote unity on the devastated European continent, his initial assumption, one widely shared in London, was that Britain could stand aloof. In Churchill's mind, Britain would sit instead at the intersection of three spheres of global influence: the empire and commonwealth, the Atlantic partnership, and Europe. It would continue to treat as an equal with Washington and Moscow. De Gaulle was similarly convinced that France could reclaim its past glory, an illusion that was to persist beyond the collapse of its power in Asia signaled by the humiliating defeat of French forces at Dien Bien Phu in 1954 and to last until French forces fled Algeria in 1963.

It was not immediately apparent that the United States and the Western European powers would forge a permanent alliance. Stalin's intentions and the West's response were not quite as obvious in 1945 as they now seem in retrospect. But beginning with George F. Kennan's "long telegram" sent from Moscow in February 1946, a growing number of U.S. officials began to warn about Soviet intentions in Europe. French and British leaders consulted on how to rebuild their power, while some voices in Washington began to call for the return of U.S. troops to Europe. Europe's leaders would both resent Washington's power and crave the security it offered them against the advance of communism. Thus, Ernest Bevin, the tireless foreign secretary in the Labour government that took power in Britain in 1945, eventually would throw all his energy into the creation of a new military alliance with the United States—and insist all the while that Britain secured a nuclear bomb stamped with its own flag.

The policy of the United States toward the continent combined great acts of generosity and strategic wisdom with a ruthless determination to stamp its own authority on the new international order. The Marshall Plan for the economic reconstruction of the continent sat alongside the often harsh terms imposed on Britain in exchange for assistance. To fury in London, in 1945 Washington summarily revoked its wartime nuclear cooperation agreement with Britain. In July 1946, the United States granted a large loan to Britain that was intended to enable it to balance the needs of domestic reconstruction and continued maintenance of Britain's extensive overseas commitments but on the condition that Britain make the pound sterling convertible—a step that proved damaging to the British economy and was seen in London as aimed at undermining the cohesion of the British Empire and Commonwealth, which was partly underpinned by the sterling bloc.

What followed—the Marshall Plan launched in 1947, the founding of NATO in 1949 as a solid front against the expansion of Soviet communism, and the Franco–German rapprochement that began with Jean Monnet's proposal in 1950 to establish a European Coal and Steel Community (the body that ultimately led to the creation of today's EU)—was not preordained. History often recalls the past in straight lines. In the Europe of the late 1940s, there were very few of those.

Two events confirmed the Europeans and Americans in their assessment of Moscow's expansionist intentions. In 1947, Stalin ordered Poland and Czechoslovakia to withdraw from talks in Paris about the economic reconstruction program that prefigured the Marshall Plan. In the following year, the Soviets blockaded Berlin. The iron curtain that Churchill had foreshadowed in his Fulton speech of March 1946 had fallen across Europe. Large numbers of U.S. troops soon would be returning to Europe, establishing the vast military infrastructure that would secure the continent against communism.

France and Britain for a time had imagined that they could go it alone. But by late 1947, Bevin was pressing for an American security commitment to Europe. In March 1948, Britain, France, and the three Benelux countries concluded the Brussels Treaty, in which they pledged to come to each other's defense in the event of an external attack. They also established the Brussels Treaty Organization, the precursor body to the Western European Union formed in 1954. Bevin hoped that the United States, impressed by European efforts at self-help, would be drawn into the alliance, which in fact happened with the North Atlantic Treaty, which was negotiated beginning in April 1948 and signed in Washington in April of the following year.

West Germany was established in May 1949 by the unification of the British, French, and U.S. occupation zones after early hopes for a settlement among the four powers over reunification of the country were dashed. Its priority was first survival and then assurance that it could be anchored firmly to the West—politically as well as economically. When Paris and London asked for a U.S. security guarantee in NATO, West Germany was initially left outside. France at first resisted U.S. pressures for West German rearmament and refused an alliance with Germany. Britain shifted sooner to see a democratic German state as an essential buffer against the Soviet Union. In the early 1950s, the French reluctantly agreed to controlled West German rearmament within the framework of a European Defense Community (EDC) and, after the EDC was voted down by the French National Assembly in 1954, to West Germany's integration into NATO the following year.

Washington believed that a more united Western Europe would strengthen the West's defenses against communism—within as well as without. When Britain stood aloof from the creation of the Franco–German coal and steel community, Secretary of State Dean Acheson urged France to assume the political leadership of the continent. As the United States pressed the cause of Franco–German rapprochement, U.S. statesmanship met that of the architects of a new Europe: Monnet and Robert Schuman of France, Konrad Adenauer of Germany, the Belgian federalist Paul Henri Spaak, and other leaders from the Netherlands, Luxembourg, and Italy. European integration offered France an opportunity to contain the new Federal Republic of Germany and assurance that the reviving German power would be locked into the Western system. Britain wanted the best of both worlds: to remain a European power but not to the extent that any commitments in Europe inhibited its global role. For France, containment of Germany was the organizing obsession.

The refusal of Britain and France to abandon their imperial pretensions was a constant cause of friction with the United States. During World War II, Roosevelt made clear his distaste for colonialism by urging, for example, an outraged Churchill to move toward independence for India, Britain's most important colonial possession. In the postwar period, U.S. officials soon recognized that there was a contradiction between their policy of building up Britain and France as bulwarks against Soviet power and continued pressures on these countries to rapidly divest themselves of the colonies on which their economic prosperity, status as global as opposed to purely European powers, and indeed their national self-confidence largely depended.

The United States provided domestic economic aid to Britain in part so that it could maintain its extensive military commitments in the Middle East from which the United States benefited and underwrote much of the cost of France's war in Indochina so that the French could stabilize their status as both a global and a European power. But tensions over how to handle colonial possessions that U.S. officials thought were owed their independence remained an irritant in Europe–U.S. relations.

This abiding tension between the Western powers was crystallized by a crisis in the Middle East. In 1956, Egypt's Gamal Abdel Nasser, casting himself as the leader of a new Arab nationalism, seized the Suez Canal from its Franco–British owners. In Britain and France, the Egyptian president's decision to nationalize the canal was both a threat to their strategic interests east of Suez and, as importantly, a powerful blow to their prestige in a region where they had long been the dominant powers. Britain saw a threat to its supply of cheap oil, and France saw a fresh challenge to its dominion in Algeria. But Washington insisted that there was insufficient provocation for the West to intervene militarily against Nasser.

In spite of warnings from Eisenhower, France and Britain conspired in an Israeli-led military intervention. The canal was seized. The victory was short lived. Amid condemnations at the United Nations and the strong disapproval of the United States, sterling came under sustained pressure on financial markets. The Bank of England struggled to support the British currency. Washington refused to come to the aid of Anthony Eden's government. Eden bowed to the U.S. demand for withdrawal of British troops. Only when the decision was taken did he inform Paris.

The Suez debacle spoke to geopolitical realities. France and Britain were waning powers. They would henceforth have to adjust to an international order shaped by the superpower standoff between the United States and the Soviet Union. It was a wrenching adjustment and one that changed decisively the political dynamic between London, Paris, and Washington. Britain had been exhausted by the war, and its retreat from empire was already well under way. The humiliation of Suez accelerated this rendezvous with reality. The conclusion that Britain drew from the debacle was that never again could it detach itself from the United States on major questions of war and peace. The "special relationship" with Washington, reaffirmed more than half a century later when Prime Minister Gordon Brown visited Obama at the White House, became the organizing principle of British foreign policy.

France drew a different conclusion. When, on November 6, 1956, Anthony Eden telephoned Guy Mollet to tell the French prime minister that Britain had bowed to U.S. pressure to withdraw, he confirmed what the French had long suspected: when the chips were down, Britain would not defy the United States. Albion had been confirmed in its perfidy. France would take a different course: it would build Europe as a counterweight to U.S. power. Germany's Adenauer, who happened to be visiting Mollet when the call from Eden came through, had an answer. "Europe will be your revenge," Adenauer told Mollet. A few months later, the six founding members of the common market signed the Treaty of Rome.

Suez was Europe's last imperial hurrah. It had been planned as an Anglo-French venture, based on the assumption that Europe could still act independently of Washington when its own vital interests were at stake. But the British retreat in the face of U.S. power had been foreshadowed. In 1944, de Gaulle had urged on Churchill a new postwar alliance: "Should England and France act together," he had said, "they will wield enough power to prevent anything being done which they themselves had not accepted or decided." But even on the threshold of victory, Churchill was doubtful, saying of the Americans, "It is better to persuade the stronger than go against them." In the aftermath of Suez, Harold Macmillan, successor as prime minister to the ill-fated Eden, drew the same conclusion.

Britain did not want to be locked out of Europe—it would press repeatedly for membership of the new club—but it looked first to the other side of the Atlantic. A secret report prepared in 1960 for Macmillan on how best to preserve British influence in the postimperial age presented the strategy in the bluntest terms: "Our status in the world will depend largely on their [the United States] readiness to treat us as their closest ally." By now, Macmillan wanted the United States to pressure the six to modify the terms on which they would have allowed Britain to enter the European Economic Community (EEC)—to come up with a special arrangement that would have allowed Britain to be both in the new community and to keep its special status with regard to the commonwealth and certain domestic policies. But the United States, which strongly backed European integration on the Brussels model, was unwilling to take this step. Even had the United States had been willing to take up the British cause, it is unlikely, after Suez, that U.S. pressure on France would have changed de Gaulle's attitude toward Britain.

Thus, Suez provided the context for the policy toward the United States pursued by Britain and France from Macmillan to Prime Minister Tony Blair and from de Gaulle to President Jacques Chirac. Britain chose subservience to Washington, France defiance. In the aftermath of the war, the United States had seen a united Europe as a buttress against communism. Returning to office in 1958, de Gaulle saw it as a counterweight to U.S. power—as long, that is, as perfidious Albion remained excluded. For his part, Macmillan's submission to Washington was not without its conceit. Britain, he mused, could serve as Greece to the Rome of the United States.

The rivalry—between France and Britain as much as between France and the United States—was played out in subsequent decades. It explained France's determination to forge ahead with European integration—and, until 1973, to lock Britain out of the new common market. It was reflected in de Gaulle's development of an independent nuclear deterrent and his decision in 1966 to withdraw France from NATO's military command. On Britain's part, it explained the decision to "buy American" to sustain its position as a nuclear power. Ultimately, the lesson drawn also explained Blair's decision to fight another war in the deserts of the Middle East some half a century later—only this second time, Britain stood alongside the United States. France sought vainly to prevent it. The Suez debacle thus shaped the three most important sets of relationships within the alliance—between Britain and the United States, between France and the United States, and between France and Britain—for the next half century.

For all that Adenauer had encouraged France in the process of European integration, West Germany was for most of the time a bystander in these arguments. In the early decades after the war its overarching priority was to anchor the Federal Republic in the emerging Euro-Atlantic community. So its instincts were Atlanticist as well as European. Economic integration within Europe entrenched the peace with France, even if at the cost of ceding political leadership of the European enterprise to Paris. Membership of NATO gave the Federal Republic security against the Soviet threat. *Westpolitik*, as Adenauer's policy would be called, also provided the framework for the "miracle" that would see West Germany emerge as Europe's most important economic power. Only in the early 1970s, when Chancellor Willy Brandt promoted the thaw in the relationship with the East, did German policymakers recover the confidence to assert an independent view. The Bonn government never gave up on the goal of reunification. *Ostpolitik*, as it was called, encapsulated the importance of a geography that required Germany to look east as well as west. It also rekindled periodic fears among the Federal Republic's allies that the Bonn government might trade neutrality for reunification.

The institution that restrained these tensions in the face of the existential threat to Europe from the Soviet Union was NATO. Even after France's

departure from the military command structure, the political alliance established by the North Atlantic Treaty in 1949 forced on its members both the
habit of cooperation and the necessity of compromise. The military alliance
was the instrument of the Western policy of containment. It did not stop
Soviet tanks from rolling into Hungary in 1956 or into Czechoslovakia in
1968. It could not prevent East Germany from building the wall in Berlin.
It stood on the sidelines when Moscow sent troops into Afghanistan. But
NATO, with its forward-based nuclear arsenal and its doctrine of flexible
response, was the essential brake on Soviet expansion westward. From the
early 1970s, it also assumed a broader political role as the alliance committed to a dual policy of maintaining both military deterrence and conducting a policy of détente and political dialogue with the Soviet Union and its
allies.

NATO did not put an end to transatlantic disputes, even those between
Britain and Washington. NATO remained silent about Vietnam, and President Johnson voiced fury at the refusal of Harold Wilson's government to
provide British troops for the war. *Ostpolitik* was seen by Richard Nixon's
administration as a potential threat to the alliance. European governments
dragged their heels in response to U.S. pressure to provide more conventional forces for the front line against Soviet communism, preferring to rely
on the U.S. nuclear deterrent.

One low point came in 1973. Secretary of State Kissinger, representing
a Nixon administration already enmeshed in the Watergate affair, declared
that this should be "the year of Europe," a moment to reshape the transatlantic alliance. For Europe, it was instead a year of crisis. A second devaluation of the dollar, the Arab-Israeli War, and oil price hikes by the Organization of the Petroleum Exporting Countries left the continent in disarray.
Washington's effort to define a new institutional relationship with Brussels
served only to rekindle Franco–British rivalries. Split over the response to
the Arab-Israeli War, the EEC likewise failed to find common positions on
the energy and economic crises.

New tensions arose in the early 1980s when a NATO decision to modern-
ize its nuclear arsenal by stationing Pershing II and cruise medium-range
nuclear missiles in Europe at times threatened to fracture the alliance.
Convinced that the West was losing ground to a militarily resurgent Soviet
Union, U.S. president Ronald Reagan adopted policies that included a substantial U.S. arms buildup, intensified economic pressure against the Soviet
Union (seen in an attempt to block construction of a gas pipeline between
Siberia and Western Europe), and an initial pullback from arms control
negotiations. The Western Europeans, who by this time had developed a
strong vested interest in closer ties with the Soviets, balked at what they
saw as Reagan's neo–Cold War policies. Britain's Margaret Thatcher shared

Reagan's suspicions of the Soviets and tended to support his policies more than did continental European leaders.

For all her love affair with Reagan, however, Thatcher raged at the U.S. president's hesitation in backing Britain's 1982 military expedition to recover the Falkland Islands from Argentina. President François Mitterrand offered Thatcher strong support in her drive to reclaim the Falklands, sharing secret technology that had earlier been supplied by France to the Argentine air force. But for Thatcher, a champion of the "English-speaking peoples," the pull of Reagan's Washington was too strong, while France continued to see its destiny as Europe's foremost power. Paradoxically, there was no great difference between Paris and London on the essential political architecture of the EU: both wanted governments to remain in the driving seat, rejecting the federalist institution building of Germany and many of the smaller EU states. But while France saw Europe as an extension of his power, Thatcher's Britain viewed closer integration as a threat to its sovereignty.

The imperative of collective defense ensured that the West weathered these storms. After the economic disarray of the 1970s, the 1980s saw Europe launch ambitious plans for a single market in goods, services, and labor. A twin-track approach of nuclear modernization and arms control negotiations with Moscow defied Soviet efforts to rupture the alliance. Reagan's apparent willingness to strike a unilateral nuclear disarmament bargain with Mikhail Gorbachev at their 1986 Reykjavik summit, after the United States had restored what Reagan called a "margin of safety" and was again interested in engaging with the Soviets, initially alarmed U.S. allies. But by 1987, the United States had signed the Intermediate-Range Nuclear Forces Treaty with Moscow, an agreement that was generally welcomed by the Western Europeans and that marked the beginning of the end of the East–West military buildup. Within a few years, the Cold War would be history.

The fall of the Berlin Wall in October 1989 and the subsequent collapse of communism in the former satellite states of the Soviet Union should have been cause for unalloyed celebration. The images of East Germans pouring through the broken concrete and the crowds celebrating freedom in Warsaw, Prague, and Budapest underscored a victory not only for the peoples of the former communist empire but also for the West's system of liberal democracy.

Success, however, also robbed the European allies of the United States of the certainties to which they had become accustomed. Without the Cold War, Europe would no longer be at the center of the geopolitical attention of the United States. Thus, as freedom in the eastern half of their continent was followed by the dissolution of the Soviet Empire, there was as much private foreboding as public celebration. The West had claimed a famous victory in the great ideological struggle of the twentieth century, but many of Europe's politicians were soon fretting about the consequences.

To some in Washington, the demise of the Soviet Empire heralded the "end of history."[3] President George H. W. Bush tried to prop up Gorbachev for as long as possible as a way of allowing reforms to continue and believed that it was important not to try scoring domestic or international political points by "dancing on the grave of communism." The mood in old Europe was even more circumspect. In London and Paris, the whispers were about the return of a dangerous past. For all the risk of a nuclear conflagration, the Cold War had delivered security. The continent's frozen landscape had imprisoned the demons of European nationalism. The division of Germany had rid the continent of the balance-of-power politics that had so often ended in war. The security of the United States had provided the essential security guarantee for integration within the EU.

Europe had prospered mightily under the protection of the U.S. nuclear arsenal. If Washington had often been irritated by the disinclination of its partner to contribute more of its treasure to the enterprise, there was little it could do. To abandon Europe would have been to cede victory to Soviet communism. The occasional transatlantic disputes had been trivial when measured against this shared endeavor.

All these calculations had now changed. In the minds of European politicians, victory in the Cold War had put collective defense in question. Did the sole superpower need Europe any longer? How much attention would it pay to its old allies in the reconfiguration of the continent? Would U.S. politicians decide that they had done their bit for alliance and that it was time to bring the troops home? Even as policymakers celebrated the defeat of communism, they worried about the future bequeathed to them by victory.

European leaders found themselves preoccupied once again with the vexing issue they thought had been banished permanently to the pages of history. The German question—how to contain the nation that sits so powerfully at the center of the continent—had returned. France had grown accustomed to exercising the political leadership of Europe. Would it now be challenged by a united Germany? Would the shift in that country's center of gravity from Bonn to Berlin see Germany turn eastward? Would the EU still be powered by the Franco–German motor? Would the fragile democracies of Eastern and Central Europe fall prey to populist nationalists? How quickly should they be brought into the EU or NATO? Would Russia collapse in on itself? The questions came thick and fast.

Thatcher and Mitterrand flirted briefly with the idea of seeking to delay German unification. The four Berlin powers technically still held a veto. Bush squashed that idea, assuring West German chancellor Helmut Kohl that he had the full support of the United States in reunifying Germany. The U.S. president also caused some offense—and much concern in London—by suggesting that the United States now looked to Germany for European leadership. France turned its mind to binding Germany more deeply into the EU; the collapse of communism was followed in short order by the Maastricht treaty promising Europe a new single currency. Britain devoted its diplomatic efforts to ensuring that a role was found for NATO that would keep the United States in Europe.

In truth, the bipolar world of the Cold War gave way to an uncomfortable and sometimes ugly interlude. Instead of grabbing the opportunities of victory, political leaders on both sides of the Atlantic retreated into their domestic preoccupations. The map of Europe had changed irrevocably, and the Western powers were obliged to respond. But their approaches were cautious and reactive. There was none of the bold idealism that had marked out the policymakers of the late 1940s.

President Bush spoke initially of the opportunity of a new world order to entrench peace and freedom across the world. The international coalition, of Arab as well as European states, assembled to expel Saddam Hussein from Kuwait in the first Gulf War of 1991, raised hopes of a new global alliance to preserve the international peace. Bush, though, was a cautious politician. He was embarrassed by leaks emanating from his own Defense Department that suggested that some U.S. planners favored a U.S. strategy of heading off the emergence of any new "peer competitors" to take the place of the Soviet Union in a new bipolar rivalry. Many in Europe rejected what they saw as U.S. pretension to a "unipolar" world, while in the United States a domestic backlash grew against Bush for his seeming neglect of U.S. domestic interests in favor of international activism. Bush himself balked at an expansive U.S. role in some regions and with regard to some issues, but in his studied pragmatism he may have let slip a chance to begin reshaping the system created in 1945.

During his 1992 election campaign, Bill Clinton focused on domestic issues, the economy in particular, but he also criticized Bush for his administration's ineffectiveness in confronting the tragedy in Bosnia. Once in office, however, Clinton proved extremely reluctant to deploy U.S. forces for broader humanitarian objectives not directly tied to U.S. national interests. Clinton withdrew U.S. forces from Somalia after a disastrous firefight in which eighteen army rangers were killed.

On the other side of the Atlantic, some considered this a moment for Europe to strut its stuff on the international stage. The EU, with its single market, common trade policy, and plans for a single currency, was already an economic superpower with a share of global output and trade rivaling that of the United States. The Maastricht treaty, with its provisions for a Common Foreign and Security Policy (CFSP), had provided the EU with an institutional framework to speak with one voice on global affairs. The only thing missing was the political will and leadership to make it work.

The violent breakup of the former Yugoslavia into its six constituent republics shattered the complacency. As the Balkans descended into a vicious war, Washington made it clear that it intended to leave this one to Europe. The United States did not have a dog in the fight, observed James Baker, George H. W. Bush's secretary of state. Luxembourg foreign minister Jacques Poos took up the challenge. Speaking for Europe as a member of the troika—the foreign ministers of the past, current, and future presidency countries of the EU Council of Ministers—Poos famously declared that "the hour of Europe" had dawned. The EU at last would show its capacity to keep the peace in its own backyard. Hope or hubris, the EU's efforts at political conciliation were lost as Bosnia and Croatia were engulfed by wars against the more powerful Serbia.

France and Britain took the political lead in responding to the crisis—if one could call vacillation taking the lead. Europe's two most powerful nations—the only two with militaries capable of projecting significant force—were ineffectual in pushing forward the EU role. Europe offered talks and troops for a UN peacekeeping force. Yet the two European nations were unwilling to deploy the military might needed to secure an effective cease-fire. To complicate things, the responses were colored by history. Paris and London harbored sympathies for the Serbs; Germany insisted on special consideration for the Croats. Washington's response to the escalating fighting was to suggest that the international community level the battlefield by lifting the embargo on arms supplies to the outgunned Bosnian Muslims. Europe resisted but also hesitated in it own efforts to broker peace. Serbia's Slobodan Milosevic, throwing the weight of the former Yugoslav army behind the Bosnian Serbs, laughed at calls for a cease-fire.

As the death toll mounted and the scenes of carnage were played nightly on the television screens of CNN, the mood in Washington hardened against the Serbs. The massacres in the Balkans came to be seen as an emblem of U.S. as well as European failure. For all its initial reluctance, the Clinton administration argued for the lifting of the arms embargo on the Bosnian Muslims to be combined with air strikes against Serbian forces. The moment of ultimate shame for Europe came in July 1995, when Dutch troops serving with the UN peacekeeping force stood aside as Bosnian Serb forces entered the town of Srebrenica. Several thousand Bosnian Muslims were slaughtered.

In late 1995, the United States finally committed its own forces to a NATO mission to rescue UN peacekeepers and to compel Serbia to a negotiated settlement. France too finally lost patience with Serbian aggression. For a brief few weeks, Paris found itself closer to Washington than did Britain. The Srebrenica massacre forced the hand of John Major's British government. London scurried into line. The Serbs were brought to heel by NATO air strikes.

Overall, the response of the European powers to the Balkans war had exposed their national prejudices, demonstrated the EU's military impotence, and damaged relations with Washington. The claim that Europe could keep the peace on its own continent had been shattered by the nightly television images of carnage in the Balkans. A war that claimed 200,000 lives and saw the return to European soil of genocide and ethnic cleansing eventually was settled only by the reluctant intervention of the United States. Europe's major powers were humbled by their inaction. But the U.S. performance was equally flawed, at least until the United States decided to act to force the settlement at Dayton in the autumn of 1995. Chirac had declared caustically of Clinton's initial caution that the leadership of the free world was "vacant." But his sarcasm spoke as forcefully to French and European vacillation.

The Dayton accord salved transatlantic wounds. It also marked out a new role for NATO as the alliance's forces took charge of peacekeeping. By the start of 1996, some 60,000 troops, a third of them American, had moved into Bosnia to keep the peace negotiated at Dayton. The successful campaign later in the decade to drive Milosevic from Kosovo would salvage a little more of Europe's pride, even if, once again, the taming of Serb ambitions depended on U.S. airpower. There was yet another glimpse in these two episodes of Europe's eternal ambivalence about U.S. power. Europeans at first grumbled about the Clinton administration's refusal to take command of events; once it did so, the same Europeans complained that Washington was insufficiently consensual.

By 1998, Milosevic had recovered his confidence and was sending Serbian troops into largely Muslim Kosovo to snuff out calls in the province for independence. By the end of that year, it seemed that events in Bosnia were repeating themselves as Kosovars were driven from their homes and over the borders to neighboring Macedonia and Albania. Tony Blair, elected in 1997 as Britain's prime minister, made a name for himself by publicly pressuring Clinton to commit, if necessary, U.S. forces to the cause of expelling the Serbs from Kosovo. In a celebrated speech in Chicago in 1999, delivered on the eve of NATO's Washington summit to celebrate the fiftieth anniversary of the alliance, Blair sought to recast the role of the Western alliance as one committed to confronting tyranny beyond its borders.[4] The British prime minister proposed a new doctrine of humanitarian intervention. Tyrants could no longer be allowed to threaten the international peace or to carry out acts of violence and genocide against their own people. In Blair's mind, NATO would be an instrument of this new internationalism. Intervention in the Balkans had already seen the alliance step beyond its founding commitment to the territorial defense of Western Europe. Blair wanted it to assume still broader responsibilities.

The speech also spoke in part to another shameful episode during the years after the collapse of the Soviet Union. As war had raged in the Balkans, the

Hutu-dominated government in Rwanda launched a genocidal attack on the minority Tutsis. France, with its strong political and cultural presence in Africa, might have been expected to take the lead in rousing international action against the slaughter. Instead, it prevaricated. Major's government in Britain turned away. So did the Clinton administration. Hundreds of thousands were slaughtered.

Beyond the Balkans, the immediate strategic challenge facing the alliance during the 1990s was to ensure that the democracy flowering in the east of the continent did not fall victim to economic chaos and the rise of new tyrannies. That meant expansion eastward of the borders of the EU and of the NATO alliance. Here U.S. impatience met European caution. The new geography of Europe might have allowed for a neat division of labor within the alliance. The EU would seek to entrench stability in the new democracies of Eastern and Central Europe by offering them a rapid path to membership of the EU—that, after all, is what it had done when Spain, Portugal, and Greece had thrown off the coils of dictatorship. Washington, for its part, would take the lead in assuring Russia that it too could prosper in a new relationship with the West.

Practice did not match theory. Europe was mired in a series of other crises; a hurricane on the foreign exchange markets in 1992 had threatened to sweep away its exchange rate mechanism and with it hopes for a single European currency; the war in Bosnia was exposing the impotence of its foreign policy. Germany was preoccupied with unification. Meanwhile, France and some others saw in the admission of Central and Eastern European states both a threat to the cohesion of the EU and a dilution of their own position within it. Thus, the EU dragged its feet on enlargement, signaling that it would probably be a decade before the former communist states met the strict criteria for membership that leaders set out at their Copenhagen summit in 1993.

The Warsaw Pact had been dissolved in the summer of 1991. Irritated by the hesitations over enlargement at EU headquarters in Brussels, Washington responded positively to applications from the new democracies to join NATO. The Europeans were corralled into agreement. Simultaneously, the Clinton administration sought to reassure Moscow that it was not seeking to encircle Russia: assurances were given about troop deployments, and Russia was invited into a formal partnership arrangement with NATO. Europeans, the Germans in particular, voiced unease about a potential backlash in Moscow (this was to come later during the presidency of Vladimir Putin) if Russia felt that it was being humiliated. Many in Washington, including the long-retired Kennan, shared these doubts. But Europe was divided, and the U.S. administration determined to press ahead. Poland, the Czech Republic, and Hungary joined the alliance in 1999. Others soon followed. By the time President Obama arrived in Strasbourg in 2009, the original NATO of twelve had become one of twenty-six. By then, most of the new entrants had also been admitted into the EU.

For all the turmoil of the 1990s, the century and the millennium closed with the alliance in better shape than many Europeans had feared. For all their initial reluctance, Europe and the United States had committed troops to the Balkans. The new democracies of Central and Eastern Europe had begun to find shelter under the West's security umbrella. Cooperation in the Balkans had given some impetus to Franco–British defense cooperation: in December 1998, the two countries signed the St. Malo agreement, which added a defense dimension to the EU's fledging CFSP. NATO had extended its purpose beyond territorial defense. In the future, as the communiqué of the alliance's 1999 Washington summit declared, it would act to safeguard "common interests" as well as territory.

It was already evident, however, that an alliance of necessity had now become one of choice. The Euro-Atlantic community could no longer rely on a common enemy to keep it together, nor, beyond the pressing concern to keep the peace in the Balkans, was there a fundamental agreement on the strategic purpose of the alliance. Sustaining solidarity in the face of divergent interests and threat perceptions would likely get harder.

When Dean Acheson wrote his memoir, he called it *Present at the Creation*.[5] The creation he had in mind was the panoply of international institutions and rules created under U.S. leadership from the rubble of World War II. As the United States prepared during the winter of 2002 to go to war against Iraq, many European policymakers concluded that they were present at the destruction.

The underlying assumptions of the post–Cold War order—that peace depended not only on the military might of the sole superpower but also on the legitimacy flowing from the international rule of law—seemed to be disintegrating. So did the bargain at the heart of the Atlantic alliance—that Europe acknowledged U.S. leadership and, in return, was accorded a voice in setting the rules. In its determination to topple Saddam Hussein, the United States seemed set on demolishing its own construction. This, in the minds of the Bush administration, was the unipolar moment of the United States: U.S. power would reshape the Middle East and beyond in its own image.

As the United States prepared to demonstrate its power, Europe confronted its weakness on the world stage. Its energies had been directed at the single-currency project and, belatedly, at opening its doors to the former communist states. Germany's preoccupation with the costly process of unification and sluggish economic growth in France and elsewhere had sapped the continent's political authority. European governments had taken and spent large "peace dividends" in the years following the collapse of communism. Commitments to the Balkans notwithstanding, their militaries were underresourced and neglected.

The transatlantic breach over Iraq was foreshadowed at a meeting in Brussels of the NATO Council only weeks after the terrorist attacks on the United States in September 2001. In an act of solidarity and an expression of shared intent, Washington's NATO allies for the first time invoked article 5 of the alliance's founding treaty: an attack on one member state would be treated as an attack on all. The West would act as one in response to the terrible act of al-Qaeda terrorism. The reaction of Paul Wolfowitz, the U.S. deputy defense secretary, who had traveled to the Belgian capital for the meeting, instead set the scene for the subsequent dangerous fracture in the alliance. The U.S. administration, Wolfowitz responded, greatly appreciated this gesture of solidarity. But it would make its own decisions on how to respond to the first attack on the U.S. mainland since 1812. "Don't call us and we probably won't call you" is how one European ambassador later described Wolfowitz's presentation.

The inescapable implication was that the United States did not intend to be encumbered by the views of its allies in hunting down Osama bin Laden. Instead, Washington would invite others to join a "coalition of the willing." The leadership of the United States—the pillar of the alliance—was to be replaced by U.S. primacy. As for Europe, in President's Bush's words, it would have to decide whether it was "with us or against us."

Bush's subsequent "axis of evil" speech, joining the regimes in Iran and North Korea with that in Iraq as enemies to be overturned by U.S. might, confirmed most Europeans in their fear that the United States was cutting loose of a rules-based system. In discussions with his European counterparts, Donald Rumsfeld, the U.S. defense secretary, scorned their attachment to old notions of international legitimacy. The attack on the U.S. homeland had rendered void any previous conventions.

The Manichaean worldview embedded in Bush's "war on terror" added to European discomfort. Britain's Blair shared some of the analysis that the West faced a generational conflict with the most extreme manifestations of Islam. It was not as much a war between civilizations as a war about civilization, Blair would say. But for most European leaders, Bush's chosen phrase seemed likely to inflate tensions with the Muslim world. Blair's own advisers shook their heads. There might be a case for removing Iraq's Saddam Hussein, but lumping together al-Qaeda with groups such as the Iraqi Baathists, the Sunni Hamas, and the Shia Hezbollah ignored the distinct motivations and ambitions of these myriad groups. The prevailing European view was that Bush was aiding his enemies by bestowing unwonted cohesion on the extremists and undue prestige on bin Laden's al-Qaeda.

To European minds, the danger was compounded by Washington's unwillingness to press for peace between Israel and the Palestinians. Under pressure from Blair, the Bush administration did pledge itself to a two-state solution in the region. During its second term, it would push the so-called Annapolis process to provide a basis for renewed negotiations. But it was obvious to all that the White House was a reluctant peacemaker. Europeans saw the Arab–Israeli conflict at the very heart of rising Muslim radicalism and called for evenhanded U.S. mediation. In the event, American policy toward the Palestinians became almost indistinguishable from that of Israel.

So the outpouring of sympathy and solidarity with the United States in the aftermath of 9/11—France's *Le Monde* had famously carried a front page headline declaring, "We are all Americans now"—quite quickly turned to disillusion and resentment. Destroying al-Qaeda's camps and pushing the Taliban out of Afghanistan was one thing. This military campaign bore the stamp of UN authorization. Ousting Saddam Hussein from Iraq without the explicit authority of the United Nations was another. Bush divided the world into friends and enemies. Public opinion in Europe, regularly stirred by the bellicose pronouncements of Vice President Dick Cheney, turned almost as quickly against the United States as it had rallied behind it during the weeks after the collapse of the twin towers. One senior British diplomat was heard to remark laconically that Bush seemed intent on reinstating the bipolar world of the Cold War: on one side stood the United States and on the other anti-Americanism.

That was not to say that Europe spoke as one. Behind the almost universal public hostility to a war in Iraq lay a much more complicated debate between and within governments. Britain would eventually back the war; so too, with varying degrees of enthusiasm, would Spain and Italy and most of the former communist states of Eastern and Central Europe. Iraq would thus succeed in rupturing Europe as well as the alliance.

Blair shared the widespread European fear that a unilateralist U.S. response to 9/11 could see the breakup of postwar Western order. But he drew a different conclusion from that of Chirac. The French president wanted to confront the United States with sufficient opposition to oblige Bush to back away from war against Iraq. He enlisted Germany's Gerhard Schröder in the enterprise. Blair thought opposition futile. Never modest about his own powers of persuasion, the British prime minister thought that he could rally the international community around a common position, even on Iraq. If Bush could be convinced to try negotiation first—in the shape of the return of UN weapons inspectors to Iraq—the Security Council could be persuaded to give its blessing to an ultimatum to Saddam.

Behind this reasoning lay two convictions: Britain, as it had concluded after that other war in the desert in 1956, had to stay close to Washington, and, as Blair had said in his Chicago speech during the conflict in Kosovo, the multilateral system could survive only if the West was prepared to see its rules were enforced. Saddam had consistently defied the United Nations; to allow him to continue would undermine its credibility. For all the subsequent controversy about exaggerated intelligence, Blair did believe that Saddam was developing weapons of mass destruction.

In truth, the divisions that emerged over Iraq pre-dated 9/11. Blair had sent British warplanes into action in U.S. bombing raids against Saddam's military infrastructure during the Clinton presidency in an effort to enforce UN weapons inspections. France, along with Russia, had backed a relaxation of sanctions against Baghdad, not least because of its extensive commercial interests in the normalization of relations with Iraq. Chirac, like Blair, also looked back to Suez: in his case, to see Europe's role as a counterweight to the United States.

The Bush administration had been viewed with deep suspicion in Europe almost from the inauguration. On his first official visit to Europe in the summer of 2001, the president had been publicly upbraided at a summit with EU leaders for his disdainful rejection of the Kyoto climate change protocol. Repudiation of the International Criminal Court and the subsequent U.S. withdrawal from the Anti-Ballistic Missile Treaty with Russia spoke to Bush's dislike of any international agreement that seemed to constrain the freedom of action of the United States.

Yet as the invasion of Iraq approached and Blair failed to secure a second UN resolution giving unequivocal backing to the use of force, the angry exchanges between European governments sometimes matched the hostility toward Bush. Blair would later accuse Chirac of seeking to use the war to topple him as British prime minister. The French president charged Blair with craven submission to Washington.

Schröder abandoned Germany's traditionally Atlanticist tilt to join Chirac in the campaign against the war. For a time, these two European leaders teamed up with Russia's Putin in a common front against Washington. Such was the febrile atmosphere of the times that there was talk, crazy talk as it was bound to turn out, of a new Paris–Berlin–Moscow axis to challenge U.S. hegemony.

Ultimately, all the big European states lost from Bush's decision to oust Saddam. Britain would find itself enmeshed in a catastrophic war of occupation; Blair, though he went on to win another election, found that siding with Bush had drained his political authority at home. Spain's José Maria Aznar sacrificed to his support for the war his government's chance of reelection. Opposition to Bush, however, also carried no political rewards. Christian Democratic Angela Merkel became chancellor of Germany after her party edged out Schröder's in the September 2005 federal elections. When Chirac's term ended in 2007, his successor was the more Atlanticist Nicolas Sarkozy, who worked to repair relations with Washington.

The abiding irony of the Iraq episode was that Britain and France found that they had come full circle since their parting at Suez. Both had been proved wrong in the conclusions they had drawn from that first debacle in the desert half a century earlier. Blair, who had backed the invasion in the hope of keeping the United States in the international system, found that Britain's post-Suez policy of acting as a "bridge" between Europe and the United States had been tested to destruction. Instead, France and Germany's implacable opposition to the war had forced Blair to choose. In backing Bush, the British prime minister ruptured his relationships with Paris and Berlin. But France likewise discovered that the central premise of its foreign policy for the previous fifty years had been flawed. The French ambition had been to build Europe as an equal to the United States. In the event, the continent divided. Spain, Portugal, and a shoal of the EU's new members in Eastern and Central Europe preferred to side with Washington rather than with what Rumsfeld called the "old Europe" of Paris and Berlin. Enlargement to the east, the French discovered, had changed fundamentally the political dynamics of the EU. More Europe no longer meant more France.

Neither Blair nor Chirac would admit these fundamental strategic failures: the habit of keeping close to Washington was too deeply ingrained in London, and the instinct to oppose was as firmly established in Paris. But their departures from office and Obama's election saw the calculations beginning to change. Although the president still valued the special relationship with Britain—Gordon Brown, Blair's successor, was among the first visitors to the Obama White House—the new administration indicated that it would be unsentimental in its dealings with its European allies. Britain would count insofar as it could bring others along with it. As for France, Sarkozy would never abandon French exceptionalism, but in taking his country back into NATO's military structures, he recognized the futility of permanent competition with Washington.

There were other forces at work destined to reshape the alliance. Europe and the United States had said good-bye to the bipolar world at the end of the Cold War. The unipolar moment that followed for the United States had proved to be just that: a moment. The rise of China and India, Russia's new assertiveness as a vital energy producer, and the emergence of new powers in Latin America and Asia were redrawing the political map. Failing states, unconventional weapons proliferation, al-Qaeda–inspired terrorism, international criminal networks, poverty, and human insecurity threatened to turn order into disorder. Inevitably, the focus of America's strategic attention turned to Asia. Hillary Clinton, Obama's secretary of state, talked of a new strategic partnership with China. The new president, committed to the withdrawal of U.S. troops from Iraq, made the fight against the Taliban in Afghanistan and Pakistan an early priority. For all his soothing words, Europe wondered where it would fit in the new U.S. worldview.

From an objective standpoint, U.S. and European interests remained coincident: peace and stability in the most volatile areas of the world, most particularly in an arc of instability running from the Horn of Africa eastward through the Middle East and Central Asia, the defeat of the Taliban in Afghanistan, a two-state solution to the conflict between Israel and the Palestinians, the separation of moderate Islam from the violent extremism of al-Qaeda, a halt to unconventional weapons proliferation, and the expansion across the world of political systems grounded in pluralism and the rule of law.

The hurricane that swept through the global financial system during the winter of 2008–2009 spoke to the same set of shared challenges. After some initial differences, the United States and Europe cooperated closely in calming the storms that had raged on financial markets since the autumn of 2008. At the Group of 20 summit in London, the leaders of developed and emerging nations, including China, India, and others, along with the United States and Europe, met to confront the economic crisis. There was an obvious shared interest in coaxing the emerging powers into the system of global institutions and laws established after 1945. China's choices over the coming decades would be critical in determining the shape of the global order; the U.S. and European interests lay squarely in persuading Beijing to become a responsible stakeholder in the institutions of global governance. Logic thus said that the partnership between the United States and Europe should be as vital a pillar of common security as it was ever during the Cold War, albeit with its objectives and capabilities recast to meet the new challenges.

A renewed alliance, however, would also have to recognize differences of strategic perception and culture. Napoleon once said that to know a nation's geography was to know its foreign policy. Add history to geography, and you get a still better picture. The lesson that Europe has taken from history and geography was that military victories brought only temporary peace.

This was not well understood in the United States. The writer Robert Kagan described the gulf between Europe and the United States as one grounded in relative power. The United States was strong, and Europe was weak: the U.S. instinct to project force reflected its capacity to do so. Europe's preoccupation with "soft power" likewise held up a mirror to its lack of military punch.[6] There was something in this analysis. Europe's armed forces were severely underresourced and lacked the sophisticated technology and intelligence resources of the U.S. military.

But a better way to understand the difference was to ask what had been the impulses that had led Europe to take a large peace dividend and the

United States to sustain its defense budget after the fall of the Berlin Wall. For Europeans, geography and history meant that security is relative, with threats divided between the tolerable and the unacceptable, the inevitable and the avoidable. A different history and geography led the United States to seek invulnerability as well as invincibility. The United States had assumed a leadership role as the guarantor of global security. Its instinct was to "fix" things; the Europeans preferred to "manage" them.

The difference has been evident in the response to Islamist terrorism. After 9/11, Washington seemed to presume that the West faced a cohesive group of violent extremists set on overturning Western values and driving the "infidels" from the Middle East. Europeans, for all their shared determination to defeat al-Qaeda, saw a less homogeneous enemy—a range of different groups, some undoubtedly sharing the violent ambitions of bin Laden but others driven by more traditional grievances. For the United States, violent political Islam represented an external threat. For Europeans, with large and sometimes radicalized Muslim populations, the danger came from within as much as from without.

Behind Europe's particular differences with George W. Bush—from the war in Iraq to his administration's reluctance to press the cause of peace between Israel and the Palestinians to the president's disdain for efforts to slow global warming—lay a clash of strategic cultures. Europe saw a post–Cold War world anchored by multilateral bargains and rules, one in which military force, though occasionally necessary, was always a last resort. Diplomacy and the deployment of soft power would come first, and, if they failed, military intervention would carry the stamp of international legitimacy. The first Gulf War fitted this model; so, in its first stages, did the expulsion of the Taliban from Afghanistan. Iraq was different.

This was a worldview treated with disdain by the Bush administration. Those around the president saw multilateralism as synonymous with weakness: as a needless constraint on a United States that was as powerful as had been any nation in human history. This United States wanted the mission to determine the coalition, not vice versa. Over time, the quagmire in Iraq tempered this view. The United States learned that to be invincible is not necessarily to be invulnerable. The diplomats of the State Department, sidelined during Bush's first term, came back into view during the second. But it was too late to properly repair the relationship with Europe.

Obama brought an entirely different perspective to the White House. In part, this was inevitable. The United States had been weakened both by the war in Iraq and by an economic crisis that had placed, at best, a question mark over its brand of laissez-faire capitalism. Lacking tact, Gordon Brown declared the much-vaunted Washington Consensus to be dead.

The new president saw a world in which the United States remained on every measure the preeminent power but one in which the rise of new great powers in Asia, the unavoidable interdependence of globalization, and the asymmetric threats presented by violent Islamist extremism required U.S. leadership to be embedded in broad alliances.

This was what Europe had asked for of the new president; when it was offered, it was less clear that Europe was ready to accept the consequences. A renewed partnership with the United States would require Europe to bear some of the burdens of global leadership: in Afghanistan, most obviously, but also in Africa, in the Middle East, and in the Caucasus and Central Asia. Even as it joined Obama in promising to revitalize the Euro-Atlantic community, it hesitated to act.

The refusal of Sarkozy and Merkel to accept Turkey as a serious candidate for future membership of the EU testified to a strategic myopia among European leaders. Internal divisions on what sort of relationship to forge with a more belligerent Russia and whether to entice Ukraine in the wider European community were further evidence of Europe's hesitations. Even in the early days of Obama's administration, it seemed that having been offered the prize of a multilateralist America, European governments were retreating from the implications.

In such circumstances, the NATO leaders meeting in Strasbourg deferred serious discussion of the future role of the alliance. The wars in Kosovo and Afghanistan had taken it beyond the original concept of territorial defense. But they had not settled the argument as to what balance NATO should strike between guaranteeing peace and security on the European continent and providing forward defenses against the new threats of the twenty-first century. Most European governments agreed with the U.S. diagnosis that defeat in Afghanistan could undermine fatally what Obama had called the most successful alliance the world had ever known. For all that, when the U.S. president announced in the late autumn of 2009 a surge in U.S. forces in Afghanistan, U.S. allies provided mostly only modest additions to their contributions to the NATO effort.

Obama's presidency confronted Europe with a challenge it would have preferred to avoid. For all that Bush's unilateralism had been despised, it had provided Europe with an alibi. As long as the United States refused to acknowledge an international system of rules, Europe could sidestep its responsibilities. In embracing diplomacy and engagement, Obama stripped Europe of its excuses.

Several tests confronted the alliance in the summer of 2009. High on the list alongside Afghanistan was Iran's nuclear ambitions. Here, once again, Obama had called Europe's bluff by announcing that, thirty years after the seizing of the U.S. embassy in Tehran, Washington was prepared to open direct negotiations with the Iranian regime. The question this asked of U.S. allies was whether they were ready to give heft to the diplomatic effort to convince Iran that it would be the loser if it acquired the bomb. Amid an avalanche of diplomatic initiatives, Obama seemed ready to break with his predecessor's unquestioning support for the Israeli government in the conflict with the Palestinians. Europeans applauded but said less about how they might contribute to a settlement that provided guarantees of Israel's security as well as a homeland for Palestinians.

By early 2010, these and other issues likely to set the path of the transatlantic relationship stood in the balance. What was clear was that Obama had been disappointed by Europe's response to his efforts to reinvigorate the relationship. The prize for Europe was plain enough: a role alongside the United States in shaping a cooperative international order. The dangers of inaction were also clear: European irrelevance in a world in which influence was shifting eastward to the rising powers of Asia. For sixty years, the Atlantic Alliance had set the terms of global economic and political development. The world they now faced was multipolar in character and threaded with complexity in its challenges. The question was how closely Americans and Europeans would work together in shaping a different future.

SUGGESTIONS FOR FURTHER READING

Grant, Charles. *Is Europe Doomed to Fail as a Power?* London: Centre for European Reform, 2009.

Lundestad, Geir. *The United States and Western Europe since 1945: From "Empire" by Invitation to Transatlantic Drift.* New York: Oxford University Press, 2003.

McCausland, Jeffrey D., and Douglas T. Stuart. *US-UK Relations at the Start of the 21st Century.* Carlisle, PA: Strategic Studies Institute, Army War College.

Serfaty, Simon. *The Vital Partnership.* Boulder, CO: Rowman & Littlefield, 2007.

Serfaty, Simon, and Sven Biscop. *A Shared Security Strategy for a Euro-Atlantic Partnership of Equals: A Report of the Global Dialogue between the EU and the United States.* Washington, DC: Center for Strategic and International Studies, 2009.

Shapiro, Jeremy, and Nick Witney. *Towards a Post-American Europe: A Power Audit of EU-Russia Relations.* Berlin: European Council on Foreign Relations, 2009.

Tombs, Robert, and Isabelle Tombs. *That Sweet Enemy: Britain and France.* London: Pimlico, 2007.

Vasconcelos, Alvaro de, and Marcon Zaborowski. *The Obama Moment: European and American Perspectives.* Paris: European Union Institute for Security Studies, 2009.

4

Europe and Russia

Strategic Partnership and Strategic Mistrust

John Van Oudenaren and Ronald Tiersky

STRATEGIC PARTNERSHIP, STRATEGIC MISTRUST

Russia's relationship with Europe is a geopolitical story of major conse-quence that goes back centuries to the beginnings of the modern European order. Tsar Peter the Great (1682–1725) attempted to modernize Russia's economy and technology while protecting the country's authoritarian po-litical system from contamination by European Enlightenment ideas and culture. In subsequent centuries, Europe confronted a Russia that alternated between periods of introspection and retreat and aggressive moves toward Europe along its western frontier. Following its rise to power after unifica-tion in 1871, Germany was the major European power confronting Russia. Germany's national expansionist policy was the major cause of World War I, and Hitler's monomaniacal attempt to subordinate all of Europe to the Third Reich led to World War II and the Holocaust. Both wars were disasters for Russia as well as for Germany.

Russia's twentieth-century history was a succession of collapses. The tsar-ist empire collapsed in World War I and the Russian Revolution, out of which came the Bolshevik takeover and seven decades of crushing commu-nist rule. The communist regimes in Russia and Eastern Europe collapsed in the largely peaceful revolutions of 1989–1991. The Soviet Union itself dis-solved in December 1991. The result is what we see today: the continuing chaotic aftermath of the dismembered Soviet communist empire. Russia, geopolitically alone again, struggles to right itself and regain its position as a great power, surrounded by hostile or semifriendly countries almost all of which fear the potential resurgence of Russian expansionist nationalism.

From the 1950s on, Russia, in the form of the Soviet Empire, had to deal with two new geopolitical factors. The first was European integration, meaning the voluntary joining of the countries of Western Europe into what eventually became today's European Union (EU). The second factor was the North Atlantic Treaty Organization (NATO), an alliance created in 1949 that was basically a U.S. military security guarantee of Western Europe against the Soviet threat. After the collapse of the Soviet Union, the ex-Soviet bloc communist regimes in Central and Eastern Europe joined both NATO and the EU, which meant the extension of these organizations up against Russia's own borders. After threatening the West for decades, Russia itself was threatened—or at least saw itself as such. This geopolitical turnabout produced the underlying tension that characterizes European–Russian relations today.

Historically, it is hardly surprising that today's Russian leaders feel that the country's recent experience constitutes a defeat of historic proportions that must be rectified. Russian leader Vladimir Putin has said that the Soviet Union's collapse was the greatest geopolitical catastrophe of the twentieth century, by which he meant the scale of the event rather than nostalgia for Stalinist totalitarian politics and society. Today's Europe–Russia relationship cannot help but be full of fears and resentments. These relations can be positive in certain ways, but mistrust persists even when common interests mean that both sides benefit from certain initiatives. Europe and Russia are condemned by geography, history, and the very different natures of their domestic systems to a combination of wary cooperation and scarcely disguised hostility. Europe and Russia cannot be easy allies, but neither has an interest in being implacable adversaries.

Europe–Russia conflicts not only involve clashes of particular interest; they also reflect fundamentally different conceptions of the basis on which the EU–Russia relationship should be built. Europe sees itself as the leading proponent and example of international relations conducted on the basis of multilateral norms, permanent institutions, and adherence to the rule of law. It sees its fundamental mission with regard to Russia as that of bringing Russia into a law-based system that is perceived as beneficial to Russia itself but in which the EU will wield great influence. Russian elites also claim to be strong proponents of institutions and the rule of law, but they do not accept as universally valid norms and rules that appear to disadvantage Russia and in which Russia had little say in drafting. These rules, if followed, would seem to consign Russia to a low rung on the international economic and political hierarchy from which it could climb, if at all, only slowly and by hard work. Russia wants nothing to do with this scenario.

Moscow's attempt to restore Russian national self-confidence and foreign policy assertiveness in the past few years under Putin and, since his election in March 2008, under President Dmitry Medvedev is intended to reassert the idea that Russia is a great power. Russia should not be treated as a collapsed superpower let alone just another country to Europe's east. Rather, it must be treated as a "strategic partner" of the EU, tacitly aligned with it in building a new international order based on the principle of multipolarity, in other words, a world order in which the United States cannot be a hegemonic power.

The best example of this aspect of EU–Russian relations was in the run-up to the Iraq War in 2002–2003. France and Germany allied with Russia in the UN Security Council in opposing the George W. Bush administration's plans to invade Iraq to overthrow Saddam Hussein and change the regime. Britain and, at the time, Italy and Spain were uncomfortable with this anti-U.S. alliance of convenience, as were the Central and Eastern European states on the eve of their planned accession to the EU in 2004. The Russians themselves seemed unsure about being outdone by putative allies of the United States in the vehemence of their opposition to U.S. policy, and Putin himself was less willing than French president Jacques Chirac or German chancellor Gerhard Schröder to burn his personal bridges to Bush. Despite all this, the possibility of a European–Russian challenge to U.S. dominance had been sketched out.

THE EU–RUSSIA RELATIONSHIP

If Russia under Putin and Medvedev has settled on a reasonably clear and consistent (if not always tactically skillful) policy toward Europe, the same cannot be said of the EU, which, nearly two decades after the breakup of the Soviet Union, continues to struggle to define a coherent policy toward Russia. The EU at times has treated Russia as just another of the weak and dependent states along its periphery, to be offered access to the EU single market and privileged political ties in exchange for commitments to align its domestic and international policies with norms set in Brussels. At other times, both Brussels and the member states have emphasized Russia's identity as a great power and tried to forge with Moscow the kind of "strategic partnership" that Europe claims to be building with China, India, and other regional powers in the emerging multipolar world and that Russian leaders themselves have regarded as befitting Russia's status as a major power.

The inconsistencies and contradictions in EU policy reflect the inherent difficulty of shaping policy toward a Russia whose post–Cold War weakness has been difficult to reconcile with its former imperial greatness. They also reflect divisions among the EU member states about policy—divisions that have widened since the accessions in 2004 and 2007 of ten former communist countries of Central and Eastern Europe, all of which are more exposed to Russian political, economic, and potentially military might than the countries of "old Europe" and which harbor deep suspicions of Moscow growing out of the Soviet era.

In the early 1990s, the EU institutions and the member state governments were, like everyone else, súrprised by the sudden collapse of Soviet power and scrambled to formulate a policy toward Russia and the other Soviet successor states. In the fall of 1992, the Council of Ministers approved a mandate for the European Commission to negotiate a Partnership and Cooperation Agreement (PCA) with the government of the Russian Federation. Signed at the Corfu summit in June 1994, the agreement did not go into effect until December 1997 as the EU withheld ratification because of Russia's war to put down separatist insurgent forces in the Caucasus region of Chechnya. Underpinning implementation of the PCA as the cornerstone of the EU–Russia relationship was an extensive program of grant aid, the Technical Assistance to the Commonwealth of Independent States (TACIS) program launched in 1991. Other elements of European policy toward Russia included the provision of loans from the newly established European Bank for Reconstruction and Development (EBRD), integration of Russia into the Council of Europe to promote democracy and human rights, and the institutionalization of the Organization for Security and Cooperation in Europe as a pan-European forum to resolve border disputes and minority rights questions. The PCA with Russia was similar to the Europe Agreements that the EU concluded with the former communist countries of Central and Eastern Europe in that it created a framework for EU technical and financial assistance and for cooperation in the economic, trade, financial, political, cultural, and scientific spheres, with a heavy emphasis on alignment of Russian norms and legal practices with those of the EU. Unlike the Europe Agreements, however, the PCA did not imply a membership perspective for Russia or the other former Soviet republics.

The distinction between the PCAs and the Europe Agreements reflected a set of political decisions about the future architecture of the European order. With Chancellor Helmut Kohl of Germany in the lead, the EU declared itself in favor of extensive enlargement of the EU to the east and the southeast, eventually to include all states west of the old Soviet border, plus the three Baltic republics of Estonia, Latvia, and Lithuania, which had been seized by Stalin in 1940 and incorporated into the Soviet Union. EU expansion would not, however, go so far as to encompass the former Soviet Union (the Baltic republics excepted), which would retain a sort of loose identity under the cover of the Commonwealth of Independent States.

Subsequent developments have shown the difficulty of attempting to build a relationship with Russia and the other Soviet successor states on the basis of this architectural design. Moscow was never reconciled to being denied all influence in an EU- and NATO-dominated order that would extend up to its western borders, while countries such as Ukraine never accepted that they could be denied the prospect of membership in the EU and NATO and permanently assigned to a grouping that Russia, by virtue of its size, location, and natural resource base, inevitably would dominate. Fundamentally, however, the EU has remained true to the decisions made in the early 1990s. The big EU countries have been unwilling to extend a clear membership perspective to Ukraine or other post-Soviet states if only because this would necessarily embroil the EU in unresolved conflicts with Russia. In contrast, even in the darkest days of the wars in former Yugoslavia, the EU has held out the prospect that all the countries of the Balkans eventually will be accepted as members provided that they make the requisite internal reforms to meet EU standards.

After a slow start due to the delays in ratifying the PCA and Western Europe's own preoccupations with enlargement, the Balkans, and internal reform, the EU turned to Russia with a sense of urgency in the first half of 1999. This was in response to the Russian financial meltdown of August 1998 and the Kosovo War in the spring of 1999, in which Russia opposed the Western effort to forcibly separate Kosovo from Serbia on humanitarian grounds but ultimately participated in brokering the peace and provided troops to the NATO-led peacekeeping force sent to the province.

At its session in Cologne in June 1999, the European Council adopted an EU Common Strategy for Russia, the first time this policy instrument, newly established under the Treaty of Amsterdam, was used. The strategy declared that Russia and the EU "have strategic interests and exercise particular responsibilities in the maintenance of stability and security in Europe, and in other parts of the world" and proposed that "the strategic partnership develop within the framework of a permanent policy and security dialogue designed to bring interests closer together."[1] Russia presented its own "Medium-Term Strategy for the Development of Relations between the Russian Federation and the European Union (2000–2010)." These two documents formed the basis for the announcement, at the October 1999 EU–Russia summit, that the parties agreed that "developing an EU-Russia strategic partnership will contribute substantially to peace, stability and economic prosperity in Europe as a whole and will help it to meet the challenges of the next millennium."[2]

A variety of mechanisms were established or adapted to give substance to this partnership, the most important of which were the twice-yearly summits between the Russian president and his EU counterparts. At the October 2000 summit in Paris, the two sides agreed to institute a regular dialogue on energy, leading to the establishment of an EU–Russia Energy Partnership. At the same meeting, President Putin, Chirac (in his capacity as rotating EU president), and the two responsible officials from Brussels, European Commission president Romano Prodi and Common Foreign and Security Policy high representative Javier Solana, signed a joint declaration in which they agreed to develop a continuing strategic dialogue and to intensify consultations on arms control and disarmament, nonproliferation, and crisis management.

At the May 2001 summit, the two sides agreed to establish a "Common European Economic Space" embracing Russia and the EU. In October, it was agreed to establish a high-level group charged with defining "the core elements which will need to be put in place in order to create a Common European Economic Area." At the St. Petersburg summit in May 2003, the EU and Russia agreed to create four "common spaces" within the framework of the PCA. These were the Common Economic Space already mooted in 2001; a Common Space of Freedom, Security, and Justice covering the areas of justice and home affairs; a Common Space of External Security relating to foreign and defense policy; and a Common Space of Research and Education, which also was to include culture.

At the May 2005 Moscow summit, the EU and Russia agreed to develop "road maps" setting out specific objectives and ways to implement the four common spaces. In combination with the regular summits, the road maps and the network of ministerial and subministerial forums to which they gave rise have been useful in building elements of cooperation and in resolving bilateral disputes. However, in contrast to successful EU relations in the 1990s and the early 2000s with the candidate countries of Central and Eastern Europe, implementation of the road maps has been slowed by a lack of resources and commitment on both sides and by political developments in Russia, notably the Putin regime's reversion to authoritarian politics at home: the destruction of independent media and harassment of nongovernmental organizations (NGOs), repression of parliamentary and electoral opposition parties, and Moscow's rejection of any attempt from outside to influence or even to comment on internal Russian politics. The return of authoritarianism and the shutting off of Russia from outside scrutiny was not what the EU intended to get from Moscow in exchange for expansion of the EU–Russia relationship.

Russia also has suffered setbacks and disappointments in the relationship. For example, Moscow has tried to achieve visa-free admission for its citizens into the EU, an understandable position for a government acting on behalf of an elite accustomed to vacationing, shopping, and buying property in Europe but a totally unrealistic request of EU governments concerned about an unwanted flow of Russian illegal immigrants, Russia's porous borders, and problems of illegal immigration, drugs, and human trafficking. Moscow also has been blocked in attempts to acquire stakes in European energy and technology firms and has been unable to dissuade most EU member states from recognizing Kosovo as an independent state.

RUSSIA AND THE EUROPEAN SECURITY STRATEGY

The European Security Strategy (ESS), adopted by the European Council in December 2003, lists Russia as one of the EU's five "strategic partners," along with China, India, Canada, and Japan. At the time the ESS was adopted, the defining characteristic of these designated partners from the EU perspective had less to do with shared values as they related to human rights, democracy, and the functioning of a market economy than with the putative partner's commitment to "effective multilateralism," which had become the leitmotif of EU external policy following the European clash with the Bush administration over the war in Iraq. Russia's opposition to the war, along with that of France and Germany, was seen by many in Europe as an indication that Russia was committed to a multipolar order built around the principle of multilateralism as this concept was understood in Brussels and other European capitals.

Along with his opposition to the Iraq War, Putin gained credit with European leaders by pushing through, in November 2004, Russia's ratification of the Kyoto Protocol on greenhouse gas emissions, a step that allowed the treaty to go into effect. In so doing, Putin validated the EU's claim to leadership in the fight against global warming and provided the EU and its environmental lobbies with an important symbolic victory over the Bush administration, whose rejection of Kyoto in 2001 was a major point of contention between Washington and Brussels. The European Commission pushed a number of other projects that reflected a European view of Russia as a reliable partner in building a multipolar global order. Russia was urged to promote the use of the euro in bilateral trade, beginning with the invoicing of oil and gas products, and there was talk of partnerships between Russia and Europe in space, aerospace, nuclear power, and other strategic industries.

In retrospect, however, it is clear that the EU attempt to cast Russia in the role of copillar of an emerging multipolar order built around effective multilateralism was based on illusions and bound to fail. Russia was never truly committed to many of the causes that the EU sought to promote and that it regarded as central to an effective multilateral international order. Russia did not support the International Criminal Court or the global ban on land mines. It ignored international agreements on trade and investment and refused to ratify the reform of the European Court on Human Rights and other Council of Europe conventions. There was less to Russia's ratification of Kyoto than met the eye. With Russia's greenhouse gas emissions still below the baseline levels of 1990, Russia could sell emission allowances to Europe and Japan, gaining lucrative financial benefits under the protocol's Joint Implementation Mechanism. Russia also won concessions from the

EU on its World Trade Organization (WTO) accession in exchange for ratification.

As Putin consolidated his power and began to pursue a more assertive foreign policy bolstered by a revived economy, Moscow placed new emphasis on Russia's identity as what one expert characterized as a "stand-alone great power"—one that could not be treated as a mere political and economic appendage of the EU.[3] Reassertion of Russia's great-power status inevitably involved a certain downplaying of Russia's identity as a European power and a countervailing emphasis on its global and "Eurasian" role. Already in 2001, Moscow played a leading part in the establishment of the Shanghai Cooperation Organization, a grouping of Russia, China, Kazakhstan, Kyrgyzstan, Tajikistan, and Uzbekistan that promotes security, economic, and cultural cooperation. Putin also became much enamored of the idea of Russia as one of the BRIC (Brazil-Russia-India-China) countries, a somewhat dubious grouping of developing countries that a Goldman Sachs economist predicted would come to exercise increasing influence on the global economy in the coming decades. Putin also was alert to opportunities—admittedly quite limited under George W. Bush—to revive or build a special relationship with the United States around security issues and reductions of nuclear weapons and nonproliferation that also stressed Russia's status as a global power rather than merely as the eastern wing of a "common space" inevitably dominated by the EU.

Attitudes in the EU toward Russia also began to evolve. In 2004, EU enthusiasm for closer relations with Russia was dampened by the accession to the EU of the ex-Soviet bloc states of Central and Eastern Europe, most of which were wary of Russia and mired in bilateral disputes with Moscow. By 2005, the urgency of checking U.S. power became less important in European thinking as the United States became bogged down in Iraq and the Bush administration appeared chastened by the Iraq debacle. Most important, the European strategic outlook—and specifically attitudes toward multilateralism and multipolarity—began to change, driven mainly by shifting views of China and its role in the international system.

For all the glib talk about multipolarity by leaders such as Chirac and Schröder in the early 2000s, Europe lagged behind the United States in grasping the full implications of China's rise. Relations between China and the EU began to cool in 2005. Disputes over Chinese dumping of its textile exports, China's piling up of huge trade surpluses and its attempts to lock up supplies of natural resources in Africa, and differences over Tibet and human rights cast doubt on the idea of China as a natural partner in an EU-led effort to shape a new international order based on multilateralism.

In a world in which the United States and China were the dominant powers, possibly giving rise to a new bipolar domination in international economics and geopolitics, it could be argued that Europe and Russia had greater incentive than ever to forge a strategic partnership.[4] In the commercial realm, European and especially German companies in fact did see Russia as a point of privileged access to expanding markets, opportunities for investment, and access to supplies of energy and raw materials that would help sustain Europe's position in the world economy under conditions of rapid globalization. The main effect, however, of the cooling of European enthusiasm for China was to cast doubt on feasibility of EU efforts to work with *any* of the other assertive new powers—China, India, or Russia—to build a world order based on multipolarity and effective multilateralism. European experts began to acknowledge that multipolarity did not necessarily equate to multilateralism and that European and non-European interpretations of these terms did not coincide. As one prominent expert wrote, "Newer and aspiring powers . . . have a different conception of multilateralism from that of the European Union, closer to the containment of the more powerful states and the assertion of their own sovereignty than to playing their part in building an effective multilateral system."[5]

Bilateral disputes between Russia and individual EU member states also began to increase after 2004, spilling over into the broader EU–Russia relationship. The growing number of such disputes was partly a function of the eastern enlargement that had brought inside the EU several countries with long-standing worries about Russia's interference in their affairs. In May 2007, Russia was suspected of mounting cyberattacks against Estonia in response to the relocation by the Estonian authorities of a memorial to Soviet soldiers killed in World War II. London and Moscow clashed over Russian refusal to extradite a suspect in the murder on British soil of former Russian intelligence agent turned government critic Alexander Litvinenko. Several trade and commercial disputes involving one or two member states (e.g., an export embargo on meat from Poland) or having a disproportionate effect on particular member states (e.g., Russian tariffs on wood exports that adversely affected the woodworking industries of Finland and Sweden) also spilled over into the broader Russia–Europe relationship. The EU response to such disputes was to remind everyone that, at least according to EU law, bilateral infringement on any part of the EU single market signaled a lack of respect for the market as a whole. The Russians were not always impressed by such declarations of EU solidarity, but neither was Russia able to fully isolate such disputes from the broader fabric of its relations with Europe.

THE EU'S NEW NEIGHBORHOOD AND RUSSIA'S NEAR ABROAD

The EU's policy toward Russia coexists uneasily with a broader set of EU policies toward the other post-Soviet states: Ukraine, Moldova, Belarus, and the countries of Central Asia and the Caucasus. From the time of the Soviet Union's collapse in 1991, the EU tried to treat the weakened Russia of the Yeltsin years and the other post-Soviet states as identically as possible, offering each a PCA, TACIS aid, and access to EBRD and other credits. While treating the ex-Soviet states as a group, the EU made a sharp distinction between these states and the Central and Eastern European countries that were to be offered EU membership.

By the early 2000s and the first years of the Putin presidency, however, the problematic aspects of treating Russia and the other post-Soviet states alike became apparent. Putin's arrival in power marked the end of Yeltsin's decade as Russia's leader, a period now universally considered in Russia as a historical moment of humiliating weakness. Yeltsin had been pushed by Western advice to adopt rapid large-scale privatization of Russia's most valuable economic assets, in particular oil and gas resources, in order to create, through short-order shock treatment, a liberal market economy. This led to a chaotic sell-off at bargain-basement prices of Russia's most valuable economic assets, such as oil and gas resources, to capitalist entrepreneurs, soon known as the oligarchs, who became immensely wealthy by pillaging the state with the cooperation of its senior leadership. Putin began to roll back these policies. He rejected out of hand the notion that Russia was no more than another post-Soviet state and conducted relations with the rest of the world with the conviction that Moscow's primary foreign policy goal should be to restore Russia's status as a great power and not simply pursue integration with Europe for its own sake.

Responding to changes on the Russian side and to its own enlargement to the east, the EU began to blur somewhat the absolute distinction that it once made between the new member countries of the EU and the non-Russian former Soviet republics as it began to intensify relations with countries such as Ukraine and Moldova. The EU's New Neighborhood Policy (NNP), adopted in 2003 on the eve of the historic enlargement to Central and Eastern Europe, was intended "to develop a zone of prosperity and a friendly neighborhood—a 'ring of friends'—with whom the EU enjoys close, peaceful, and co-operative relations."[6] The NNP encompassed both the countries of North Africa and the Middle East and those of the "new eastern Europe," by which was meant the post-Soviet states that sat on Russia's borders and that would not in principle become EU members.

The NNP reflected a bureaucratically driven, EU-centric view of the world and was of limited effectiveness. The countries of North Africa and the Middle East wondered what it meant for their own Barcelona process, launched with the EU in 1995.[7] Ukraine was offended at being lumped in with non-European countries, which it feared signaled the EU's intention not to grant Ukraine a membership perspective. For its part, Russia made clear that it did not want to participate in the initiative or be considered a "new neighbor," even though Russia in fact would border directly on five member states of the enlarged EU (Finland, Estonia, Latvia, Lithuania, and Poland). Rather, Russia emphasized that it regarded itself as a major power and a strategic partner of the EU that had its own interests in the new Eastern Europe and was not content to see countries such as Ukraine and Moldova treated as objects of an EU policy that was shaped without Moscow's involvement.

The "color revolutions" in Georgia and Ukraine in 2003 and 2004 crystallized the contradiction between the EU's NNP heading eastward and Russia's determination, present already under Yeltsin but much strengthened by Putin, to exert Russian influence westward in what it regarded as its own neighborhood or "near abroad." Moscow regarded the 2003 "rose revolution" in Georgia, in which the American-educated, pro-U.S. and pro-European Mikhail Saakashvilli replaced Eduard Shevardnadze as leader of the country, as a Western-orchestrated plot. The rose revolution demonstrated the danger of allowing U.S. and European NGOs to operate freely in the post-Soviet space. Moscow similarly denounced Ukraine's "orange revolution" the next year. Europe and the United States refused to recognize the outcome of a rigged election in November 2004 in which the Russian-backed candidate, Viktor Yanukovich, was said to have defeated the more Western-oriented Viktor Yushchenko. (Yushchenko had been poisoned with dioxin before the elections, the Western assumption being that Moscow was involved in an assassination attempt.) Amid huge street protests, Washington and the EU called for new elections, which the Ukrainian Supreme Court ultimately ordered and which resulted in a decisive victory for Yushchenko.

For a time, Russia continued to pursue a two-track policy in regard to external involvement in what it regarded as its near abroad, differentiating between, on the one hand, NATO and the United States, which were seen as Russia's implacable foes in this region, and, on the other, the EU, with which Russia—under certain conditions—could still find common interests and approaches. The 2005 road map for an EU–Russia "Common Security Space" declared that the two sides would cooperate in resolving the so-called frozen conflicts in the Caucasus region (Abkhazia, Nagorno-Karabakh, South Ossetia, and Transdnistria) left unthawed after the end of the Cold War. Europeans and Russians not surprisingly viewed these conflicts rather differently, and EU–Russia discussions about them made little progress toward their resolution. Nonetheless, the fact that the frozen conflicts were included in the common spaces and the road map suggested a Russian willingness to accord the EU some sort of overlapping role in its near abroad that it never would have granted NATO.

As the decade progressed, however, Moscow became more wary of EU involvement in the former Soviet space. The differences between the two sides came into sharp relief in August 2008, when Russian military forces rolled into Georgia in response to fighting between the Georgian military and Russian-backed secessionist forces in South Ossetia. The ensuing five-day war killed hundreds and left thousands of people homeless. French president Nicolas Sarkozy, in his role as the six-month rotating EU president, brokered a cease-fire agreement that called for the withdrawal of Russian troops from Georgia to positions in the separatist regions of Abkhazia and South Ossetia. Moscow also dramatically raised the stakes in the conflict by formally recognizing South Ossetia and Abkhazia as independent states.

To justify both its military action against Georgia and its subsequent recognition of South Ossetia and Abkhazia, Moscow used NATO's 1999 military action against Serbia to protect Kosovo as a precedent. This action did not have UN Security Council approval and thus was strictly speaking not legal in terms of international law. Having failed, in early 2008, to prevent the United States and several European governments from recognizing Kosovo as an independent country, Moscow invoked the Kosovo precedent in extending recognition to these political entities in the Caucasus.

The 2008 war put European governments on notice that Moscow was willing to use force to protect its special interests in a neighboring country. Russia regarded itself as having exclusive rights and "privileged interests" in the former Soviet republics to the south.[8] Following the war, Ukraine and Georgia had more reason than ever to seek the protection afforded by eventual EU and NATO membership. But the war made the EU and NATO more reluctant than ever to take on responsibilities that would put the West on a collision course with Russia. At the NATO summit in late 2008, Sarkozy and Merkel successfully blocked an effort by the Bush administration to progress toward NATO membership by adopting Membership Action Plans for these countries. European governments were clearly more reserved than the United States in their backing for the Georgian government, which was widely seen as having helped bring the conflict on itself.

At the same time, however, greater Russian assertiveness with regard to Georgia and Ukraine encouraged the EU to clarify the objectives and improve the effectiveness of its own policies toward these countries. In December 2008, the European Commission put forward a proposal for a new "Eastern Partnership" for Armenia, Azerbaijan, Belarus, Georgia, Moldova, and Ukraine.[9] The proposal called for new association agreements, including better access to the EU single market with free trade agreements, possibly leading to the establishment of a "Neighborhood Economic Community," visa facilitation to increase mobility and human contacts between these countries and the EU, and joint cooperation on mutual energy security. In addition to being Europe's answer to the August 2008 crisis in Georgia, the new mechanism was an overdue corrective to the geopolitically absurd and largely ineffective European Neighborhood Policy and a response to the demands of the new member states (Poland in particular) for a reinvigorated eastern policy as the price of going along with French president Sarkozy's much-touted Union for the Mediterranean.

The limitations of the new initiative were evident, however, in the tepid support given to it by several larger member states. The leaders of Britain, France, and Italy skipped the May 2009 summit in Prague, at which the initiative was formally launched, while the Netherlands and Germany forced a change in a Czech draft of the meeting's final document that renamed the six as "Eastern European partners" instead of "European countries," which they regarded as an unnecessarily proenlargement term.[10] Sensing the internal differences on the EU side, Moscow stayed on the offensive. Medvedev denounced the pact for its perceived anti-Russian bias: "We would not want the Eastern Partnership to turn into a partnership against Russia. . . . I would simply not want this partnership to consolidate certain states that are of an anti-Russian bent with other European states."

Tensions between Russia and the post-Soviet states remain a highly divisive issue within the EU and greatly complicate the search for a united and coherent policy toward Russia. Countries such as Lithuania and Poland are sympathetic to these countries and press for stronger EU support for them up to and including by offering them a membership perspective. France, Italy, and Germany are less supportive and are sometimes accused of following a "Russia-first" policy that sacrifices the interests of these countries for commercial benefit and out of an excess of geopolitical caution. The fact that the color revolutions have produced less reform than originally expected further complicates the issue. The Western-oriented, proreform political forces in Ukraine failed to consolidate their gains, resulting in the selection of the once-reviled Yanukovich as prime minister in August 2006, while in Georgia, Saakashvilli has proven to be a disappointment to some in the West, unjustly reviled by the Russians to be sure, but more effective in courting Western support than in effecting reforms in Georgia and himself seen as partly responsible for the conflict with Russia that erupted in the summer of 2008.

ECONOMIC AND ENERGY TIES

Following the collapse of the Soviet system and especially after the successful overcoming of the 1998 financial crisis, the EU–Russia economic relationship expanded dramatically. Russia is now the EU's third-largest trading partner (after the United States and China). Until the recent economic crisis, trade expanded at annual rates of up to 20 percent. Trade and investment ties are based on proximity and concurrent interests. The EU is the logical market for Russian exports of energy and other natural resources, while Russia, with its modernizing economy and growing middle class, is a large and geographically nearby market for European industry. EU companies have invested heavily in both the manufacturing and the services sector of the Russian economy. Germany, whose leaders are determined to sustain its traditional economic model based on exports of high-value-added manufactured goods supporting high wages, has been especially driven to exploit the Russian market. Italy is not far behind (which in part explains the otherwise curious good relationship between Putin and Italian prime minister Silvio Berlusconi). Several other EU countries have developed important niche markets for key industries in Russia.

On balance, however, the increased level of economic interdependence between the EU and Russia have failed to produce the Common Economic Space that was discussed in 2001 and that formally remains on the bilateral agenda. An EU–Russia Energy Partnership never materialized in the terms sketched out in the early 2000s, largely because Moscow was unwilling to play by rules set in Brussels, while the EU lacked the means to compel or cajole Moscow to play by these rules. Russia remains the only major world economy still not a member of the WTO, in large part because its refuses to accept the legally binding constraints on its domestic and foreign economic policies that membership would entail.

EU–Russia economic relations are marked by disputes, some ongoing and recurrent, others new and unexpected. These disputes are seen in Brussels mainly as growing out of arbitrary Russian state interference in the market, sometimes involving official refusal to follow international treaties and regimes to which Russia formally ascribes. For example, European airlines are forced to pay several hundred million euros annually to the Russian airline Aeroflot for the right to overfly Siberia on routes between the EU and Japan, South Korea, and China. These fees are incompatible with international aviation treaties to which Russia has adhered. At the November 2006 EU–Russia summit in Helsinki, Moscow committed to phasing out the charges but has since refused to discuss the issue in practical terms while European airlines are still paying 330 million euros per year. Other arbitrary and illegal actions, as seen from Brussels, include the 2006 decision to bar meat imports from Poland, allegedly for sanitary reasons but in fact a way to punish a country that Moscow sees as "unfriendly."

Energy remains the driver of the overall Russia–EU economic relationship. Energy revenues enable Russia to buy from and invest in the EU, resulting in complex patterns of economic interdependence, financial ties, and cross-border physical interconnections (mainly pipelines). A quarter of EU oil imports and more than 40 percent of gas imports come from Russia, with dependency ratios in the gas sector ranging from as high as 100 percent for Finland and Slovakia and 96 percent for Bulgaria to 36 percent for Germany, 25 percent for France, and 20 percent for Italy.[11] Russia's leverage in the energy relationship grew under Putin in the early 2000s as Moscow centralized state control over the production and export of oil and natural gas and as broader trends in the European and global energy markets favored exporters over importers. Russia has benefited from increased production of its own oil and natural gas resources as well as its role as a middleman in Caspian-area oil and gas shipped through Russia to the EU market. Rising world market prices driven by increased global demand, especially in China and India, have been an important global factor. Meanwhile, domestic production in Western Europe, especially of natural gas, has declined as fields in the Netherlands and the North Sea passed their peak production years.

Moscow has resisted attempts to reduce its leverage over EU energy supplies by refusing to ratify the transport protocol to the European Energy Charter, which would guarantee reliable supply and provide a mechanism for conflict resolution, and attempting to discourage Western efforts to build pipelines that would lessen European dependence on Russian transport routes and gas supplies. The most important of these initiatives is the so-called Nabucco pipeline, which would bring gas from Azerbaijan through Turkey to Austria via Bulgaria, Romania, and Hungary. Moscow has launched the North Stream and South Stream projects, which would bypass Ukraine and thereby give Russia the option of cutting off gas to Ukraine without disrupting the flow of gas to Western Europe—a situation likely to increase Kiev's vulnerability to Russian pressure.

Russia has increased its economic influence relative to Europe not only as a consequence of its role as a direct supplier of gas and oil to EU member states. It also has gained leverage from its role as a supplier to countries such as Ukraine, whose fate is a matter of EU concern, and from the financial power that Russia has acquired as it joined the ranks of the world's "resource nationalists" and began to pile up hard-currency reserves. In recent years, Moscow has used the energy lever against neighboring countries in ways that have affected EU interests and that have been impossible for the EU to ignore. The first major Russia–Ukraine crisis over supplies of natural gas took place in the winter of 2005–2006, when Russia's Gazprom demanded a large increase in the price Ukraine paid for Russian gas and a shift from barter to cash payment. Ukraine initially refused to pay, and Gazprom interrupted shipments. Ukraine responded by siphoning gas destined for the EU area from the transit pipelines in a way that affected supplies to several European countries. A compromise agreement got the gas moving again, but Europe had been put on notice that the security of its energy supplies could not be viewed apart from the Russia–Ukraine relationship as well as from the EU's relations with both countries.

In late 2006, Moscow threatened to cut off the supply of oil to Belarus through the Druzhba pipeline in a dispute over payments and pricing, a step that again would have affected the flow of energy to the EU area. The crisis was defused by a bilateral arrangement between Russia and Belarus that established a weak "early warning mechanism" regarding possible supply disruptions affecting EU consumers. In the midst of yet another of the by now familiar Moscow–Kiev disputes over natural gas prices, in January 2009 Russia once again cut off supplies to Ukraine, interrupting supplies to Europe. Tens of thousands of consumers in EU member countries were left without heat in the dead of winter. EU negotiators helped broker a compromise that gave something to both sides: higher prices to Russia for its gas and higher transit payments to Ukraine for gas moving from Russia to Europe.

Russia's meteoric rise, in less than a decade, from insolvent debtor to major international creditor all but eliminated erstwhile EU financial assistance as a leverage factor in the EU–Russia relationship. In the 1990s, EU aid to Russian economic development had created some measure of influence in Moscow's decision making, what the EU refers to as "positive and negative conditionality." The large EU aid program for Russia—TACIS—ended in 2006. The EU still funds various small projects (studies, seminars, and pilot projects of various kinds) relating to institutional, legal, and administrative reform and to social assistance in particular regions (the Arctic, Kaliningrad, and the North Caucasus) and underwrites joint institutions and initiatives such as the European Studies Institute in Moscow and the participation of Russian students and academics in EU research and exchange programs. But these projects, while they may have some effect over time in promoting the EU's reform agenda in Russia, are too small and scattered to affect the calculations of the Russian government or, in many cases, even of the ministries directly targeted by EU assistance. Meanwhile, Moscow has set up a sovereign wealth fund, patterned after those maintained by China and the Persian Gulf energy exporters, that has attempted to invest in Europe, raising the specter of "reverse leverage" in Russia's relations with Europe.

The collapse of world energy prices as a consequence of the international financial crisis that began in the fall of 2007 initially seemed to take the swagger out of Russian foreign policy. Russian revenues from oil and gas sales plummeted with the decline in demand caused by the global great recession. Moscow could not avoid using a large part of its hard-currency reserves to prop up the ruble in an attempt to limit the damage to Russia's own economy. The legitimacy of the increasingly authoritarian Putin–Medvedev regime rested on the resumption of economic growth, hence jobs and rising prosperity at home.

But Russian foreign policy, at least in its neighborhood, grew more rather than less assertive during this period of economic downturn. Hard times in Russia were even harder in the near-abroad area. In the words of one observer, "Basically Russia sees the crisis as an opportunity to increase its influence in the post-Soviet space. . . . They think this is the right time to act."[12] The EU is of course not without leverage of its own in dealings with Moscow. Russia's own gas and oil fields are aging, and sustaining Russia's position as a major exporter of energy will require intensive new investment in the maintenance of existing fields plus huge new exploration in Siberia. Much of this investment and the accompanying expertise are likely to come from Western Europe, but actually exercising this leverage would require a fully unified European economic and political strategy toward Russia that would bind all the member states—something that the EU still has not managed to achieve.

HUMAN RIGHTS IN THE EUROPE-RUSSIA RELATIONSHIP

Compared with economic and strategic factors, democracy and human rights play secondary roles in Russia–Europe relations, either in the policies of particular European countries or in those of the EU as a whole. Foreign policy "realists" generally endorse this approach. In their view, international relations ought to be a matter of adjusting the relations between states in the world order. In contrast, foreign policy idealists believe that democratic states should be actively concerned with the domestic systems of other states because, besides being the right thing to do, the historical record shows that well-established liberal democracies hardly, if ever, fight wars against each other.

EU policy toward Russia, like that of the United States, mixes elements of realism and idealism. The EU claims that it operates with a special concern for human rights, democracy, and international law. Progress on democracy promotion and human rights is important to maintaining the EU's collective image of itself as a "normative power," capable of exerting positive influences on other powers, particularly those on its own periphery. In practice, however, the EU is often no better than the United States on human rights issues—at times perhaps worse because the EU abjures big-stick diplomacy.

Much of the pressure for human rights concerns in European foreign policy comes from influential European and international NGOs and interest groups that lobby member state governments and the EU and other policymaking institutions. The European Parliament is a particular focus of lobbying. The EU works for democracy and human rights in Russia through the European Initiative for Democracy and Human Rights (EIDHR), which was established in 1994 and began operations in Russia in 1997. Renamed the European Instrument for Democracy and Human Rights in 2006, the EIDHR has funded more than 250 projects involving nongovernmental and educational institutions. As in the case of comparable U.S. programs, however, success is quite limited, above all because the Putin government actively discouraged the work of such outside organizations. Freedom House began classifying Russia as "not free" in 2005, tracking a trend that culminated in the hollow parliamentary elections of December 2007 in which the Putin government, assured to win by a huge majority, nonetheless censored the media, beat up and jailed highly visible opposition leaders such as former world chess champion Gary Kasparov, and monopolized the public debate in favor of Putin's United Russia Party. The March 2008 presidential elections were in a way even worse, as Putin basically installed Medvedev as his successor but stayed in power by the constitutional ruse of assuming the post of prime minister as offered to him by the new president.

This was a perfectly legal if fundamentally anticonstitutional solution that Moscow defended by intoning the new principle of "sovereign democracy," the claim that Russia has developed its own unique form of democracy whose inviolability is an aspect of Russia's national sovereignty that outsiders must accept. Sovereign democracy could be seen as reflecting a new version of Slavophilism, the centuries-old claim that there is a distinctive, mystical Russian soul that its government must protect.

In terms of institutionalized relationships, Russia and the EU hold twice-yearly meetings on human rights issues within the framework of the agreement to develop the Common Space of Freedom, Security, and Justice. Since the first consultations in November 2004, Europeans have put on the agenda a growing range of issues—from Moscow's wars in Chechnya and the North Caucasus to censorship of media and freedom of expression and the imprisonment or murder of investigative journalists.[13] The Russians have replied with assertions of moral equivalence, citing the discriminatory treatment of Russian minorities in the Baltic countries as well as the general treatment of minorities and illegal immigrants in the EU. (Moscow gives the same sort of reply to U.S. criticisms of Russian human rights standards.) The February 2009 consultations ended in high drama when Putin, newly ensconced as prime minister, clashed publicly with European Commission president José Manuel Barroso at a Moscow press conference. Barroso expressed EU concerns about alleged contract killings that may involve the Russian government at some level, while Putin shot back with a litany of familiar charges against the EU.[14]

THE SEARCH FOR A POLICY

The Europe–Russia relationship has not been particularly cordial, and it is not likely to become much more so in the near future. The strategy of integrating a weakened postcommunist Russia into an EU-inspired European order of stability and prosperity, the driving force behind the common spaces project, has failed. The alternative approach of building a strategic partnership with Russia around a shared commitment to multilateralism also has failed. The first strategy foundered because, while Russia is not quite a reborn great power, neither is it just another post-Soviet country. The second strategy failed because neither Europe nor Russia has an interest in combining in a way that would alienate itself completely from the United States and because Russia and the EU have very different understandings of concepts such a multipolarity and multilateralism.

In this situation and absent any fundamental Russian challenge that would change the strategic equation, each EU country continues much as it has in the past, focusing first of all on its own national interests often in disregard of broader EU interests. In a November 2007 "power audit" of EU–Russia relations, the European Council on Foreign Relations identified five groups of member states with regard to EU policy toward Russia. First are the "Trojan horses," which defend Russian interests in EU forums (Cyprus and Greece). Second are "strategic partners," which have special bilateral relationships with Russia that they privilege over EU solidarity (France, Germany, Italy, and Spain). Third are "friendly pragmatists," which maintain good relations with Russia and give priority to their business interests (Austria, Belgium, Bulgaria, Finland, Hungary, Luxembourg, Malta, Portugal, Slovakia, and Slovenia). Fourth are the "frosty pragmatists," which also emphasize good relations and close business ties but which are more willing to criticize Russian human rights abuses and foreign policy actions (Czech Republic, Denmark, Estonia, Ireland, Latvia, the Netherlands, Romania, Sweden, and the United Kingdom). Last are the "new cold warriors," which are hostile to engagement with Russia and prepared to block progress in EU relations with Moscow (Poland and Lithuania).

Poland is the largest former Soviet bloc country, one whose history with Russia is particularly tragic not only in World War II but going back to the three partitions of Poland in 1772, 1793, and 1795. That Poland is often unfriendly to Russia is therefore not surprising. Along with Lithuania, it is the country in the EU most alert to signs of neoimperial Russian aggressiveness. In this respect, the Poles play an effective restraining role in EU internal political discussions about Russia. Germany has its own unhappy history with Poland and must reckon with Polish concerns about Russian attempts to play on internal differences within the EU that might disadvantage the Poles. But the Germans have not been fully responsive to Polish concerns. They have not, for example, made a priority of creating a unified EU market in natural gas, even though such a market would go far to eliminate Moscow's ability to use natural gas supply as a lever against individual EU member states.

In recent years, the new cold warriors and the strategic partners in the EU have faced off over the issue of renewal of the PCA with Russia, which, under its original ten-year term, technically expired at the end of November 2007. In November 2006, Poland vetoed a mandate to the European Commission to begin negotiations on a new agreement. Poland dropped its objections in early 2008, following a change of government in Warsaw and a resolution of the still inflammatory issue of Polish meat exports. But Lithuania, which alone among the EU member states had been backing the Poles on the mandate issue, continued to block the start of negotiations. Three of the four big countries—France, Germany, and Italy—won the day by assuring Lithuania that the Russians would be pressed on issues relating to energy security, the security of Moldova and Georgia, and Lithuanian grievances against Moscow going back to the Soviet period.

Russia has made clear that it regards the original PCA as a one-sided agreement, effectively imposed on Russia during its period of maximum weakness in the 1990s. To emphasize that any new agreement will not be a mere renewal or amendment of the PCA, the EU and Russia have formally dubbed the target of their efforts the "New Agreement," an empty, formalistic designation that speaks volumes about the current impasse in EU–Russia relations. The EU would like to preserve as much of the old PCA as possible—to secure a reasonably watertight legal agreement that will underpin and in turn be underpinned by other binding arrangements, such as the transit protocol to the Energy Charter Treaty, Council of Europe conventions, and, assuming that Russia eventually accedes to the WTO, the vast body of international trade law produced by the Uruguay Round and earlier rounds of the General Agreement on Tariffs and Trade. Russia, in contrast, prefers a new and more political (and less legalistic) approach that would serve the dual objective of establishing Russia as an equal, perhaps even the dominant, power when it comes to setting the European agenda as well as helping Russia escape from legal obligations that, if observed, are seen in Moscow as harmful to the country as a whole and to the interests of powerful, rent-seeking individuals and institutions whose voices are heard in the Kremlin.

The differences between these two approaches were on display at the May 2009 EU–Russia summit in Khabarovsk, which ended in acrimonious exchanges over energy and foreign policy. Medvedev stated that Russia had no intention of ratifying the Energy Charter Treaty but suggested that Russia and the EU incorporate provisions (presumably more to Russia's liking) on energy in the New Agreement under negotiation. For its part, the EU stuck with the charter, with Barroso stating that "we should rely on existing agreements. We should not question the present energy security system in Europe."[15] Along the same lines, trade commissioner Catherine Ashton stated unequivocally that the EU would not sign a new bilateral agreement with Russia unless Moscow joined the WTO, which would mandate the lifting of the tariffs imposed in November 2008, the elimination of the Siberian overflight payments, and other measures long demanded by Brussels. Russia gave no ground in these discussions. Medvedev refused to rule out another cutoff in gas supplies to Ukraine, both expressing the Russian leadership's prevailing contempt for Ukraine by doubting Kiev's ability to pay for its gas imports and protesting "the attempts in some countries" to exploit the EU's new Eastern Partnership against Russia.

The same Russian determination to set the agenda in Europe rather than just respond to EU and transatlantic initiatives is apparent in Moscow's proposal for a new pan-European security order, an idea first floated by Medvedev in speeches in June and July 2008. Speaking in Berlin, the Russian president claimed that "Atlanticism as a single basis for security has exhausted itself." The new strategic concept should be a "single Euro-Atlantic space from Vancouver to Vladivostok," a global vision that implied that the United States would be included. The new Russia idea would recognize that the United States is a permanent power in the European equation but would also create the presumption of some kind of subordination of NATO within a larger security concept. A new Treaty on European Security of unprecedented scope would, Medvedev said, offer the EU a leading role: "A strategic partnership between Russia and the EU could act as the so-called cornerstone of a Greater Europe without dividing lines, which would include intensive economic inter-penetration on the basis of agreed 'rules of the game,' including in the fuel and energy sector and the high-tech field. We are open to this, we are ready for this."[16]

In late November 2009, the Russian government put forward the draft of the proposed European Security Treaty. It contained vague and open-ended provisions that Western governments were certain to reject (e.g., article 2.1: "A Party to the Treaty shall not undertake, participate in or support any actions or activities affecting significantly the security of any other Party or Parties to the Treaty").[17] But some European governments may be interested in discussing Russian ideas for a new security architecture. Europeans have every interest in not allowing Russia to use a grand political proposal as a way to circumvent the kind of commitments to the rule of law that the EU seeks in a new bilateral agreement with Moscow or in Russian accession to various binding multilateral agreements and treaties. But the idea of making the EU and Russia copillars of a new European architecture could have some appeal in Europe, especially in a country such as France, which would like a larger, independent role for itself in international affairs. It also might provide a way around the current NATO–Russia impasse, which gives the United States what some Europeans consider an inordinately large influence in Europe's security relations with Russia.

CONCLUSIONS AND OUTLOOK

EU policy toward Russia is at an impasse, one that is unlikely, in the absence of radical domestic reform in Russia, to see a breakthrough. Since the mid-1990s, the EU has pursued two partly complementary, partly contradictory approaches in policy toward Russia. One is the integrationist approach, embodied in the PCA and the project for the common spaces. It entails Russian rapprochement with the EU short of membership, based on accommodation to EU norms and acceptance of an EU-centric agenda. The other approach, embodied in the concept of strategic partnership, treats Russia more as an autonomous and equal great power, capable of pursuing its own agenda with the EU. In making "effective multilateralism" the pivot of this partnership, however, the EU has continued to display the same implicit sense of superiority that underlies the common spaces project. In the final analysis, effective multilateralism is an EU rather than a Russian concept, albeit one that Russian elites are urged to accept as in their real and long-term interests.

By now it is clear, however, that the EU lacks the strength to impose on Russia a relationship that, however artfully dressed up, is in essence unequal and implies an exclusive right of Brussels to set the bilateral agenda. The EU is, by most quantitative and qualitative indicators, the larger and stronger power in the EU–Russia relationship. But this strength has limits and is difficult to turn into usable foreign policy leverage. Europe depends on Russia for markets and energy, and the divisions among and within the member states regarding Russia prevent a unified, clear, and consistent policy. EU decision-making structures, at least in foreign policy matters, are still weak and nonbinding.

European political and business leaders by and large are not part of the transnational network of "power, dependency, and rent seeking" through which Russia has maintained and extended its influence in countries such as Ukraine and Moldova.[18] But certain leaders are not immune to cutting special deals with Russia for political, psychological, and even financial gain. Berlusconi's political posturing with Putin and Medvedev, Sarkozy's activism during the Georgia crisis, Czech president Vaclav Klaus's anomalous "Russophilia," and, not least, Schröder's incongruous involvement following his departure from public office as a high official in the North Stream project all come to mind.

If such factors make it impossible for the EU to pressure or cajole Russia into accepting the kind of relationship with Europe that Brussels would prefer, they pale beside the weaknesses and self-delusion that underpin Russian policy toward the EU. Russia's leverage over the EU is largely negative. It derives in large measure from Russia's readiness to ignore or play fast and loose with European and global norms—to refuse to sign or ratify agreements, ignore agreements that Russia has signed and ratified, bully neighbors, break contracts, deploy financial assets in ways that fail to meet European standards of transparency and adherence to the rule of law, and, in the final analysis, use force in ways that Europe fundamentally rejects. For all the wishful thinking and self-serving aspects of the EU approach to Russia, Brussels is in essence correct. In the long run, Russia cannot prosper in the global economy or increase its political influence by force of intimidation or military action.

The current impasse in theory could be broken. For the EU, the way forward has been viewed as a simple matter of getting to yes—of getting the Russians to make the internal reforms and external adjustments needed to implement the common spaces and the strategic partnership on terms defined in Brussels. But this clearly has not happened and most likely will not happen in the next several years. The rise of younger, more self-confident Russian leaders—the Putins, Medvedevs, and their successors who emphasize "sovereign democracy" and Russia's right to define its own interests and its own place in the world—suggests that such an outcome is less likely today than it was a decade ago.

For the Russians, frustration with the current impasse has led to a search for new forums, new institutional mechanisms, and new issues that somehow will give Russia agenda-setting power in its relations with Europe and in Russia's overall foreign policy. Examples include Moscow's fascination with the BRIC grouping, with the G-20 process, and with BRIC as a component of the G-20. Others include Medvedev's proposal for a treaty establishing a post-Atlantic security structure in Europe and Moscow's call, in the wake of the financial crisis, for reform of the international monetary system and the need to downgrade the role of the dollar as the world's reserve currency.

But Russia's economic weight and geostrategic relevance are unlikely to be sufficient to result in more than symbolic advances in any of these areas (with the partial exception of a new European architecture). Russia's gross domestic product and population constitute a small fraction of those of the BRIC grouping. China and India hardly need association with Russia to assert their place on the international stage. When a Chinese official even hints at a shift in Beijing's attitude toward the dollar, markets tremble. When Medvedev engages in one of his periodic rants against "the artificial, unilateralist monopoly on key segments of the world economy," they shrug.[19]

With Russia too weak to compel European acceptance of a new institutional framework and a new agenda for Russia–EU relations but too strong to be pressured or cajoled into acceptance of an agenda and norms set in Brussels, fundamental changes in the relationship are unlikely. Trade will grow, driven by mutual economic interests. People-to-people contacts of all kinds will continue to develop, facilitated by proximity and economics. And the two sides will muddle through on security issues. But the current impasse in Russia–EU relations is likely to continue.

SUGGESTIONS FOR FURTHER READING

Allison, Roy, Margot Light, and Stephen White. *Putin's Russia and the Enlarged Europe*. London: Wiley-Blackwell, 2006.
Legvold, Robert, ed. *Russian Foreign Policy in the 21st Century and the Shadow of the Past*. New York: Columbia University Press, 2007.
Leonard, Mark, and Nicu Popescu. *A Power Audit of EU-Russia Relations*. Berlin: European Council on Foreign Relations, 2009.
Lucas, Edward. *The New Cold War: Putin's Russia and the Threat to the West*. New York: Palgrave Macmillan, 2009.
Mankoff, Jeffrey. *Russian Foreign Policy: The Return of Great Power Politics*. Boulder, CO: Rowman & Littlefield, 2009.

5

Europe–China Relations

A Delicate Dance

David Shambaugh

The China–Europe relationship has traversed a long and complicated history. When the then European Community of nine members formally established diplomatic relations with the People's Republic of China in 1975, the relationship was a minor shadow of what it has become today. The relationship has particularly burgeoned since the late 1990s, although it has a history that far pre-dates the past decade.

THE HISTORICAL LEGACY

China's relations with Europe take place against a long historical backdrop.[1] From the Chinese perspective, it is an ambivalent history. The ambivalence became manifest, on the one hand, in the imperial encroachment by the European powers (particularly England, France, Germany, and Portugal) beginning in the eighteenth century. This involved the onslaught of European traders, missionaries, and "gunboats." The European powers established "treaty ports" up and down the China coast, where "extraterritoriality" was practiced; that is, foreigners were not subject to domestic Chinese law, and Chinese were subject to European law. The British also foisted opium onto China. When Canton commissioner Lin Zexu sought to expel the British opium traders, Britain responded with force. The result was the 1840–1842 and 1858–1860 Opium Wars and a series of "unequal treaties" imposed on China after its defeat. With these European activities in China, *national humiliation* became an animating element in Chinese society—and modern Chinese nationalism was born. The Chinese sought to *reject* all things associated with European imperialism.

93

On the other, hand, however, Europe offered a model of *emulation* for China in these years. As China wrestled with its impotence in the face of European power, the Qing government embarked on a policy known as the Self-Strengthening Movement (1861–1894). This period was characterized by the policy of "selective learning" from Europe. This strategy went under the rubric of "Western learning for application, Chinese learning for [cultural] essence" (*Zhongxue wei ti, Xixue wei yong*). Animating this policy was the Chinese search for the secrets to the European industrial revolution. Thus, the Qing leaders embarked on a conscious policy to learn from Europe—which involved dispatching students to study in European academies and universities. As the Qing leaders were particularly motivated to learn the sources of European military prowess under the policy of building "shipyards and arsenals," the majority of these students were sent to study various aspects of engineering, naval science, and military-related subjects. However, once in Europe, not all students dutifully followed the curriculum. Several began reading more broadly into European philosophy, politics, and social thought. They quickly discovered the key linkage between critical thought and the scientific method and between democracy and modernity. This set of realizations sparked a generation of Chinese—beginning with the 1898 Hundred Day Reforms and ending with the 1919 May Fourth Movement—to believe that the sources of China's backwardness and the key to its modern future lay in the nature of its political system; that is, they advocated the abolition of the imperial system in favor of a liberal republican form of government. Ostensibly, the Chinese Revolution of 1911 (*Xin Hai Geming*) produced this transition.

Thus, Europe offered an ambivalent model—rejection and emulation—for the China of the nineteenth century. This ambivalence would continue into the 1920s, highlighted by the passing of Shandong province from German to Japanese control at the Versailles conference in 1919 (which sparked the May Fourth Movement and modern Chinese mass nationalism) but also the national government's attraction to German and Italian fascism.

When the nationalists were finally overthrown and retreated to Taiwan in 1949, the Chinese Communist Party (CCP) and new People's Republic of China inherited this ambivalent legacy of relations with Europe. But, for the CCP, the former element was dominant. That is, Mao and other Chinese communist leaders were deeply influenced by Lenin's 1917 theory of imperialism—which was a convenient explanation for China's plight as well as a blueprint for revolution.

THE COLD WAR YEARS

On coming to power in October 1949, few European countries formally recognized the new People's Republic. Only the Scandinavian states did so, although the United Kingdom did so without establishing an embassy in Beijing. The signing of the Sino–Soviet alliance in February 1950 further sealed the divide, as Beijing threw its lot in with the "socialist bloc" led by the Soviet Union. This meant that it had ties with the communist states of Eastern Europe but not the democratic states of Western Europe. China was granted observer status in the Soviet-dominated Council for Mutual Economic Assistance. By 1960, China's total trade turnover with Eastern European countries totaled $640 million, reaching a high of $670 million in 1958. East German, Polish, and Czechoslovakian technicians built scores of factories in China during the 1950s. Sino–Eastern European political relations during much of the decade were less positive. They were shaped largely by Sino–Soviet relations and Mao's problems with Soviet leader Nikita Khrushchev in particular. Intrabloc relations grew progressively strained over the course of the decade. The year 1956 was a pivotal one because of Khrushchev's denunciation of Stalin at the Soviet Communist Party's Twentieth Congress as well as the uprisings in Hungary and Poland. There was also a brief "thaw" in China's relations with Western Europe as a result of the 1954 Geneva Conference on Indochina. The 200-strong Chinese delegation to Geneva was led by Premier Zhou Enlai, but it also contained numerous officials intent on initiating commercial ties with Western European companies. China was at that time in urgent need of a wide range of goods that the Soviet Union and its Eastern European satellites could not provide: rubber, petroleum, high-quality iron and steel, nonferrous metals, machines and machine tools, cotton, medicines, coarse grains, and so forth. Following the Geneva Conference, despite the absence of diplomatic relations, China and Western European countries began to ply surprisingly large commerce and trade in nonstrategic goods. West Germany became China's largest noncommunist trading partner during the 1950s, achieving $162.3 million in bilateral trade in 1958, while Chinese trade with Britain and France totaled $125 million and $55.1 million, respectively, in the same year.

The balance of the Cold War years were characterized by one overriding characteristic in China–Europe relations—they were *derivative* of the broader Cold War and relations with Moscow and Washington and thus were unable to develop their own autonomous and independent dynamics.[2] The open rupture of Sino–Soviet relations in 1960 had a definite impact for China's ties with Eastern Europe, as Eastern European technicians and military advisers were withdrawn along with Soviet ones. Party-to-party ties were severed with all Eastern European communist parties except Albania and Romania, as China's only friends were Enver Hoxha and Nicolai Ceausescu. Trade dropped off precipitously, although diplomatic relations were maintained. China's relations with Western Europe during the 1960s were also initially influenced by the Sino–Soviet split, as Western European communist parties (and their links to Moscow) became a conundrum for the Chinese. On a state-to-state level, French president Charles De Gaulle's diplomatic recognition of China in 1964 was a symbolic breakthrough for Beijing, but not much came of it substantively. It did facilitate a modest increase in bilateral trade—as was also the case with West Germany—but a combination of China's internal convulsions during the Cultural Revolution and U.S. pressure blocked any significant expansion of commercial and diplomatic ties through the remainder of the decade.

The 1970s witnessed the blossoming of full diplomatic relations with the balance of Western European states. Following the American opening to China in 1971–1972, Western European governments moved quickly to establish comprehensive ties with Beijing. The European Community (forerunner to the European Union) extended recognition to China in 1975 (conversely, China was the first communist country to recognize the European Community), and it conferred preferential trade status on China in 1978. This status and a series of bilateral accords helped boost the total volume of Sino–Western European trade to $5.8 billion by the end of the decade. It was not until after Mao's death in 1976 that a rapprochement began with Eastern Europe—but this remained limited to Yugoslavia and Romania.

If the 1970s was the decade in which China and Western Europe reestablished contact, it was during the 1980s that relations were fully normalized. Yet, even though they were normalized diplomatically, bilateral ties continued to lack real depth and an independent dynamic. The last years of the Cold War and China's continuing opposition to the Soviet Union continued to cast a shadow over ties. But as Mikhail Gorbachev began to initiate a rapprochement with Deng Xiaoping and China in the mid- to late 1980s, there finally emerged some scope for China and Europe to begin to forge their own relationship free from the influence of the geopolitics of the Cold War.

Unfortunately, this opportunity was abruptly aborted by the events of 1989—both in China and in Eastern Europe. Western European governments reacted sternly to the Chinese military crackdown on June 4, 1989—imposing a freeze on official exchanges, a ban on all arms sales to China, and a stiffly worded statement condemning the violence and use of force in Beijing. Several leaders of the prodemocracy movement secretly escaped to Europe (mainly France). Then, in the autumn of 1989, the Berlin Wall was breached, and the German Democratic Republic (GDR) collapsed, together with a series of "dominoes" across Eastern Europe. The CCP reacted with alarm to these dramatic events. Throughout the autumn of 1989, the CCP leadership watched in shock and trepidation as the Communist Party states in Eastern Europe experienced popular uprisings and, one after another, fell from power. Ironically, the first communist regime to lose power did so on June 4—the very day of the martial law crackdown in Beijing. As the Chinese military shot its way through the streets of Beijing, voters in Poland peacefully went to the polls and gave the ruling Communist Party a resounding and humiliating defeat in National Assembly elections. The subsequent denouements of other ruling communist parties across Eastern Europe were not as peaceful or smooth as in Poland.

Thus, the twin events in Beijing and across Eastern Europe during 1989 caused a significant rupture in China's ties with *both* Western and Eastern Europe. Then, two years later, the Soviet Union collapsed—only fueling the strains and paranoia in China's leadership.[3] It was not until about 1995 when Sino–European relations began to renormalize after the EU dropped all remaining post-1989 sanctions against Beijing (except the arms sales embargo) and the European Commission began to fashion a new China strategy.

SINO–EUROPEAN RELATIONS TODAY

Over this period, the China–Europe relationship has grown to be both extensive and intensive. Consider some examples. Negligible trade and investment has grown more than sixty-fold since 1978 to the astonishing point of Europe being China's number one trading partner, while China ranks second for Europe. Total two-way trade reached €326.4 billion (approximately $425.6 billion) in 2008, with a rapidly growing trade surplus of €169 billion in China's favor. In the past five years (2003–2008), trade has soared by $300 billion. Europe has also become the largest source of technology and equipment transfer to China, transferring a total of 22,855 "technological items" to China by June 2006.[4] This amounts to about half the total technology that China imports from abroad every year. Extensive scientific collaboration also takes place, including energy and space cooperation.[5]

In the field of education, there are now more Chinese students (nearly 200,000 in 2009) studying in European institutions of higher education—more than anywhere else in the world. Academics enjoy a wide range of interaction via various mechanisms, such as the China-EU Think Tank Roundtable Mechanism. Exchanges between a broad range of European political parties and the CCP take place regularly, as the CCP has long been interested in (and has assiduously studied) the experiences of European social democratic parties.[6] Tourism is also booming: more than a million Chinese visit Europe every year.[7]

From minimal official interaction, the diplomatic relationship is now broad and deep. This entails annual summits with the EU presidency, EU troika foreign ministers, and individually with the main member states. Thirty-two sectoral dialogues take place between the European Commission officials and Chinese ministries annually to discuss detailed areas of collaboration while candidly discussing differences in areas such as human rights.[8] Similar interactions occur bilaterally between China and EU member states. The two sides also collaborate extensively on a range of international issues in the United Nations and other contexts. In 2003, the EU and China proclaimed a "comprehensive strategic partnership." In a May 2004 speech in Brussels, Chinese premier Wen Jiabao defined the meaning of this partnership:

> It is a shared view of the two sides to work for a comprehensive strategic partnership. By "comprehensive," it means that the cooperation should be all-dimensional, wide-ranging and multi-layered. It covers economic, scientific, technological, political and cultural fields, contains both bilateral and multilateral levels, and is conducted by both governments and non-governmental groups. By "strategic," it means that the cooperation should be long-term and stable, bearing on the larger picture of China-EU relations. It transcends the differences in ideology and social systems, and is not subjected to the impact of individual events that occur from time to time. By "partnership," it means that the cooperation should be on equal footing, mutually beneficial and win-win.

Beijing has also agreed to individual "strategic partnerships" with France, Germany, and the United Kingdom.

China is also a significant recipient of European Union overseas "cooperation assistance" (external aid)—with the EU spending €250 million on such cooperation projects during the four-year period 2002–2006.[9] In January 2007, when European Commissioner for External Relations Benita Ferrero-Waldner visited Beijing to launch negotiations on a new comprehensive China–EU "Partnership and Cooperation Agreement" (PCA),[10] further agreements were reached totaling €62.6 million in support of a Europe-China School of Law at Tsinghua University, the EU-China Project on the Protection of Intellectual Property, and the Europe-China Business Management Training Project. European foreign direct investment into China has also been substantial and has supplemented cooperation assistance. According to Chinese sources, by the end of 2006, the EU has invested in 24,033 projects in China, with a contractual value of $92.8 billion and actual realized investment of $50.56 billion.

While the relationship has developed dramatically since establishment of formal relations in 1975, the state of relations today is even more astonishing and impressive when one considers that it is only since 1995 that it has really blossomed. Prior to that time, the relationship was beholden to broader international forces—particularly the Cold War and Sino–Soviet antagonism. China–Europe relations were dominantly derivative from these broader factors. This all began to change, though, around 1995, when two events occurred:

- The EU dropped all sanctions (except military arms sales and defense technology transfers) dating from the June 4, 1989, incident in Beijing.
- The European Commission unveiled the first of its several subsequent policy papers (communications) on China.[11]

More broadly, six other factors contributed to the post-1995 surge in the relationship:

- The limiting effects of the Cold War passed, and the relationship could finally begin to develop on its own, free of the shadow and influence of the U.S.–Soviet rivalry.
- There is hardly any Taiwan lobby in Europe, as in the United States, to influence the public and politicians—and there is no "Taiwan issue" between European governments and China, as all faithfully subscribe to the "one-China principle."
- Europe has no military presence or few security interests in East Asia (unlike the United States).
- There existed a considerable (but not total) identity of views between Beijing and Brussels concerning the desired nature of the international order and system.
- There exist great complementarities of commercial and economic interests.
- The China strategy/policy mapped out by the European Commission in several policy documents between 1995 and 2006 offered a benign view of China's rise and identified a range of areas for collaboration.

Taken together, these factors collectively influenced the Sino–European relationship beginning in the mid-1990s and contributed to its dramatic growth over the past decade.

But what about the future? How are China–Europe relations likely to develop? What are the key variables that will affect the evolution of the relationship going forward?

MOVING FROM HONEYMOON TO MARRIAGE

After a decade of rosy rhetoric and steadily improving ties, China–Europe relations have entered a more complicated and difficult phase. Since late 2006, it seems that the relationship is passing from the "honeymoon" into the "marriage" phase. Some disputes have erupted, and both sides are beginning to realize the complexities of the relationship, the fact that they do not see identically on many issues, and that outside factors and actors impact their relationship. Both the atmosphere and the substance of the relationship have changed over the past several years.

The arrival in office of German chancellor Angela Merkel, French president Nicolas Sarkozy, and British prime minister Gordon Brown have also contributed to the changed atmosphere, as they are all more skeptical of China than their predecessors. Thus, the change of governments among Europe's "Big Three" and admission of the "New Twelve" former communist Central European states into the EU have also been a factor in Europe's reorientation. There is thus greater convergence of perspectives and policies toward China across the continent today than for many years. The acrimony arising out of the arms embargo imbroglio of 2004–2005 has been replaced with a stronger sense of unity and political purpose. This became true across the Atlantic as well, as the new EU mood better matched the China "hedging" policies of the Bush administration and the growing anger in Congress over a wide variety of trade-related matters.

The European public mood has also been affected by publicized incidents of Chinese industrial espionage and attempted hacking into the computer networks of the German Chancellor's Office and the British Foreign Office (as well as the U.S. Pentagon) and by concerns over human rights in China (particularly Tibet). Criticisms of China's government and human rights record have always been harsher among many of the new EU member states in Central Europe—particularly the Czech Republic, Poland, and the Baltic states—as they tend to view Beijing through the prism of their communist past and are also more sympathetic to secessionist forces in Taiwan, Tibet, and Xinjiang.

European corporations are also increasingly voicing their frustrations with China. A variety of discriminatory trade and investment practices plague European (and other) businesses in China—particularly the continuing widespread theft and pirating of intellectual property as well as numerous market access barriers to China's financial services industries, distribution networks, and protected "strategic industries."

There are thus a variety of reasons for the bloom to have come off the rose, and a variety of strains have emerged in the relationship. The release in October 2006 of the European Commission's latest official communication on China and the accompanying policy paper on EU–China trade and investment signaled and made explicit many of the concerns about China that had been bubbling beneath the surface in Europe.[12] In the communication, for the first time in such a policy document, the European Commission made a number of requests of China:[13]

- "open its markets and ensure fair market competition";
- "reduce and eliminate trade and non-tariff barriers";
- "level the [commercial] playing field";
- "fully implement WTO obligations";
- "better protect intellectual property rights";
- "end forced technology transfers";
- "stop granting prohibited subsidies";
- "work on clean energy technologies";
- "be a more active and responsible energy partner";
- "ensure balance in science and technology cooperation";
- "[recognize] the international responsibilities commensurate to its economic importance and role as a permanent member of the UN Security Council";
- "better protect human rights";
- "[ensure] more accountable government";
- be more "results oriented with higher quality exchanges and concrete results" in the human rights dialogue;
- ratify the UN Covenant on Civil and Political Rights;
- enter into formal dialogue with the EU and "improve transparency" concerning aid policies in Africa;
- "maintain peace and stability in the Taiwan Strait";
- improve "transparency on military expenditures and objectives";
- "comply with all non-proliferation and disarmament treaties";
- "strengthen export controls of WMD [weapons of mass destruction]-related materials."

This laundry list of requests gave the 2006 communication a harder edge than any of its predecessors, but it also reflected the new sobriety in Europe concerning certain aspects of China's policies and behavior. The European Council ratified the communication at its meeting on December 11, 2006, and produced its own twenty-three-point list of observations and concerns about the relationship.[14]

These documents took China's government and Europe watchers by surprise. Both the tone and the substance of the documents reflected a departure from the effusive rhetoric and lofty goals set forth in previous communications and led some notable Chinese Europe watchers in Beijing to accuse Brussels of adopting confrontational or "containment" policies similar to what they sometimes perceive from the United States. Privately, Chinese Foreign Ministry officials apparently assured their official European counterparts that they "understood" European concerns and were not overly alarmed by the tone or the substance of the communication. The Chinese decision to move ahead with negotiations on a new EU–People's Republic of China PCA and the warm reception given EU external relations commissioner Benita Ferrero-Waldner in launching the negotiations in January 2007 are perhaps indicative of the more pragmatic official reaction. Nonetheless, the EU documents did reflect a change in tone, substance, and approach to China from past precedent.

More difficulties arose subsequent to the changed tone and substance of the relations emanating from Brussels in November–December 2006, 2007, and 2008. The most noteworthy was the ballooning EU trade deficit with China, which reached €169.6 billion in 2008—which is growing at the alarming rate of €15 million per hour (according to then–EU trade commissioner Peter Mandelson). The rate of growth in the EU's deficit with China now exceeds the rate of growth of the U.S. trade deficit; if current trends continue, the aggregate EU deficit will surpass that of the United States by 2010. As a result, throughout 2007, Mandelson escalated his criticism and made a series of visits to Beijing.

Then, in September 2007, just after she returned from a state visit to China, Angela Merkel became the first German chancellor to receive the Dalai Lama in an official capacity in an official residence (the Chancellor's Office). This enraged Beijing (and drew public criticism from her predecessor, Gerhard Schröder), which suspended a series of governmental exchanges with Berlin until a private exchange of letters smoothed out the tensions. Merkel, herself a product of the former communist GDR, adopts a much stronger stand on human rights with Beijing than her predecessor Schröder. She subsequently indicated that she would not attend the opening ceremony of the Olympic Games to protest China's March 2008 crackdown on the uprising in Tibet.

The Tibet issue has resonated deeply among European publics. Well before the March 2008 uprising and subsequent crackdown by Chinese security forces, Europeans supported the Dalai Lama and the cause of Tibetan independence (although the Dalai Lama himself does not). The Tibet issue immediately became fused with the Olympic Games—and the running of the Olympic torch through Athens, London, and Paris. In all three cities, the ceremonies were disrupted by pro-Tibetan and anti-Chinese demonstrators. Various European parliaments passed motions condemning China, and a series of European leaders (notably, Vaclav Havel) criticized Beijing publicly. Havel, Merkel, and Sarkozy all boycotted the opening ceremony of the Olympics, although Gordon Brown was present for the closing ceremonies (as London is the next host city). For its part, Chinese national pride was injured by these incidents (particularly in Paris), resulting in an upsurge of Internet nationalism and public protests. The French chain Carrefour was boycotted by Chinese citizens for several months.

The decision by French president Sarkozy to meet the Dalai Lama in the fall of 2008 added to the strain and resulted in China's decision to "punish" him and France for the action. As part of the "punishment," China announced the cancellation of the China–EU Summit due to be held in Lyon in December 2008 (the capstone to the rotating French presidency). When Chinese premier Wen Jiabao toured several European countries in early 2009 in an effort to stabilize deteriorating ties, his itinerary purposively circumnavigated France.

Thus, the trade and Tibet issues have added to the sober mood in Europe over the broad range of issues noted previously. The "marriage" phase of Sino–European relations has clearly begun, and it will be interesting to see how the two sides manage their new difficulties.

SHAPING THE FUTURE OF SINO–EUROPEAN RELATIONS

Looking to the future, what variables will likely shape EU policy toward China? Seven sets of variables can be identified.

The first is the impact of trade on the European economies and workforce. With a huge EU trade deficit with China, high unemployment rates in several countries (especially France, Germany, and Italy), hollowed-out tertiary industries (particularly in the Mediterranean countries), and relative lack of economic competitiveness in the twelve new EU member states, European economies are increasingly feeling the "China factor." Thus far, the trade issue has not received the political traction that it has in the United States, but voices of concern and protectionism can be heard across the continent. These economic concerns can quickly snowball and possibly have a series of negative consequences—economically and politically.

The second variable is the degree of Chinese responsiveness to the numerous issues of concern noted in the 2006 communication. These are not demands, but they are more than "markers." They are serious requests put forward by the European side, in the spirit of partnership, to advance the China–Europe relationship. To be sure, China has its requests too—notably, lifting the arms embargo and granting of market economy status—that the EU needs to take seriously and be responsive to.

The third variable concerns relations between the EU member states and the European Commission and Council and between the European Parliament and the Commission/Council. Prior to the release of the 2006 communication on China, it was apparent that civil society, the China expert community, and nongovernmental organizations in several member states were unsettled and discontented with the European Commission's ambitious and optimistic view of China. Many accused the Commission of being naive. The manner in which the EU Commission and Council (mis)handled the arms embargo issue, creating an intra-European and transatlantic policy fiasco, only emboldened the critics of Brussels' China policy. These criticisms have continued since that time—adding to the public disenchantment with China across Europe.[15]

It seems that the European Commission seriously reflected on this subterranean discontent between 2004 and 2006, undertook a rethinking of the relationship and a reexamination of Europe's interests, and incorporated its findings in the new 2006 communication. This, it would be assumed, will better position the Commission and Council with the member states but also with voices heard in the European Parliament. As a result, China's "free ride" in Europe is over.

A fourth factor that will shape Europe's policy toward and relations with China will be the pace and scope of internal reforms in China. The EU has invested heavily—politically, financially, and rhetorically—in assisting China in a wide range of reforms. This has been the core of the EU's approach to China and what sets the EU apart from the United States and other nations in its dealings with China. The EU has viewed China primarily through the prism of a developing country and transitional nation—in the midst of multiple reforms aimed at marketizing the economy, globalizing the society, and pluralizing the polity. In these reforms, Europeans believe that they have much to share with China—given their own histories as welfare states and, more recently, the transition from socialist systems in Central Europe. This orientation differs markedly from the U.S. approach to the "rise of China"—as Americans tend to be exclusively concerned about the *external* manifestations of China's rise, while Europeans seem more concerned about its *internal* conditions.

Fifth, Europe now expects more from China in terms of contributing to global governance. This is made clear in the 2006 communication. The EU welcomes China's recent contributions to UN peacekeeping operations, UN reform, nonproliferation, and resolving the North Korean nuclear crisis and generally Beijing's new diplomatic activism. But at the same time, the EU is deeply concerned about China's support for nondemocratic states and its "value-free diplomacy" and "no-strings-attached" aid programs with such states, particularly in Africa and with Myanmar (Burma). Similarly, the EU is closely monitoring Beijing's worldwide quest for energy resources and raw materials. China may not yet be a global power, but it is increasingly a global actor. As such, Europe (and other nations) will be looking to Beijing to help address many of the challenges and crises that afflict the international order.

The sixth variable affecting European policies toward China is the U.S. factor and the new role that relations with China play in the transatlantic relationship. One positive side effect of the arms embargo imbroglio has been that a greater appreciation of China–Europe relations began to take hold in the U.S. government and, concomitantly, a greater sensitivity and appreciation of U.S.–China relations and U.S. security commitments in East Asia developed in Brussels and other European capitals. As such, the "China factor" is now lodged more deeply in transatlantic relations. There now exists considerable consensus and broad agreement between the United States and the EU on a range of issues pertaining to China. It is apparent that the commonalities across the Atlantic concerning China far outweigh any differences.

Finally, unexpected issues—like Tibet—can arise to trouble the relationship. The European concern over the human rights situation in China will gain greater salience over time. Another factor is that, unlike U.S.–China relations, there is no strategic basis to China–EU ties. That is, there are no security issues in the relationship—as the EU is a nonactor in Asian security.

LEARNING TO LIVE WITH COMPLEXITY

The Sino–European relationship and "strategic partnership" remains an important one in world affairs and is, on the whole, a very positive one. Nonetheless, despite all the positives, it is also evident that the relationship has begun to emerge from its honeymoon phase. It is also evident that the changed—more sober—climate in relations comes primarily from the European side. In fact, when one reviews the rapid progress in relations over the 1995–2005 decade, it is evident that the EU had been the catalytic force in the relationship and played the role of ardent suitor. Brussels pursued Beijing more than vice versa. But, similarly, the lust seems to have begun to wear off more quickly on the European side.

Going forward, the two sides will need to lower their expectations somewhat; clarify their rosy rhetoric; learn how to live with, narrow, or manage their differences; and develop the mechanisms to build a truly sustainable long-term marriage.

SUGGESTIONS FOR FURTHER READING

Godement, François, and John Fox. *A Power Audit of EU-China Relations*. London: European Council on Foreign Relations, 2009.

Shambaugh, David. *China and Europe, 1949–1995*. London: SOAS Contemporary China Institute, 1996.

Shambaugh, David, Eberhard Sandschneider, and Zhou Hong, eds. *China-Europe Relations: Perceptions, Policies, and Prospects*. London: Routledge, 2008.

6

Europe, the Mediterranean, and the Middle East

A Story of Concentric Circles

Nathalie Tocci and Benedetta Voltolini

The Mediterranean and the Middle East look very different from the two sides of the Atlantic. These regions represent Europe's southern neighborhood, not unlike Central and South America to the United States. Geographical proximity affects the conduct of European policies in the area in two principal ways. First, proximity leads to a blurring of and tight interlinkage between the normative and strategic objectives of the European Union (EU) in the region. In the European discourse, the promotion of a peaceful, prosperous, and stable Mediterranean and Middle East is viewed as complementary or even necessary to meet the EU's strategic aims, be these the pursuit of commercial interests, the management of migration flows, the fight against terrorism and organized crime, or the securing of energy supplies. Second, proximity conditions the foreign policy instruments at the EU's disposal in view of the EU's nature as a nonstate actor and its struggle to define a foreign policy in the neighborhood that is distinct from its enlargement policy. It is often said that the eastern enlargement has been the EU's major foreign policy success, whereby the magnetic attraction of the EU exerted significant influence on the transformation and transition of the former communist countries to the east. Yet over the past decade, the EU has become trapped in its own rhetoric, replicating the model of enlargement with some countries while in most cases devising "light" versions of the accession policy by applying the method of enlargement without the prospect of EU membership itself.[1] In turn, many of the EU's policy instruments in the neighborhood, including in the Mediterranean and the Middle East, are marked by the characteristic European mix between integration and foreign policies.

Geographical proximity to the southern Mediterranean and the Middle East has thus affected both the EU's policy objectives and its policy instruments in the region. This has led to a typically European construction of the Mediterranean and Middle Eastern regions in concentric circles, which may not appear intuitive across the Atlantic. This chapter aims to unpack the southern Mediterranean and Middle East as approached by the EU by focusing on three subregional cases: within the closest circle to the EU, we analyze the case of Turkey as an accession country; moving to the next circle, we examine Israel and the Occupied Palestinian Territory, which fall beyond the remit of enlargement yet remain anchored in the framework of EU contractual relations such as the Euro-Mediterranean Partnership and the European Neighborhood Policy; finally, we turn to Iran and Iraq in the last circle, as Middle Eastern states with whom the EU's policy approach falls squarely beyond the remit and logic of European integration. The underlying question tackled here is whether a pattern emerges between, on the one hand, the EU's definition of Mediterranean and Middle Eastern subregions with its accompanying policy aims and instruments and, on the other, the EU's impact on these regions and the influence of external actors, first and foremost the United States.

WITHIN THE ORBIT OF ENLARGEMENT: TURKEY

Turkey, like Cyprus and Malta up until the 2004 enlargement and currently alongside the western Balkans, gravitates within the orbit of enlargement. The end point of Turkey's EU membership, while agreed back in 1999, remains highly contested within several European capitals, whereby member states such as France, Austria, and Germany, while valuing highly relations with Turkey, remain unconvinced that full membership is the desirable end point.[2] Yet the official line towed in Brussels and thus the official EU policy framework applied to Turkey since Turkey was accorded EU candidacy in 1999 remains that of enlargement. This has had implications regarding both the EU's policy objectives toward Turkey and its policy instruments. It also has had significant implications on the EU's impact on Turkey and on the role of the United States in EU–Turkey relations.[3]

Approaching Turkey through the Lens of Enlargement

Viewing Turkey as a prospective or potential member state has led to a congruence between the EU's strategic interests and its normative objectives. Turkey has always been pivotal to European security interests, both during the Cold War, when it stood as a bulwark against Soviet expansionism, and thereafter, as it serves as a potential beacon of westernized democracy, peace, and stability in the midst of the turbulent Middle East and Eurasia. As such, EU actors have had a long-standing interest in Turkey's democracy and human rights record, its internal stability, and its foreign policy orientation. Yet beyond these general foreign policy aims and interests—largely shared across the Atlantic—the specific political and economic transformation of Turkey has become imperative for the EU in view of the inclusion of Turkey in the accession process in 1999. The prospect of membership and thus the prospect of Turkey's entry into EU institutions and decision-making structures have raised exponentially the importance of promoting Turkey's domestic transformation. The EU does not only desire a democratic, stable, and developed Turkey. It cannot afford to allow anything but a democratic, stable, and developed Turkey into its fold because of the implications on the EU's internal political, social, and economic cohesion.

The inclusion of Turkey in the accession process also has meant not merely that the EU is interested in promoting Turkey's modernization, democratization, and westernization but also that it is specifically concerned with Turkey's "EU-ization."[4] Aspiring to promote Turkey's EU-ization has entailed three sets of objectives. First, Turkey's compliance with the political criteria elaborated at the 1993 European Council in Copenhagen is necessary to open accession negotiations with a candidate country. These criteria include the stability of institutions; the respect for human and minority rights, democratic principles, and the rule of law; the existence of a functioning market economy; and the capacity to cope with competitive pressure and market forces within the EU. When applied to candidate Turkey, these criteria, spelled out in the European Commission's successive progress reports and accession partnership documents, have repeatedly stressed the need to guarantee nondiscrimination and the freedoms of thought, expression, association, peaceful assembly, and religion. The EU has called for the abolition of the death penalty, the eradication of torture, and the respect for rights and standards in trials and detention periods. Beyond individual human rights, the European Commission has made specific demands on governance and cultural and minority rights. It has called on Turkey to ensure effective, transparent, and participatory local government. It has insisted on Kurdish broadcasting and education. It has also called for administrative and judicial reform, for a rebalancing of civil–military relations, and for bridging regional disparities through a socioeconomic development plan that would improve health, education, infrastructure, and water facilities in the Kurdish-populated southeast.

Second, Turkey's EU-ization entails its harmonization with the EU's *acquis communautaire*, that is, the adoption and implementation of the entire body of EU laws, rules, and regulations spanning all policy domains of European integration. Harmonization with the *acquis* represents the nuts and bolts of the accession negotiations, divided into thirty-five policy "chapters" that candidate Turkey alongside the European Commission "open" and "provisionally close" by reviewing Turkey's adoption and implementation of the relevant minutiae of the *acquis*.

A third specific EU objective regarding Turkey and formulated within the context of accession is that of ensuring that the EU's "integration capacity" can withstand the entry of candidate Turkey. Whereas the question of the EU's absorption or integration capacity has been part of the EU's approach to enlargement since 1993, it has become an issue of prime political concern in the context of Turkey's accession process. This is because Turkey represents a somewhat "different" candidate to most European policymakers and citizens. Its size, location, and strategic significance set it apart from previous candidates, for good and bad. Hence, the question that looms high in the minds of European policymakers is the impact that Turkey's membership would have on EU institutions, on the goods and services market, on labor markets, on the EU's budget projections, and on EU foreign policy. Whereas on some of these questions the benefits of membership are self-evident, on other questions European policymakers see the need to tackle potential areas of concern through efforts undertaken both by Turkey and by the EU.[5]

Promoting EU Objectives through the Accession Policy

Turkey's first contractual relationship with the then European Economic Community (EEC) dates back to 1963, with the signature of the association agreement. The agreement envisaged the establishment of a customs union and opened the door to accession if and when the political and economic conditions were met. In 1987, following gradual political stabilization and economic liberalization of Turkey after the 1980 military coup, Turkey submitted a formal request for full membership. But partly because of the EEC's internal task of completing the single market and partly because of the problematic state of Turkish democracy and the mounting violence in Turkey's southeast, in 1989 Ankara's application was rejected, and Turkey's European future was put on hold.

The end of the Cold War brought about radical changes to Turkey's environment. Turkey's role as western sentinel against Soviet expansionism ended, ushering the way to a new period of mounting instability in the Middle East and Eurasia.[6] Turkey consequently underwent an intense period of soul-searching, assessing alternative geostrategic options such as pan-Turkism or regional leadership in the Middle East and Eurasia. Ultimately, the domestic debate converged on a renewed emphasis on the EU project by the mid-1990s. Turkish political démarches intensified, lobbying for inclusion in the EU customs union. Turkey's pressures were matched by Washington, which also pressed member states to deepen ties with Turkey.

The EU accepted, and in 1996 the EU–Turkey customs union entered into force, marking the beginning of higher levels of economic integration and, in Ankara and Washington's eyes, the prelude to membership.

The positive atmosphere created by the conclusion of the customs union agreement rapidly deteriorated, however, in 1997. Despite strong pressure from Ankara and Washington to upgrade EU–Turkey relations into the accession process, the 1997 European Council in Luxembourg underlined that Turkey did not meet the standards for candidacy and offered instead a "European strategy" based on the exploitation of the integration prospects foreseen under existing contractual relations—the Association Agreement. Unlike 1989, this second rejection, together with the EU's finger-pointing at Turkey's deficiencies, was perceived in Ankara as a clear case of discrimination. In response, Turkey froze its political dialogue with the EU and threatened to withdraw its membership application and integrate with the internationally unrecognized Turkish Republic of Northern Cyprus. The goal of full membership was not abandoned, however, and the Turkish establishment began displaying a dichotomous approach to the EU that it would consolidate in the years ahead. While the government stepped up its campaign to obtain candidacy, the domestic political debate was rife with criticism of the EU.

The tide turned with the 1999 Helsinki European Council, when Turkey's long-sought candidacy was recognized. Given the downturn in EU–Turkey relations in the 1997–1999 period, the member states acutely felt the need to move forward in EU–Turkey relations, and there was a growing sense within the EU of the need "not to lose Turkey." Alongside this, strong pressure was exerted by the Clinton administration in the United States to grant Turkey candidacy. The European Council in Helsinki recognized Turkey's candidate status yet stopped short of opening accession negotiations, arguing that the country first had to fulfill the Copenhagen political criteria. In turn, the European Commission was given a mandate to monitor progress and to draft a first Accession Partnership for Turkey, recommending areas for reform. The EU also adapted its financial assistance to Turkey, redirecting aid to provide more explicit support for Turkey's reforms.

The acceleration of Turkey's reform momentum, particularly since late 2001, spilled over into EU–Turkey relations, especially when the Copenhagen European Council in December 2002 concluded that it would determine whether and when to open accession negotiations with Turkey in December 2004. The approaching green light for the opening of negotiations set the target and the time line for the reform program of the new Justice and Development Party (AKP) government elected in November 2002. Turkey's progress in reforms under the first AKP government meant that the December 2004 European Council's verdict was that Turkey "sufficiently" fulfilled the political criteria and that accession talks could begin in October

2005. EU actors, however, appreciated the need to sustain Turkey's reform process over the course of the negotiations. Hence, the European Council foresaw a continuing EU role in determining Turkey's reform priorities through updated accession partnerships, monitoring compliance through the European Commission's progress reports, and threatening to suspend negotiations in the event of a stalling or backtracking of the reform process. In addition, the negotiating chapter on the "judiciary and fundamental rights" impinged directly on political reforms. All seemed in place for an ongoing virtuous dynamic.

Yet since the opening of accession negotiations in 2005, the 1999–2005 golden years in EU–Turkey relations seem to have come to a (temporary) halt, as the relationship has slipped back into a vicious dynamic resembling more the 1997–1999 period. Turkey's accession negotiations have been proceeding at a snail's pace, with twelve out of thirty-five chapters opened in five years and only one chapter (science and research) provisionally closed. In addition, France has informally vetoed the opening of several other chapters on the grounds that these are too closely linked to the prospect of full membership, about which Paris is openly negative. Moreover, accession talks, increasingly entangled with developments in the Cyprus conflict, risk grinding to a halt lest a solution on the eastern Mediterranean island is found. On the grounds of Turkey's nonimplementation of the amended customs union protocol to include the Republic of Cyprus in the EU–Turkey customs union, the EU in fact decided in December 2006 to suspend negotiations with Turkey on eight chapters of the *acquis*. In the autumn of 2009, the European Council was scheduled to review Turkey's accession process in relation to Turkey's (non)implementation of the Additional Protocol extending the EU–Turkey customs union to Cyprus. While the December 2009 European Council averted a much-feared train wreck in Turkey's accession negotiations, the Damocles sword of Turkey's ratification of the Additional Protocol continues to hang over Ankara's head. Insofar as Turkey links its extension of the customs union to southern Cyprus to progress in the Cyprus peace process or at the very least to the lifting of the EU's isolation of northern Cyprus—an unkept promise by the EU since 2004—the Cyprus quagmire is becoming increasingly entangled in EU–Turkey relations.

Understanding the EU's Impact on Turkey

The EU's impact on Turkey and its EU-ization can be understood by analyzing three factors. First and foremost is the EU's capability and more specifically the relevance of the EU's accession framework with all the instruments and incentives embedded in it. Here we note how, as and when Turkey switched from the framework of association and the customs union to that of the accession process, the EU's impact on Turkey's domestic transformation magnified. EU actors became increasingly sensitive to Turkey's domestic shortcomings in the 1990s. Indeed, during negotiations over the customs union, EU actors attempted to exert pressure on Turkey regarding its internal political situation. An important example occurred in 1995 when, following the arrest of several Kurdish deputies, the European Parliament (EP) delayed the ratification of the customs union agreement. Yet on the whole Turkey, relegated to the framework of the customs union in those years, snubbed EU pressure, and limited itself to slightly modifying a controversial article of its antiterror law, unblocking the EP's ratification.[7] Likewise, during the 1997–1999 period, when Turkey was kept out of the enlargement process, there was little progress and incentive to pursue domestic political reforms in Turkey. The only steps forward were the minor amendments in the penal code, the reduction of police custody for suspected crimes, and the removal of military judges from serving in state security courts. In sharp contrast, as and when Turkey moved into the framework of accession, the instruments and incentives embedded in this framework granted the EU far greater influence over Turkey's domestic transformation.[8] The carrot on offer was no longer merely trade related but entailed the entry into the EU in all its policy dimensions and institutions. Hence, after a slow start in 2000 and 2001, Turkey's reform momentum accelerated in the 2001–2005 period. The first major breakthrough came in October 2001 when thirty-four constitutional articles were amended. An even more acute turning point came in August 2002, when the Turkish parliament approved a far-reaching legal harmonization package, including the abolition of the death penalty; the right to broadcast and teach in languages other than Turkish; the liberalization of the freedoms of speech, association, and assembly; and the recognition of religious minorities' property rights. As Turkey struggled to gain its "date" to begin accession negotiations, incentives for reform peaked, and consequently 2003 and 2004 were the highest-intensity years of the reform process. In those years, another major constitutional reform, five additional legislative packages, a new penal code, and numerous laws and regulations modified many of the most restrictive features of Turkey's legal and political system.

A second critical determinant of the EU's impact on Turkey and its EUization is made up of the interests of member states and the manner in which these have imperiled the incentive embedded in the "technical" and "objective" accession process. The EU's influence on Turkey is bedeviled by the Turkish suspicion of Europe's reluctance to include Turkey in its club. Until 2002–2003, EU skepticism was rarely voiced in the open. With a few notable exceptions, European declarations normally focused on Turkey's shortcomings in the areas of democracy and human rights. However, as and when the prospects of Turkey's membership became more tangible with the approaching launch of accession negotiations in 2005, the underlying interests and positions of the member states came to the fore. Key personalities in France voiced their fears that Turkey's entry would dilute the EU's loosely defined *"esprit communautaire"* and push the EU's borders into the volatile Middle East and Eurasia. Actors in Germany, France, the Netherlands, and Austria have argued that Turkey's economic development would entail high levels of redistribution of EU funds to Anatolia, would bankrupt the Common Agricultural Policy, and would lead to an invasion of "Turkish plumbers" into the EU. Greece and more recently Cyprus have mobilized EU conditionality to win bargaining points in their bilateral disputes with Turkey. Least noble of all, politicians, political parties, and journalists across the EU have been reluctant to embrace a country with an allegedly "different" culture and religion. The skepticism of the member states has been compounded by other intra-EU problems, such as the EU's constitutional crisis and its so-called enlargement fatigue, which have cast dark shadows over Turkey's EU future. This does not mean that the EU has secretly decided against Turkey's membership. Yet the absence of a strong European commitment to Turkey's membership has fueled Turkey's insecurity, bolstering nationalist and conservative views that argue that Turkey should be cautious in passing reforms given that Europe will never accept Turkey into its club. The more the political concerns of the member states "pollute" the accession process, the less effective is the EU's impact on the domestic transformation and EU-ization of Turkey.

The third determinant of the EU's impact is the evolution of Turkey itself. In the post-2005 period, the reform momentum in Turkey slowed down, partly in response to the EU's wavering commitment to Turkey's membership yet largely because of domestic developments in Turkey itself. Since 2005, we have seen a worrying wave of prosecutions limiting the freedom of expression of activists and intellectuals and a resurgence of violence in the southeast. Particularly since 2007, the acrimonious power struggle between different domestic forces in Turkey has come to the fore, epitomized by the crisis over the election of President Abdullah Gül in 2007, the judiciary's closure case against the ruling AKP party in 2008, and the Ergenekon case in 2009.[9] Viewed from a different angle however, Turkey, having undertaken groundbreaking reforms on paper in 2002–2005, has since then been undergoing the "real" domestic transformation in its political, economic, and social structures and belief systems. Like any transformation, this entails complex and multifaceted power struggles between and within different sectors of society, the outcome of which cannot be ensured.

Yet what can be ascertained is that the EU, in the context of its accession policy, has acted as a necessary trigger for this process of domestic transformation to begin. Since 2005, the EU has largely lost its leverage, principally in view of its wavering commitment to Turkey's accession and partly because Turkey is currently embroiled in its own domestic battles.

Yet as long as Turkey remains anchored to the accession process, the EU is likely to remain the major source of external influence on the country's domestic transformation. In this respect, the influence of other actors, including the United States, is limited. Whereas the United States, under the Clinton, Bush, and Obama administrations, has repeatedly voiced its strong commitment to see Turkey in the EU, the influence that the United States has exerted on EU–Turkey relations since 1999 has been limited. The Clinton administration was pivotal in securing Turkey's entry into the customs union and the granting of Turkey's candidate status. Yet with the entry of Turkey in the accession process, EU–Turkey relations have become a domestic affair, both for Turkey and for the EU, on which external actors, including the United States, have limited influence. This is true both for the Bush administration, which garnered little sympathy in the EU or in Turkey, and for the Obama administration, whose ratings across Europe are decisively high.

STRADDLING EU INTEGRATION AND FOREIGN POLICY: ISRAEL AND THE OCCUPIED PALESTINIAN TERRITORY

Moving one circle away from the EU, we find the countries of the southern Mediterranean, that fall beyond the remit of the EU and the accession process. Here we include the southern Mediterranean countries of the "Euro-Mediterranean Partnership" (EMP), a multilateral policy framework launched in 1995 and intended to foster functional cooperation in the region. In July 2008, the EMP was incorporated in the French-inspired Union for the Mediterranean, which, like the EMP, is meant to promote mutual interest cooperation between the two shores of the Mediterranean in specific soft-policy domains. In this geographical circle, we also find the southern dimension of the European Neighborhood Policy (ENP), a policy intended to deepen bilateral relations between the EU and its neighbors across all policy domains yet with the proviso that the upgrading of relations would stop short of full membership. Geographically, this circle includes the countries of the Maghreb (Morocco, Algeria, Tunisia, and Libya) and the countries of the Mediterranean Middle East (Egypt, Israel, Jordan, Lebanon, Syria, and the Occupied Palestinian Territory [OPT]).[10] In order to shed light on the EU's aims, instruments, and impact on this region, the following section focuses on the case of EU relations with Israel and the OPT.

EU Normative Objectives beyond the Enlargement Framework

The EU's declared objectives in Israel and the OPT are based on two normative pillars that have consolidated over the decades into a clear view of the conflict and its resolution. The first pillar consists in securing Israeli and Palestinian rights to self-determination. The EU historically recognized Israel's right to statehood, living in peace with its neighbors within secure and internationally recognized boundaries. The European position toward the Palestinians was articulated progressively over the decades. Beginning with open-ended support for Palestinian self-determination in the 1980 Venice Declaration, by the end of the Oslo process at the Berlin European Council in 1999 the European Council advanced its support for a Palestinian state. With the eruption of the second intifada in 2000, the EU felt strong enough to further articulate its vision for peace, namely, the creation of two states living in peace within internationally recognized borders. The state of Palestine would be established in the West Bank, East Jerusalem, and the Gaza Strip along the 1967 borders (with minor and mutually agreed adjustments if necessary) and would be viable, independent, sovereign, and democratic. Despite the ever-diminishing prospects of such a state, the EU has remained steadfast in its commitment.

The second set of EU objectives regards the importance of respecting human rights and democratic principles and international law. Most EU declarations on the conflict since the 1970s have, on the one hand, condemned Palestinian acts of "terrorism," pointing to the relevant violations of international law, while, on the other, condemned Israeli settlements, the construction of which contravenes the Fourth Geneva Convention. During the Oslo years, the EU kept relatively silent, particularly about the accelerated pace of settlement construction in the OPT, for fear of "disturbing the peace process." However, with the outbreak of the second intifada, the EU intensified its calls for a halt to and reversal of settlement construction and denounced a whole array of human rights and international humanitarian law violations, ranging from Palestinian suicide bombings to Israeli incursions, extrajudicial killings, forms of collective punishment, and construction of the barrier in the West Bank. Finally, since Israel's disengagement from the Gaza Strip in 2005 and the political separation between the Hamas-controlled Gaza Strip and the Palestinian Authority (PA)/Fateh–controlled West Bank in 2007, condemnations of Israel's military incursions and the closure of Gaza and of Hamas's indiscriminate launching of rockets into bordering Israeli towns have featured prominently in EU declarations.

Hence, by the turn of the century, EU declarations clearly stipulated both the EU's vision of the Middle East and the means necessary to achieve it. The aim was that of two states on the basis of the 1967 borders. The means were negotiations and respect for human rights, democracy, and international law. More than a vision, the attainment of these goals has been viewed as an integral element of the EU's security interests and strategy as spelled out in the EU's European Security Strategy.[11]

EU Policies in Israel and the OPT:
Diplomacy, Capacity Building, and Contractual Relations

In order to contribute to the fulfillment of these normative and strategic objectives, the EU has deployed its policy instruments in Israel and the OPT under three main headings: diplomacy, capacity building, and contractual relations. Whereas the first two policy headings are more typical of EU foreign policy, EU contractual relations retain strong elements of the EU's integration policy, representing a "light" version of the accession process.

The first policy heading is diplomacy, which is conducted in the context of the EU's Common Foreign and Security Policy (CFSP). The EU's diplomatic role in the Middle East includes multilateral and unilateral initiatives. Following the 1991 Madrid conference, EU multilateral diplomatic involvement took the form of chairing the Regional Economic Development Working Group and cochairing several other working groups. In 1995 and in the context of the Oslo peace process, the EU launched the EMP in which both Israel and the PA are included. With the end of the Oslo process, the EU has also acquired a more structured role in multilateral mediation, most notably with its participation in the Quartet, the grouping of the EU, the United States, Russia, and the United Nations charged with brokering a Middle East peace. Moving to unilateral frameworks of action, we find the EU's declaratory diplomacy, which entails the issuing of public statements and démarches both during meetings of the Council of Ministers and the European Council and in response to specific facts and events. We also find the roles of the CFSP high representative Javier Solana and the special representative for the Middle East peace process. The EU's diplomatic involvement in the conflict has been secondary and as such only minimally influential. The EU has, through its steadfast commitment to Palestinian self-determination since the 1980s, contributed greatly to placing on the international agenda the objective of establishing a Palestinian state.[12] However, EU operational diplomacy has taken the lead in the conflict only on specific crisis management initiatives rather than in regard to the overall mediation of a settlement, which has remained firmly in the hands of the United States.

A second policy heading is that of assistance to the Palestinians. We include under this heading both financial aid, primarily disbursed by the European Commission, as well as European Security and Defense Policy (ESDP) missions deployed under the CFSP pillar. EU aid to the Palestinians has been disbursed to support "state" building (or "state" survival) and economic development (or economic subsistence).[13] Since 1971, EU aid has been channeled to Palestinian refugees through the UN Relief Works Agency. In 1987, this was complemented by assistance to Palestinian civil society. In the context of the Oslo process, the member states stepped up their economic support to the Palestinians, this time directed primarily to the PA. In 1994–1998, the EU committed ECU 400 million in grants. It committed a further €600 million in 1998–2002. Through these monies, the EU financed the establishment of PA institutions as well as key infrastructure projects, such as the Gaza airport and seaport. However, since the mid-1990s and particularly since the turn of the century, EU aid has increasingly taken the form of humanitarian assistance and payments to cover the PA's recurrent expenditure in view of the progressive implosion of the PA and the accelerating dedevelopment of the OPT. Since 2000, average EU annual transfers to the Palestinians have risen substantially, reaching almost €1 billion in 2009 if member state contributions are included.

Yet alongside this rise in aid necessary to sustain an increasingly dysfunctional PA and prevent an impending humanitarian crisis in the OPT, since 2006 EU assistance to the Palestinians has also become increasingly politicized. In view of Hamas's victory in the 2006 Palestinian Legislative Council elections and its subsequent entry into the PA, the EU, alongside its Quartet partners, imposed conditionality on the new government. In view of the inclusion of Hamas on the EU's list of terrorist organizations since 2003, some form of conditionality was inevitable. Yet the Quartet went beyond calling on the new government to renounce terrorism and insisted on three "principles" (an end to violence, recognition of Israel, and acceptance of previous agreements). EU diplomacy in the context of the Quartet failed to induce compliance by Hamas and, in response the EU, taking the lead from the United States, boycotted the PA government and withheld assistance to it. The policies of boycott, sanctioning, and closure pushed the OPT to the humanitarian and economic brink. In response, at the EU's insistence, the Quartet agreed on a Temporary International Mechanism (TIM), through which funds would be channeled to the OPT while bypassing the Hamas-led PA government. While the boycott paralyzed the PA, thus worsening the economic and humanitarian situation in the OPT, the TIM and the surge in aid that came with it pulled Palestine one step back from a humanitarian catastrophe. The rising levels of assistance through the TIM, however, also entailed the dedevelopment of the governance structures of the would-be Palestinian state, in particular with a recentralization of power in the hands of the presidency and security forces loyal to the presidency. Above all, the withholding of funds to the Hamas government and the channeling of funds to the structures under control of the presidency contributed to an increasingly acrimonious polarization between Fateh and Hamas, which culminated with Hamas's "victory" in Gaza and Abbas's control over the West Bank.

Another aspect of capacity building is the role of the EU in Palestinian security sector reform. Here we find two missions deployed under the ESDP. Since 2005 (although practically since 2007), EUPOL-COPPS has provided civil police training and equipment and has engaged in the reconstruction of Palestinian security and judicial facilities (i.e., prisons, courts, and police stations). Whereas EUCOPPS contributed to improved law and order in the West Bank, it failed or, rather, could not succeed in inspiring an overhaul of the security sector, which remained fundamentally stalled by the Fateh–Hamas divide. In turn, Palestinian security forces in the West Bank remained politicized, lacking democratic accountability. They engaged in human rights abuses, arbitrary arrests, and detentions, particularly against hundreds of Hamas members and supporters in the West Bank (much like Hamas has done with its Fateh opponents in Gaza). Furthermore, the efforts of the Palestinian civilian police were stalled by the frequent Israeli military incursions in the same cities in which PA forces were deployed. The EU attempted to remedy this by sponsoring human rights training programs among police forces. But these microinterventions were a drop of water in an ocean. Alongside EUCOPPS and in the context of the November 2005 U.S.-brokered Agreement on Movement and Access, the EU also engaged in border monitoring at the Rafah crossing (the crossing point for the movement of people between the Gaza Strip and Egypt) through its border monitoring mission EUBAM. While not having executive power over who could cross through Rafah, EUBAM was mandated to operationally monitor, verify, and evaluate PA performance in border management as well as to build border and customs capacity through training, equipment, and technical assistance. EUBAM has de facto ceased to be operational since June 2006 in view of Israel's noncompliance with the terms of the 2005 Agreement on Movement and Access. With EU monitors unable to reach Rafah, the crossing was closed most of the time between June 2006 and June 2007. EU cajoling only led to its occasional opening up until the Hamas takeover of Gaza in June 2007, when the crossing was permanently shut.

A final policy heading at the EU's disposal, which resembles more the logic and method of the accession process, is the EU's bilateral contractual relations with Israel and the Palestine Liberation Organization (PLO) and the PA.[14] The EU's contractual ties with Israel have been progressively upgraded since the 1960s. The first European Community trade agreement with Israel dates back to 1964. Further preferential trade agreements were signed in 1970 and in 1975. In 1995, Israel and the European Community signed a Euro-Mediterranean association agreement that entered into force in 2000. Israel's association agreement, which is set within the framework of the EMP and entered into force in 2000, is extensive. It covers political dialogue, free trade in industrial and select agricultural products, freedom of establishment, free movement of capital, the harmonization of regulatory frameworks, and social and cultural cooperation. Israel has more recently also signed additional agreements on procurement, agriculture, scientific and technical cooperation, aviation, and space. Turning to the Palestinians, the EU, building on the 1986 regulation giving rise to a separate preferential import regime for Palestinian products, signed an interim association agreement with the PLO in 1997, providing for the partial liberalization of trade. However, as opposed to EU–Israel relations, the implementation of the EU–PLO agreement has been grossly ineffective because of Israel's nonrecognition of and, thus, noncooperation in the functioning of the agreement. Finally, both Israel and the PA are included in the ENP. Particularly in the case of Israel, the ENP Action Plan spells out a long list of EU benefits, ranging from reinforced political dialogue to economic and social cooperation, trade and internal market integration, and cooperation in justice and home affairs and in the areas of transport, energy, environment, information society, research, and civil society. Implementation of the EU-Israel Action Plan has accelerated over the years, whereas the EU-PA Action Plan remains largely a dead letter.

As far as contractual relations are concerned, EU leverage on the Palestinians has been minimal in view of the de facto nonimplementation of interim association agreement and the ENP Action Plan. Likewise, in the case of Israel, despite the valuable "carrots" on offer through contractual relations, the EU has opted not to use its potential leverage on Israel in the service of its objectives in the region. Despite the grave human rights and international law violations perpetrated by Israel, no attempt has been made to impose negative conditionality, let alone sanctions, on Israel. As in the EU's relations with other southern Mediterranean countries, the EU has expressly stated its preference for "constructive engagement" with Israel. Hence, regardless of Israel's widespread human rights abuses and violations of international law, the EU has never seriously contemplated suspending the association agreement. However, far more common in the EU's constructive engagement with third countries, including those of the southern Mediterranean, has been the idea of positive conditionality. While only partially applied elsewhere, this approach has not been implemented toward Israel at all. Carrots rarely have been dangled and normally have been simply given regardless of Israel's conduct. In the ENP Action Plan, there has been no attempt to formulate positive political conditionality toward Israel. Yet by far the most serious and atypical way in which the EU has related to Israel has been its progressive bending to Israeli policies that contravene international law to the extent of risking to acquiesce in Israeli policies and distorting its own law in order to accommodate illegal Israeli practice. The dispute over the preferential export of Israeli goods produced in settlements is one case in point. By turning a blind eye to the problem, the EU has signaled to Israel that European Community law is up for political bargaining and has cast doubt over the EU's own commitment to the rules and values it rhetorically promotes.

Understanding the EU Impact on Israel and the Palestinians

The EU, as a secondary external actor in the region, could not have represented the major determinant in the evolution of the conflict. Yet, in light of the EU's highly developed bilateral relations with the parties, has the EU put its policy means to the best use? The answer is largely negative. In a structural context of Israeli dominance and Palestinian weakness, there has been a diminishing prospect for the establishment of a viable Palestinian state in view of Israel's accelerating colonization of the OPT. Despite its declaratory support for a two-state solution, EU policies have reinforced this trend. Over the Oslo years, the EU supported the PA and the peace process without paying much attention to the PA's performance and Israel's human rights and international law violations resulting in its expanding grip on the OPT. Since then, EU efforts have mitigated the humanitarian effects of the conflict by pouring aid into Palestine. Yet aid to Palestine and acquiescence to Israel have supported the deteriorating trends on the ground.

What explains the EU's negative impact on the conflict? In terms of capability, the EU has disposed of significant instruments to influence positively the conflict. Compared to the EU's contractual ties with other noncandidate countries, both Israel and the PA rank high on the EU's list of priorities, judging by the relationships they enjoy. Furthermore, both Israelis and Palestinians accord high importance to their relations with the EU. Israel is a small country whose openness to international trade is key to its economic survival. The EU is Israel's largest trading partner, accounting for one-third of Israeli exports and around 40 percent of Israeli imports. The political value attributed by Israel to the EU is far more controversial but arguably more important. Since the turn of the century, Israelis have frequently referred to the "crisis" in EU–Israel relations. Israel's strategic relationship with the United States has also overshadowed the murkier political ties with the EU. However, Israel lives at the EU's doorstep, it is surrounded by real and perceived enemies, and the United States remains on the other side of the Atlantic. Beyond the rhetoric, Israel's links to Europe are valued highly, and the desire of finding a place of belonging in Europe (rather than in the Middle East) is deeply embedded in the Israeli Jewish majority (of European descent). The subjective value of EU ties with the Palestinians is also high. In economic terms, the EU represents by far the largest donor to the Palestinians. Without EU aid since 2000, the PA may well have collapsed. Politically, Palestinians frequently accuse Europe of its inadequate political role. However, they would warmly welcome a stronger European involvement given their view of the U.S. bias in favor of Israel and their appreciation of the multifaceted weaknesses of the Arab world. But Israel and Palestine do not aspire to join the EU, and their exclusion from the accession process limits potential EU influence. The influence that the EU could exert on the parties is likely to be lower than on candidate country Turkey.

A second factor to explain the EU's impact on the conflict is the EU's internally competing interest agenda. It would be mistaken to view the EU's advocacy of a rights-bound, two-state solution in the Middle East as being hypocritical. Yet while the EU might genuinely support these normative ideals, its concomitant pursuit of narrower interests has induced it to deploy its policies paradoxically in contradiction to its objectives. In the Middle East, the EU has viewed the protection of Israel and close relations with it as a high-order priority. Europe's history of anti-Semitism has generated a deep-felt preference, particularly in some member states, to foster close relations with Israel and promote its security. Although the EU has repeatedly underlined that a two-state solution is the only long-term guarantee of Israel's security, the EU majority has also wished not to antagonize Israel through concrete responses to its conduct in the conflict. This has occurred to the extent of bending the EU's own laws and rules for the sake of accommodating (illegal) Israeli policies.

A third set of reasons explaining the EU's impact relates to the external environment and more precisely to domestic forces in Israel and the OPT and by U.S. policy in the region. The evolution of the conflict is above all dictated by domestic factors rather than by the EU.[15] More specifically, the flaws in the Oslo process, which came to a head at the Camp David II summit; the unwillingness of Arafat to rein in the intifada in its early stages; and the subsequent escalation of violence and colonization of the OPT underlie the shift away from a two-state solution and the mounting violation of human rights and international law. In particular, since 2000, several interrelated features have constrained the EU's role. In Israel, the feeling of existential threat aroused by Palestinian suicide attacks explained the government's free hand in crushing the Palestinian uprising in open disregard of rights and law. The growing Israeli popular desire to "disengage" from the Palestinians and the rising awareness of the "demographic threat" posed by them underpinned the "separation barrier" in the West Bank, the Gaza disengagement, and the progressive closure of the Gaza Strip. The 2006 Lebanon War, Hamas's takeover of Gaza in 2007, and escalating tensions between Hamas and Israel triggered Israel's military offensive in Gaza in December 2008–January 2009 and the end of any peace process worthy of the name.

Finally, the EU's imperative to maintain cooperation with the United States on the Middle Eastern dossier has meant that the EU has constantly accommodated the line followed by Washington. In other words, unlike the case of Turkey, where U.S. insistence regarding Turkey's European future is often viewed with annoyance by Europeans (who view the matter as an exclusively internal one), when it comes to the Middle East, the picture changes radically. EU policy toward Israel and the OPT, while being endowed with potentially influential and independent policy instruments, constantly seeks to dovetail with the U.S. approach to the region. During the Oslo process, this meant that regardless of the parties' conduct on the ground, the EU's priority of keeping the U.S.-sponsored peace process alive meant refraining from criticizing the actions of the parties to the conflict. After Oslo, it has led to a considerable EU focus on Palestinian capacity building only when and to the extent that this was the main tune played in Washington. Once that tune changed (following the election of Hamas), the EU first boycotted the Hamas-led government and then opted to support its unelected Fateh branch in the West Bank. It remains to be seen whether under the Obama administration U.S. policy in the region will change in form and above all in substance and, if so, whether and how the EU will follow suit.

THE STRUGGLE TO DEFINE FOREIGN POLICY BEYOND THE NEIGHBORHOOD: IRAN AND IRAQ

Because of their distance from the EU, Iran and Iraq fall within neither the remit of accession nor the EMP and ENP. This means that the EU can rely on a smaller and less influential set of instruments toward these two countries. More specifically, EU policies toward Iraq and Iran relate to CFSP measures—mainly diplomatic initiatives and declarations—as well as trade and humanitarian assistance. The EU's relations with both countries thus entail looser forms of cooperation that do not have, to date, a contractual basis insofar as no agreements have been signed between the EU and Iran and Iraq.

In terms of EU objectives, although the EU's aims and interests are specified in relation to each country separately, in practice the EU views the stability of the region and the development of economic and trade relations with it, especially in the energy and raw material sectors, as prime common objectives. Beyond this strategic component, the EU has also declared its normative commitment to promoting democracy, the respect of human rights, and the nonproliferation of weapons of mass destruction in both countries. Beyond the formulation of common objectives, EU policies toward Iran and Iraq, while not formally linked, can be viewed as being closely intertwined not only because they belong to the same subregion in the eyes of Europeans but also because EU policy toward one can be viewed as the mirror image of policy toward the other, with 2003 representing the turning point in EU positions toward both countries.

An Intertwined Story Determining Goals and Policies Pursued

Unlike the United States, which broke ties with Iran after the 1979–1981 embassy hostage crisis in Tehran and opted for a policy of containment and sanctions, the EU and its member states have always kept open channels with Iran. More specifically, in 1992 they developed a "Critical Dialogue," defined as such because it dealt with all issues of prime concern—terrorism, human rights, and the fatwa issued against the British writer Salman Rushdie—yet "Iranians both listened and were listened to."[16] Relations were not easy, and in 1996, EU–Iranian relations reached a breaking point over the "Mykonos case."[17] Yet the incident was soon overcome with the election of Mohammed Khatami in the 1997 presidential elections, which ushered the way to a new start in EU–Iran relations under the 1998 "Comprehensive Dialogue." This forum was meant to host bilateral meetings dealing with democracy and human rights issues, terrorism, and nonproliferation and to explore cooperation in the fields of drug control, refugees, and the energy sector. In view of Khatami's reelection in 2001, the EU opened the prospect of enhancing relations with Iran through a Partnership and Cooperation Agreement (PCA), with a first meeting between the parties taking place in 2002. Yet negotiations over the PCA were conditioned on progress in talks over four political issue areas—the Middle East, human rights, terrorism, and nonproliferation—discussed in the context of the Political Dialogue Agreement. By linking the economic to the political track and thus exerting positive conditionality on Iran, the EU attempted concomitantly to pursue its strategic and commercial objectives alongside its normative goals. A series of human rights roundtables and discussions were held over the next two years alongside parallel talks on the PCA. Yet by 2003, progress was hampered by a shift in the international context, driven by a change of tune played in Washington, with the Bush administration branding Iran as part of an "axis of evil" as Khatami's government was losing public support.[18] The situation deteriorated further in 2003 when Iran's nuclear program became the dominant issue on the international agenda. Since then, the EU, setting aside all other matters related to the PCA and the Comprehensive Dialogue, focused its attention on the nuclear question. By 2005, both negotiations on the PCA and the Comprehensive Dialogue were suspended, and their resumption was explicitly linked to progress in resolving the Iranian nuclear question.

Interestingly, when it comes to Iraq, a reverse story can be told over the same time span, that is, between the 1990s and 2003. After the Gulf War, the EU not only did not enjoy contractual relations with Iraq as in the case of Iran, thus eliminating the prospect of structured dialogue as well as positive conditionality, but also imposed negative conditionality—an economic embargo—on Iraq. The embargo lasted from June 1990 (UN Security Council [UNSC] Resolution 661) to May 2003 (UNSC Resolution 1483) and consisted of freezing financial resources and suspending all trade relations (except for medicine and some food products justified on humanitarian grounds). Indeed, the EU applied UNSC resolutions imposing sanctions on Iraq and argued that bilateral relations could be reconsidered only when Iraq abided by those resolutions.[19] EU–Iraq trade, which was almost nonexistent between 1991 and 1996, rose in 1997 under the Oil-for-Food Program.[20] Between 1992 and 2003, the only other policy pursued by the EU consisted of delivering humanitarian assistance. The European Commission provided €157 million in humanitarian aid between 1992 and the 2003 war and was the single largest donor to Iraq after the United Nations. Sanctions on the one hand and humanitarian assistance on the other thus represented the only two aspects of the EU's Iraq policy up until 2003. Even more starkly than in the Iranian case, 2003 was a critical turning point in the EU's approach toward Iraq: not only were the member states bitterly divided over participation in the U.S.-led invasion, but following the invasion and occupation, EU policy toward the country changed significantly, opening the way to a comprehensive and structured relationship with Iraq.

The role reversal in the EU's Iran and Iraq policies over the same period is not accidental but rather tightly interlinked. More specifically, the EU's policy toward Iran was also—but not only—the consequence of the EU's internal and transatlantic rift over the war in Iraq. Thus, not only was the EU driven by its strategic and normative interests toward Iran, but also the Iranian nuclear question and the EU's involvement in it became instrumental to bridge the transatlantic divide and restore unity between the member states and thus self-confidence in EU foreign policy.

The Iraqi question was highly divisive above all because of the "you're either with us or against us" rhetoric and style of the Bush administration, which obliged member states to position themselves either for or against the war, thus rendering the differences between them stark.[21] Although the issue rose on the U.S. agenda immediately after the September 11 attacks, the European Council turned its attention to it very late in the day at the meeting held in December 2002 in Copenhagen, which set aside the question of the war and limited itself to supporting the United Nations and calling on Iraq to comply with UNSC Resolution 1441. The fact that the European Council debated Iraq only a few months ahead of the invasion did not help forge a European consensus. At the same time, the delay in the European Council's discussion on Iraq was due, inter alia, to the existing divisions between the member states on the question. The division into two camps had in fact started taking shape months beforehand, when German chancellor Gerhard Schröder unambiguously excluded German military intervention in Iraq in support of the United States. A similar stance was adopted by French president Jacques Chirac, who championed a European and diplomatic approach to the problem. The division between the member states, deridingly dubbed by U.S. defense secretary Donald Rumsfeld as a division between "old Europe" and "new Europe," had less to do with an appreciation of the Iraqi problem as such and more with the appropriate response to it.[22] On the one hand, Germany and France led the group of member states that opposed the recourse to military means, calling for a more nuanced and humanitarian response to the problem and the imperative of seeking a more consensual approach to it internationally;[23] on the other hand, member states such as the United Kingdom, Italy, Spain, and most Eastern European member states championed the more aggressive military line toed by Washington. For many Europeans, the invasion of Iraq epitomized the lowest point in the search for a European CFSP.

Yet precisely because the member states were so badly burned by the war in Iraq, the lessons drawn from it were applied, mutatis mutandis, to the Iranian nuclear dossier. The Iranian nuclear question represented a golden opportunity for the EU to mend fences within the EU and thereafter also across the Atlantic. With the door left wide open by the refusal of the United States to engage directly with Iran, Europeans walked straight through it, with Germany, France, and the United Kingdom taking the lead and launching a new format to deal with the Iranian nuclear issue: the so-called E3. Initially, the EU was not directly involved in negotiations. The E3 effectively negotiated on behalf of the EU without its formal authorization, causing some resentment, especially among other large member states, such as Italy, which felt unfairly excluded from the initiative.[24] Yet by 2004, the EU as a whole officially supported the E3's initiative, and CFSP high representative Javier Solana was formally included in the group, which became known as E3/EU. The E3/EU deployed typically European instruments and logics to the problem, exerting diplomatic pressure on Iran and engaging in "carrot-and-stick" strategies. The EU thus offered economic and technological cooperation in return for Iranian compliance with international demands. Moreover, the EU also used the stick of the referral of the nuclear dossier to the UNSC, a step that was initially avoided in favor of negotiations and dialogue. The objective was to restore the authority of treaty-based international arrangements, to avoid a possible military confrontation between the United States and Iran, and to hedge against intra-EU divisions as in the case of Iraq.[25] Over its first eighteen months, the E3 succeeded in containing the nuclear problem and reached two agreements: the Tehran Agreement in 2003 and the Paris Agreement in 2004. However, in August 2005, diplomatic relations started deteriorating as Iran resumed the activities related to the enrichment of uranium, which is a necessary step for the production of energy but is a process that can also be used for military purposes. The EU retaliated by supporting sanctions alongside the United States. In turn, the International Atomic Energy Agency referred the Iranian case to the UNSC. Since then, the E3/EU initiative has been incorporated into a new international format comprising also the United States, Russia, and China.[26] The EU has thus backed UNSC resolutions imposing sanctions on Iran as a result of its noncompliance with the obligations under the Nuclear Nonproliferation Treaty. At the same time, diplomacy has persisted, and attempts to reach a compromise were made in 2006, 2008, and 2009, none of which persuaded Iran to suspend its enrichment of uranium.

By contrast, in Iraq the situation developed the other way around: since 2003, the EU has abandoned its narrow and punitive form of engagement and embraced a more comprehensive approach. The intra-EU fragmentation caused by the war was repaired following the toppling of Saddam Hussein's regime, as the EU moved into a terrain it is more accustomed to: reconstruction and efforts to establish a new Iraqi administration through financial assistance, support for the United Nations, and deploying the ESDP civilian crisis management mission EUJUST LEX, which aimed at training Iraqi officials within the criminal justice system. In addition to bilateral assistance, the EU also contributed to the establishment of a multidonor instrument for channeling international support for the reconstruction process in Iraq: the International Reconstruction Fund Facility for Iraq. By June 2004, the European Commission set out a framework for its multifaceted engagement with Iraq, including electoral assistance, political cooperation, and bilateral agreements, to be applied as and when the political transition and security climate in the country improved.[27] In line with this approach, in 2006 the EU launched negotiations on a PCA with Iraq that were concluded in 2009, yet beyond this the EU still struggles to define and above all implement a well-structured strategy toward Iraq.[28]

Explaining EU's Impact on Iraq and Iran

The EU's impact on both Iraq and Iran is limited in view of the distance of these countries from the EU. With this proviso in mind, the EU has nonetheless had an impact on both countries, an impact that can be understood by turning to a set of conditioning factors.

First are the interests and objectives sought by the EU, which have included material self-interests such as the pursuit of raw materials, trade benefits, and the stability of the region, alongside normative goals, such as the respect for international law, the promotion of democracy, and the respect for human rights. Insofar as the pursuit of national interests has often led to intra-EU divisions, the normative dimension has acted as the necessary glue favoring a common policy. In the case of Iran, this was achieved precisely because of the nuclear question, in view of the presence of a common unifying norm against nonproliferation. By contrast, the Iraq War, which most Europeans saw as an act of aggression devoid of legal legitimacy, lacked this international law dimension, thus leaving the member states bitterly divided in their pursuit of separate national interests. Once the invasion became a hard reality, the member states reconverged

Nathalie Tocci and Benedetta Voltolini

on the norm of reconstruction, which constrained their exclusive pursuit of narrowly defined self-interests and aided the search for a common position.[29]

Second, the menu of policy instruments at the EU's disposal also goes far in explaining the EU's role and impact on these two countries. In the case of Iran and Iraq, the EU could not rely on its power of attraction, embedded in the accession and neighborhood policies, and thus could not make an effective use of conditionality. The EU did try to exert its influence through the offer of cooperation agreements, but the benefits on offer in these agreements are simply not valuable enough to endow the EU with effective leverage on these countries. The case of Iran in particular highlights the limited range of coercive options at the EU's disposal, which span from withholding rewards to supporting UN sanctions, without any in-between tools to exert leverage.[30] Moreover, EU conditionality and the hierarchical relations that it establishes between the EU and the targeted state can be easily rejected by the latter, which does not have much to lose by compromising its relations with the EU, pressing instead for a more balanced partnership.[31] Furthermore, the EU is unable to offer high incentives in the field of security, which remains a U.S. prerogative. Particularly in the Iranian case, security benefits are of the essence to explaining the EU's limited leverage on Tehran, which remains concerned primarily with the role played by the United States. In the case of Iraq, the EU's potential to influence the country rose after the invasion. Whereas prior to 2003 the EU could only apply sanctions and deliver humanitarian assistance, after the overthrow of Saddam Hussein's regime, the ground was cleared for the EU to engage with instruments and policies it is more familiar with, namely, state-building and postwar reconstruction measures. In this context, it was also possible for the EU to launch negotiations on the PCA with Iraq, thus being able to use economic instruments, which represent the strongpoint of European foreign policy.

Third and most important, EU policies toward Iraq and Iran have been conditioned by the external environment, determined by the domestic situation within these two countries alongside the preponderant role played by the United States in the region. In the Iranian case, although the Critical Dialogue had contributed to a gradual shift in Iranian behavior, the EU's influence was successful primarily because it interlocked with President Ali Akbar Hāshemi Rafsanjāni's approach to moderate Iran's line and encourage interaction with the EU. Similarly, the Comprehensive Dialogue was enabled by the "reformist" successor to Rafsanjāni, President Mohammad Khātami, who created a favorable setting for the Comprehensive Dialogue to take place. The EU's policies were in line with Khātami's reform agenda and his policy of liberalization in the political, cultural, and economic domains. Moreover, the emerging debate on Islam, human rights, and democracy among Iranian intellectuals also eased EU influence on Iran on these issues.³² However, as and when the nuclear issue became the dominant feature in EU–Iran relations, prime decision-making power was granted to Supreme Leader Ali Khamenei, who decides on matters of critical importance on the basis of the wider national consensus. The relationship has further deteriorated following the election to the presidency of Mahmoud Ahmadinejad in 2005 and reelection in 2009 in view of the president's confrontational rhetoric toward the West. As for Iraq, under Saddam Hussein's rule, EU leverage was extremely limited in view of the wider international context governing EU relations with Iraq. After the invasion and regime change in Iraq, the new pro-Western authorities turned for support from the EU, opening the way for a more comprehensive and influential EU role in the country.

Finally, the external actor that has called the shots in both Iraq and Iran has been the United States, and the EU, out of will or sheer need, has reacted and responded to Washington's policies. Transatlantic relations have shaped and also divided EU member states as far as the war in Iraq was concerned. Many member states and above all the eastern members did not have an independent Middle East foreign policy as such, and thus the prime factor determining their stance was their perceived need to support the United States in the region. The EU as a whole was only able to step into the postinvasion situation engaging in a familiar division of labor with the United States whereby the former is concerned with humanitarian, governance, and economic affairs, while the latter remains firmly in control of security questions. Following the Iraq debacle, the Iranian nuclear crisis became the EU's opportunity to reconstitute its internal cohesion and mend fences with the United States, which was in turn handicapped by its military overreach and its absence of diplomatic relations with Iran.³³ Yet even in the Iranian case, since 2005 the EU's independent policy toward Iran has shifted back toward the more familiar "the United States leads and the EU follows" approach typical of EU policy in the Middle East more widely. This happened as transatlantic relations improved while EU–Iranian relations worsened.

CONCLUSIONS

EU policies in the Mediterranean and the Middle East are shaped by the construction of the region in the minds of Europeans. This construction has consequences for the aims pursued and instruments deployed by the EU within a wider context of an EU that struggles to define a foreign policy that is thoroughly distinct from its integration policies. This struggle is often derided by outsiders—and with good reason if we compare the role of the

EU to that of major state actors. Yet the EU is not a state, and its developing foreign policy is the mirror image of its continuously evolving "domestic" integration policy. To the extent that the EU is still in a stage of construction on the "inside," it is only natural that its approach toward the "outside" remains riddled with ambiguity and confusion.

When it comes to Europe's southern neighborhood, this ambiguity has meant that the EU has been able to develop an independent and at least partially effective policy toward those countries transiting from the outside to the inside, that is, the candidate countries. The case of Turkey highlights both the power of the accession policy and its limits yet where the limits are almost exclusively determined by internal factors within both Turkey and the EU rather than by external factors and actors.

When moving to the next concentric circle, that of the EMP and the ENP, we note how the EU's uneasy mix between integration and foreign policies has nonetheless generated significant potential to influence the southern shores of the Mediterranean. However, the EU has often been unable to make good on this potential in view of the subordination of its policy instruments to other internal interests and external pressures. The Israeli–Palestinian case can be read in this light: not as a case of EU weakness driven by its ineffective policy instruments but rather as a case in which the EU has chosen to deploy the instruments at its disposal at the service of other, unstated goals and interests, determined primarily by its relations with Israel and across the Atlantic.

Finally, both Iraq and Iran are countries that fall squarely beyond the EU's magnetic power of attraction. Thus, the EU could not play a leading role in this subregion, lacking a consistent and comprehensive foreign policy distinct from its integration policy. In turn, the tendency to follow the lead of the United States has been preponderant, with the EU stepping into the policy gap only as and when Washington has either opted to take a backseat or actively invited European engagement.

SUGGESTIONS FOR FURTHER READING

Bicchi, F. *European Foreign Policy Making toward the Mediterranean.* New York: Palgrave Macmillan, 2007.

Joseph, J., ed. *Turkey and the European Union: Internal Dynamics and External Challenges.* New York: Palgrave, 2006.

Kelley, J. "Promoting Political Reforms through the ENP." *Journal of Common Market Studies* 44, no. 1 (2006): 29–56.

Le More, A. *International Assistance to the Palestinians after Oslo: Political Guilt; Wasted Money.* London, Routledge, 2008.

Sabet-Saeidi, S. "Iranian-European Relations: A Strategic Partnership?" In *Iran's Foreign Policy: From Khatami to Ahmadinejad*, edited by A. Ehteshami and M. Zweiri, 55–87. Reading, MA: Ithaca Press, 2008.

Tocci, N. *The EU and Conflict Resolution*. London: Routledge, 2007.

Van Ham, P. "The EU's War over Iraq: The Last Wake-Up Call." In *European Foreign Policy: From Rhetoric to Reality?*, edited by D. Mahncke, A. Ambos, and C. Reynolds, 209–26. Brussels: P.I.E., 2004.

Verney, S., and Ifantis, K., eds. *Turkey's Road to European Union Membership*. London: Routledge, 2009.

7

Europe and Globalization

Internal and External Policy Responses

Paul Taylor

For Tony Blair, globalization began at home. Meeting a visiting group of Brussels journalists at the start of Britain's six-month presidency of the European Union (EU) in July 2005, the then prime minister trumpeted the example of the utilities supplying his official residence in the heart of London's government district. "The electricity in Number 10 Downing Street is supplied by a French company, the water by a German company. The gas is supplied by four companies, three of which are not British," he boasted.[1]

Blair was contrasting Britain's relaxed, welcoming attitude to foreign ownership and France's allergic reaction to the prospect of a foreign hand controlling any of its national industrial champions. That same month, there was an outcry in France after a stock exchange rumor, never confirmed by either company, that Pepsico, a giant U.S. soft-drink company, was considering a takeover bid for Danone, France's leading maker of yogurt and other milk products. There were calls for Parliament to be recalled from its summer recess to deliberate on "the Danone affair."

In the name of "economic patriotism," then French prime minister Dominique de Villepin issued a decree requiring government permission for foreign companies to buy a controlling stake in one of eleven strategic industrial sectors. Yogurt was not among them. De Villepin personally engineered a merger between privately owned French water and gas utility Suez and government-controlled Gaz de France to prevent Suez from falling into the hands of an Italian conglomerate. In 2004, Nicolas Sarkozy, then French finance minister, took a state shareholding in ailing engineering company Alstom, which builds France's high-speed TGV trains and power stations, to prevent it falling into the hands of Germany's successful Siemens Corporation.

133

The French are happy to see their own corporations take over foreign firms but deeply suspicious of any outside bid for French companies, even from a close European partner such as Germany or Italy. Foreigners are welcome to invest in the French stock market as long as they do not seek to control French companies.

The Franco–British dichotomy on foreign ownership is typical of wider divisions in Europe's approach to globalization, rooted in history. The British, for centuries a seafaring trading nation, have broadly embraced globalization as an unstoppable, benign economic revolution that brings prosperity at home and spreads development abroad. The French, on both left and right, steeped in the tradition of a state-directed, mercantilist economy, tend to view globalization as a more menacing process requiring strong political management to limit social damage.

For nearly two decades following the fall of the Berlin Wall, the former view mostly held sway in the EU. But the global financial crisis that began in 2007 called into question free market economic thinking and posed a serious test to Europe's commitment to an open economy, threatening to throw globalization into reverse. It was a stark reminder that past periods of economic openness in Europe were brought to a halt by recession, revolutionary or nationalist politics, and war.

THE EU AS A MODEL

The EU is at the center of this debate. Europe was itself both a precursor and a model for globalization, combining free trade within a community of nations with multinational governance and enforcement. The 1957 Treaty of Rome enshrined the principle of freedom of movement of capital, labor, goods, and services, known as "the four freedoms." It took decades to turn that promise into reality, even among the six founder members of what was then called the European Economic Community—France, West Germany, Italy, the Netherlands, Belgium, and Luxembourg—and the task is still not complete, notably in the services sector.

The founding treaty created a customs union with a common external tariff. It delegated responsibility for negotiating all external trade agreements to the executive European Commission. With security guaranteed by a large U.S. military presence during the Cold War, Western Europe prospered as a common market with tariff barriers to protect its agriculture, in particular, against competition from third countries. In the 1950s, when Europe was still recovering from the decimation of World War II, the rationale for agricultural protectionism was a perceived need to achieve self-sufficiency in food production. When subsidized farming yielded large, unsellable surpluses in grain, beef, butter, and wine in the 1970s and

1980s, the EU subsidized bulk exports to the Soviet Union or developing countries, sparking trade disputes with the United States and other food exporters such as Canada and Australia. Chiefly because of vested interests in France, Germany, and Italy, it took the EU decades to reduce the real value of farm subsidies, curtail export subsidies, and reform the system of payments to farmers to stop incentivizing overproduction.

The same mixture of internal openness and external protection persists today, particularly in agriculture, although the EU has substantially reduced its tariffs and claims to be the most open trading area in the world. Arguably as important as its tariffs and quotas is the EU's arsenal of health, food safety rules, and technical standards that goods must satisfy to enter the European market. In many areas, the EU has become the regulatory standard setter for the world since anyone wishing to export to its market, the world's biggest trading area, must comply with its norms. The EU continues to add to these regulations, for example, through a law mandating the registration, evaluation, and authorization of some 30,000 chemical substances, which took effect in 2008.

Critics say that "Fortress Europe" is still resisting global free trade, and its Common Agricultural Policy continues to cushion subsidized European farmers against competition from exports from developing countries. Furthermore, nongovernmental organizations, such as development pressure group Oxfam, blame subsidized EU food exports for undercutting farming in Africa and parts of Asia. Former World Bank chief economist Joseph Stiglitz contends that "the United States and Europe have perfected the art of arguing for free trade while simultaneously working for trade agreements that protect themselves against imports from developing countries."[2]

Europe embarked in earnest in the mid-1980s on the integration of its internal market, the most ambitious exercise in open borders and multinational governance of its time. The creation of the single market gave substantial extra regulatory powers to the European Commission, charged with ensuring the proper implementation of a swathe of new free market legislation enacted jointly by member states and the European Parliament. It gave the European Court of Justice (ECJ) the power to fine countries that breach EU open market rules. The European model of a transnational level playing field enforced by the rule of law has many admirers. The main drawback is that the enforcement procedures operate in slow motion. It can take three years for the ECJ to uphold a European Commission complaint against a member state for violating the treaty, by which time facts have been created, for example, blocking a cross-border takeover.

The European Commission has sweeping powers to regulate cross-border mergers, abuses of market dominance, state aid to business, and anticompetitive behavior, such as price-fixing and market-sharing cartels. While Europeans regularly protest against U.S. extraterritorial legislation applied to

European companies (e.g., if they invest in Iran), the EU has not hesitated to use its competition powers globally, ostensibly in defense of competition in the European market. For example, it fined U.S. software giant Microsoft nearly $1 billion and ordered it to change its business practices, based largely on complaints by rival U.S. firms. The EU executive also barred two major U.S. corporations from merging in 2001, stopping General Electric from buying fellow U.S. company Honeywell. In 2007, it stymied a proposed merger of the world's two biggest mining conglomerates—one based in Australia, the other in Britain—by raising competition objections.

The 1986 Single European Act, which launched a major legislative program to complete the EU internal market for goods, involved arguably the biggest transfer of power from nation-states to supranational institutions in history. The 1991 Maastricht Treaty on European Union, which paved the way for a single European currency, was the logical next step toward economic and monetary union. It aimed to eliminate currency risk in the single market, putting an end to a cycle of devaluations in which member states sought or were forced by market pressure to improve their competitiveness in relation to Germany, the bloc's biggest economy, by making exports cheaper and imports more expensive.

Europe also served as a model for globalization by continuously expanding its zone of prosperity and security to embrace new member states that meet the criteria of democracy, the rule of law, and a functioning market economy and were prepared to adopt its onerous rule book. From six nations in 1957, it expanded to nine in 1973, ten in 1981, twelve in 1986, fifteen in 1995, and, more recently, twenty-five in 2004 and twenty-seven in 2007. In Western Europe, only oil-rich Norway, Iceland (which eventually applied to join in 2009), and wealthy Switzerland chose to stay out, paying an annual levy to Brussels for access to the EU's single market and accepting its rules.

Joining the EU involves a huge legal and social upheaval, as the Poles, Romanians, and Hungarians have recently learned. It entails a significant voluntary limitation of national sovereignty in many policy areas. Candidates must adopt more than 80,000 pages of community legislation regulating everything from air and water pollution to state aid to industry, transportation safety, and the independence of the judiciary and of competition authorities. Newcomers become full members with equal rights from day one, even if benefits are sometimes phased in over a transition period. Slovenia and Estonia have a vote on EU decisions that affect them. Switzerland, a nonmember, does not.

The EU has been an economic success story which other regions of the world—Southeast Asia, Latin America, Africa and the Arab states of the Gulf—have sought to emulate in their own way, usually with a much lesser degree of political integration. It has made Europe by any measure one of the big winners of globalization.

THE EU AS A WINNER OF GLOBALIZATION

A 2008 study by U.S. analysts Daniel Hamilton and Joseph Quinlan[3] highlighted how Europeans have gained from globalization in terms of trade, investment, portfolio flows, employment, income and labor mobility, low inflation, cheap credit, real growth in gross domestic product (GDP), and technological diffusion. They noted that the fifteen-nation EU's share of world exports increased from 40.8 percent in 2000 to 41.7 percent in 2006 and that its share of exports of manufactured goods rose to 47.1 percent. Much of the increase in trade has been with the EU's periphery—Eastern Europe, Russia, Turkey, the Middle East, and Africa—rather than with China and India. Europe's business relationship with the United States remains bigger than its dealings with the whole of Asia. American firms invested nearly three times as much in Ireland alone in 2000–2006 as they did in China and more than eight times as much as they did in India.

European companies have been among the greatest beneficiaries of globalization, building new markets in fast-growing countries near to Europe and in emerging economies further afield. European automakers assemble vehicles in Asia, the Middle East, and Latin America as well as Europe. The two top-selling cars in China in 2007 were German Volkswagen models assembled in Shanghai. A senior French auto executive confided that while his company made and sold cars in France, "we don't make money in France anymore."[4] Many European multinationals have reduced their production costs by manufacturing or buying components and assembling products in low-cost locations while retaining much of the know-how and the profit in their home country. Finland's Nokia Corporation, the world's biggest mobile phone manufacturer, was a prime example of this global supply chain. A Nokia cell phone contains some 900 components sourced in more than forty countries. It is assembled in China and sold in more than eighty markets around the world. The profits accrue largely to Finland.

The single European market helped give European companies the scale, efficiency, and habits of cross-border integration needed to compete and succeed in a globalized economy by maximizing their comparative advantage. The Swiss Economic Institute's Index of Economic Globalization[5] puts nine European countries in the top ten "most economically globalized" nations and twenty-three in the top thirty. Unsurprisingly, the smaller EU countries, which have long been used to having an interdependent open economy, were at the top, while the larger European countries were lower in the table—Britain in twenty-seventh position, France thirtieth, Italy thirty-third, and Germany thirty-fifth.

The findings of an Organization for Economic Cooperation and Development (OECD) indicator of how advanced industrial countries are able to cope with globalization made more worrying reading for EU countries.[6] The criteria included labor and product market flexibility, educational achievement, active labor market expenditure, immigration, innovation, and the rate of creation of new companies. Among the Europeans, the Nordic countries—Sweden, Finland, and Denmark—scored best, followed by Britain, the Netherlands, Austria, and Belgium. Poland, Greece, Italy, Portugal, and Hungary were at the bottom of the pile. A range of studies by different organizations, including the European Commission, the OECD, and the World Economic Forum, highlight a north–south divide in which the Nordic countries, Britain, Ireland, the Netherlands, and Belgium appear best placed to profit from economic globalization, while southern and southeastern Europe lag in terms of innovation and research and development, networked industries, Internet penetration, financial services, and market liberalization.

The march of globalization has changed centuries-old European trade patterns, for example, in shipping and port services. Traditional Mediterranean ports such as Marseille in France and Naples and Genoa in Italy, with high-cost unionized dock labor, are losing business to highly automated container-ship hubs such as Malta, Algerciras in Spain, and Gioia Tauro in Italy, where goods from East Asia, shipped through the Suez Canal on big container ships, are offloaded onto smaller vessels that ferry them to north European ports for just-in-time delivery. European companies such as Denmark's A. P. Moller-Maersk and France's CMA-CGM are leaders in the container revolution, but China's Cosco shipping company is breaking into the market and invested €300 million in 2008 to build and manage for thirty-five years from 2015 a container hub in the Greek port of Piraeus, destined to serve the fast-growing Black Sea region.

THE ANTIGLOBALIZATION MOVEMENT

Even before the global financial crisis, the EU had become a focus of resentment among those, especially in Western Europe, who considered themselves victims or potential losers of globalization. Many citizens feared developments linked to globalization and were pessimistic about the outlook for the values, institutions, and policies that have underpinned postwar Europe's success and way of life. Opinion polls, such as the regular Eurobarometer series conducted for the European Commission, testify to the growth of these fears in the mid-2000s, with more EU citizens regarding globalization as a threat to their jobs rather than an opportunity. The rise of negative views of globalization in Germany, the world's number one exporter and Europe's most industrialized economy, was particularly striking. Many critics of globalization argued that it made a "race to the bottom" in labor standards, social policy, and welfare provision inevitable.[7]

The "No" campaigns that defeated the EU's draft constitution in 2005 referendums in France and the Netherlands were spearheaded by left-wing and far-right opponents of globalization who blamed "Brussels" for failing to protect workers against job losses, industrial decline, an influx of cheap labor, and the relocation of production to Eastern Europe, North Africa, and Asia. Other factors played a role in both votes, notably the unpopularity of incumbent governments. But hostility to what French campaigners called "a Europe open to all winds" was a central feature of the debate. In the Netherlands, the backlash was against a perceived loss of national identity and control, whereas in France, it was more overtly against free trade and investment and against the enlargement of the bloc, which had brought in ten poorer, mostly Central and Eastern European member states in May 2004. Rather than rejecting provisions of the constitution, designed to give the enlarged EU stronger, more efficient leadership and a more democratic decision-making system, many French people were actually voting against the original principles of the Treaty of Rome—the "four freedoms."

The bogeyman crystallizing resentment of globalization in the French referendum campaign was not a Chinese factory worker or an Indian call-center employee but the (largely mythical) "Polish plumber." The fear was that migrants from the new ex-communist member states were taking French jobs and undercutting wages and welfare benefits in wealthy Western Europe. There is little statistical evidence that enlargement has in fact depressed wages in Western Europe. Official figures show that unemployment has fallen, the overall employment level has risen, and real wages have increased modestly on average at the same time that the region absorbed some 9 million immigrants between 2000 and 2006. Ironically, Germany, where real wages fell or stagnated during that period, was the EU country that maintained a ban on admitting workers from the new member states longest.

Rosy figures for exports, GDP, and employment do not mean that there are no losers from globalization in Europe. Factories have closed, and manufacturing jobs have been lost, particularly at the unskilled and low-skilled end of the value chain. Traditional crafts have suffered from competition from emerging economies with lower production costs. But while trade unionists, politicians, and the media have highlighted the human suffering in such cases, they tend to ignore the fact that many more jobs have been created than lost in Europe in the age of globalization. As important politically as the actual losers are the larger number of workers and families who feel that their living standards are threatened by global-ization. A fast-changing economy has made expectations of employment, health care, welfare provision, and pensions more uncertain in an aging society. As Irish economic historian Kevin O'Rourke noted in an essay for the Bruegel think tank, "If unskilled workers in rich countries believe that they are being hurt by globalization, this could be sufficient to produce an anti-trade backlash, regardless of the accuracy of these beliefs."[8]

According to statistics compiled by the European Restructuring Monitor, an agency funded by the European Commission, the number of jobs lost to all forms of industrial restructuring in EU member states in 2003–2006 ac-counted for 1.2 percent of the total number of people in employment. Less than one-twelfth of those job losses were due to "delocalization"—moving production to a lower-cost location.

There has been a small number of highly publicized cases, notably in France, of employers threatening to transfer production to another country to pressure workers to accept longer working hours or reduced pay. Trade union officials say that even when such threats are not explicit, the risk of "offshoring" to lower-cost new EU member states, neighboring countries, or Asia often weighs on wage negotiations in Western Europe.

There was an outcry in Germany in 2008 when Nokia of Finland decided to close the last German cell phone factory and transfer production to new EU member state Romania. The dispute pitted German trade unionists against their Finnish and Romanian comrades. The head of Nokia's Euro-pean works council, Mika Paukkeri of Finland, defended the decision, say-ing that the company's overall situation in Europe and its need to remain competitive had to be taken into consideration. Labor costs in Romania were far lower. The German state of North Rhine-Westphalia ordered Nokia to repay subsidies it had received to retool the plant in Bochum.

Efforts to safeguard Western European employment, safety, and work time standards in the face of globalization were at the heart of fierce debate in the European Parliament in 2005 over a proposed EU law to liberalize the provision of services across borders. The initial draft directive proposed by then Internal Market Commissioner Frits Bolkestein angered organized labor and left-wing groups because it enshrined the so-called home country principle, whereby a company providing services in any EU state could do so while complying with the laws of its country of origin rather than the member state where the services were provided. Critics said that this so-called Frankenstein Directive would legalize a race to the bottom in labor standards, wages, and working hours. The European Parliament removed the home country principle from the much-watered-down final version of the law it adopted.

A test case of concerns that companies from new, eastern member states were using EU law to undercut labor standards and wages in Western European countries occurred in Sweden in 2004. Swedish trade unions block-aded a construction site in a town near Stockholm, where Latvian workers from a Riga-based company called Laval were renovating a school. The unions complained that the company was undercutting Swedish collective agreements on wages and working time. The company said that it was com-plying with EU law, notably the free movement of services, nondiscrimi-nation on grounds of nationality, and the Posting of Workers' Directive. The ECJ ruled in 2008 that the blockade violated the freedom to provide services enshrined in the EU treaty. Unions could not take industrial action to impose terms in the absence of legally enforceable national provisions. However, the court did recognize that opposing so-called social dumping could constitute a legitimate ground for collective action. Both trade unions and employers were dissatisfied with the ruling, which was seized on by critics of globalization.

Organized opposition to globalization in Europe began to grow in the late 1990s, mainly in France and Italy on the political left, although far-right parties in both countries had long argued for trade protectionism and sending immigrants back to their home country. In a best-selling 1997 book titled *L'horreur economique* (Economic Horror), French novelist Vivi-ane Forrester denounced "the dictatorship of the market" and advocated "adapting to globalization not by training ourselves to submit to it but by freeing ourselves of its demands." A radical farmers' leader, Jose Bové, became the mustachioed "Asterix the Gaul" figurehead for the movement after he was jailed briefly for wrecking a McDonald's restaurant in a 1999 protest against genetically modified crops. He lumped together geneti-cally modified organisms and multinational capitalism with the evocative French word *malbouffe* (junk food).

Bové ran for president in 2007 and won nearly half a million votes, 1.32 percent of the total. His antiglobalization vandalism had echoes of the Lud-dite movement of English textile workers in the early nineteenth century who protested, often by smashing steam-driven machines such as looms, against the technology of the industrial revolution, which they felt was killing their jobs. The principal objection of the Luddites was against the introduction of new wide-framed automated looms that could be operated by cheap, relatively unskilled labor, resulting in the loss of jobs for many skilled textile workers. They also opposed the deregulation of prices.

An international campaign group known as ATTAC, an acronym for the Association for the Taxation of Financial Transactions to Aid Citizens, was established in 1998 to demand "democratic control" of the financial markets and a tax on speculation to fund development. It also opposed further liberalization in the World Trade Organization (WTO) negotia-tions as well as regional free trade zones, such as the North American Free Trade Area and the EU's plans for a Euro-Mediterranean free trade area.

The movement, which called itself "altermondialiste," implying an alternative form of globalization, was spearheaded by leftist French intellectuals such as Bernard Cassen, director of the monthly newspaper *Le Monde Diplomatique*. ATTAC's grassroots network became a multipurpose protest organization, mobilizing against all forms of trade and economic liberalization, labor market flexibility, privatization of the energy sector, the EU constitution, and economic partnership agreements between Europe and the African, Caribbean, and Pacific states.

Antiglobalization demonstrations, which sometimes turned violent, became a regular feature of major international gatherings such as a 1999 WTO ministerial meeting in Seattle, the annual Davos World Economic Forum of business and political leaders, and regular summits of the EU and the Group of Eight (G8) industrialized nations. Violence reached a peak in 2001 when a protestor was killed and several were injured in clashes with police at a G8 summit in Genoa, Italy. Antiglobalization demonstrations in Europe subsided as economic growth revived in the mid-2000s, but the political influence of antiglobalization arguments endured, prompting governments in France, Italy, Germany, Greece, and even Ireland, one of the biggest beneficiaries of "offshoring" of business services, to advocate protectionist measures against imports of Chinese textiles, furniture, shoes, and steel products and, in the Irish case, Brazilian beef.

THE POLICY DEBATE

When French president Sarkozy took over the EU's rotating presidency in July 2008, he pledged to promote "a Europe that protects" and a revived talk of a "community preference" in trade while denying that he advocated protectionism.[9] He accused the European Commission of being "naive" in its trade policy and blamed EU trade commissioner Peter Mandelson personally for the rejection of the Lisbon Treaty, the successor to the defunct EU constitution, in a referendum in Ireland in June 2008. Opinion polls and a postreferendum survey suggested that hostility to free trade was not a major factor in the Irish vote. After receiving a series of concessions from their EU partners—none of them concerning trade—the Irish voted in October 2009 in favor of the treaty, which finally came into force in December 2009.

Sarkozy had already succeeded in deleting mention in the Lisbon treaty of "free and unfettered competition" among the core objectives of the EU. He argued that it was just another means to attain the objective of economic growth and not an end itself. Mandelson was the most outspoken member of the EU executive in urging Europeans to embrace globalization, arguing that Europe and the rest of the world had enjoyed unprecedented prosperity thanks to the "openness boom" unleashed since the fall of communism in 1990. In a speech to the Work Foundation in London in March 2007, he put the case this way:

> The protectionist argument is that the only way to preserve employment in Europe is to wall up the single market and forget the rest of the world. This not only ignores the supply chains that feed that market, but also the huge and growing aggregate global demand that is, in large part, driving it. We have much more to gain in chasing a piece of that much larger global pie than in looking inwards, only to our own market.
>
> The point of competitiveness should be to maintain the economic strength to pay for our social models and the provision of public goods. . . . The idea that competitiveness means paring back the state strikes me as a purely ideological statement rather than one that reflects the real world.[10]

Some of the EU's internal critics contend that the EU has been overtaken by globalization. Gordon Brown, when he was Britain's chancellor of the exchequer (treasury secretary) in 2005, told visiting Brussels journalists that the EU was a great idea whose time had passed. Creating a regional free trade zone had been a giant step forward in the 1950s, but what mattered now was tearing down European barriers to globalization and allowing market forces to take their course, he said.

Brown softened that view somewhat after becoming prime minister in 2007. In a speech early in 2008, he acknowledged that the EU remained central to Britain's prosperity but said,

> The countries and continents that will succeed in the new era of globalization will be those that are open rather than closed, for free trade rather than protectionism, are flexible rather than rigid, and invest in high skills and the potential of their people. My vision of Europe moving forward is global Europe—not just an internal single market that looks inwards but a driving force of the new fast-changing global market place. An open, outward looking, flexible global Europe competing on and prosperous because of its skills, its innovation and its creative talents.[11]

The Franco–British dichotomy on foreign ownership and free trade is broadly typical of a north–south divide in European responses to globalization. Sweden, Denmark, the Netherlands, Britain, and Ireland are usually the most enthusiastic proponents of open markets, foreign investment, and the free movement of workers and services, perhaps partly because of their history as seafaring, trading nations—although Ireland, with a powerful farmers' lobby, is in the protectionist camp when it comes to agriculture. France, Italy, Portugal, Greece, and sometimes Spain are the most protective of their industry and agriculture. Germany, Austria, and Belgium are often in the middle ground, keen to protect their labor markets and avoid an influx of unskilled foreign workers but eager to enable their consumers to benefit from cheap imports that boost purchasing power and keep inflation low.

When the EU enlarged to admit eight former communist Central and Eastern European countries in 2004, only Sweden, Britain, and Ireland immediately allowed unrestricted access for workers from those countries. France opened its labor market for them only in 2008, and Germany waited until the bitter end of a seven-year transition period to lift restrictions.

Some of the fiercest policy debates about globalization took place in the relatively arcane area of the EU's trade defense instruments for dealing with goods "dumped" on the European market. The EU imposed a series of punitive duties on Asian-made goods, ranging from shoes to plastic bags, that it deemed to be sold below cost price. These struggles often involved the conflicting interests of European industries, member states, consumers, and the EU's overall policy objectives. The EU definition of "dumping," in line with world trade rules, reflects the complexity of the issue. Three conditions must be met for the bloc to impose antidumping duties on imports:

1. A finding of dumping: the export price at which the product is sold on the EU market is shown to be lower than the price on the producer's home market.
2. A material injury to European industry: the imports have caused or threaten to cause damage to a substantial part of the industry within the EU, such as loss of market share, reduced prices for producers, and resulting pressure on production, sales, profits, productivity, and so forth.
3. The interests of the EU: the costs for the EU of taking measures must not be disproportionate to the benefits.

However, in the age of globalization, such decisions become even more complex. What does the term "European industry" mean when European companies manufacture goods in China or Thailand and ship them to the EU? How does the EU weigh the interests of its domestic producers against those of European consumers or against other policy objectives, such as building a cooperative overall relationship with a major emerging economy such as China or fighting climate change?

One case that highlighted many of these dilemmas concerned energy-saving lightbulbs. The European Commission came under pressure in 2007 from Germany and its electrical manufacturer Osram, part of the engineering group Siemens, to extend antidumping duties on Chinese energy-saving lightbulbs first imposed in 2001. It was opposed by Dutch consumer electronics group Philips, which imports such lightbulbs from China. Both companies manufacture the energy-saving bulbs in Europe as well as

China. The dispute came just as EU leaders agreed to require all European households to switch to energy-saving bulbs by 2011 as part of a drive for energy efficiency designed to combat global warming. The European retailers' lobby urged the bloc to axe the tariffs, saying that they cost consumers €2 billion ($3.2 billion) a year at a time when electricity bills were going sky-high and households were being encouraged to save energy. Mandelson favored scrapping the 66 percent duty. After a lengthy battle among member states, the EU decided to extend the antidumping duty for one year rather than the five-year period for which such penalties usually run.

The depth of differences between member states forced the trade commissioner in January 2008 to drop a proposed reform of antidumping policy that would have taken greater account of broader economic interests than those of domestic European producers. Fresh battles loomed over Chinese steel and chemicals that were sharpened by the global financial crisis and the ensuing recession.

THE POLICY RESPONSE: INTERNAL

European governments became increasingly aware at the turn of the twenty-first century that they needed to adapt their economic, social, and education policies to remain competitive in a rapidly globalizing economy. They were falling behind the United States and Japan in key measurements such as public and private investment in research and development, the number of patents registered, and broadband Internet connections. The advent of social democratic modernizers to government in Britain, Germany, the Netherlands, and Sweden provided the impetus for the adoption of an ambitious but somewhat unfocused economic reform program known as the Lisbon Agenda at an EU summit in the Portuguese capital in March 2000. Proclaiming their intention to overtake the United States within a decade, EU leaders set the strategic goal of making Europe "the most competitive and dynamic knowledge-based economy in the world" by 2010.

"The EU is confronted with a quantum shift resulting from globalization and the challenges of a new knowledge-driven economy. These changes are affecting every aspect of people's lives and require a radical transformation of the European economy. The Union must shape these changes in a manner consistent with its values and concepts of society and also with a view to the forthcoming enlargement," the Lisbon Declaration said.[12] "The rapid and accelerating pace of change means it is urgent for the Union to act now to harness the full benefits of the opportunities presented. Hence the need for the Union to set a clear strategic goal and agree a challenging program for building knowledge infrastructures, enhancing innovation and economic reform, and modernizing social welfare and education systems."

Among the goals the leaders set were the following:

1. Spend 3 percent of GDP out of public and private funds on research and development (R&D) by 2010 (R&D spending remained unchanged at 1.8 to 1.9 percent of GDP in 2000–2007)
2. Achieve an employment rate of 70 percent of the working-age population by 2010 from 61 percent in 2000 (the overall employment rate had crept up to 65.4 percent in 2007, with a more impressive increase in the number of older workers in employment and a decline in long-term unemployment)
3. Complete the integration of Europe's financial markets and ease cross-border investment (significant progress achieved with the exception of a law on cross-border takeovers that left major loopholes)
4. Establish a simple, cheap Europe-wide European Community patent by 2001 to put European inventors on equal terms with the protection granted by key competitors (still not achieved in 2009 because of linguistic disputes)
5. Liberalize the EU telecommunications market and take initiatives to make high-speed Internet access cheaper and more widespread, especially for schools and public services (largely achieved)
6. Remove barriers to trade in services throughout the EU (achieved only very partially in 2005 with the adoption of a watered-down law after a bitter battle and demonstrations against cheap labor from new member states)
7. Speed up liberalization in areas such as gas, electricity, postal services, and transport (slow progress due to rearguard resistance, notably by France)

If those measures were implemented, EU leaders said, an average economic growth rate of around 3 percent should be a realistic prospect. Partial implementation may have helped Europe's trend growth rate improve over the decade. The EU achieved 3.1 percent in 2006 and 2.9 percent in 2007, but the average growth rate in 2000–2007 was a more modest 2.1 percent a year. The new member states and more flexible economies such as Britain, Sweden, and Denmark grew faster than the three core members of the euro zone—Germany, France, and Italy. The global recession that began in 2008 hit the EU hard. After a meager 0.9 percent growth in 2008, the European economy contracted by an estimated 4 percent in 2009.

Unlike the internal market program, the Lisbon Agenda lacked any binding enforcement mechanism, relying on a system known as the "open method of coordination." This provided for the drafting of annual national action plans, peer review among member states, the sharing of best practice, and the "naming and shaming" of laggards by the European Commission.

Since governments, notably the Germans, did not like being criticized by Brussels, the Commission effectively dropped that approach when the policy was streamlined in 2005. The goal of being the most competitive and dynamic knowledge-based economy by the end of the decade was also quietly jettisoned.[13]

While the Lisbon Agenda failed to ignite an economic revolution, it did provide political cover for governments to take sometimes unpopular measures to make their labor markets more flexible, increase overall employment levels, combat youth unemployment, keep older people in work longer, and improve training and lifelong learning opportunities. The most successful European countries were those, especially in the Nordic region, that spent the most on education and used public funds to support and retrain workers who fell out of employment rather than using rigid labor laws and subsidies to preserve outdated industries on social grounds.

By 2007, all EU countries including France had come to embrace, at least rhetorically, a Danish employment policy known as "flexicurity." This buzzword combined easy hire-and-fire laws with generous unemployment benefits, active retraining, and incentives to return to work. The aim was to protect the worker, not the job, since few people if any could expect to keep the same job for life in a fast-changing globalized economy. Backed by the European Commission, EU employers and trade union organizations agreed in 2006 on a set of principles to promote best practice in "flexicurity" across Europe while taking account of each country's specificity.

John Monks, general secretary of the European Confederation of Trade Unions, embraced the concept even though he acknowledged that "flexicurity" was a swear word in some parts of the labor movement, where some dubbed it "flexploitation."[14] While unions liked the big investment of public money in people who fell out of work, employers liked the fact that it was simple and less costly to fire a worker. How easily transferable the model is from an affluent, high-tax, homogeneous society such as Denmark to other European countries remains to be seen.

The EU began to compensate some of the losers of globalization by creating a European Globalization Adjustment Fund in 2007 to provide up to €500 million a year in temporary assistance, mostly in the form of retraining support, for workers whose jobs are transferred abroad. European Commission president José Manuel Barroso proposed the initiative to assuage the French and Italians after bitter debate over legislation to liberalize cross-border services in the EU, which was a factor in the French referendum defeat of the European constitution. However, the fund was more a political palliative than a genuine policy instrument. In the first two years, it paid out just €94 million in cofinancing to local authorities in France, Italy, Germany, and Spain.

THE POLICY RESPONSE: EXTERNAL

In its external relations, the EU sought to manage globalization and to smooth its sharp edges by developing a system of global governance modeled loosely on its own structures. It negotiated "strategic partnerships" with a range of players, including the main emerging economies—China, Russia, Brazil, India, Mexico, and South Africa as well as Japan and Canada. It built or tried to build bloc-to-bloc relations with a range of regional organizations including a group of African, Caribbean, and Pacific states that are mostly former European colonies, the African Union, the Association of Southeast Asian Nations (ASEAN), and the South American common market (Mercosur). Closer to home, it created a web of trade, cooperation, and aid agreements with Eastern European and Mediterranean countries through the European Neighborhood Policy and the Euro-Mediterranean process. Through these accords, the EU sought to stabilize its surroundings by granting market access and extending cooperation to countries that commit themselves to EU-prescribed market-based economic reforms, legal security, and human rights. In practice, the accords have often fallen short of the desired goals because governments, military, and business elites in the partner countries see the EU's goals as a threat to their interests or grip on power. Moreover, the EU's attachment of human rights and governance conditions to aid and economic ties with African countries fueled resentment of former colonial masters among African elites and put Europe at a disadvantage when China began in the early 2000s to pursue an aggressive resource diplomacy, handing out unconditional aid and building roads and prestige projects in return for long-term commodities contracts. President Abdoulaye Wade of Senegal told a visiting EU official, "When the Europeans offer to support a road-building project, I have to fill in dozens of forms with all sorts of irksome conditions. When the Chinese offer to build me a road, the next morning I look out of my window and there they are building the road." Wade sent his first child to the Sorbonne University in Paris and his second to the University of Beijing.[15]

Europe was a key driver in the creation in 1994 of the WTO, successor to the General Agreement on Tariffs and Trade, which provides not only a framework for negotiating multilateral trade deals but also a dispute settlement mechanism to uphold the rules. The Europeans' commitment to the WTO has not stopped them, at times using every procedural device in the book to delay and circumvent rulings that go against them in disputes panels, such as over EU tariffs on bananas designed to protect former European colonies from competition from U.S.-backed "dollar banana" producers in Central America. This longest-running world trade dispute was finally settled in December 2009.

On the political front, the EU dedicates substantial financial and political resources to the United Nations, which it views as the guardian of international law and of rules-based multilateral cooperation on issues ranging from peacekeeping to development, climate protection, and promoting public health. However, while the European Commission represents the twenty-seven member states in the WTO, the EU has been unable to agree on a unified system of representation at the United Nations, the International Monetary Fund (IMF), and the World Bank. National interests in retaining acquired rights and positions of power still prevail over the desire to aggregate and maximize European influence in global forums. Britain and France refuse to even consider yielding the permanent seats on the UN Security Council that they won at the end of World War II in favor of a single European seat, which would be the logical consequence of the development of a common European foreign policy.

The Lisbon treaty gave the EU for the first time the legal personality required to sign treaties. The EU's foreign policy high representative gained the right to address the Security Council, provided that the member states agree. But that remains a far cry from the kind of joint representation that has given the EU such strong influence in international trade negotiations.

THE START OF DEGLOBALIZATION?

The financial crisis that began in the United States in 2007 and spread around the world in 2008, felling banks, freezing credit markets, and causing a collapse in demand, posed the biggest challenge to globalization since the end of World War II. It raised unprecedented problems for the EU, highlighting the degree to which national governments, not the EU, remained in control of financial and economic policy. The EU's political and economic cohesion and its commitment to open markets came under a real-life stress test.

International trade negotiations stalled in 2008 because of a dispute over agricultural trade safeguards between the United States and India in which the EU was a powerless bystander. The volume of world trade began to contract in the third quarter of 2008 for the first time since the early 1980s. Trade finance dried up as overleveraged banks restricted lending in a panic measure to avoid insolvency. The EU continued to call for a rapid conclusion of the Doha round of WTO trade liberalization negotiations, but it had insufficient leverage over the other main players to achieve its desired outcome. Protectionist measures began to creep in not in the form of higher tariffs or smaller import quotas but rather in moves such as antidumping duties on a wider range of Chinese goods and a resumption of subsidized exports of EU dairy produce.

Western European banks, desperate to cover losses at home, started to repatriate capital and stop the flow of credit to their subsidiaries in Asia and the new EU members in Central and Eastern Europe, putting those countries' currencies and debt under strong pressure. The economies of countries such as Latvia, Hungary, and Romania were severely strained by suddenly having to plug big imbalances of payments as debt refinancing dried up.

With individual Western European governments committing tens of billions of euros to rescue big, cross-border banks, ministers were understandably keen to ensure that taxpayers' money was used to sustain domestic lending and preserve jobs at home. This sort of creeping "financial protectionism" was rarely spelled out in writing—not least because such conditions would fall foul of EU rules policed by the European Commission. But leaders from Britain's free-marketeering Gordon Brown to the head of Greece's central bank made clear in public comments that banks' first loyalty must be to their home country. Greek central bank governor George Provopoulos warned his country's banks, which had ventured profitably into neighboring Balkan states, that they must no longer use domestic deposits to provide credit in those countries. "They cannot take money from Greek depositors to fund those markets," he said.

The EU turned out to be ill equipped to deal with this kind of financial deglobalization. The initial response was a raft of uncoordinated national measures, some of which had unintended beggar-thy-neighbor consequences on EU partners. For example, Ireland was the first EU state to offer an unlimited guarantee on bank deposits after the collapse of Icelandic banks led to the beginnings of panic withdrawals by savers. The initial Irish guarantee covered only deposits in six Irish-based banks and not savings in other European banks on the same high streets of Dublin or Cork. That triggered a wave of withdrawals from banks not entitled to the Irish guarantee, prompting Britain to complain to the European Commission, which eventually forced Ireland to change its legislation in line with EU rules.

The European Commission came under fierce pressure from governments to set aside its state aid rule book, at least temporarily, and approve immediately national rescue schemes for banks and mortgage lenders. EU regulators working overtime approved most of the more than fifty plans within a few days. However, when Brussels raised concerns about restrictive conditions or potential distortions of competition, the EU executive was subjected to political blackmail and abuse. This came not just from countries such as France, with a track record of hostility to EU competition policy, but also from traditional free marketeers such as Sweden. "The Commission has not been constructive. I do think we have to call off these legions of state aid bureaucrats," Swedish finance minister Anders Borg thundered in December 2008.

The EU's state aid regulations allow governments to provide emergency rescue aid to companies in difficulty on condition that they restructure after six months to compensate for the distortion of competition caused by the injection of public money. That restructuring typically involves spinning off some profitable businesses or reducing the volume of a company's activities. However, the financial crisis forced the European Commission to extend the deadlines since the economic emergency that prompted the aid was still as acute, and it was close to impossible for banks to sell off assets in such markets. It is too early to judge the long-term impact of EU competition rules and national restructuring of the banking sector on globalization, but it is clear that banks are likely to emerge from the crisis with less freedom and less appetite to engage in global financing.

The crisis threatened to reopen an east–west divide in Europe that had been gradually healing after two decades of economic convergence policies following the fall of communism in the east. Neighbors such as Ukraine, outside the EU, were rebuffed by Brussels when they requested aid and were urged to seek IMF rescue packages. New EU members not yet in the euro zone, such as Latvia, Hungary, and Romania, received more favorable treatment. Several were granted low-interest loans from the EU to help them over balance-of-payments deficits, but they were forced to seek IMF assistance first, partly to ensure that the Washington-based fund took the political flak for austerity conditions imposed on recipients. Latvia, for example, was forced to cut public sector workers' pay by 15 percent, prompting violent protests. Its GDP was forecast to decline by at least 12 percent in 2009, almost three times as sharply as the worst-hit economies of Western Europe.

Countries inside the euro zone, which grew to sixteen members when Slovakia joined in 2009, received a schizophrenic message from the European Commission, the European Central Bank, and Germany, the EU's biggest paymaster. First, they were reminded that the EU treaty expressly forbids a bailout of a member state by the EU or its central bank. Then they were told that if a euro zone country got into serious payments problems, it could count on the help of the euro zone but were given no details of how this would work. And, finally, they were admonished to take tough austerity measures themselves rather than have even more stringent fiscal adjustment imposed on them as a condition for a euro zone rescue. Four euro zone countries—Portugal, Ireland, Greece, and Spain—had their sovereign credit ratings downgraded by international ratings agencies, increasing the risk premium they had to pay investors to borrow. This premium reflected the market perception of the risk of a sovereign default, however unlikely that may have seemed to economists.

The financial crisis gave a new urgency to the issue of regulation of cross-border banks and financial institutions in Europe and globally. The sight of tens of thousands of Britons standing in line to withdraw their savings from the stricken Northern Rock mortgage lender in September 2007 raised tricky questions as to what would happen if there were a simultaneous run in several countries on one of the forty-three cross-border banks and insurance companies that control most financial services in the EU.

In the late 1990s, the EU had created a complex system of coordination among national banking, insurance, and securities supervisors, but national governments opposed any transfer of power to these pan-European bodies. Ironically, the big banks wanted a more streamlined European system of supervision to reduce costly reporting requirements they faced in all the EU countries where they operated, but politicians were unwilling to give up national control of financial regulation. Britain, home to the world's second-largest financial center, the City of London, was strongly opposed to any single European regulator. Supported by Germany's powerful central bank, the Bundesbank, London argued that national governments and central banks were the lenders of last resort and must therefore retain the final say.

Yet the crisis revealed a flaw in the system that fueled stronger demands for pan-European financial regulation. EU single-market rules allowed banks from any state in the European Economic Area (the EU, Iceland, and Norway) to set up branches across Europe using their home country registration as a "passport." This enabled loosely regulated Icelandic banks, based in a ministate with 270,000 citizens, to advertise aggressively in Britain, Belgium, and the Netherlands, taking in deposits worth billions of dollars. British regulators could do nothing to curb their activities and had to rely on Reykjavik's supervision. When the banks collapsed in 2008, it was British, not Icelandic, taxpayers who had to pick up the tab to compensate British savers.

As with the banks, EU countries chose national rather than European solutions when it came to rescuing ailing automobile makers, some citing U.S. emergency loans to the big auto manufacturers in Detroit as a reason for offering their own aid packages. This unleashed an expensive subsidy war to prop up a sector with a chronic production overcapacity in a shrinking market. In some cases, subsidies were evenhanded. For example, both France and Germany gave a premium to motorists who scrapped an old car (more than ten years old in France and nine in Germany) and bought a new, cleaner vehicle. This benefited all carmakers regardless of nationality. Indeed, half the money in Germany was spent on foreign cars. But direct government loans to loss-making national manufacturers threatened to distort global competition in the auto market and undermine the viability of profitable companies.

Europe's carmakers were among the winners of globalization, with European marques penetrating fast-growing new markets such as Russia, China, and Brazil. But when it came to handing out taxpayers' money to support auto manufacturers, some governments sought to attach national strings. French president Sarkozy stipulated that a condition for state loans of billions of euros to Renault and Peugeot-Citroen was that they should not close any factories or make layoffs in France. The clear implication was that any closures or job losses would have to occur in other countries where the two firms make cars, such as the Czech Republic, Slovakia, and Romania. Sarkozy spelled it out in a 2009 television interview: "I want to stop offshoring and if possible promote onshoring. If we give money to the automobile sector for restructuring, we don't want to hear that another factory is moving to the Czech Republic or elsewhere. . . . Creating a factory in the Czech Republic to sell cars in France is not justified." Under EU rules, attaching such conditions to state aid to business is illegal.

The comment caused a diplomatic incident between Paris and Prague and prompted the European Commission to insist, in return for approving French aid to the car industry, that all such conditions be removed. They no longer exist on paper, but French officials say that automobile executives have given a moral commitment. Germany also offered billions of euros in state loan guarantees to troubled carmaker Opel, the European arm of fallen U.S. auto giant General Motors, on condition that it maintained all four German production sites, falling foul of the European Commission, which forced Berlin to pledge that the money was available without geographical conditions.

When the financial crisis began to bite, Sarkozy responded by creating a €20 billion French sovereign wealth fund to protect key companies from being swallowed up by the credit crunch or bought up cheaply by foreign interests. He urged other EU states to follow suit, through none did. Among the first beneficiaries of the French fund was Valeo, a key maker of components for the French car industry, supplying both Renault and Peugeot-Citroen.

France was not alone in being concerned about the implications of state-controlled funds, mostly from autocratic oil- and gas-producing states, buying control of the crown jewels of European industry at fire-sale prices in the crisis. While EU law allows the free movement of capital in principle, including investment from third countries, it makes exceptions for reasons of national security, defense, and property ownership and allows member states to restrict the flow "on the grounds of public policy or public security" and in emergency situations. Germany traditionally restricted investment only in the areas of defense and encryption, but the government drafted a law in 2008 creating the equivalent of the U.S. Committee on Foreign Investment with power to review and block investments of more than

25 percent in all areas of the economy on grounds of national security or public order. Ironically, the biggest single foreign investor in the top forty quoted French companies in 2008 was a sovereign wealth fund from an oil-producing state—the Norwegian Government Pension Fund.

THE EU, THE CRISIS, AND GLOBAL GOVERNANCE

The EU's external political response to the financial crisis was to call for a new system of global economic governance that would set common rules to prevent a recurrence of the regulatory failures, excessive risk taking, and global economic imbalances that caused the crash. Europe sought to remake the world in its own image as a community of law with binding financial regulations. This was most clearly the case in the fight against climate change, on which the EU sought a binding global agreement to cut emissions of greenhouse gases blamed for global warming, with an international trading mechanism for permits to emit carbon dioxide.

Sarkozy, as holder of the EU presidency, took the lead in pressing for a first global economic summit of leaders of the Group of 20 (G-20) nations, including the emerging economic powers of Asia, the Middle East, Africa, and Latin America. The meeting, which took place in Washington in November 2008, heralded a changing international order, with countries like China, India, Brazil, and Saudi Arabia given a full role for the first time at the world's top economic table. The program agreed at the unwieldy four-hour summit, which was consumed largely by opening speeches, was less ambitious than the "refoundation of capitalism" demanded by Sarkozy or the "new Bretton Woods" advocated by British prime minister Brown. But it did launch an incremental process of reform of international financial institutions and the adoption of a set of principles for global financial governance.

The Europeans played a key role in persuading a reluctant United States and Japan to recognize new realities and admit the newcomers to the inner sanctum of economic decision making, previously limited to the Group of Seven—the United States, Japan, Germany, Britain, France, Italy, and Canada—with Russia attending political but not financial meetings. However, the Europeans were unwilling or unable to streamline their own overrepresentation in such bodies, which was an increasing anomaly. There were no fewer than eight European delegations in the G-20, each with as much speaking time as China. The idea of a single European seat at the world's top tables has been implicit in the process of European integration ever since the bloc agreed in 1991 to create a single currency and conduct a common foreign policy. But it rubs up against the inconvenient realities of national power and ambition.

Britain and France have been permanent, veto-bearing members of the UN Security Council since its inception in 1945. Germany and Italy, the defeated powers of World War II in Europe, are excluded. Germany has had a seat at the Western world's top economic table since the Group of Five nations was created in 1975. Italy gate-crashed that grouping after its creation. In the IMF, European countries still have more votes and seats than any other region of the world. In 2008, mighty China's voting power in the IMF was similar to that of little Belgium or Switzerland. By tradition, the managing director of the IMF is a European, while the president of the World Bank is an American.

At a second summit of the G-20 in London in April 2009, world leaders agreed in principle to reform IMF quotas and voting rights by 2011 to give a bigger say to the emerging and developing countries. They also declared that the heads of the international financial institutions would henceforth be selected on merit, although Washington and Brussels have many ways to influence the choice. The Europeans won a commitment that no market, financial instrument, or institution would go without supervision or regulation. This included specifically credit ratings agencies, hedge funds, and other pools of capital, a euphemism for private equity funds. France and Germany led a drive to outlaw tax havens—often microstates that used banking secrecy to attract investors seeking to evade tax in their home country and in some cases to launder the proceeds of crime, drugs trafficking, and undeclared work. The G-20 agreed to the publication of a blacklist of such "noncooperative jurisdictions," with the prospect of sanctions if they did not accept minimum standards for sharing information with the tax authorities of other countries. Most tax havens moved fast to avoid being on the blacklist, but some, including Switzerland and Luxembourg in Europe, were furious at being named on a "gray list" of states that had promised to clean up their act but had not yet done so.

The United States and Britain had traditionally been indulgent with tax havens, some of which had historic links with them, partly because British and U.S. banks made liberal use of those fiscal oases to reduce their own tax liabilities. But the financial crisis and the advent of U.S. president Barack Obama, who as a senator had proposed a bill to crack down on tax havens, gave the Europeans their opening.

The EU did not wait for the outcome of the G-20 process of reforming international regulation to advance with legislation of its own. Under strong pressure from the European Parliament, France, and Germany, the European Commission put forward proposed directives on bank capital requirements and the registration and supervision of (overwhelmingly U.S.) credit rating agencies. In addition, the EU executive proposed legislation in 2009 to regulate hedge funds and private equity firms and to change accounting rules to avoid amplifying financial instability. By moving ahead on their own, the Europeans hoped to achieve the kind of regulatory "first-mover advantage" that they had seized in the 1980s by setting what became the global technological standard for mobile telephones. Other countries were forced to comply with the European regulation if they wanted to compete in the EU market—the biggest internal market in the world.

Whether this will prove equally effective in the financial sector remains to be seen. Like water, money tends to flow around obstacles and seek the path of least resistance. Rather than making Europe the global standard setter for financial regulation, the wave of legislation now in the EU pipeline could drive capital to new financial centers outside Europe, just as the heavy-handed U.S. Sarbanes-Oxley Act of 2003, drafted in haste after the Enron accounting scandal, reduced the number of listings on the New York Stock Exchange and drove companies to list in London.

EUROPE AND THE FUTURE OF GLOBALIZATION

At the time of writing, the global financial crisis was still in full swing. It was not clear whether the great leap forward in international prosperity wrought by globalization, with rapid GDP growth in developing and industrialized countries, low inflation, and high levels of employment, had ended for a prolonged period or just for a year or two. While there was much talk of "deglobalization"—a reversal of the open international economic system—the reality was far less stark. Within the EU, the initial impact of the crisis was to underline the role and responsibilities of national governments rather than of the EU and its collective institutions. Nevertheless, the EU treaties and international trade pacts to which the Europeans subscribed have prevented any retreat into 1930s-style protectionism. The EU's single market has come under stress from national subsidies to banks and industries, but governments remain committed to respecting the bloc's competition laws and world trade rules.

It seems certain that finance will become less globalized in the short term. Banks and companies will face strong political pressure, at a time of increased unemployment, to preserve lending and jobs in their home base rather than investing overseas. The dwindling of financial flows to developing countries and the precipitous slump in European demand for imports from those nations are bound to change the patterns of globalization in the short run. Export powerhouses such as China will have to produce more for domestic consumption and ship less to Europe and the United States in the next few years. Global supply chains will have to be adapted to reduced Western demand. The risk of more serious economic conflict, for example, over currency exchange rates or commodity shortages or between countries running big current account surpluses and those with large deficits, cannot be ruled out. Acutely aware of those risks, the G-20 leaders pledged to avoid competitive devaluations, eschew protectionist trade measures, and work to reduce global financial imbalances. But the brutal dynamics of the crisis are bound to test those commitments.

Furthermore, the fight against climate change poses huge challenges for global governance. The EU typically approached the problem by devising a legally binding framework for cutting greenhouse gas emissions by at least 20 percent by 2020 from 1990 levels, deriving 20 percent of electrical power from renewable sources and achieving a 20 percent cut in energy use through efficiency measures. These so-called 20-20-20 goals were enshrined in EU legislation, with monitoring by the executive European Commission and the threat of fines for countries that exceeded their targets. The central mechanism for achieving these goals is the EU's Emissions Trading Scheme, a carbon market in which companies buy and sell permits to emit greenhouse gases that are rationed by the Commission to meet the EU's policy goals.

The EU offered to go further and accept a mandatory 30 percent cut in carbon emissions if other major emitters signed up to equivalent binding reductions in UN climate change negotiations in Copenhagen in December 2009. At that conference, the Europeans failed to achieve any commitment from other powers to specific figures for emissions reductions, to a legally binding treaty on climate protection, or to the creation of a World Environmental Organization with similar powers to the WTO. The Swedish environment minister, who was one of the EU negotiators, called the outcome—a nonbinding political declaration to limit global warming to a maximum of two degrees Celsius from preindustrial times without specific targets for emissions reductions—a disaster.

In Copenhagen, the European model of rules-based global governance with a supranational body to enforce compliance was rejected by the rising powers—India and China—as well as by the United States, where even a Democrat-controlled Senate looks askance at any infringement of national sovereignty. If the EU is unable to persuade the United States, China, India, and other emerging nations to join Europeans in making binding reductions in greenhouse gas emissions, there is a risk that it will resort to trade restrictions against countries with less strict environmental standards.

As we have seen, European public support for globalization was already in decline before the financial crisis struck because of concerns over job losses and a perceived threat to labor, social welfare, and environmental standards. Those anxieties are likely to be aggravated by rising unemployment, tax increases, and welfare benefit cuts to finance the huge budget deficits incurred in the crisis. Anger over job losses, widening social inequality, and public sector wage cuts imposed because of the crisis fueled demonstrations and political instability in several EU countries in 2008–2009.

European governments will need to pay more attention to social justice
and frame policies to reduce inequalities of wealth and income that have
widened in the past twenty years if they are to maintain public backing for
free trade and open markets.

The crisis raises other uncertainties about the sustainability of the model
of globalization that has prevailed for two decades. Ronald Findlay and
Kevin O'Rourke argue persuasively that geopolitics was as important as
technological advances in creating the conditions for past periods of economic globalization. Nineteenth-century globalization was more a result
of British military superiority and of the geopolitical stability created by
the Congress of Vienna after the Napoleonic Wars than of the steam engine
and advances in maritime transport. "The great globalization boom of
1815–1914 can be seen as being in large part due to the establishment of
a new geopolitical order as a result of Britain's military triumphs over the
main western European rival, France, and the establishment of British naval
hegemony over the oceans of the world."[16]

The technological vectors of the economic revolution of the past twenty
years have been the Internet, cheap telecommunications, mobile tele-
phony, networked affordable computers, mass air travel, and low sea and
air transportation costs. The geopolitical conditions were created by the
collapse of the Soviet Union and the unchallenged military supremacy of
the United States, whose economic model was prescribed to the world by
international financial institutions in what became known as the "Washington Consensus." Contrary to some hubristic forecasts, this was not the
end of history. The financial crisis and the wars in Iraq and Afghanistan
ended that phase of unipolar U.S. ascendancy, although U.S. military might
remains unmatched. The crisis is ushering in a more multipolar but not
necessarily a more stable world. Growing competition for scarce resources,
high energy prices, the impact of climate change, and asymmetrical threats
such as sea piracy and terrorism all could disrupt the permissive environment for economic globalization.

The European response is to seek negotiated forms of global governance,
binding all nations to a set of common rules for environmentally sustainable economic development. But the EU does not have the diplomatic,
military, or economic means to enforce such a disposition, and it may also
lack the collective political will. Emerging powers such as China and India
and a resurgent Russia may regard Europe as weak and naive. The failure
to achieve binding agreements on either trade liberalization or climate protection in 2009 was a setback for the EU model and highlighted the extent
to which global solutions are no longer in European hands. Whether the
EU progresses toward its goal of a multilaterally regulated form of globalization will depend more on decisions taken in Washington, Beijing, and
perhaps New Delhi than on compromises reached in Brussels.

SUGGESTIONS FOR FURTHER READING

Bhagwati, Jagdish. *In Defense of Globalization.* New York: Oxford University Press, 2007.

Glyn, Andrew. *Capitalism Unleashed: Finance, Globalization and Welfare.* Oxford: Oxford University Press, 2006.

Stiglitz, Joseph. *Making Globalization Work.* New York: Norton, 2006.

Wolf, Martin. *Why Globalization Works.* New Haven, CT: Yale University Press, 2004.

8

France

Nostalgia, Narcissism, and Realism

Ronald Tiersky

More than any other European country, France wants to have a distinctive, global voice in international affairs. Britain and Germany are each in their own way equally important European powers, but since the founding of the Fifth Republic by Charles de Gaulle in 1958, only Paris, not London or Berlin, seeks to speak on the global strategic stage.

The French dilemma has always been to fill the gap between its goal of international leadership and the means necessary to achieve it. France by itself has neither the resources nor the strategic weight to go it alone. And in attempting to lead Europe diplomatically, French activism runs up against Germany's understandable foreign policy caution and Britain's diminished ambition and lingering commitment to its special relationship with the United States. Thus, French foreign policy often has an urgency about it that irritates other governments rather than attracting them.

The result is a peculiarly French existential diplomatic anxiety and foreign policy frustration that is typified by the current president, Nicolas Sarkozy, whose performance reflects a nostalgic fascination with de Gaulle's international influence. France, if it is to be truly France, must lead, or at least it must try. By contrast, the British and Germans have largely given up the idea that they are global powers. France's continuing international dilemma is therefore to conceive a more realistic foreign policy, yet without abandoning the idea that France has a special role to play in the world and without giving up the hope of rallying Germany and Britain behind it.

Against this background, in the long run the European Union (EU) is the key to French geopolitical fulfillment. France alone is only a second-rank diplomatic power and a second-tier economy (nevertheless the fifth or sixth largest in the world). But to the extent that French diplomacy can represent common European interests and attitudes, France can use the European stage as a geopolitical amplifier and multiplier of French influence.

In building the EU internally over the past five decades, France and Germany, the so-called Franco–German tandem, drove the European integration process and guided its direction. In foreign policy, French presidents have been more tempted to go it alone because in the superpresidentialized French system, the man at the top has so much unconstrained power. In the long run, however, France must be a good European citizen, if only because national interest is tied up with the EU's success. If European integration fails, inevitably so does France.

ELECTED MONARCHY: THE FRENCH PRESIDENCY AND FOREIGN POLICY

The first fact about French foreign policy is that it is made almost entirely by the president himself, far more so than in any other democratic system. In the parliamentary systems of countries such as Britain, Germany, or Spain, leaders must reckon with built-in counterpowers, for example, the balance of opinion inside their own party or parliamentary majorities that are interparty coalitions rather than the absolute majority of a single party. In a coalition government, the defection of one of the parties, even a small one, can depose the prime minister. In the cases of Margaret Thatcher and Tony Blair in Britain, a prime minister can even be ousted by an internal party revolt. In the U.S. system, presidents never entirely control even their own party in Congress, and they often must deal with a Congress controlled by the other party. The making of U.S. foreign policy is always a tug-of-war rather than an exercise of fiat in the hands of an elected monarch.

In the Fifth Republic institutional setup created by de Gaulle, there are two possible political configurations at the top. In one case, presidential and parliamentary majorities match. As long as the president controls a majority in parliament, he has complete autonomy in foreign policy because of a history of unusually strong party subordination to the president's wishes. But when parliamentary elections produce a majority hostile to the president, the president and prime minister fight for control of policy. In the French semipresidential semiparliamentary regime, key aspects of the constitution are ambiguous, and while there is still a presumption of presidential dominance in strategic affairs, in a "cohabitation" of right and left (or left and right), foreign policy that requires parliament's approval can turn into a war of maneuver.[1]

The political weakness of the cohabitation governments was such that politicians decided to do something about it. To turn the French system into a completely presidential regime would have meant abolishing the job of prime minister and the entire parliamentary aspect of the regime. It would have meant creating a Sixth Republic. Instead, the electoral system was changed to maximize the probability of matching presidential and parliamentary tendencies. The president's term in office was shortened from seven years to five (i.e., the length of the parliamentary term), and presidential elections now are held immediately before parliamentary elections rather than after in order to maximize the chances that the presidential result carries over into a complementary parliamentary result. A mixed team at the top is still possible but less likely than before.

French Presidents and French Foreign Policy

Three presidents stand out as particularly important in Fifth Republic foreign policymaking: de Gaulle, François Mitterrand, and the current president, Nicolas Sarkozy.

1958–1969: Charles de Gaulle

De Gaulle was modern France's "great leader," comparable to Franklin Roosevelt in the United States or Winston Churchill in Britain. De Gaulle was twice a political savior who brought his country "back from the abyss," as he described it. In 1940 during the Blitzkrieg German invasion of France, de Gaulle escaped to London in daring circumstances where he created a French government in exile and organized the Resistance movement that miraculously replaced the collaborationist Vichy regime when France was liberated. The news film of General de Gaulle leading a victory parade down the Champs Elysées from the Arch of Triumph to the Paris City Hall is iconic, a vision of France reborn.

De Gaulle temporarily presided over the postwar French government but resigned in January 1946 because he could not win support for the creation of a presidential-style regime. He left politics, to return only in 1958 when he was called back by parliament to save France a second time at a low point in France's disastrous colonial war in Algeria. He then was able to impose the new, presidential-centered constitution that he had been unable to win at the end of the war. Presidential supremacy began with foreign policy. De Gaulle swept up total authority from parliament and the parties to resolve the Algerian question, which everyone agreed had become a matter of national crisis. Seeing that keeping Algeria French was a futile enterprise, de Gaulle's government agreed to Algerian national independence in 1962. With this second national salvation, de Gaulle's charisma was reestablished, the legitimacy of the Fifth Republic was established, and France had become a country of unquestioned control of foreign policy by the president.

De Gaulle's goal was to rebuild French status and influence in the world order. France could not match the U.S. and Soviet superpowers, but de Gaulle, through skill and intransigence, could oblige the bigger powers to reckon with him and thus with France.

The first concern was to reestablish France's foreign policy independence and credibility. De Gaulle understood perfectly that for as long as the Soviet Union was a threat, France and Europe needed the U.S. security guarantee. He also knew that France, Britain, and the United States were natural allies on the world geopolitical chessboard. His strategy was to demonstrate that France could be an ally of the United States without saluting every memo from Washington—to show that with careful implementation, France could have its own foreign policy.

Even in the Cold War straitjacket, he reasoned, Paris might tempt the Soviets into a separate, limited détente with France, if only because he seemed to be giving them the possibility of manipulating France against the United States. By inserting himself as a semi-independent player into the Washington–Moscow game, de Gaulle was thinking big and, without question, running a risk.

But there was the ultimate protection of the U.S. nuclear guarantee of European security. In a sense, the strength of the United States could be used as a lever to assert French and European autonomy. De Gaulle also believed that France's example could give courage to other Western European governments, in which case France would become the unquestioned diplomatic leader of the continent.

Because he made so much of French and European independence, de Gaulle was perceived in Washington as personally anti-American, which he was not. A realist, de Gaulle knew perfectly well how much France and democratic Europe owed the United States from its role in World Wars I and II. His great worry, indeed anguish, was that France and Europe were finished as world powers. In his *War Memoirs*, de Gaulle recounted his meeting with Franklin Roosevelt's emissary Harry Hopkins just before the Big Three conference at Yalta in February 1945 (to which France, i.e., de Gaulle, was not invited). Hopkins said that the U.S. lack of confidence in France, even in a France led by de Gaulle, was due to "the stupefying disappointment we suffered when we saw France collapse and surrender in the disaster of 1940." De Gaulle, who had the same view of the French demise, said to Hopkins that, however this might be, "the United States does not give us the impression that it regards its own destiny as linked with that of France, that it wishes France to be great and strong, that it is doing all it can to help her to remain or become so once again. Perhaps, in fact, we are not worth the trouble. In that case, you are right. But perhaps we shall rise again. Then you will have been wrong. In either case, your behavior tends to alienate us."[2]

This was the core of de Gaulle's complaint with the United States. In the words of political scientist Stanley Hoffmann, Gaullism was always "more an attitude than a policy."[3] While resentment at the structure of power itself may be permanent, foreign policy itself must be adapted to particular situations. As president from 1958 to 1969, de Gaulle reoriented French foreign policy in several respects.

First, he put France on the right side of decolonization. After World War II, France tried to maintain its empire, but its expeditionary army was defeated in Indochina by Ho Chi Minh's communist/nationalist forces. The end came in the disastrous French defeat at Dien Bien Phu in March–May 1954. In Algeria, the anticolonial National Liberation Front pushed the French out in a war that began in 1954 and ended only with de Gaulle's historic turnabout agreeing to Algerian national self-determination. Shrewdly making a virtue of necessity, de Gaulle thereafter made France the representative among the big powers of the worldwide anticolonial movement against the remnants of imperialism.

Second, de Gaulle reoriented French policy toward the East–West conflict. De Gaulle never lost sight of the fact that in the Cold War, French and Western European security depended on the United States. His initial attempt at détente with the Soviet Union in 1959–1961 interested Moscow insofar as it tended to decouple Western Europe from the United States. But the Cuban missile crisis of October 1962 showed the limits of French diplomatic and political room for maneuver. De Gaulle was furious over the crisis because he believed that it meant a "return to Yalta," meaning the unshakeable division of Europe that eliminated the possibility of a Western European/Russian detente. In 1964, de Gaulle surprised Washington and Moscow by making France the first Western country to recognize communist China. De Gaulle's spectacular Cold War decisions presaged and helped inspire moves toward the East by other Western leaders, including West German chancellor Willy Brandt's *Ostpolitik* with the Soviet bloc beginning in 1969 and the surprise opening by U.S. president Richard M. Nixon (who greatly admired de Gaulle) to China in 1973.

Third, de Gaulle reoriented French policy toward Europe. De Gaulle's European policy was based on three priorities. First was reconciliation with West Germany. In January 1963, he signed a historic Franco–German treaty of friendship, economic cooperation, and political solidarity with German chancellor Konrad Adenauer. The treaty buried Franco–German hostility and amounted to French legitimation of West Germany's return to Europe.

The second aspect of de Gaulle's European policy concerned Britain. De Gaulle believed that Britain would never be fully European because all its history set it apart from the continent and because its postimperial Atlanticism meant that it would always act as a Trojan horse for U.S. interests in

European affairs. Britain refused to join the European Economic Community at its inception in 1958 but only a few years later, seeing its success, applied for membership. De Gaulle, quite naturally in his estimation, vetoed the British in January 1963. Subsequently, of course, the question of whether Britain is fully European has never been taken off the agenda.[4]

The third aspect of de Gaulle's European policy was adherence to the principle that European integration must be a projection of national sovereignty rather than an attempt to dissolve sovereignty in an elitist, bureaucratic structure presided over by an unelected group of technocrats. This meant intergovernmental agreements embodied in treaties rather than a federal European state with a constitution.

De Gaulle and the North Atlantic Treaty Organization

The most spectacular of de Gaulle's foreign policy moves was his decision in 1966 to take France out of the integrated military command of the North Atlantic Treaty Organization (NATO). It seemed to be a repudiation of Western solidarity. But de Gaulle's objective in leaving the central military command was not to take France out of the Atlantic alliance. NATO is not simply a military alliance; it is a political alliance with a military force. France continued to be represented in the North Atlantic Council, participating in all aspects of the alliance except the military command structure.

For de Gaulle, NATO was "a system whereby the Allies contributed their forces to a strategy drawn up in Washington."[5] France, to the contrary, had to be able, if necessary, to defend itself. In the nuclear age, no country could be counted on to risk its own destruction, even to help out an ally to which it was bound by solemn treaty. De Gaulle doubted that any U.S. president would actually risk Washington and New York to save Paris. Accordingly, France had to have its own nuclear weapons. France detonated its first nuclear bomb in 1960. Soon it had a small but independent and sufficient nuclear deterrent.

The United States had tried to discourage France from developing an independent nuclear deterrent. The Eisenhower administration had offered to station U.S. nuclear weapons in France on a dual-key basis, meaning that they could not be fired without U.S. approval. De Gaulle refused, telling Eisenhower's secretary of state, John Foster Dulles, that "if you agree to sell us bombs, we shall be happy to buy them, provided that they belong to us entirely and unreservedly."

As a result of the 1967 Arab–Israeli Six-Day War, de Gaulle changed France's policy in the Middle East as well. Israel's unexpected defeat of the combined Egyptian, Syrian, and Jordanian armies and its occupation of the Sinai Peninsula and the West Bank of the Jordan River suddenly made the small country seem the stronger power. De Gaulle immediately embargoed arms shipments to victorious Israel. France had long supported Israel's security and had even secretly helped the Israelis develop nuclear capacities. At the same time, France had special relations with the Arab countries for oil and geopolitical influence. De Gaulle thought that his shift on Israel demonstrated a policy of French evenhandedness and balance. Israel naturally perceived the French turnaround as a betrayal. Among the big European powers, the new policy put France at odds with West Germany, a strong supporter of Israel since its creation in 1948. French attitudes toward Israel have been controversial ever since.

In retrospect, de Gaulle was the seminal European leader of the second half of the twentieth century. He put the issue of Europe's independence on the agenda even before the Cold War ended. His defiance of U.S. predominance had many admirers, not only in Europe. His criticism of European lack of political will was resented by some Europeans but tacitly acknowledged by all. His insistence on the primacy of nation-states rather than federalism in European integration defined the debate as to how integration should be structured. And his foreign policy determination, however much he failed to shake the primacy of the superpowers, became a measuring rod for post–de Gaulle European leadership.

Georges Pompidou and Valéry Giscard d'Estaing

The presidencies of de Gaulle's successors, Georges Pompidou, who was president from 1969 to 1974, and Valéry Giscard d'Estaing, president from 1974 to 1981, were modest compared to de Gaulle's. There were notable developments, but the 1970s were mired in international economic stagflation, stagnation in European integration, and permanent crisis in the United States, including the defeat of the United States in Vietnam, President Nixon's resignation, and Jimmy Carter's largely unsuccessful foreign policy.

Pompidou had been de Gaulle's last prime minister. Despite his Gaullist pedigree, Pompidou lifted de Gaulle's veto of Britain's application to join the European Community. In 1973, the United Kingdom joined the Community, along with Ireland and Denmark. Pompidou thought that a successful Europe needed Britain, that the European Community needed enlargement, and that Britain would react well to being taken into the Community, even if the British special relationship with the United States would complicate matters. The Franco–German core would keep the Community anchored.

Valéry Giscard d'Estaing's presidency began with high hopes. Elected at only forty-eight years old, a liberal-conservative, and the first non-Gaullist president, Giscard d'Estaing appeared to be a kind of French John F. Kennedy. He claimed to favor a federalist United States of Europe and, in collaboration with Helmut Schmidt, the chancellor of West Germany from 1974 to 1982, initiated the informal European Community summit meetings that evolved into today's European Council. Franco–German agreement was more than ever the basis of continuing European integration. Whenever France and Germany negotiated, their compromises—those of agricultural and Mediterranean France and industrial and northern European Germany—embodied essential interests of the other member countries.

However, despite Giscard's federalist intentions, France's European integration policy remained essentially Gaullist, one of pursuing national interests with precious little inclination to sacrifice for the greater European good. The 1970s also were the time of revolutions against the postfascist regimes in Spain and Portugal and against the military regime in Greece. "Euro-communism," the ominous rise of the French and Italian communist parties into electoral positions where they might enter the government, added to uncertainties.

Soviet power was on the rise across the globe as well. In the early 1970s, Secretary of State Henry Kissinger was grimly telling intimates that his job amounted to managing a relative shift in international power relations, from the global preeminence of the United States to more of a balance with a more powerful and assertive Soviet Union. By the late 1970s, the Soviet Union was intimidating the European countries with new intermediate-range ballistic missiles, and in 1979 Moscow, to the surprise of Jimmy Carter's hopeful Soviet policy, launched its invasion of Afghanistan.

François Mitterrand's Foreign Policy

Some presidents are faced with epoch-making events. In the case of François Mitterrand, it was the sudden collapse of communism in 1989–1991. The crux of Mitterrand's presidency was whether a socialist president would fundamentally change French foreign policy or whether national interests as defined since de Gaulle had become a national consensus.[6]

Mitterrand's government involved an alliance of his Socialist Party with the French Communist Party, which at that time still dominated the French left. The communists had 20 percent of the electorate and controlled the strongest political organization in the country, the CGT trade union movement. Although most people were unaware of it, Mitterrand was a longtime anticommunist. But he needed communist votes to get elected and took the risk of alliance with the communists. The alliance posed some danger that France might have been destabilized, which would have meant a major crisis for NATO and the European Community. But the Communist Party's votes were absolutely necessary for any left-wing candidate to win a majority.

Three aspects of Mitterrand's program were particularly controversial. First was his intention to nationalize the banking sector as well as several of France's largest corporations in order to reorient the economy in a more socialist direction. Second was a huge Keynesian government fiscal stimulus, a great risk because at the same time the Reagan administration in the United States and the Thatcher government in Britain had mounted deflationary, recessionary policies to lower inflation rates that had been heading toward an astonishing 20 percent. The third worry was, para-doxically, the unlikely prospect that Mitterrand's socialism might actually succeed. France would become some kind of a socialist economy at odds with the European Community economy.[7] It was not clear how the dis-crepancy could be resolved.

Quickly, however, Mitterrand's policies resulted in financial disaster for France and the abandonment of his socialist reflationary program. The U.S. and British economies rebounded sharply beginning in 1982, but the French economy nose-dived. Because of excessive deficit spending and the fact that increased purchasing power often bought imports rather than French products, inflation skyrocketed, and the French franc collapsed. One dollar had been worth five francs in 1981; in 1985, it bought ten.

Unless Mitterrand dropped socialist economics, France, one of Europe's largest economies and key to the whole process of European integration, would at least be obliged to leave the European Monetary System, with unpredictable consequences for the entire organization of the European Community. By 1983, events were out of Mitterrand's control, and he had the good sense to recognize his lack of economic realism. Socialism was abruptly swept under the rug, and French voters returned the Socialist Party to power in 1984 because of Mitterrand's personal popularity and his unex-pectedly strong Atlanticism at a key moment in Cold War tensions. In this election, the communists lost 20 percent of their electorate to the socialists and quit the government in humiliating circumstances on their way to be-coming a fringe party after having been the dominant force on the French left for decades. If nothing else, Mitterrand had achieved a long-standing goal—to make the Communist Party irrelevant.

Mitterrand's pro-NATO stance in the so-called Euro-missile crisis of 1979–1983 reinforced his domestic political legitimacy and France's At-lanticist credentials. Not only was it a defeat of the French communists; it also helped turn back Soviet policy in Europe. The Euro-missile crisis tested the stability of the European strategic equilibrium established in the Cold War. Once the Soviet Union had exploded its first nuclear weapon in 1949, the pursuit of military advantage on either side progres-sively lost all sense. The arms race became essentially a continuing test of political will between NATO and the Soviet bloc. The Euro-missile crisis was just the latest episode.

In the 1970s, the Soviet Union increased its nuclear geostrategic pressure on Western Europe with faster and more accurate SS-20 medium-range missiles based on Soviet territory. They could hit any target in Western Europe but not reach the United States.[8] The SS-20s, according to Moscow, were no new threat. NATO believed that Moscow, by creating a new threat to Western Europe alone, wanted to put into question the U.S. commitment to intervene in case of war.

The Europeans therefore asked Washington for new U.S. intermediate-range missiles in Western Europe as a show of U.S. political commitment. The Carter administration offered Pershing II missiles not unlike the SS-20s. Moscow reacted furiously. In Western Europe, hundreds of thousands of antinuclear peace movement demonstrators marched in cities in the five NATO countries where the missiles would be deployed. The huge opposition to the Euro-missile deployment in Western Europe was, one writer said, "the most impressive display of populist muscle in the postwar era."[9]

President Ronald Reagan reaffirmed the U.S. commitment to deploy on European territory. West Germany's decision was crucial. The conservative government led by Helmut Kohl needed parliamentary approval for deployment, and even some deputies in his own coalition were not certain to support it.

In this situation, Mitterrand's support was particularly important because he was a left-wing president and thus presumably was for détente and a French role of intermediary between east and west. Moreover, prevailing geopolitical winds in the 1970s were blowing in Moscow's favor, and no missiles were scheduled for French territory. The French president could have played foreign policy subtleties, but like de Gaulle in the Cuban missile crisis, he made the right strategic decision for Atlantic solidarity.

Mitterrand's unreserved support for deployment of NATO Euro-missiles surprised a lot of people who thought that he might play politics to make France special. To the peace movement, he said, "I'm against the Euro-missiles just like you. Only I notice that the new missiles are on the other side while the peace demonstrators are on our side."[10] In January 1983, he addressed the German parliament at a crucial moment in the German debate: "The Soviets with their SS-20 missiles are unilaterally destroying the equilibrium in Europe. . . . I will not accept this and I recognize that we must arm ourselves to restore the balance. . . . Whoever is staking a bet on decoupling Europe from America jeopardizes the . . . balance of power and thus the preservation of peace."[11] Kohl's government then won the Euro-missile vote by a single ballot.

Mitterrand and European Integration

Mitterrand had been in favor of European integration from his earliest days in politics in the Fourth Republic. But in adopting socialist politics in the

1960s, he made impassioned speeches denouncing the European Community's capitalism. His pro-NATO Euro-missile policy, plus his decimation of the Communist Party in French politics, had settled the question of whether he was a foreign policy realist who understood France's national interests.

After a decade of stagnation, European integration was thus relaunched, powered as usual by the Franco–German tandem now comprised of a left/right consensus of reformed French socialists and a conservative German government. The ideological struggle in Western Europe about the content of European integration, part of the so-called end of ideology in Western societies as a whole, was coming to a close. At the same time as Mitterrand and Helmut Kohl got integration going again, Mikhail Gorbachev arrived in power in Moscow. The stage was being set for the collapse of communism and German reunification, although virtually no one—including the leaders—knew what was coming or how quickly events would develop.

By 1987, Gorbachev's signature innovations, glasnost (government transparency and telling the truth) and perestroika (economic reforms to try to salvage the collapsing economy), had already begun to destabilize the Soviet system. The Central and Eastern European Soviet bloc regimes began to totter as well. Gorbachev's sincerity about ending the Cold War led to the 1987 treaty signed with President Reagan eliminating all medium-range nuclear missiles in Europe (i.e., the Euro-missiles).

Mitterrand, like Thatcher, Reagan, and even Kohl, had no idea that the end of communism was approaching. (Gorbachev himself obviously did not.) Each Western government soon faced the most important geopolitical events since World War II. Mitterrand, like the others, had to redefine his country's foreign policy in the changing European order, a revolution without war. In particular, Mitterrand had to decide how France would deal with German unification.

Events went quickly. The Berlin Wall fell in November 1989. Communist East Germany collapsed in the summer and fall of 1990. The two Germanys unified in October 1990. Without firing a shot or even negotiating about it, the former communist East Germany became part of the European Community because it was now part of a single Germany. It was the first former Soviet bloc country to join the West.

Mitterrand had always said that the goal of France's European policy, as de Gaulle had said before him, was to get "beyond Yalta," that is, to reunify the opposed blocs of Cold War European geopolitics. Getting "beyond Yalta" had been easy to advocate as long as it was impossible. Now, the hidden agenda in the Cold War emerged. Mitterrand and other historically minded French leaders, plus Margaret Thatcher in Britain and the new non-communist Polish leaders, turned out to have doubts about the wisdom of re-creating "Big Germany."

A divided Germany in a divided Europe had been a nightmarish situation for Eastern Europeans, but to the French and British (and many U.S.

leaders) it had seemed a safer Europe than one where the United States and the Soviet Union would fight for control of Germany and Germany might have its own nationalist ideas. (The French writer François Mauriac had famously said that he loved Germany; in fact, he loved Germany so much that he was "glad there were two of them.") Mitterrand and especially Thatcher wanted at least a slowed-down course of events that would end with a watered-down East German/West German confederation rather than a potentially overpowerful reunified Germany. The only Western leader to unequivocally support chancellor Kohl's rush for German reunification was U.S. president George H. W. Bush. Even his own national security adviser, Brent Scowcroft, opposed outright unification because no one could guarantee that a reunified Germany would not return to an expansionist policy.[12] At the very least, Mitterrand and Thatcher worried that a Big Germany would inevitably dominate the European Community.

However, total reunification became impossible to stop when literally a few million East Germans moved quickly to West German territory. At that point, Mitterrand, in an odd and significant turn of phrase, said that "I am not afraid of German unification."

German Reunification and the Maastricht Treaty

Kohl knew that Germany had to reassure France, Britain, Poland, the United States, and, not least, the expiring Soviet Union that the new Germany would be a good European citizen. German goodwill in terms of European integration produced the Maastricht treaty, of which Kohl and Mitterrand were the primary authors. The bargain was essentially that France would endorse German reunification, thus legitimizing it, and that Germany would bind itself inside Europe more than ever by joining a new monetary union and political union.

The Treaty on European Union (i.e., the Maastricht treaty) was really two treaties, one on political union, the second on monetary union. Political union, in which the European Community was renamed the European Union, installed reunified Germany at the center of unified Europe. Monetary union launched the process by which the common currency, the euro, was created in 1999. It was a successful, historic realignment of European geopolitics. In political terms, Helmut Kohl provided the essential guarantees that the new, larger Germany would be European rather than nationalist. The new European Union created a European citizenship complementary to national citizenship and many other innovations in political and legal integration.

What Germany had to digest was monetary union, meaning that the Germans had to give up the fabled deutsche mark for a new European currency whose solidity in the financial markets was anything but guaranteed.

The deutsche mark had been West Germany's pride for decades, a kind of patriotic symbol that had the value of the national flag that Germans for obvious reasons felt reticent about displaying. The strong mark expressed Germany's economic health; giving it up for a European currency meant that Germany would likely have to pay for the bad economic management of other governments.

Mitterrand wanted monetary union and a European currency precisely because the French tendency to inflation (not least his own mistakes in the early 1980s) would be constrained and other EU countries, especially the weakest economies that remained competitive only through recurring devaluations, would be disciplined by its rules. France and other countries would benefit from wealthy Germany's disproportionate contribution to the EU budget, such as for the farm subsidies of which the big agrobusinesses of wealthy France were, remarkably, the largest recipient.

Mitterrand and Kohl came to an agreement in which, once again, the Franco–German tandem organized the other EU countries. Whenever France and Germany could agree on some major innovation, other countries could accept it because the two big continental powers in themselves embodied the various major European interests: agricultural France and industrial Germany, Catholic Mediterranean France, and Protestant northern European Germany.

After Maastricht, Mitterrand's health deteriorated sharply when prostate cancer first diagnosed in 1981 came out of remission. The last few years of his presidency, a new cohabitation government, were a painful personal as well as political struggle. Mitterrand and conservative Prime Minister Eduoard Balladur worked together, but French foreign policy went through a period of vacillation. In the worst episode, the Mitterrand/Balladur government did little to prevent or limit the genocide in Rwanda, a country where France had a strong influence historically and in which there was a small French military force that could have prevented at least some of the killing.[13]

Foreign Policy under Jacques Chirac

President of France for twelve years, Jacques Chirac left office with a mixed record. In domestic affairs, his presidency was a model of time lost in making badly needed social reforms in France. He was more successful in foreign policy but mainly in following up European integration projects launched during the Mitterrand presidency.

Chirac's personal style grated on other leaders and governments. It was supposed to remind people of de Gaulle's solemnity and gravitas, but he came across as pompous and lightweight. From time to time, Chirac advocated a Gaullist-inspired multipolar world order that would balance out

U.S. dominance, but he never did much about it. Chirac's premise was, as one commentator put it, that Washington "would take even more seriously allies who took themselves seriously."[14] In principle, this was true, but nobody was much convinced that Paris was now serious.

Chirac's single moment of international glory was to oppose the George W. Bush administration's invasion of Iraq to overthrow Saddam Hussein. "War," he declared at one point, "is always the worst solution." A supposedly Gaullist-inspired leader should have known that sometimes war is not the worst solution. On the one hand, he and Chancellor Gerhard Schröder of Germany appeared as the political representatives of a nearly worldwide rejection of the Bush policy that abetted a growing anti-American feeling at the time. On the other hand, most European governments, as opposed to their public opinions, backed the invasion. Central and Eastern European government support for the Bush policy was often a kind of reciprocity for the central role of the United States in facing down the Soviet Union during the Cold War. In this episode, Chirac's action was a caution for future French foreign policy. France, one writer said, "learned a tough lesson: it cannot unite Europe against the U.S."[15]

With respect to the wars in former Yugoslavia, Chirac and European governments in general did worse. They were unable to keep the peace even in their own Balkan backyard. They failed to stop the nationalist wars between Serbs and Croats and the Serb attacks on the Muslim Bosnians. In the end, it was Chirac himself who successfully implored U.S. president Bill Clinton to intervene with American airpower to stop the Serbs in Bosnia in 1995 and who again supported U.S. intervention against the Serbs in Kosovo in 1999.

There was a lot to do in terms of EU business as well. Chirac worked well enough with Schröder and his successor, Chancellor Angela Merkel, but Franco–German dynamism in EU affairs faded. Chirac was in office when the common currency came into being in 1999, but this was a project that Mitterrand and Kohl had launched in the Maastricht treaty. These were also the years of the double enlargement of NATO and the EU. Chirac supported NATO membership for the former Soviet bloc countries, but this was a U.S.-driven enterprise. He was less enthusiastic about EU membership for these same Central and Eastern European countries, partly because of the usual French worry about increased German power at the expense of France. Eastern Europe was, after all, historically a German sphere of economic and political influence.

The "return to Europe" of the Central and Eastern European countries had to involve EU membership. It was historical justice, and it provided thicker protection from Russia in addition to NATO membership. The Chirac years hardly enhanced France's reputation as a leader in European integration. On the other hand, the eastern enlargement has not been as damaging to French interests as initially was feared in Paris.

NICOLAS SARKOZY AND FRENCH FOREIGN POLICY TODAY

When Nicolas Sarkozy was elected French president in May 2007, the change in mood was palpable. Sarkozy, twenty-five years younger than Chirac, full of ideas, energy, and ambition, wanted to make France into the spearhead of Europe's return to influence. This meant turning the page on Franco–American distrust, pushing French political culture beyond its obsession with Gaullist intransigence in relation to the United States, and overturning the idea that it was necessary to choose between Europeanism and Atlanticism. Sarkozy's idea was that France would be more influential internationally and in Europe by working with the United States rather than trying to counterbalance it.

For the United States, Sarkozy was the best news to come out of Europe in several years. British prime minister Tony Blair's dogged defense of U.S. policy in Iraq had destroyed his credibility at home. Merkel, a staunch transatlantic friend of the United States, had little influence outside Germany. The Italian prime minister, Silvio Berlusconi, was Atlanticist and pro-American but also unpredictable and marginal in European affairs.

Sarkozy's arrival on the international scene had an immediate impact at the European leadership level. At home, he worked hard and with some success to turn around the anti-U.S. sentiment built up during the Bush administration years. His relationship with George W. Bush had been cordial but shallow. Bush anyway would be out of office in a year.

Barack Obama's election delighted Sarkozy—and the French people. Sarkozy saw the chance to create a special relationship with a leader as dynamic and forward looking as himself, perhaps even to install France as the favorite European ally of the United States. However, after a few months, Sarkozy seemed frustrated with the fact that the new U.S. president was not singling France out. "No European leader has worked harder to mend ties with America, nor had so much to do," as one newspaper put it.[16] On his first trip to Europe, Obama repeated the usual refrain: France was the "oldest ally" of the United States and Britain its closest. Sarkozy's successful six-month EU presidency in the last half of 2008 had made France once again Europe's diplomatic driving force. But the French president had excessive expectations about how important even a renewed, very pro-U.S. France could be.

The Two Pivots of French Foreign Policy

In the Sarkozy era, French foreign policy as always has two main areas of interests, Europe and transatlantic relations (i.e., relations with the United States). However, France as always wants to play a significant role on the world scene as well, and this means making Europe more of a global player.

In 2008, before the financial crisis, the French economy in nominal terms had a gross domestic product (GDP) of about $2.8 trillion, the fifth largest in the world. Among European countries, it was behind only Germany ($3.7 trillion) but ahead of the United Kingdom ($2.7 trillion) and Italy ($2.3 trillion). (China and Japan are the world's second- and third-largest economies.) The total EU GDP was over $18 trillion, significantly higher than the U.S. GDP of about $14 trillion. Like all EU countries, France's foreign trade takes place mainly with other EU countries. The remarkable increase in such trade over the past fifteen years has been to a considerable extent the effect of the completion of the EU's single market under the "1992" program.

Germany is France's largest trading partner, accounting for 15 percent of French exports and 19 percent of imports. The intensity of Franco–German trade is a signal of the general importance of Franco–German ties at the core of the EU historically. By contrast, Britain takes about 8 percent of French exports and accounts for about 6 percent of French imports. Britain's largest trading partners are the United States and Germany, one indication of the United Kingdom's heavier orientation to the transatlantic relationship.

France's economic prosperity depends on the prosperity of its EU partners, just as the strength of French political influence depends largely but not entirely on its ability to mobilize EU support for its diplomacy, in particular with respect to the United States. While the transatlantic economic relationship was for decades by far the most profitable in the world, the rise of China and other powerful trading economies has diminished its importance somewhat.[17]

France and NATO

From the beginning of his presidency, Sarkozy wanted to improve relations between France and the United States, always a reliable indicator of France's global influence. This was not just a matter of getting along better in that, in Sarkozy's view, better relations with Washington were in the French national interest. Rehabilitating the image of the United States in France and that of France in the United States represented two sides of a coin.

France's uncomfortable position in NATO—inside the political alliance but outside the integrated military command structure—was a perennial source of friction ever since de Gaulle created this situation as a way to show that France could be an ally of without being dominated by the United States. As with de Gaulle, neither political nor military solidarity was ever really at issue. Even de Gaulle would surely have voted to invoke article 5, the "all-for-one, one-for-all" pledge, of the NATO Treaty after the September 11, 2001, attacks on the United States. In post–Cold War

NATO (and UN) military operations, France has played a significant role, one that Sarkozy has intensified.[18] In April 2009, in an anticlimactic end to fifty years of controversy, the French military returned to NATO's integrated command structure. There was perfunctory Gaullist criticism, but the country as a whole seemed not to care very much about the change.

Two arguments were made against the move: first, it would mean that at key moments France would face intense pressure to go along with unwelcome U.S. and British policies and, second, that to rejoin the NATO integrated command was to give up a symbol of French independence. "Symbols count," as France's former socialist foreign minister Hubert Védrine put it.[19] Sarkozy's counterargument was that this legacy of Gaullism created more distrust of France than respect. In the view of Washington and London, France's real goal was to beef up the EU's security and defense structure in order to shift the transatlantic balance away from NATO.

The French reentry could affect controversial issues such as enlargement of NATO. For example, France, Germany, and certain other European governments oppose bringing Ukraine and Georgia into the alliance, which the Bush administration supported as a way of protecting these countries against Russian pressure, including even military action, as had happened in the Russia–Georgia war of the summer of 2008. Whatever Washington would be prepared to do, Europeans do not want to be under treaty obligation to defend these countries in case of renewed hostilities with Russia.

Ukrainian and Georgian membership discussions ought to be the occasion to define the respective roles of NATO and the EU in defense and security matters. NATO's strength is in broad military operations, such as the mission of the International Security Assistance Force (ISAF) in Afghanistan. The EU has a lot of experience in peacekeeping, law enforcement, police training, and energy and health security. Here NATO and the EU can complement each other, although the issue of potential U.S./European disagreements about NATO missions will remain.

Counterterrorism operations are an area where France, at least since 9/11, has an outstanding record, even though in earlier decades the pattern was more mixed. Up to and into the 1980s, French governments sought to preserve French territory as a sort of sanctuary "both for and from international terrorists," as one study put it. Terrorist groups, such as the Palestine Liberation Organization, "would have nothing to fear and nothing to achieve in France"; they could operate with impunity as long as they left France itself in peace.[20] When France did become a target in 1986, government policy became a matter of accommodation in which French governments reportedly made secret deals with Syria, Iran, and terrorist groups, including ransom of terrorists. From 1987 to 1994, French territory was by and large left alone. In the 1990s, French governments moved from accommodation to active suppression of terrorist groups because the civil war in Algeria led to actions by the Armed Islamic Group in France against the hated former colonial power. From there, the policy moved to prevention, meaning active counterterrorist operations in which French military and secret services became highly expert.

In response to 9/11, Chirac immediately upgraded French international participation in counterterrorism operations. Cooperative efforts in this area were affected not at all, even during the Paris–Washington conflict over the Iraq War. France is central to the EU's Europol organization and leads European efforts inside Interpol and all the other points of contact among the world's intelligence operations. Sarkozy is himself a former interior minister (police and homeland security), so he was familiar with these operations. France has spearheaded intensified EU counterterrorist operations as well as stricter immigration controls on EU borders and arrangements to deport illegal immigrants. Immigration control is complicated because it has to be dealt with at both the national and the EU level given that a person entering any EU country can travel visa free throughout the EU's territory.

France and the EU

Sarkozy's plan to put France back in the center of European and transatlantic relations meant that Paris had to become once again the driving force in EU politics. The very afternoon of his inauguration, Sarkozy went to meet Chancellor Merkel in Berlin, a way of showing that Germany was France's first European partner and that he intended to reenergize the Franco–German tandem. The two could hardly have been more different personalities. Sarkozy's hyperenergetic pace was not Merkel's style at all; to Sarkozy, Merkel's supercautious style seemed the wrong temperament at the wrong place at the wrong time. The two had to get on with each other if Europe was to play a bigger role internationally, but it was not certain that Merkel had this in mind. Sarkozy and the dour British prime minister Gordon Brown were also opposite poles temperamentally.

With Sarkozy pushing hard, the European Council adopted the Lisbon treaty and set in motion the ratification process in the twenty-seven member states. This "minitreaty" kept the main changes of the more ambitious constitution that French and Dutch voters rejected in 2005 referendums. Lisbon solidifies the EU structures and makes decision making more efficient. It increases the European Parliament's powers, and majority voting is extended to new policy realms. An EU foreign minister position is created, and, most visibly, the EU Council presidency is strengthened by replacing the purely administrative six-month presidency with a two-and-a-half-year term, renewable once, that creates the possibility of real political leadership.

With regard to relations with Russia, Sarkozy took center stage in negotiating a cease-fire in the Russia–Georgia war in the summer of 2008. He could not have succeeded unless Moscow wanted to use his services, yet this episode showed that an activist, big-country EU president gives the EU a public face and an international profile. Subsequently, in January 2009, even though the French presidency had ended, Sarkozy showed up in the Middle East trying to negotiate a cease-fire in the Israel–Hamas war in Gaza. He went as the president of France, but his involvement in the crisis confused Europe's profile since an EU mission led by the new Czech presidency was there at the same time, along with the president of the EU Commission, José Manuel Baroso.

Further EU expansion is a particularly charged issue in France. The main question is membership for Turkey. Like Merkel, Sarkozy opposes Turkish membership but favors offering almost everything else to Ankara in a special arrangement. His arguments are familiar: Turkey is geographically not in Europe, its 72 million population (huge by EU standards) is largely poor and would require enormous subsidies from an EU hardly able to finance current accounts, Islam as a religion is not at issue except that to admit such a large Muslim population risks unpredictable situations, and if Turkey joined, the EU's borders would be extended to Iraq, Iran, and Syria.

Sarkozy is more tolerant in matters of religion and culture than many people realize, and he understands Turkey's geopolitical importance and the animosity that complete rejection would create. The French-sponsored Union for the Mediterranean (UM), established on Sarkozy's initiative in July 2008, is to encompass North African and Middle Eastern Mediterranean countries in a development relationship of overlapping circles in which Turkey would be the leading non-EU member country. Ankara was incensed by the idea, seeing it rightly as an attempt to sidetrack Turkey's membership. Hardly mollified with assurances that the UM was not an alternative to but a stepping-stone toward membership, Ankara nonetheless accepted if only to show flexibility. Whether this increases Turkey's chances of joining the EU is doubtful since opposition to Turkish membership is the consensus view in France and Germany.

Ukraine's case for membership is more promising than that of Turkey. Ukraine is a crucial country for the EU because it is the main transit country for natural gas coming from Russia. Moscow believes that it cannot afford to "lose" Ukraine, even to the EU if not to NATO. Paris is open to Ukraine's candidacy, much more so than Berlin. Germany's economic relations with Russia, including dependence for one-third of its natural gas, make it an uncomfortably Russia-careful country. Both France and Germany oppose NATO membership for Ukraine and for Georgia because these are unstable countries that have unsettled border and other conflicts with Russia.

Other Foreign Policy Priorities

France and Russia

Russia is Europe's greatest security challenge. Whether Russia is considered to be a European or a Eurasian country, Europe's eastern question will not be easily resolved. The historic German question is closed, but Russian goals and methods are still unpredictable, and Russia's overall relation to the entire EU area continues to be full of problems. Under the governments of Vladimir Putin and Dmitri Medvedev, Russian domestic politics in the past decade have become less chaotic than in the 1990s during the Boris Yeltsin presidency. But the country has also become more authoritarian, sometimes brutally so, and foreign policy in its southern neighborhood region, where EU enlargement is heading, has become what diplomatic language calls "more assertive."

Russia is important in French and EU foreign policy calculations in three ways: as a supplier of energy, as an unpredictable geopolitical neighbor, and as an important actor in international geostrategic negotiations in which EU countries are also involved, for example, in the so-called Quartet that has the mission of furthering a Middle East peace.

Sarkozy's Russian policy combines critical and conciliatory tactics to try for leverage and to play to different audiences. For him, relations with Russia are an occasion to show that French diplomacy can have independent international influence. He first criticized the authoritarian turn in Russian politics to bolster his Atlanticist and human rights credentials. But when Putin's United Russia Party won the December 2007 parliamentary elections, sometimes literally beating up the opposition forces, Sarkozy alone among democratic leaders congratulated him on the victory. Then Sarkozy accused the Putin/Medvedev government of "complicating" world affairs with petro-dollar chicanery and manipulation of Russia's natural gas exports. When the brief Russia–Georgia war erupted in August 2008, it was Sarkozy who showed up to negotiate a cease-fire between Moscow and Tbilisi.

France and the Greater Middle East

During the period from the 1830s to the 1960s, France had a complex and sometimes sorry history in the Middle East. Both despite and because it was a colonial power, France's *politique Arabe* was designed to convince Arab governments that France was their most sympathetic European partner. Many French leaders still believe that they understand the historical Middle East more deeply and with greater nuance than others, in particular the United States. The fact that Washington's influence more or less marginalizes that of Paris is yet another aspect of French geopolitical frustration.

France was given the League of Nations mandate in Syria at the end of World War I. More or less alone, France created Lebanon as a separate country in the 1920s in order to give Lebanese Christians a safe haven and to restrain Syrian influence. Chirac was personally invested in the largely unsuccessful attempt to keep Lebanese politics independent from Damascus in order to preserve France's role there but also because he was particularly close to the anti-Syrian former Lebanese prime minister Rafik Hariri, who was brutally assassinated, apparently with Syrian involvement, in February 2005. The assassination provoked an anti-Syrian uprising on the streets of Beirut, leading to the "Cedar Revolution" and the withdrawal of Syrian troops in 2007.

Sarkozy has continued France's rejection of Syria's meddling in Lebanon, adding to U.S. pressure brought by the Bush administration. In the 2008 Lebanese presidential election, Damascus made a large gesture to the West by finally accepting the idea of a consensus president as opposed to a pro-Syrian one. This was the point at which Washington decided to engage diplomatically with Syria. Sarkozy invited Syria's leader Bashar al-Assad to Paris, giving him a controversial honored place in the Bastille Day celebrations, to show him that Syria could be welcome in the West if it stayed out of Lebanese politics and diluted its relationships with Iran (including its underwriting of Hezbollah, whose exile organization is located in Damascus).

Sarkozy condemned Hezbollah and Hamas in Gaza as terrorist organizations, but, in the usual French attempt to be balanced, he also said that both have a social base and recognizable political objectives and thus a certain legitimacy that has to be reckoned with. Once again, the activist diplomat Sarkozy tried to mediate a truce during the Israel–Hamas war in Gaza in the winter of 2008–2009. His position was that Hamas's incessant firing of rockets into Israel led to a justified Israeli military response because no country could accept permanent attacks however small in actual damage. Nevertheless, he also said that Israeli destruction in Gaza was entirely disproportionate to the cause.

France, through the EU, is a member of the Quartet of outside powers (the United States, the EU, Russia, and the United Nations) seeking to resolve the Israeli–Palestinian conflict. It supports the road map developed by the Bush administration and tries to influence events through bilateral diplomacy. French policy has tended to see the Israeli–Palestinian conflict as the key to bringing peace to the Greater Middle East. The Bush administration, by contrast, worked more on the assumption that the road to Jerusalem went through Baghdad and then, once Saddam Hussein was overthrown, through Tehran.

The French attitude toward Israel has changed significantly in recent years. Chirac already had quietly improved French diplomatic relations with Israel. Sarkozy has spoken openly and unapologetically about Israel's security dilemmas, and French media and public opinion polls also indicate a more sympathetic French attitude toward Israel. At the same time, French financial support for the Palestinian Authority continues at a substantial level. In 2007, Paris even hosted a major international donor conference to support the authority. And Sarkozy, like the Obama administration, has increased pressure on Israel to stop settlement construction and to negotiate a two-state solution to the conflict.

As is the case for the other Western countries, in the past few years Iran has moved to the center of the French diplomatic radar screen—because of its nuclear program; its relationships with Syria, Hezbollah, and Hamas; and the June 2009 uprising following the fraudulent presidential election victory of Mahmoud Ahmadinejad. During the Chirac presidency, Paris, London, and Berlin sent their foreign ministers several times as a three-man team to negotiate with Tehran a deal under which Iran would agree to halt its objectionable nuclear activities in exchange for economic, political, and other benefits. This effort was not successful. The Iranians were not particularly interested in the Europeans, making clear that only the United States mattered to them. The lack of success of this troika mission (derided by some critics as "the three dwarves") seemed to confirm the EU's perennial diplomatic weakness. Chirac himself reportedly said in private that "an Iran with one or two nuclear bombs wouldn't be intolerable."

But French policy on Iran suddenly hardened when Sarkozy arrived in power. His position was that Iran was a matter of the gravest international security concern, including for France. His rejection of the Iranian nuclear program matched the intensity and rhetoric of the Bush administration rather than the more cautious language of Britain and especially Germany. He endorsed proposals for stricter economic and political sanctions to increase the pressure on Tehran. Echoing U.S. Republican presidential candidate John McCain, Sarkozy said that "the only thing worse than military action to stop an Iranian weapons program would be a nuclear Iran." Given all this, the Bush's administration's unexpected decision in 2008 to join diplomatic conversations with Tehran put Sarkozy off balance because Paris had not been consulted or even told in advance of this important change in U.S. policy. Sarkozy's reaction to the fraudulent Iranian presidential election of June 2009 was again more dramatic than that of other EU leaders. "These elections are dreadful news," he stated. "The Iranians deserve something else . . . the extent of the fraud is proportional to the violent reaction" against it.

Like all European powers except for the British, the French have played a limited military role in the war in Afghanistan against the Taliban and al-Qaeda. Among France's total 3,750 troops there, only about 1,000 French soldiers are permanently deployed within the multinational ISAF mission in the south of the country, which is run under NATO and UN auspices. The French mission has been more to train Afghan military and police forces and to hold territory rather than a combat role. About 200 French Special Forces soldiers were part of the original Enduring Freedom campaign in northern Afghanistan looking for al-Qaeda leaders, but in 2006, Chirac, to the dismay of the United States, decided to pull these forces out. Critics argued Chirac simply wanted to minimize the political risk at home of French casualties.

Declining support in French public opinion for the Afghan War paralleled the trend in every other country involved, including the United States. In reaction to the September 11, 2001, attacks, French public opinion fully supported the invasion of Afghanistan and continued to be supportive—or at least indifferent about it—for several years. The war, it seemed, was far away, and French casualties were negligible. Then, in August 2008, ten French Special Forces soldiers were killed in an ambush near Kabul, the worst toll of French military casualties in two decades.

France's highly esteemed Special Forces units are known for their high morale and combativeness, and they understand the risk of casualties. French public opinion, however, reacted strongly to the unexpected losses and turned sharply against the war. Nevertheless, Sarkozy's secure majority in parliament voted to continue the mission.

The most recent turning point came when President Obama decided, in November 2009, on a "surge strategy" in Afghanistan, such as had worked in Iraq, and asked for increased European military commitments to complement the surge in U.S. forces. France, with other governments, had sent a few hundred more soldiers on a temporary mission to help guarantee the security of the September 2009 Afghan presidential election, in which Hamid Karzai won in an election tainted by massive fraud. Sarkozy aggressively denounced this election as he had that of Ahmadinejad in Iran, saying that France "would not send a single additional soldier" to Afghanistan because the war had to be won by the Afghans themselves. By the end of 2009, of the 10,000 troops Obama sought, only 7,000 had been promised, 5,000 from NATO allies (with Britain making by far the largest commitment) and 2,000 from countries outside the alliance. France and Germany did not commit to providing additional troops, although they did not rule out doing so in the future.

France and Africa

French colonialism and postcolonial influence in Africa is a long, often sad history that can only be touched on here. In a few West African countries that used to be French colonies and remain under unofficial influence, French forces continue to operate discreetly but effectively. During the

Mitterrand and Chirac presidencies, small French military contingents protected some governments and helped to oust others, Ivory Coast and Chad
being two examples. French arms sales were also significant, with recently
revealed illegal sales to Angola, the "Angola-gate" scandal, having resulted
in the trial and conviction of a former high-ranking Gaullist minister.

Sarkozy has redirected French military policy in Africa. France's military
presence in sub-Saharan Africa has been reduced while it has been increased in the Horn of Africa and the Persian Gulf. A new French outpost in
Djibouti faces Iran across the gulf, an example of Sarkozy's overall attempt
to increase French influence in the Middle and Greater Middle East.

Sarkozy also has tried to improve France's reputation as a friend of African development. But a major speech in Dakar, Senegal, that was intended
to be fraternal and respectful fell flat because of a poetic but often patron-
izing tone, including a hard-to-translate sentence to the effect that "Africans
have not yet become sufficiently part of History."

France and China

French left-wing intellectuals for years had a romantic but largely irrelevant idea of Mao's China that combined orientalism and socialism. In
contrast, de Gaulle's diplomatic recognition of Maoist China was a matter
of cold-eyed foreign policy realism. France still is viewed positively in Beijing, but China's greatest enthusiasm for Western leadership is reserved for
Richard Nixon and Henry Kissinger, the authors of the unexpected opening
of the United States to China in 1972.

Sarkozy's China diplomacy can be regarded as yet another attempt at
balance. On his first Asian trip in November 2007, Sarkozy emphasized exports rather than human rights. The Chinese reciprocated with $20 billion
in orders for French companies. But in March 2008, Sarkozy declared that
he would not attend the opening ceremonies of the Beijing Olympics—so
important to China's international reputation—unless Beijing met with
the Dalai Lama or his representatives to discuss the Tibet conflict. Sarkozy
ultimately did go to Beijing but as the EU rather than French president. Ig-
noring Chinese warnings of the consequences, Sarkozy then met in France
with the Dalai Lama. Beijing responded by canceling an EU–China summit
meeting and, apparently, a certain number of business deals between Chinese state enterprises and French companies. When Chinese prime minister
Wen Jiabao visited five EU countries, he excluded France and included
Germany—despite the fact that German chancellor Merkel also had met
with the Dalai Lama. In effect, Beijing showed that it would punish France
for Sarkozy's grandstanding at China's expense, while it was prepared to
accommodate the equally critical but less dramatic German government.
Beijing's realism also reflected the fact that Germany's industrial exports are

much more significant for China than are France's, yet another problem of matching ends and means.

CONCLUSION

Nicolas Sarkozy's presidency is an almost perfect example of the difficulties any French president faces in gaining support for French international leadership and greater geopolitical ambition. France, when the president is willing to take risks, can have a strong declaratory foreign policy because of the unique freedom of action of the presidential office. France, in other words, can be uniquely assertive among the big European countries.

But any French president also faces the web of limitations created by the very nature of European foreign policy decision making. Whether the decision-making site is the European Council or bilateral or multilateral negotiations outside the EU framework, France can hope to play a central world role only if there is a common European strategic view and a common political will to act on it. In other words, France can succeed only if and when the major European governments follow its lead. No other European government can even aspire to this kind of leadership. For the foreseeable future, this means that Europe can have a united foreign policy only if France is at the core of it.

And in this respect, there is a double problem. First, Britain and Germany have their own foreign policies and national interests, and the rules of the European Council's strategic decision making remain based on national sovereignty. Second, the British prime minister and the German chancellor, indeed all other European leaders, are themselves hemmed in by the various checks and balances of domestic parliamentary government. (Tony Blair's "presidential" decision on the Iraq War is the exception that proves the rule.) A final complication is that almost every major foreign policy problem in which the Europeans are involved also involves the United States. Each big European state has its own bilateral relationship with Washington to nurture, and the EU–NATO relationship is yet another dilemma.

However, a new opportunity for France has been created by the world financial crisis that began in late 2007. Europeans, in particular Sarkozy and Britain's Brown, have taken a leading role in shaping the role of governments in dealing with the various parts of the international financial system that urgently need structural reform. Brown and Sarkozy were particularly vehement in denouncing the big banks for their foolhardy behavior, and Brown, a former finance minister, made the first big proposal for reform of the international financial system. Sarkozy then followed Brown's lead in announcing a one-time 50 percent tax on bankers' bonuses over about $40,000. In the climate change negotiations leading up to the Copenhagen

summit of December 2009, Sarkozy and Brown sometimes seemed to be
working in tandem. Taking a different tone from his earlier lionizing of
Obama, Sarkozy even began to criticize or bait the American president
about the modesty of U.S. commitments to international efforts to limit the
damage of climate change. Conceivably, economic and financial globalization, in particular their potential damage to fragile aspects of the international system, may present France and the Europeans in general with new
opportunities to play more important roles in the world order.

SUGGESTIONS FOR FURTHER READING

de Gaulle, Charles. *The Complete War Memoirs of Charles de Gaulle.* New York: Simon
    and Schuster, 1964.
———. *Memoirs of Hope: Endeavor and Renewal.* New York: Simon and Schuster,
    1971.
Hoffmann, Stanley. *Decline or Renewal? France since the 1930s.* New York: Viking
    Press, 1974.
———. "Two Obsessions for One Century." In *A Centuries Journey: How the Great
    Powers Shape the World,* edited by Robert A. Pastor, 63–89. New York: Basic Books,
    1999.
Knapp, Andrew, and Vincent Wright. *The Government and Politics of France.* 5th ed.
    London: Routledge, 2006.
Maclean, Mairi, and Joseph Szarska, eds. *France on the World Stage: Nation-State
    Strategies in the Global Era.* New York: Palgrave Macmillan, 2008.
Sarkozy, Nicolas. *Testimony: France in the Twenty-First Century.* New York: Pantheon,
    2007.
Schabert, Tilo. *How World Politics Is Made: France and the Reunification of Germany.*
    Columbia: University of Missouri Press, 2009.
Tiersky, Ronald. "France Returns to Center Stage." *Current History* 107, no. 707
    (March 2008): 99–104.
———. *François Mitterrand: A Very French President.* 2nd rev. ed. Lanham, MD: Row-
    man & Littlefield, 2003.

9

The United Kingdom

Old Dilemmas and New Realities

John Van Oudenaren

THE IMPERIAL LEGACY

At the end of World War II, Prime Minister Winston Churchill contemplated how Britain, exhausted by the great wars of the century and faced with two continental giants—the United States and the Soviet Union—whose power was still on the rise, could maintain its status in the front rank of nations. Churchill's answer was to see Britain as positioned at the center of three geopolitical circles, playing a special role in each: the British Empire and Commonwealth, which he saw as persisting in revitalized form into the postwar era; the special relationship with the United States, forged during the two world wars and based on unbreakable bonds of language, culture, and shared history; and a close relationship with a Europe that Churchill hoped to see united and economically and politically revived, in large part under British leadership. In the postwar era, none of these circles took shape in precisely the form that Churchill envisioned, but a residue of each—indeed, in the case of Europe far more than a residue—survives and continues to shape a distinctive British approach to the world.

The British Empire broke up with a suddenness that in retrospect is not surprising—the world wars and the worldwide rise of nationalism spelled the end of European imperialism—but that many politicians did not anticipate and that some, including Churchill himself, very much regretted. Britain granted independence to India and Pakistan in 1947 and withdrew from Palestine in 1948. Decolonization in Southeast Asia and Africa followed in the 1950s and early 1960s. The seminal event in British postwar history was the Suez crisis of 1956, in which the government of Prime Minister Anthony Eden tried to defend what it believed was a strong legal and moral claim to ownership of the Suez Canal by joining with France and Israel in a military attack on Egypt, whose leader, Gamal Abdel Nasser, had nationalized the canal. The United States refused to back its British and French allies in this venture, which ultimately collapsed for political and economic reasons.

While Britain remained an important military power with bases in the Middle East and elsewhere outside Europe, the debacle at Suez marked the end of Britain's aspirations to remain a great power with the ability to act autonomously around the world. Harold Macmillan, who replaced Eden as prime minister, drew the lesson that henceforth Britain should avoid finding itself on the wrong side of the United States on any major foreign policy issue—a policy that generally has been followed by all British leaders since.

The imperial legacy and scattered bits of empire that Britain retained after the 1960s have played a diminishing role in British foreign policy over time, but conflicts and crises growing out of this glorious past have continued to pop up with a certain unpredictable regularity. Examples include the role that Britain played in brokering the Lancaster House Agreement, which brought black majority rule to Zimbabwe in 1980; the Falklands War with Argentina in 1982; the tensions with the United States over the 1984 U.S. invasion of Grenada (a member of the Commonwealth); ongoing sparring with Spain inside the European Union (EU) over Gibraltar; the long negotiations with China to end British rule of Hong Kong by 1997; and even such lesser issues as London's recent criticism of the government of Bermuda (a nonsovereign territory whose foreign affairs are still Britain's responsibility) for accepting prisoners released from the U.S. base at Guantanamo, Cuba.[1] The thorny problem of Northern Ireland also has been an ongoing preoccupation of British foreign (and domestic) policy in recent decades—a drain on British defense resources, an enormous distraction for policymakers, and a complication in relations with the United States and the Republic of Ireland.

The official name of the British foreign ministry, the Foreign and Commonwealth Office, carries with it the implication that the members of the Commonwealth are not truly "foreign." This is largely a political fiction, but the Commonwealth does provide a useful forum through which Britain exercises a certain residual influence. Fifty-three independent countries are members of the Commonwealth, which promotes democracy and human rights and other forms of cooperation through heads of state and ministerial meetings and a secretariat based in London. Queen Elizabeth II is the titular head of the Commonwealth, and sixteen of the organization's members still have the British monarch as their head of state. For virtually all members of the Commonwealth, however, including Britain itself, the organization is not the primary focus of its foreign policy but rather an adjunct to the more important regional organizations to which these countries belong.

In addition to the Commonwealth, Britain retains sovereignty and ultimate political control over a number of territories and dependencies around the world. They include Diego Garcia, part of the British Indian Ocean Territories that the United Kingdom leases to the United States as a major military base to project power into the Middle East; Ascension Island in the South Atlantic, which hosts one of the five ground stations around the world for the U.S. Global Positioning System; and territories in the Caribbean, Pacific, South Atlantic, and British Antarctica. Also strategically important are the Sovereign Base Areas on Cyprus, which Britain retained after granting Cyprus independence in 1960.

However, the real legacy of empire and Britain's former status as a great power is not the Commonwealth or these scattered dependencies but rather Britain's role as one of the five permanent members of the UN Security Council. This gives Britain a voice—and potentially a veto—in every important international issue that comes before the world's supreme legal body. This in turn translates into special influence with the United States (as well as influence and resentment in Europe). Having tested its first nuclear device (in part the product of close cooperation among Britain, Canada, and the United States during World War II) in October 1952, Britain was also the world's third nuclear power. As one of the three original nuclear weapons states, the United Kingdom became, along with the United States and the Soviet Union, a formal cosponsor of the UN nuclear arms control regime, which included the Limited Test Ban Treaty of 1963 and the Nuclear Nonproliferation Treaty (NPT) of 1968 and which continues in the periodic NPT review conferences.

A final legacy of empire worth noting—and one with potential foreign policy implications—is the racially, ethnically, and religiously diverse character of the British population. All European countries, whether or not they had overseas empires, have increasingly diverse populations as a consequence of labor- and crisis-driven migration, so empire as such does not explain the fact of such diversity. But history does explain why minorities in Britain have been drawn disproportionately from South Asia and the West Indies rather than, as in the case of Germany, from Turkey or, in the case of France, from North Africa. Britain's population is approximately 8 percent nonwhite, with 4 percent of the population South Asian and 2 percent black. Like the rest of Europe, Britain is nominally Christian and overwhelmingly secular, but approximately 8 percent of the population professes Islam—a level that has led to speculation about the effect that Britain's internal religious composition might have on its foreign policy and in particular its involvement in conflicts with Islamic insurgents in Iraq and Afghanistan.

BRITAIN AND EUROPE

The confusion and mutual disappointment in Britain's relations with Europe go back to the early postwar era. Churchill had spoken in favor of a united Europe as far back as 1930. In June 1940, he tried to stave off France's surrender to Nazi Germany by offering to establish a full union between France and Britain. In his Zurich speech of September 1946, he electrified Europe with his call for the creation of a United States of Europe. At the time, Churchill was the leader of the Conservative opposition, and the Labour government of Clement Attlee showed little interest in participating in a united Europe. Like the Conservatives, Labour politicians still saw Britain as a great power that need not place itself on a par with the continental powers, all of which had been defeated and occupied in the war. Labour politicians also had a particular fear that international entanglements, especially with Christian Democratic–dominated European powers, might impinge on Britain's freedom to build socialism at home.

Churchill's return to power in 1951 briefly raised hopes that Britain would take up the cause of European integration, but London declined to join the European Coal and Steel Community when it was formed in 1952 and later the European Economic Community (also known as the European Community [EC]) established under the 1957 Treaty of Rome. As Foreign Secretary Anthony Eden remarked at the time, to join a federation on the continent of Europe "is something which we know, in our bones, we cannot do."[2] Impressed by the initial successes of the EC and, equally important, unable to enlist the support of Washington for any of the alternative architectures for Europe with which the British had been experimenting in the late 1950s, Prime Minister Macmillan reversed course and applied for membership in the EC in the summer of 1961. But by then, it was too late. France under President Charles De Gaulle had cemented its political leadership of the EC and was convinced that it could build a political and economic bloc in continental Europe to challenge "Anglo-Saxon" domination of the West and transcend the bipolar U.S.–Soviet rivalry that structured international politics. Under a variety of pretenses, all of which came down to the fact that the United Kingdom was not sufficiently "European," de Gaulle vetoed Britain's application to join the EC in January 1963 and again in May 1967.

Not until January 1973 did Britain manage to secure its place in Europe. The somewhat hapless Labour government of Harold Wilson, in power from 1964 to 1970, struggled with sterling devaluation, Britain's economic decline relative to continental Europe, and retrenchment from military commitments outside Europe left over from the era of empire. De Gaulle resigned in 1969. France was becoming interested in counterbalancing the rising power of West Germany in the EC by bringing Britain into the EC.

The Tories returned to power in 1970 under Prime Minister Edward Heath, who, under these more favorable political circumstances, successfully concluded the negotiations with the Six to secure British membership in the EC's first enlargement (Denmark and Ireland also joined at that time).

Britain's relations with the EC (and subsequently the EU) have since traversed an often-rocky path. On his return to power in 1974, Wilson sought to renegotiate the terms of Britain's accession and called a referendum on continued British membership. The vote took place in June 1975, with the pro-EC camp carrying the day with a surprisingly large majority of the electorate—67.2 percent—voting in favor of staying in the EC, with only 32.8 percent against. But while Britain made clear that it had no intention of leaving the organization, it was distinctively unenthusiastic about attempts over the next two decades, led by the Franco–German pairings of Valery Giscard d'Estaing and Helmut Schmidt and François Mitterrand and Helmut Kohl, to propel the EC forward toward new forms of economic and political union. Prime Minister James Callaghan, who succeeded Wilson in 1979, declined to join the European Monetary System (EMS) initiated by Giscard and Schmidt (in close cooperation with, ironically, the first—and so far only—British European Commission president, Roy Jenkins). Callaghan also began to complain about the size of Britain's net contribution to the EC budget.

Callaghan's successor, Conservative prime minister Margaret Thatcher, turned Euroskepticism into a high political art that continues to shape British and international perceptions of the United Kingdom's relationship with Europe. A fiscal conservative, Thatcher harangued her fellow European leaders about the size of Britain's contributions to the EC budget, all but paralyzing EC business until she managed to secure, at the Fontainebleau session of the European Council in 1984, a permanent annual rebate of Britain's contribution to the budget.

Thatcher was unenthusiastic about the efforts by European Commission president Jacques Delors, Kohl, and Mitterrand to "relaunch" the European Community in the 1980s and was furious at being outmaneuvered at the June 1985 session of the European Council, at which the Italian presidency engineered the convening of an intergovernmental conference (IGC) by the simple expedient of a majority vote among the assembled heads of government. Britain voted against the motion to call the IGC, which nonetheless carried by a seven-to-three vote (Denmark and Greece joined Britain in opposing the call for an IGC). Once engaged in the IGC, however, Britain played a constructive part in its main work: the negotiation of a treaty containing a binding commitment to complete the European single market by the 1992 target date through the elimination of remaining barriers to the free movement of goods, services, capital, and people. Such "negative integration" was compatible with Thatcher's free market ideology and promised to be economically beneficial to Britain, whose economy was already more open than those on the continent and which was well positioned to benefit from the liberalization of services such as banking, finance, and consulting, industries in which Britain was relatively strong.

Thatcher was far less enthusiastic about proposals for enhanced "positive integration" and in particular the idea advanced by Delors and the European Commission that completion of the single market required the next logical step: full economic and monetary union and the adoption of a single European currency. In her September 1988 speech to the College of Europe in Bruges, Belgium, Thatcher rejected what she saw as plans to create a European superstate that would negate the identities of the individual member states:

> My first guiding principle is this: willing and active cooperation between independent sovereign states is the best way to build a successful European Community. To try to suppress nationhood and concentrate power at the centre of a European conglomerate would be highly damaging and would jeopardize the objectives we seek to achieve.
>
> Europe will be stronger precisely because it has France as France, Spain as Spain, Britain as Britain, each with its own customs, traditions and identity. It would be folly to try to fit them into some sort of identikit European personality.[3]

Britain opposed the creation of the single European currency. Instead, it promoted an alternative scheme, the "hard ECU," which involved an effort to transform the existing European Currency Unit (ECU), which essentially was an accounting device (a unit of value composed of a basket of EC-country currencies) into a real currency of sorts. The British scheme to develop the ECU into a parallel currency to the national monies still in circulation in the end pleased no one. To the continental advocates of EMU, it was a transparent ploy to derail the formation of a single currency through what leaders such as Delors, Kohl, and Mitterrand saw as the only possible way: a supreme act of political will on the part of the European governments. To the diehard British Euroskeptics, on the other hand, it went too far in that it at least admitted the possibility that Britain would adopt a European currency, albeit after a process of evolution rather than through a single political act.

Britain finally joined the Exchange Rate Mechanism (ERM) in October 1990. But Thatcher's skepticism about the EC continued to grow, tinged by a Germanophobia that grew more pronounced as the Berlin Wall fell and Germany marched toward unification. Thatcher's views became an increasingly divisive issue within the Conservative Party and led to the resignation, in November 1990, of Thatcher's respected deputy prime minister, Sir Geoffrey Howe. In his resignation speech, Howe delivered a strong attack on

Thatcher's erratic and emotional approach to the EC, which he argued was damaging Britain's economic interests. Howe's vocal critique set the stage for a Conservative Party revolt against Thatcher, who in November 1990, failed to win reelection as leader of her party and was forced to resign as prime minister.

Thatcher's successor, John Major (who as chancellor of the exchequer had been the main exponent of the hard ECU scheme) adopted a change of tone and promised to put Britain "at the very heart of Europe." But Major adhered to what had been Thatcher's "red lines" on European integration, and his government proved to be a very tough negotiating power in the two IGCs of 1990–1991 that led to the establishment of the EU. In addition to slowing the momentum toward creating an autonomous European foreign and security policy, Britain secured exceptions for itself in two areas: EMU and the Social Charter. These were both areas in which Britain was not prepared to accept the political consequences of completely blocking progress toward the deeper and more comprehensive integration desired by the French, Germans, and other member states but in which it was prepared to accept such integration only to the degree that it was allowed to opt out of certain laws and policy mechanisms in order to preserve its national autonomy.

The Maastricht treaty stipulated that, as early as 1997 and in any case no later than January 1, 1999, the member states of the union would move to the third and final stage of EMU: the adoption of the euro and the phasing out of their national currencies. Britain had the option of participating in the third stage of EMU, but it was under no obligation to do so. A separate protocol attached to the treaty specified that the United Kingdom "shall not be obliged or committed to the third stage of economic and monetary union without a separate decision to do so by its government and parliament" and that it "shall retain its powers in the field of monetary policy according to national law."[4]

If the United Kingdom decided (as was widely expected) not to adopt the single currency, it also would not participate in the European System of Central Banks or the European Central Bank that was being set up to manage the euro. Against this background, the debate in Britain over EMU came to be framed in large part in terms of the question of whether the preservation of national sovereignty secured in this and other opt-outs was worth the loss of British influence over broader European policy that opting out inevitably entailed. This question has retained its relevance as federalist-minded forces on the continent were determined to press ahead with more extensive schemes for integration regardless of British presence. In many ways, this question continues to be the key one in British policy toward the EU although one whose urgency has tended to fade somewhat as the integration project has lost momentum.

The Social Protocol was a pet project of Delors, a European socialist who believed, with the support of political allies in the European Parliament and member state governments, that the probusiness, free market emphasis of the 1992 program had to be counterbalanced by new Europe-wide rules and policies that would guarantee the interests of workers. At its December 1989 session in Strasbourg, the European Council adopted the Charter of Fundamental Social Rights of Workers (the Social Charter), which listed twelve principles, ranging from the right to a fair wage to inclusion of the disabled to a decent standard of living for older people. In the Maastricht negotiations, a number of member states led by France, Belgium, and Italy pressed for incorporation of the Social Charter into the EU treaties, a step that would make the declaratory, nonbinding principles adopted in Strasbourg a legally binding document that would give the EU new powers to pass EU-wide directives in the area of social policy, which the member states then would be required to implement through the adoption of national legislation.

Thatcher was opposed to what she regarded as unwarranted interference in British domestic affairs, as was much of the British business community, which saw in the charter a threat to the deregulated, free market environment that had enabled Britain to improve productivity and attract foreign investment in the 1980s and to begin closing the gap in per capita gross domestic product (GDP) that had opened up between Britain and the continent from the 1950s to the 1970s. With the Conservatives dug in on this issue, the Social Charter became one of the hardest-fought issues of the Maastricht negotiations. In a last-minute compromise, the negotiators agreed to an arrangement under which all member states except Britain would adopt a separate protocol that was appended to the Maastricht treaty and that would allow these eleven states to adopt binding social directives that then would have to be implemented by the eleven at the national level. Known as the Social Protocol, this document was similar to the protocol on EMU in that it resulted in a certain differentiation among the member states with regard to the *acquis communautaire* but in this case did so by the device of allowing all member states except Britain to *opt in* to certain forms of integration rather than allowing Britain to *opt out*, which was the case with EMU.

In addition to EMU and the Social Protocol, Britain hung back from the most extensive forms of cooperation in the so-called third pillar of the EU, known as Justice and Home Affairs. In 1985, Belgium, Germany, France, Luxembourg, and the Netherlands signed the Schengen agreement, which abolished border controls among the signatory states while establishing enhanced controls at what became the "Schengen border." Although it was effected outside the formal structures of the EC, the Schengen agreement was in line with the 1992 program and the EC goal of removing all internal barriers to the movement of people as well as of goods, services, and capital. Other member states acceded to the agreement in the early 1990s, but Britain, as an island nation with a strong tradition of controlling its own borders, did not. Britain continues to operate its borders outside the Schengen system, although in other respects it participates fully in EU third-pillar activities, notably EU-level actions in the fight against terrorism, drug trafficking, and other cross-border threats.

British skepticism about EMU, already firmly entrenched in the 1980s, deepened in the financial crisis of 1992, when Britain was forced to suspend participation in the EMS that it had only recently joined at such high political cost. In June 1992, voters in Denmark rejected the Maastricht treaty, raising doubts about whether the treaty would go into effect and whether EMU would be realized. Speculators began to dump the weaker European currencies in the expectation that they eventually would be forced to devalue against the German mark. Britain borrowed $14.5 billion in marks to bolster its reserves, and the Bank of England raised its minimum lending rate to 12 percent, with very damaging effects on the British economy, all in an effort to keep the pound within the two-and-a-quarter-percent range required by EMS/ERM. Meanwhile, German officials, worried about the inflation associated with a reunification-induced economic boom, refused to lower Germany's high interest rates, which economists in Britain and elsewhere saw as the basic cause of the pressure on the pound and other European currencies. On September 16, Britain left the ERM/EMS, having suffered bruising political and economic losses that would make tighter economic—and political—integration with Europe more difficult to achieve in the future.

A final area in which Britain hung back from the more expansive integration plans of its continental partners was in foreign policy. Britain went along with the establishment, as the "second pillar" of the EU, of a Common Foreign and Security Policy (CFSP) based on strengthened consultations among the member states on foreign policy and the undertaking, by unanimous decision, of joint actions. But the British resisted French attempts to promote a European defense identity. The result was an ambiguous compromise in the treaty that provided for the "eventual" framing of a common defense policy without specifying how or in what timeframe this would come about. The treaty declared that the Western European Union (WEU), which previously had not been linked to the structures of the EC, was an "integral part of the development of the European Union" and provided a mechanism under which the WEU could "elaborate and implement decisions and actions of the Union which have defense implications." But British negotiators rejected a merger of the WEU with the EU as a way of providing the EU with the nucleus of a defense capability. In subsequent years, Britain worked to uphold the primacy of the North Atlantic

Treaty Organization (NATO) in European defense matters, a stance that the French in particular found enormously irritating, and to regard the WEU as a secondary institution that at best could serve as a bridge between NATO and the EU rather than function as the nascent defense arm of the EU.

While skeptical of the "deepening" of the EU through an expansion of its powers and the extension of policy competence to new areas, the United Kingdom strongly favored "widening" the EU to new member states. In contrast to the French, for example, who were concerned about the costs of enlargement, the competitive threats that new members would pose to French industry and agriculture, and the political dilution of the EU that taking in new members might entail, the British were early and strong supporters of bringing the Central and Eastern European countries into the EU—so much so that federalist-oriented Europeans suspected the British of wanting to expand the EU so as to preclude, once and for all, the creation of a strong Europe that could be built only on the basis of a shared cultural and political identity. This attitude toward widening extended to British views on Turkey, whose candidacy for EU membership Britain supported, in contrast to the stances taken by France and Germany.

After the assertive and triumphal years under Thatcher in the 1980s, the 1990s were not a happy time for British foreign policy. Two former British foreign secretaries, Lord Carrington and David Owen, served as UN mediators in the Balkans but were unable to bring peace to the region—in Owen's case, as he argued in his memoir, in large measure because of lack of support from the United States, which was reluctant to consider the de facto ethnic partitioning of Bosnia-Herzegovina.[5] Along with France, Britain was a major provider of peacekeeping forces to the Balkans under UN mandate, but these forces failed to stop the conflict in Bosnia in the early 1990s. Tensions ran high with the United States, which was critical of the European effort even though unwilling to commit its own forces in the Balkans, and within Europe, where Britain and France were seen as leaning toward Serbia, while Germany and Austria were seen as motivated by more pro-Croat leanings. Not until 1996 and the Dayton peace agreements made possible by a new level of U.S. and NATO involvement did this situation take a turn for the better.

The departure of Thatcher also failed to resolve the differences within the Conservative Party over policy toward Europe. Britain managed a successful EU presidency in the second half of 1992, making progress, among other things, on EU enlargement, a codified definition of "subsidiarity," and smoothing over lingering Danish objections to provisions of the Maastricht treaty.[6] But bickering over Europe and the euro continued within the Conservative Party and rendered party statements on Europe increasingly incoherent and off-putting to the British public as well as causing concern to partners in the EU. These factors, along with the exhaustion and the accumulated weight of scandals small and large from nearly two decades in government, provided an opening that the opposition Labour Party finally was able to exploit in the elections of 1997.

LABOUR RETURNS TO POWER

During its seventeen-year period in political exile, Labour had undergone a significant revolution in its thinking about Europe. While pockets of Europhobia continued to exist within the party, the Conservative Party's aggressive advocacy of U.S.-style free market capitalism had swung much of the opposition in favor of European-style regulation and social safety nets. For Tony Blair, who had taken over the party in 1994 and sought to modernize it by jettisoning old dogma about state ownership of industry, British leadership in a progressive Europe was a perfect way to win over middle-class voters tired of Conservative Party bickering and incoherence on the issue of Europe.

Following Labour's May 1997 electoral victory, Blair took office as prime minister, just in time to lead Britain in the final weeks of the negotiations toward the Treaty of Amsterdam, the first significant revision of the treaties agreed at Maastricht. Blair announced that Britain would adhere to the Social Protocol that the Conservatives had spurned and that the United Kingdom would accept all the directives that the other member states had passed to implement the charter and would transpose these directives into British law. This shift allowed the protocol to be integrated into the amended EC treaty, ending at least one of the anomalies that had been introduced at Maastricht as a result of the split between the more and less integration-minded member states.

At the same time, however, Amsterdam introduced a new anomaly in the *acquis*—one that grew out of the reluctance of Britain and a few other member states to go along with the proposals of the more integration-minded states to enhance the role of the EU in the area of justice and home affairs. Concerned at the ineffectiveness and the lack of legal clarity of the policy process under the third pillar, France, Germany, and the other more integration-minded member states were determined to incorporate the Schengen agreement into the Treaty on European Union. But preserving Britain's right to police its own borders was a key policy objective of the Major government and one that was taken over wholeheartedly by Labour on its assumption of power. In the end, Britain (along with Ireland) secured an opt out from what became the new border regime of the EU, while the continental countries were required to dismantle their internal border controls by 2004.

On the key issue of the euro, the new government proceeded very cautiously. Labour adopted a stance toward the euro that on the surface was more positive than that of the previous government, stating that the decision to join was a matter for Parliament and possibly a national referendum to decide. But Gordon Brown, the chancellor of the exchequer, devised a set of five tests—having to do mainly with the business cycle and whether the British economy would gain from adoption of the euro (including effects on the competitive position of the City in London, the British equivalent of Wall Street)—which, in addition to the convergence criteria set by the Maastricht treaty itself, would determine whether Britain would join. The five tests were sufficiently demanding to make it unlikely that the government soon would recommend joining the euro.

Blair adopted a more forward-leaning posture on CFSP, although this occurred not immediately but over a period of months in response to changing circumstances on the ground and Blair's own disappointment at the failures of both NATO and the EU in dealing with crises in the Balkans. At a session of the European Council in October 1998, Blair called for "fresh thinking" on European defense cooperation and floated several possible institutional reforms, including possible full merger of the WEU into the EU, which Britain previously had opposed. In December of the same year, Blair and Chirac met in a small town on the French seacoast and issued their pathbreaking St. Malo "Declaration on European Defense," in which they called for the development of an EU capacity for "autonomous action" in the field of defense.

The shift in Britain's position did not, government spokespersons insisted, signal any turning away from Britain's strong support for NATO and a continued U.S. role in European security but rather a search for new European options and capabilities to supplement those of NATO and the United States. The background to the change in British policy was a renewed flare-up of violence in the Balkans, in this instance a crackdown by Serb forces on restive ethnic Albanians in the Serb-ruled province of Kosovo. While urging, in the end successfully, the United States and NATO to get involved in the conflict, Blair was frustrated at the paucity of options at his disposal for influencing the course of events in Kosovo and at Europe's seemingly complete dependence on the United States to resolve a crisis in its own backyard—an early experience that led him to see the virtues of an autonomous European capability.

Along with the adjustment in policy toward CFSP, the other important change in British foreign policy brought about by Labour was the shift to a more "moral" foreign policy, in line with Labour's roots in the British churches, its ties to the Cold War disarmament movement, and the sympathy of the European left for the developing world and the cause of global economic justice—all tendencies that represented a change from the Conservative emphasis on Realpolitik, promotion of British national interests, maintenance of ties to the United States, and support for British business interests. An early indication of this change came with Britain's embrace of an international treaty banning land mines then being promoted by Canada and Norway and a coalition of "like-minded" small and middle powers. Britain previously had been among the strongest opponents of such a treaty, which the British military saw as an unwarranted limitation on its ability to conduct military operations and which was also rejected by the United States, which wanted to retain land mines as defensive weapons along the border between North and South Korea. But Blair and his advisers were swayed by pressures from the British anti–land mine campaign, whose unofficial leader had become Princess Diana, who traveled to Angola in January 1997 as a guest of the British Red Cross and who endorsed the ban as a humanitarian measure.

A similar dynamic played out with regard to the International Criminal Court (ICC), which was being negotiated in a series of conferences and UN-sponsored working groups. The British government under Major was not opposed to the creation of an ICC, but it stood with the Clinton administration in rejecting a court that was not firmly under the political control of the UN Security Council and that was not bound by certain procedural guarantees ensuring that NATO soldiers on peacekeeping or other intervention missions would never be prosecuted for war crimes. The new Labour government dropped British opposition to what the United States continued to regard as unacceptable aspects of the court, and Britain—unlike the United States—was among the majority of countries from around the world that voted for the statute establishing the court when it was adopted in Rome in July 1998.

This emphasis on what Blair and his colleagues saw as morality in foreign policy remained a theme in British foreign policy throughout the Blair years and was seen most clearly in two other areas: aid to the developing world and policy toward global warming. Blair steadily increased the size of the British foreign assistance budget (both in absolute terms and as a share of GDP) and, as host and chair of the July 2005 G-8 summit in Gleneagles, Scotland, pushed for renewed efforts to meet the UN Millennium Development Goals (scheduled to be reviewed at a special summit in September 2005) and managed to broker an agreement to double aid by the G-8 to Africa in the 2004–2010 period.

As an EU member state, the United Kingdom is obliged to contribute to meeting the EU's overall target under the Kyoto Protocol of an 8 percent reduction in greenhouse gas emissions from the base year of 1990 by 2008–2012. Between 1990 and 2005, eleven of the fifteen preenlargement EU member states reported increases in emissions rather than declines. The United Kingdom was one of four member states actually to cut emissions and to meet its Kyoto-mandated target of a 12.5 percent reduction in national emissions. It also made a subsequent unilateral pledge to cut emissions by 20 percent from the 1990 base year by 2020. Even more ambitiously, the British government adopted a plan to cut emissions by 60 percent by 2050, a figure that was later raised to a still more ambitious 80 percent.

One of Blair's most significant foreign (and domestic) policy achievements was the 1998 Good Friday Agreement between Britain and Ireland, which, after decades of violence, represented a huge step toward the final resolution of the Northern Ireland problem. The agreement established a new governing structure for Northern Ireland, required the Republic of Ireland to amend its constitution to drop its claim to the north, and specified that any future change in the political status of the north would be achieved by exclusively nonmilitary means and would require the consent of the population. The Clinton administration played a direct role in brokering the agreement—a role that was facilitated by and in turn helped to strengthen the strong personal bonds between the Clinton and Blair governments at various levels.[7] The EU was less directly involved, but European integration clearly provided the background conditions for a settlement by muting the importance of sovereignty and territoriality, promoting economic convergence between Britain and Ireland, and providing regional aid to all parts of Ireland.

BRITAIN AND MILITARY INTERVENTION

Britain's embrace of the land mine treaty, the ICC, and Kyoto all contributed to the relative diplomatic isolation of the United States and lent credibility to the charge of "unilateralism" that became the core of the standard European critique of U.S. foreign policy in the late 1990s and especially after January 2001 and the inauguration of George W. Bush. In other respects, however, Blair stuck very closely with the United States in a way that helped prevent U.S. isolation. This was especially the case with regard to the use of force, which Blair strongly believed was justified to uphold international law and, in extreme circumstances, to deter or defeat national governments from attacking their own populations.

In December 1998, the United Kingdom joined with the United States in undertaking Operation Desert Fox, a four-day bombing campaign against Iraq mounted in response to Baghdad's refusal to comply with UN Security Council resolutions. This was at a time when France and Russia, fellow members of the Security Council, were resisting any effort to crack down on Saddam Hussein and calling for the lifting of the economic sanctions imposed on Iraq for noncompliance with Security Council resolutions. In the spring of 1999, Blair became one of the strongest voices in NATO for intervention to stop the Serb attacks on the Kosovars. Moreover, once NATO was committed to military action, Blair used his influence, in private meetings with Clinton and in a high-profile speech in Chicago in April 1999, to insist that NATO had no choice but to prevail in Kosovo, even if doing so required a costly and bloody intervention by NATO ground troops—something that Clinton had ruled out at the start of the war but that he was forced to reconsider as the air campaign wore on without producing the desired change in the behavior of Serbian dictator Slobodan Milosevic.

In May–June 2000, Britain deployed some 700 elite troops, backed by ships and additional personnel offshore, to Sierra Leone to prop up a failing UN peacekeeping mission and protect British nationals in the chaos-ridden country. This mission was undertaken outside the UN and NATO frameworks but involved extensive informal cooperation with the United States (which assisted by airlifting UN peacekeepers) and with Jordan and India, which provided the most effective peacekeeping forces. It was widely regarded as a success that helped to save lives and bring a modicum of stability to the former British colony.[8]

Much like Thatcher, who had worked with President George H. W. Bush after the collapse of communism to define what Bush memorably called a "new world order," Blair closely aligned Britain with the policies of the George W. Bush administration following the September 11, 2001, terrorist attacks on New York and Washington. He did so out of a genuine sense of solidarity but also to ensure that Britain would play a central role in what was certain to be another recasting of the international order. While the United States was much criticized for spurning most European offers of military help after the 9/11 attacks, it welcomed British participation in the war to topple the Taliban government in Afghanistan and to eliminate the bases from which al-Qaeda had planned the terrorist attacks on the United States. British submarines launched cruise missiles in the initial attacks in October 2001 on targets in Afghanistan, and British special forces joined their U.S. counterparts in the assaults on al-Qaeda and Taliban strongholds. Subsequently, Britain remained heavily engaged in the Afghan peacekeeping and reconstruction effort, with a particular focus on counternarcotics activity.

Blair's most controversial foreign policy decision was his backing for the Bush administration's 2003 war to topple Saddam Hussein in Iraq. Like other Western leaders, Blair appears to have genuinely believed that Iraq possessed weapons of mass destruction. He also shared Bush's view that Iraq's continued defiance of UN Security Council resolutions was corrosive of international order and believed that once the United States was determined on a particular course of action—and Bush clearly was set on war with Iraq—it was important for Britain to side with the United States to shape the nature of the U.S. action rather than to mount an opposition from outside that in any case was likely to be futile.

But if these were Blair's initial calculations, they soon were overshadowed by a bitter struggle for power within Europe in which France, supported by Germany, sought to use the unpopularity of the Iraq War to cement French leadership of Europe around Chirac's anti-American agenda and to marginalize Britain as a force in Europe. This intra-European struggle was waged in the confines of the Security Council, where, by a curious coincidence, four of the five largest EU member states happened to be represented during the run-up to the war: Britain and France as permanent members and Germany and Spain as nonpermanent members elected from the West Europe and Others Group of UN member states. Blair successfully pressed the Bush administration to delay the invasion and made an all-out push to win Security Council approval for the move against Iraq. Such approval was blocked by Russia and especially France, however, and in the end Britain, along with Australia and Poland, was one of a handful of countries to participate in the U.S. invasion.

At the height of combat operations, Britain had 46,000 troops in Iraq. The war became increasingly unpopular in Britain, especially once it became apparent that Saddam Hussein did not possess weapons of mass destruction and as the chaos in Iraq (and casualties to British soldiers and Iraqi civilians) mounted. During the more than five-year occupation of Iraq, the British army was responsible for the southern zone centered in Basra. Initially, there was a great deal of talk in Europe and elsewhere about the success of the British effort (compared to the perceived faltering U.S. efforts in more violence plagued areas such as Baghdad and Anbar province), supposedly based on peacekeeping and policing skills gained in Northern Ireland and the Balkans and the general European advantage over the United States in the exercise of "soft power." In the end, however, the British effort in southern Iraq was perceived as less than a success, as British forces failed to deal with mounting violence in their sector and withdrew to garrisons near the airport to avoid casualties and as reconstruction and development efforts, hindered by poor leadership and lack of resources, lagged behind those undertaken by U.S. forces in other parts of Iraq.

THE POST-BLAIR ERA

Labour managed to win the elections of May 2005, in part because of continued disarray in the Conservative opposition, but the rising discontent with the war and a public weariness with Blair after a decade in office contributed to his decision, in May 2007, to resign from office and to turn the reins of power over to Brown, a longtime Labour Party collaborator and sometime rival. A free market economist by inclination, Brown was known as being more skeptical than Blair about European integration, the euro in particular, and aspects of the transatlantic relationship.

For the most part, the new prime minister maintained continuity in British policy. In March 2008, Brown presented to Parliament Britain's first comprehensive national security strategy, "the first time the Government has published a single, overarching strategy bringing together the objectives and plans of all departments, agencies and forces involved in protecting our national security."[9] The document identified as security challenges terrorism, proliferation of nuclear weapons and other weapons of mass destruction, transnational organized crime, global instability and conflict and failed and fragile states, and civil emergencies and called for all agencies of the government to work together to meet the threats and risks arising from these challenges. The document strongly reaffirmed a British commitment to multilateralism and a rules-based international system but was evenhanded with regard to the relative priority to be accorded to the United Nations, the EU, and NATO in British policy.

As the global economic crisis that began in the United States in 2007 spread to Europe and the rest of the world, Brown, a former finance minister, seemed well placed to assert a leadership role in the global economic system. With U.S. influence limited by the lame-duck status of the Bush administration and the presidential election campaign (and by the fact that U.S. subprime mortgage lending and other excesses were seen around the world as the cause of the global economic meltdown), Brown seized the initiative and convened a summit of the G-20 countries to discuss anticrisis measures and reform of the international financial system. British regulators also proved quick and innovative in taking steps to calm the collapsing financial markets. But Brown's ability to play a leadership role soon foundered as the magnitude of Britain's own domestic economic problems became apparent, which in turn undermined Brown's domestic political standing and seemed to ensure that it was only a matter of time before Labour was voted out and the Conservatives returned to power.

Britain's ability to "punch above its weight," both globally and in the EU, in the past several decades has depended on strong political leadership (with Thatcher and Blair in particular known for their forceful personalities) and astute diplomacy as well as Britain's ability to project military power (unique in Europe) and the recognized strengths of its intelligence agencies. But Britain's influence also has rested on its relatively strong economic performance. In the period between 1996 and 2005, British GDP grew at an average annual rate of 2.8 percent, compared with 2.0 percent for the euro zone and a sluggish 1.4 percent for Germany (1.5 percent for Italy). Gone were the embarrassing days in the early 1980s when Italy seemed poised to overtake Britain as Europe's third-largest economy (after

Germany and France). Rather, the United Kingdom was gaining on France, making up ground that it had lost in the 1960s and 1970s. More than the continental countries, still highly dependent on traditional manufacturing industries, Britain was making a successful adjustment to a postindustrial economy based on finance, services, as well as some manufacturing. This was exemplified by a prosperous London, which vied with New York to be the financial capital of the world.

These relative gains suddenly appeared to be in danger in the crisis of 2007–2009. As elsewhere in Europe and around the world, economic growth turned sharply negative, and unemployment surged in Britain in 2008–2009. The distinctive feature of the British economic scene, however, was the collapse of public finances and the staggering public deficits that mounted under Brown. A combination of falling tax revenues, spending on bank rescues and other crisis-related measures, and other factors resulted in the British deficit rising to 12.4 percent of GDP in fiscal 2009, approximately double the level in the main continental countries.[10] High deficits were expected to persist for years to come and to lead to a large increase in public sector net debt. The dire financial outlook, combined with disarray in the Labour Party linked to unhappiness with Brown and a scandal involving parliamentary expense accounts, nearly led to the fall of the Labour government in June 2009.

The possibility that Brown might be forced to resign and call early elections was a matter of some importance for the EU and British–EU relations. The Conservatives, who were all but certain to win the elections, had pledged to hold a referendum on the pending Lisbon treaty, which most likely would have been rejected by the British voters, throwing the EU back to "square one" in the efforts to reform the EU's basic treaties that had been under way since the European Constitutional Convention of 2002–2003. In the end, the danger passed, as Brown survived and the Conservatives pledged not to reopen the question of Lisbon after their return to power if the treaty were approved by Parliament under the outgoing Labour government.

Brown's political difficulties did, however, once again highlight the enduring strength of British Euroskepticism, as the June 2009 elections to the European Parliament, in large part as a protest against the government, became a powerful expression of anti-EU sentiment. The British Independence Party, whose program called for the withdrawal of Britain from the EU, edged out Labour for second place in the elections, winning thirteen seats in the European Parliament. The British Nationalist Party, a racist, right-wing party likely to embarrass Britain in Strasbourg, also elected two members of the European Parliament, its first breakthrough to representation at the European level. Moreover, the Conservative Party, which won the highest number of seats, further accentuated its Euroskepticism by withdrawing, after twenty years, from the moderate Christian Democratic European People's Party grouping in the European Parliament and aligning instead with anti-EU parties from Poland and the Czech Republic.

The deteriorating financial situation also raised questions about whether Britain could maintain its expansive foreign policy and defense commitments—with the general consensus being that it could not. British foreign aid was likely to remain at a relatively high level (0.41 percent of GDP in 2008), but further large increases were unlikely. Questions arose about whether, for example, it might be necessary to shift spending from Africa to climate change, both of which were British foreign policy priorities in which the United Kingdom had sought to lead Europe and the world. The most difficult trade-offs were certain to be in the defense area. In 2008, Brown's first full year as prime minister, Britain had some 8,300 troops deployed with International Security Assistance Force in Afghanistan, 4,100 troops in Iraq, and smaller numbers of soldiers in the Balkans (Kosovo and Bosnia). In December 2008, the prime minister announced the phased withdrawal of British forces from Iraq, and in April 2009 Britain ended all combat operations in Iraq with the handover of the Basra area to U.S. forces.

By July 2009, British fatalities in Afghanistan reached 185, surpassing the losses sustained over six years in Iraq. Amid rising public concern about the level of casualties, Brown became embroiled in a public spat with the top general in the British army, who charged that funding for British troops was inadequate and questioned whether a shortage of helicopters was undermining the effectiveness of the British military effort and possibly contributing to the casualty rate. But Brown stood his ground and sided with the treasury rather than the army in refusing large increases in spending or the number of troops deployed. The government also deferred a decision on the modernization of Britain's strategic nuclear submarine—the Trident—until after the 2010 elections. Meanwhile, in what to some was an irritating reminder of the price that sometimes needed to be paid to play the European game, Britain continued to pour billions of pounds into the purchase of the European military transport plane, the A-400, which was four years late and vastly over budget, and the Typhoon Eurofighter, which some defense commentators saw as a project driven by industrial policy with limited military utility.[11]

RELATIONS WITH EUROPE

Tony Blair, a politician sometimes known in Britain for his good luck, dodged a bullet in 2005. While committed to the reform and streamlining of the EU, the British government viewed with some concern the vigorous constitution-building efforts under way in EU in the early 2000s. When the draft Constitutional Treaty was adopted in 2004, Blair was committed to putting what had come to be known as the "European Constitution" to a test with the British public through a referendum. It was widely thought that the referendum might fail in Britain, while it would be approved by the parliaments and, in those countries that also planned to hold referenda, by the electorates of the other member states.

While the failure to ratify by any one state was legally sufficient to block the entering into effect of the treaty, there was widespread talk in Europe of a two-speed Europe emerging from the constitution-adopting process. Led by France, Germany, and the other countries of the euro zone, a group of continental European countries would forge ahead to form a core Europe built around the euro, a common defense and foreign policy, and common immigration policies. Those few countries (e.g., Britain and Denmark) that failed to ratify might be consigned to an outer circle, participating in the single market and EU regulations but enjoying progressively less influence over the EU as a whole. This was a very negative scenario for the British and one that the Labour government long had tried to head off. Blair's positive moves on European defense, while motivated by genuine concern about defense issues, also were an attempt by Blair and his advisers to position Britain at the center of a key European policy area at a time when it was partly marginalized by its nonadoption of the euro. As it happened, the French and Dutch voters killed the Constitutional Treaty before the British electorate had its chance to vote, heading off the specter of marginalization in a two-speed Europe. The European Constitution was replaced by the scaled-down Lisbon treaty, which the British Parliament ratified without major difficulty.

Nonetheless, maintaining British influence in Europe is likely to be an ongoing concern to any government in London, as the more integration-minded states on the continent will continue to press ahead with projects about which the British are likely to remain more skeptical. Another issue over which Britain and some of its continental partners differ concerns Turkey and EU enlargement in general. Unlike France and Germany, Britain continues to support Turkey's EU candidacy, which was underscored by Queen Elizabeth's state visit to Turkey in May 2008 and the accompanying statements by the British foreign secretary that the French proposal for a Union of the Mediterranean could not be a substitute for full membership for Turkey.

Differences with other European states over the future of Europe will continue to draw attention to Britain's long-standing "special relationship" with the United States. The conventional wisdom—formed by EU-minded analysts, academics, and former policymakers in continental Europe, the United States, and indeed Britain itself—holds that going back to the 1950s, Britain had to choose between its close alliance with the United

States and wholeheartedly going into Europe, that it unfortunately allowed an Atlanticism at times bordering on subservience to block its choice for Europe, and that it was then forced repeatedly to opt for Europe—as in the decision by Macmillan in 1961 to apply to join the EC or in Blair's embrace of CFSP—belatedly and on worse terms than could have been had at earlier points. While containing elements of truth, this view is at best a caricature. It is not supported by a careful reading of the historical record and overlooks the extent to which Britain sought to avoid having to choose between the United States and Europe. Britain in fact at times resisted fairly brutal pressures from Washington to move closer to Europe. These pressures were strongest in the late 1950s and in the early 1960s, but they are a recurring theme in U.S. policy and in the U.S. policy debate over Europe.

Rooted as they are in the commonly voiced claim that Britain's holding back from Europe is a major factor standing in the way of the EU emerging as a powerful actor on the international scene that can serve as a U.S. "partner" and relieve Washington of its burdens around the world, these views are unlikely to disappear soon, either in the United States or in Europe. Such views also overlook the degree to which British policy toward the United States is not only (perhaps not even primarily) about the United States but also about Europe. A Europe in which NATO is marginalized and U.S. influence is reduced inevitably will be a Europe in which British influence also is reduced. Paris and Berlin inevitably would come to call the shots—on domestic as well as foreign and defense policy—in such a Europe. Far from any great love toward or subservience to the United States, the special relationship can be seen, like British openness to EU enlargement, as part of Britain's pursuit of a certain idea of Europe.

Along with the contested interpretation of the special relationship, several other issues are likely to complicate Britain's relations in and with Europe. One concerns the streamlining of international institutions. London supports efforts to make existing international institutions, "from the UN Security Council to the World Bank . . . more ambitious, effective and representative."[12] But it is not clear that Britain is prepared to move in the direction of consolidated EU representation in bodies such as the International Monetary Fund or the UN Security Council—as hoped for by the more integration-minded EU member states and that is seen elsewhere in the world as a possible long-term solution to the problem posed by Europe's strong overrepresentation in international institutions and the resulting underrepresentation of other parts of the world, Asia in particular. Like France, Britain has resisted any talk of consolidating the EU's representation on the Security Council into a single seat and has backed the bid by Germany (made in conjunction with Brazil, India, and Japan) for a permanent seat, a step that would move the EU further away from rather than in the direction of a single representation.[13]

Another long-term challenge concerns devolution. While the success of the EU and of European integration undoubtedly has created a context in which the Northern Ireland problem could be tackled, it also has created an environment in which many subnational entities—from the Catalans in Spain to the Slovaks in the former Czechoslovakia, to, at one time, the Northern Italians in "Padonia"—can aspire to operate as independent nation-states, bypassing historic national capitals to deal directly with Brussels, which increasingly is the locus of lawmaking and decision making in Europe for many issue areas. While the breakup of the United Kingdom is hardly imminent, the existence of a vocal Scottish Independence Party, well represented in the European Parliament in Strasbourg, will be another complicating factor for any British government as it seeks to forge a coherent Europe policy and maintain its influence within the EU.

CONCLUSIONS

Of the "three circles" identified by Churchill in the 1940s, the one that is likely to be most important for the future of British foreign policy concerns Europe. Here, as in the past, Britain faces a number of familiar dilemmas that it must address against the background of changing international and domestic circumstances. One dilemma concerns the old problem of trying to balance Britain's desire to have an active, global, and partially independent foreign and defense policy, befitting Britain's history as a great power and empire, with its increasingly stretched financial and human resources. The extent to which Britain can make up these deficits in and through Europe will be a key question.

A second challenge concerns the trade-off between loss of autonomy and loss of influence that comes from nonparticipation in aspects of the European integration project. Britain could increase its influence in Europe by, for example, adopting the euro, but this would result in the loss, both real and apparent, of a certain degree of policy autonomy. As long as the European integration project continues to move ahead, no matter how slowly, how to strike the right balance between influence and autonomy will be a question for British governments.

Finally, the relationship with the United States will be a key consideration, important both in its own right and as something that conditions how governments and publics in Europe and beyond view Britain as a partner.

With elections scheduled for no later than May 2010, these were all issues set to figure in the ongoing national debate stretching back to 1945 on Britain's role in the world—one that seemed all but certain to continue well into the twenty-first century.

SUGGESTIONS FOR FURTHER READING

George, Stephen. *An Awkward Partner: Britain in the European Community.* 3rd ed. New York: Oxford University Press, 1998.

Mannin, Michael. *British Government and Politics: Balancing Europeanization and Independence.* Lanham, MD: Rowman & Littlefield, 2010.

Thatcher, Margaret. *Downing Street Years.* New York: HarperCollins, 2003.

Williams, Paul. *British Foreign Policy under New Labour.* Basingstoke: Palgrave, 2006.

Young, Hugo. *This Blessed Plot: Britain and Europe from Churchill to Blair.* Woodstock, NY: Overlook Press, 1999.

10

Germany

Ascent to Middle Power

Helga A. Welsh

In the first few months of 2009, the global financial and economic crisis preoccupied most political analysts and the news, but as Germany entered yet another "super election year," other topics competed: European, local, regional, and national elections as well as the election of the federal president by a federal assembly. Defining moments in the history of postwar Germany were commemorated as well: sixty years ago, a new constitution was launched that today symbolizes the success of Germany's democracy. The twentieth anniversary of the opening of the Berlin Wall in November 1989 recalled the peaceful revolutions in East Germany and Central and Eastern Europe.

In other ways, 2009 was business as usual. The September 2009 elections ended the four-year coalition government between the two major political parties: the Christian Democratic Union/Christian Social Union (CDU/CSU) and the Social Democratic Party of Germany (SPD). The electoral campaign was fought over domestic, not foreign and security, concerns and widely regarded as lacking political passion. Continuity in foreign policy objectives prevails even after the inauguration of a new coalition government between the CDU/CSU and the liberal Free Democratic Party (FDP) one month later. Even the allocation of governmental positions was predictable. Since 1966, when the first grand coalition government was formed, the junior partner has filled the position of foreign minister rather than the party that has governed Germany longer than any other, the CDU, while the chancellor and defense minister positions are always in the hands of the party with the largest number of seats in the national parliament, the Bundestag. Following this coalition scenario, in the fall of 2009, Angela Merkel (CDU) remained as chancellor, and Karl-Theodor zu Guttenberg

(CSU) assumed the role of defense minister. Guido Westerwelle, chairman of the FDP, became vice chancellor and foreign minister.

To explain why Germany succumbed to Hitler's totalitarian rule in the interwar period, historians have frequently employed Germany's enigmatic historical development and compared it to other Western nations such as the United Kingdom and France. In 1945, Germans were called on to radically break with a past that had led to war, devastation, and genocide. The ensuing decades laid the groundwork for foreign and security policy to this day: multilateralism, emphasis on soft power, and pursuit of policy goals by civilian means. This political culture combines clear rejection of the past with commitment to the West based on the political and economic success of the western part of the country. The communist East had to declare political and economic bankruptcy in 1989, reinforcing tendencies to write German history as West Germany's history. Its foreign and security policy prevailed following unification of the two German states in October 1990.

Since 1990, global changes and the advancement of European integration from a Western club to now encompassing most of Eastern and Western Europe with a widening policy scope and greater international clout have profoundly influenced the conduct and goals of German foreign and security policy. No new vision or strategy has emerged, but significant adjustments to the time-proven and cherished principles of multilateralism, soft power, and civilian means have allowed Germany to claim a space among the major international players.

FROM DEFEAT TO THE FRONT LINE OF THE IRON CURTAIN

Germany's evolution from outcast to respected international partner and from division to union suggests a straight line, but this view obscures many significant domestic and international junctures. On May 7, 1945, Germany surrendered unconditionally; sovereignty was completely in the hands of the victorious Allies: the United States, the United Kingdom, the Soviet Union, and, later, France. They agreed to divide Germany into four zones of occupation; Berlin, the former capital of Germany, was carved up into four sectors. An Allied Control Council was set up as the military governing body, but its effectiveness was limited from the very beginning because of sharp ideological and policy differences among the victorious four powers. On the surface, they pursued identical goals of denazification, demilitarization, decentralization, and democratization in a defeated Germany, but the implementation and ultimate political outcomes differed substantially.

Allied Control Council negotiations between the Western powers and the Soviet Union broke down in 1947 and, combined with developments in Eastern and southern Europe, marked the beginning of the Cold War. Berlin, the former capital, was surrounded by territory occupied by the Soviet Union and later the German Democratic Republic (GDR), and West Berlin's vulnerability was dramatically exposed in 1948. In response to actions by the Western powers to merge their territories, Stalin imposed a blockade by closing all access routes to the western sectors of Berlin. Showing the resolve of the West, the United States supplied goods through the famous Berlin airlift. In May 1949, the Federal Republic of Germany was founded, uniting the western zones into one country; Bonn became the capital. In October, the Soviet Union and the communist government in the Soviet Zone of Occupation declared the creation of the GDR. What was seen as a provisional arrangement would prevail for four decades. Berlin remained a sore spot: it did not officially belong to either state, and the four Allied powers maintained troops along with special rights and responsibilities. It was the place where the Soviet Union, together with its East German comrades, tested the West's resolution.

Allied rights limited the sovereignty of both German states even after their foundation, yet they moved from pariah to partner more quickly than could have been expected. As pawns in the emergent superpower rivalry, they depended on the security interests of their major alliance partner—the Soviet Union for East Germany and the United States for West Germany. They were also indispensable as the literal front line in the East–West conflict, providing opportunities to regain international rights.

As the official successor state to the Third Reich, West Germany inherited profound liabilities. Its strategy to regain international respectability relied on clear demarcation from previous expansionist and militaristic policies and close cooperation with the United States, reconciliation with France, and support for European integration efforts. The Western allies now saw the Soviet Union rather than Germany as their major enemy. Skillfully gaining their trust, Chancellor Konrad Adenauer (CDU) began to integrate West Germany into Western alliance structures and closely cooperated with France. First steps were taken toward engaging Israel in a special relationship and paying reparations. Adenauer also held the position of foreign minister until 1955; he is at times called the father of (West) Germany, and his successors are often judged against his policy acumen and political style.

On the other side of the iron curtain, GDR leaders also saw themselves as part of a new Germany; their persecution under the Third Reich and the implementation of Soviet-style communism were adduced as evidence that they represented the "better Germans." The rest of the world was more skeptical; for many years, the GDR was shunned and lacked international legitimacy. Just how anxious their fellow communist neighbors in Central and Eastern Europe felt was not open to debate as official socialist solidarity took precedence under the umbrella of the Soviet Union.

A divided Germany seemed less threatening to its Western European neighbors. Many foreign observers shared the cynical sentiment famously expressed by French novelist François Mauriac; he "love[d] Germany dearly," leading him to "hope there will always be two of them."¹ By 1955, each state was integrated into its respective alliance and had regained most of its sovereignty. West Germany became one of the founding members of the European Coal and Steel Community (1952) and joined the North Atlantic Treaty Organization (NATO) in 1955; East Germany became a member of the Council for Mutual Economic Assistance in 1950 and joined the Warsaw Treaty Organization in 1955. Membership in these alliance structures functioned as a control mechanism but also allowed participation. NATO's goal was said to be keep Russia out, the United States in, and Germany down, but security from Germany also provided security for Germany.

To focus on such outcomes as integration into alliance structures, international respectability, and, in 1990, unification overlooks the debates that surrounded those developments. Within West Germany, integration into European organizations and remilitarization and membership in NATO aroused heated controversies. While all major political parties rallied around anticommunism and unification, their priorities differed. For Adenauer, integration with the West took priority over national unity; the path toward unification should contain communism and prove the superiority of the Western model. For the main opposition party, the SPD, national unity took precedence. It was suspicious of Adenauer's close alliance with the United States since it advocated a socialist model of development until a policy shift in 1959 (Godesberg program). In this climate, repeated offers by the Soviet Union to advance German–German relations proved both tempting and disruptive. Although the SPD and the CDU, in particular, fought bitter battles, West German neutrality or the adoption of a bridge function between East and West were never credible policy alternatives.

Reconciliation between Germany and France was central to European integration efforts after World War II. After three wars in less than a century, the future of Europe depended on cooperation between the two archenemies. The vision of reconciliation articulated by Robert Schuman, Jean Monnet, and, after some hesitation, Charles de Gaulle on the French side and Adenauer on the German side paid off: out of necessity, the two countries started to share power in Europe, and a war between them has long been unthinkable. Now linked not only by high politics but also by a network of grassroots cooperation across the border, they are also each other's most important trade partners. Their efforts to promote European integration united them even when their ultimate objectives differed. French interest was driven by its desire to control Germany and to usurp the leading position in Europe, which was to become an extension of French power. For Germany, reconciliation with France was the admission ticket into the international community and depended on support for European integration. Early European integration efforts also balanced the interests of a largely agricultural France with those of a more industrialized Germany.

The Franco–German alliance that emerged from this arrangement revealed different visions for Europe. Under de Gaulle's leadership, a Europe of the fatherlands prevailed; that is, national power should not be constrained. In addition, France should lead, and the influence of the United States in Europe should be curtailed. In contrast, German leaders advocated a federated Europe, the transfer of power to supranational organizations, and close relations with the United States. De Gaulle's aspirations divided the German political elite, in particular the ruling CDU/CSU, into Gaullists and Atlanticists, a division that is occasionally still felt today. For Adenauer, close cooperation with France was insurance against possible tides in U.S. foreign policy. For those who favored the United States, such as Ludwig Erhard (CDU), the father of the social market economy, French economic policy was too protectionist and its foreign policy too nationalist. They felt that the United States provided security guarantees that no other power could provide. In reality, policy choices were restricted, and differences were more a matter of emphasis: successive German governments have supported a delicate balance between Paris and Washington that holds today. The Elysée Treaty, ratified in 1963, was the symbolic cornerstone of reconciliation between Germany and France, but its preamble reinforced Germany's close cooperation with the United States.

Against the backdrop of Soviet influence in the eastern part of the country, U.S. influence in the West was perceived as benevolent. Its armed forces provided a security shield that allowed focus on economic recovery, and, although contested, Americanization brought modernization to West Germany and much of Western Europe. The admission of the Federal Armed Forces (*Bundeswehr*) into NATO in 1955 ended an acrimonious debate within and outside of Germany. In an effort to deflect the rejection by the French National Assembly of a European Defense Community that included Germany, the Paris Agreements (1954) officially restored the sovereignty of West Germany, recognized it as the only legitimate representative of Germany, and invited it to join the Western European Union and NATO. The Federal Republic had become crucial to deterring the immediate threat of communism; Americans, who had no experience of German invasion on U.S. soil, found Germany's rearmament easier to accept than did its European neighbors, but the past threw alarming shadows, and there were caveats. Germany could not pursue atomic, biological, or chemical weapons, and its armed forces could not exceed 500,000 soldiers, who would be fully integrated into NATO. Unification could be pursued only by peaceful means, and the former occupying powers retained their rights to station troops in Berlin. These external limitations would later be self-imposed.

Within West Germany, resistance against remilitarization was fierce; pacifists, trade unionists, Christians, intellectuals, and Social Democrats united under slogans such as "count me out." An active and varied peace movement prevailed until the end of the Cold War. On various occasions, hundreds of thousands of West Germans joined in peace marches and signed resolutions against nuclear weapons and the arms race. Protests peaked following the NATO double-track decision of December 1979, which envisioned deployment of additional nuclear weapons on West German territory in response to the Warsaw Pact's deployment of new SS-20 rockets.

The Soviet Union exploited lingering fears among Central and Eastern European neighbors to oppose West German rearmament by forming its own military alliance, the Warsaw Treaty Organization, with East Germany as a member. East–West relations deteriorated throughout the 1950s. In 1953, demonstrations in East Germany and, three years later, in Hungary were brutally suppressed by Soviet troops. In 1968, reform efforts were crushed by Warsaw Pact military intervention in Prague; the principle of socialist solidarity was reinforced by the so-called Brezhnev doctrine.

In Germany, the wounds of the country's division into two separate states were fresh and open, and families were divided; daily, hundreds of people fled across the border from East to West. From the very beginning in 1949, West Germany viewed East Germany as illegitimate since communism was ruthlessly imposed on its people; the state was not meant to exist. For West German politicians, relations between the two states were not deemed *foreign* but of special inner-German character. They were also largely limited to trade relations; high politics among the major representatives of the two German states did not take place. West Germany also reinforced its claim for sole representation of all Germans with concrete actions; should a country recognize the GDR as a sovereign state, West Germany terminated relations. As the dominant partner—in terms of population and economic and political influence—for years it successfully limited the international role of East Germany to fellow socialist countries. However, enforcing this policy became increasingly difficult as time went on.

The building of the Berlin Wall in August 1961 ushered in an ice age in relations between East and West with high humanitarian costs as it rendered the border impermeable. Pressure mounted to improve relations with the communist neighbors in the East. Realizing that progress toward improving inner-German relations required Soviet approval, shortly after its inauguration in the fall of 1969, a coalition government between the SPD and the FDP launched policy initiatives to improve relations with the Soviet Union, Poland, Czechoslovakia, and the GDR. For his efforts, Chancellor Willy Brandt (SPD) was awarded the Nobel Peace Prize in December 1971. At home, the so-called new *Ost- und Deutschlandpolitik* led to heated controversies since it required the de facto recognition of East Germany under the construct "two states in one nation." It also raised suspicions among alliance partners that West Germany might turn eastward. In 1972, the defection of members of parliament from the governing coalition allowed a first-ever vote of no confidence against a sitting chancellor in the *Bundestag*. When the vote narrowly failed, the CDU/CSU opposition questioned the constitutionality of the Basic Treaty between East and West Germany in the Federal Constitutional Court. The treaty passed this hurdle, and, once ratified, relations between the two German states expanded but remained strained. In 1973, the GDR was finally recognized on the international stage, and the two German states took seats in the United Nations. West German reconciliation with communist Eastern Europe and the Soviet Union had commenced but its closure had to wait until the 1990s.

Unification occurred with little advance warning. The German sociologist Wolf Lepenies referred to the collapse of communism in East Germany and subsequent unification as unprecedented: "How could they happen? How did they happen?"[2] Chancellor Kohl (CDU) has been credited with using a window of opportunity that opened in 1990 to advance unification of the two German states. It rested on the allied partners' approval, and the Soviet Union, France, and the United Kingdom expressed reservations. Only the U.S. government brought unconditional approval to the negotiating table. It took the lead in the "Two-Plus-Four" talks between representatives of both German states and the four allied partners. Soviet concerns about a unified Germany's entry into NATO and the withdrawal of Soviet troops were mollified by legal assurances and financial assistance.[3] After some hesitation, Kohl agreed to officially recognize the existing German–Polish border, allaying Polish fears about a revision. The negotiations ended successfully, but they revealed considerable apprehension about Germany's future role in Europe from opposing ends: would German leaders aspire to dominate Europe, or would they abandon their commitment to European integration?

The fall of the Berlin Wall in November 1989 signified the end of the Cold War. Questions of territoriality and sovereignty were resolved with the signing of the Two-Plus-Four Treaty. Germany was now surrounded by friendly states, and traditional security concerns receded. The defined bipolar Cold War order had come to an end. But what would take its place and what role Germany would play in the years to come was unclear.

THE END OF THE COLD WAR AND THE QUESTION OF POWER

There is wide agreement that the end of the Cold War substantially changed Germany's political environment but less on whether and to what extent policies adequately reflect those changes and what the consequences have been for its role in the world. According to some observers, German foreign policy has been marked by a continuity in goals and methods that survives unification and big changes in the international environment and still falls short in a realist framework that accentuates national interests and autonomy. Others see a gradual shift to a more assertive foreign policy with neorealist overtones but wonder how it can still fall short in sharing the military burden in trouble spots around the world. Both of these camps are divided over the sources of change and continuity and the extent of change. Ironically, both continuity and change have been widely debated.

The pillars on which German foreign policy rests—multilateralism, soft power, and civilian power—are not static but frameworks that must be filled by meaning and actions and adjusted to a changing international environment. Multilateralism refers to a policy of "never alone" in the pursuit of foreign and security policy goals. Major decisions are made in concert with other international players. The active incorporation of international organizations and alliances, important in all political pursuits, becomes indispensable in military actions.

The concept of soft power refers to persuasion rather than coercion. It is attractive to others because it uses diplomacy, compromise, and incentives to achieve desired goals. Similarly, civilian powers use politics before force and emphasize that foreign and security policy should be part of a civilized discourse that fosters democracy, human rights, and the rule of law. Historian James Sheenan defines them as states with the ability but no interest in waging war.[4] The devastating experience of warfare in the first half of the twentieth century influenced the transformation of Western European states into civilian states although underwritten by the security guaranteed by the United States, which also allowed them to sidestep major military allocations and to focus on economic integration in the European Community.

The overlapping concepts of civilian power, soft power, and multilateralism aspire to the ideal; instances arise in which states do not fully comply with them. They are not limited to one country or organization; for example, the Common Foreign and Security Policy (CFSP) of the European Union (EU) also highlight them. Further, civilian powers that uphold soft power and multilateralism do not necessarily practice unqualified pacifism, refraining from all military force or engagement, or apply these values for exclusively altruistic motives. National interest can be pursued via channels that differ from traditional policy positions that associate power with force. The political shift from hard to soft power after World War II paved the way for Germany's reentry into the civilized world and international respectability.

Germany is nonetheless different from rival powers in Europe, such as France and the United Kingdom. The concepts of multilateralism, soft power, and civilian power have a centrality in policymaking and discourse that is specific and unparalleled due to the darkest chapter in its history: the Third Reich. Political rhetoric is infused with this legacy and the resulting moral obligations. In 1945, the chance of becoming a *normal* power seemed remote if not impossible. Jürgen Habermas refers to a crucial "dialectic of normalization": if Germans want to consider themselves normal, they must be aware of just how different their history has been.[5] Clear and lasting demarcation from the Hitler regime and the nationalistic and authoritarian traditions that allowed his rise to power became sine qua non. Since the actions of the Third Reich discredited the military, renunciation of militaristic attitudes was a major goal of successful reeducation efforts after World War II. Political socialization emphasized peaceful conflict resolution and the benefits of international cooperation and reconciliation. Reestablishment of patriotism and national pride as legitimate forms of political allegiance took time, further confused by the division into two separate states. The massive buildup of soldiers and weapons on German territory during the Cold War deliberately discouraged military force; fear of an outbreak of war between East and West infiltrated policymaking. The policy of "never again" to engage in war is now rooted in German consciousness and explains its strategic culture of restraint in military matters.

Germany is also a particularly effective proponent of soft power backed up by hard power, in particular, economic influence. It is a trade superpower and often designated the world export champion. Its economy is by far the largest in Europe and the fourth largest in the world. Alone, it counts for one-fifth of the gross domestic product of the EU. Foreign policy remains heavily influenced by economic and export imperatives. As the most important economic power in Europe, Germany and its performance are exposed to particular international scrutiny. When its economy sputters, Europe as a whole is affected.

Today, most analysts consider Germany a reliable and respected partner, and such negative aspects as economic and financial problems may actually make it more normal. Even the Holocaust has been Europeanized, although the memory of it still holds a special place in German discourse and policymaking. Beverly Crawford points out that *normalization* can be used as code word when Germany puts national interests first and acts against alliance partners.[6] Tensions remain between Germany's role as a normal country and its unique combination of soft power reinforced by hard power.

Nonetheless, the role that Germany is expected to play in the international arena is contingent on its power potential. Unification and the end of the Cold War have ended some constraints, but to what extent have they enhanced its relative power? Some observers emphasize its resources in terms of population, central location in Europe, sovereignty, economic power, and world standing. Others point to the twin strains of German unification and globalization; despite the resulting increase in size and population, its cherished systems of welfare, economy, and education, to name a few, have been under stress.

Such changes as greater assertiveness, attention to national interests, or involvement in military operations can be viewed as variants of the same policy principles updated for a new international environment; they result from adaptation pressures and reveal pragmatism and incremental change. They may signal that Germany is finally becoming a normal country whose actions resemble those of its neighbors, but nuances matter, and its international role is scrutinized from different perspectives: some want it to be more involved, while others still need reassurance of its modesty. Designations vary accordingly: it has been called a great power, a major power, a regional hegemon, a middle power, a European power, an uncertain or precarious power, a reluctant power, and a quiet power.

The German discourse is revealing. Only in recent years has the concept of power reentered the political vocabulary, replacing *Machtvergessenheit* (forgetting about power). Power cannot be strictly measured; it is a relative term that must take into account verifiable indicators, such as economic and military clout, as well as the willingness to use it and other people's perceptions of it. How German policymakers and citizens perceive their role in the world and how their power should be used are significant. According to a 2009 survey of German foreign policy experts, 81 percent of respondents either fully or partially agreed that Germany is a middle-level power, and more than 70 percent agreed that it plays a leading role in the EU. Only about a third thought it a leading power (*Führungsmacht*).[7] The questions carefully avoided any reference to Germany as a great power. A middle power has recognized influence beyond its region. It relies heavily on diplomacy and multilateral solutions to international problems, with Germany as a case in point. The respondents to the elite study seem to agree: 95 percent considered membership in the EU very important, and around 90 percent considered membership in NATO, the United Nations, the G-8, and the World Trade Organization very important or important.

Implicit in discussions about continuity are perceptions of identity and role; in particular, if soft power is one major tool of influence, reputation in the international community matters. In the past, the German economic system, which powered economic recovery and provided a high standard of living, was a model. Globalization and the challenges of unification have shown the limits of the social market economy, although in discrediting pure neoliberal economic polices, the current economic crisis may justify a new "third way." The success of certain aspects of its political system—for example, the mixed electoral system—has been transferred to other regions of the world.

The discourses of continuity and change affect four major foreign policy areas: Germany's involvement in the EU, its security strategy, its transatlantic partnership, and its relations with Russia. In contrast to its influence within Europe, its global influence in bilateral relations remains biased in favor of its role as a trade power, but it has stepped up its role as a multilateral player in the United Nations, the World Bank, the International Monetary Fund, and the World Trade Organization.

MULTILATERALISM AT WORK: GERMANY AND THE EUROPEAN UNION

After unification, fears about Germany's future role in Europe were at opposite extremes: would its leaders retreat from the EU to pursue national interests and to exploit its location and historical ties with Central and Eastern Europe, or would they try to shape Europe? Kohl went to great pains to reassure the world that the commitment to European integration would be firm. In his words, German unification and European integration were sides of the same coin, intimately linked, and German politicians have not contemplated a change in policy: European integration is central to an understanding of Germany's foreign policy. It has special status, as evidenced by the fact that the German constitution mandates the transfer of sovereign powers to intergovernmental institutions, including a mutual collective security system and the EU.

The strategy of multilateralism, particularly integration into the EU, has worked well for Germany. It facilitated rehabilitation on the international scene and reconciliation with its neighbors. While the political rewards were always tangible, Germany's export-driven economy benefited from economic integration from the outset. Germany may pay more into the EU budget than it receives, but in 2008, 64 percent of exports went to EU members and 72 percent of imports came from them. Most political elites in Germany acknowledge the symbolic and real benefits of European integration. The major parties, the CDU/CSU and the SPD, agree widely on EU policy, differing mostly in their stance toward Turkey's potential membership in the EU. The conservative party favors a "privileged relationship," while the Social Democrats are in favor of full membership. Only those on the ideological fringes, left and right, are openly Euroskeptic; parties to the extreme right express outright hostility, but their electoral success has always been limited, and they do not enjoy representation in the national parliament, the *Bundestag*. All chancellors have made Europe central to their leadership, albeit with variations. Both Adenauer and Kohl fostered close relationships with their French counterparts, Charles de Gaulle and François Mitterrand, respectively. In his memoir, former chancellor Helmut

Schmidt (SPD) refers to French president Valéry Giscard D'Estaing as a close friend and reminds readers that the entwined historical experiences of their countries were vital to their commitment to European integration. In the 1970s, the close cooperation between Schmidt and D'Estaing led to the European Monetary System, which paved the way to the European Economic and Monetary Union (EMU) and direct elections to the European Parliament.

The 1998 elections brought generational change to parliament and government and—a first—a coalition between the SPD and Alliance 90/The Greens. Politicians who had not experienced World War II were at the helm. History had bestowed and political socialization reinforced commitment to Europe. It was promoted with vigor by rebel–turned–foreign minister Joschka Fischer (Alliance 90/The Greens) and backed by Chancellor Gerhard Schröder (SPD), who made headlines with his more assertive policy style. Merkel, raised in communist East Germany, has internalized responsibility toward Europe in equal measure. Her commitment to European integration and leadership of the EU in the spring of 2007 were recognized in 2008, when she received the prestigious Charlemagne Prize (*Karlspreis*), joining an illustrious group of European leaders from Jean Monnet to Valéry Giscard D'Estaing and, only once, in 2002, an idea—the euro.

Continuity does not imply that relations with and attitudes toward the EU have remained static. It is a quite different organization today than it was in 1990. It encompasses twenty-seven member states, and its leadership has become increasingly complex. Its wide-ranging areas of activity far exceed the initial goals of economic and monetary union. While membership always touched daily life, the common currency, ease of travel, and student programs that foster educational mobility, to name just a few areas, have transformed it. Now, through its CFSP and Common Security and Defense Policy (CSDP), the EU has entered the realm of international politics. The goals and strategies associated with these policies strongly mirror German discursive influences by emphasizing civilian and soft power. They also allow Germany to engage in military operations apart from NATO. The effectiveness of the CFSF/CSDP is often questioned. But despite its shortcomings, the new international position of Europe has enhanced rather than limited Germany's room to maneuver.

Yet the transfer of new powers to the EU has also raised concerns within Germany about the continued erosion of national sovereignty. The debate culminated during the ratification of the Treaty of Lisbon, which resurrected important elements of the ill-fated Constitutional Treaty. After its ratification in the German parliament, lawmakers and politicians on the left and right challenged its constitutionality on several counts, with some pointing to the loss of power for national parliaments and courts and others challenging the democratic legitimacy of the EU. In a much-anticipated ruling, in June 2009 the Constitutional Court affirmed the treaty's compliance with the Basic Law but demanded greater participatory powers for the national legislative bodies, the *Bundestag* and the *Bundesrat*, in European affairs.

National parliamentary elections were less than three months away, and the government wanted to resolve the matter speedily before election day; on the international stage, the ratification by all twenty-seven member states should not be held up any longer by Germany, which, after all, had been one of the main architects of the treaty. Thus, domestic and international pressure ensured the speedy passage of new legislation in September 2009. Several new laws spell out the revised role of the two houses of parliament in relation to the EU and augmented obligations by the German government to inform members of parliament about ongoing European projects. The court's ruling was widely interpreted as setting tighter limits on European integration. Not surprisingly, Euroskeptics hailed it a success for their cause, whereas advocates of European integration lamented the tone of the judgment, which, they claimed, was reminiscent of nationalist rhetoric thought to have been condemned to the dustbin of history.

The Franco–German relationship is still at the core of European integration efforts but undergoes highs and lows. Germany is no longer the junior partner but has equal status. Any major EU decision requires compromise between the two and their willingness to work jointly to build consensus among the members. Two cases in point: when Germany held the Council presidency in the spring of 2007, French president Nicolas Sarkozy actively promoted the German agenda for the Treaty of Lisbon among reluctant EU members. When France led the EU in the fall of 2008, Sarkozy and Merkel helped broker a cease-fire in the military conflict between Russia and Georgia.

Germany's global interests and interactions are limited but expanding, not least because of the opportunities that the EU provides. In alignment with its preference for multilateral actions, German leaders aspire to broker mediations honestly and to build coalitions. They notably did so in negotiations to bring the Central and Eastern European countries into the EU and NATO. German politicians played an important role in keeping Russia involved in the wars in the former Yugoslavia in the 1990s; Germany's leadership role was also crucial in developing the Stability Pact for Southeast Europe, which combined economic and political incentives to advance peace in the war-torn region. The force is multiplied when Germany acts as part of the E-3 with the United Kingdom and France, as in its involvement in the Middle East Quartet (the United States, Russia, the United Nations, and the EU) and nonproliferation talks with Iran. However, as Hanns W. Maull shows, Germany's overall record in coalition building is mixed; while it has regained its willingness to act as broker, the political environment has become more difficult and less predictable, not the least because the EU itself now has to accommodate twenty-seven voices.[8]

For some, Germany's international actions reflect its new power and make it a regional hegemon; they emphasize the "uploading" of German preferences to the EU but also its willingness to shoulder a "disproportionate share of the regional burden of institutional cooperation."[9] Others emphasize the give-and-take in European integration; while Germany is a major power in Europe, the two-way process of Europeanization is both enabling and constraining. Policy actors can "upload" their preferences to the EU level, but they also have to "download" common policies that may force national adaptations. Europeanization is never a zero-sum game. All too often, German power is tied to its economic performance. If it is strong, the argument runs, it enhances power; if it shows signs of weakness, German power declines. This reliance on economic performance reveals vulnerability and asymmetry in the concept of German power.

Germany's embeddedness in European institutions allows it to take leadership roles that are not perceived as threatening or too threatening. Over time, the process of reconciliation has advanced much farther with Western European countries than with its Eastern neighbors. The reconciliation with France may serve as a benchmark, but for Central European nations, such as Poland, an equal measure of trust and cooperation has not been established. A lingering unease explains a tendency to overdraw conclusions from singular events. For example, during the economic crisis in the spring of 2009, the media in Paris and Brussels nicknamed Merkel Madame Non when she blocked EU stimulus packages to Eastern Europe. Immediately, pundits asked whether Germany would abandon its supportive role of Central and Eastern Europe.

The German political landscape has also changed. The public is more reserved in its attitude toward the EU than the elites, but, in survey after survey, a majority of respondents attests that membership has been good for the country, and Germans are proud to be European. As for all member states, support for the EU increases with higher levels of education; younger people are more supportive than people over age sixty. Germans strongly support a greater role for the EU in environmental and energy concerns and the fight against terrorism. They favor progress in developing a common foreign policy and common defense and security policy (79 and 82 percent, respectively) but strongly oppose, with citizens in France, Austria, and Luxembourg, the recent EU enlargements, which they feel have weakened the organization. Paradoxically, German politicians were particularly instrumental in advancing EU enlargement, while their public was skeptical at best and disapproving at worst. A similar picture emerged a decade ago when Germans criticized adoption of a common European currency.[10]

These examples demonstrate that elite-driven European integration represents a challenge to its leaders and that they have not been entirely successful in framing the discourse to reflect the benefits of certain actions. For example, Germany's strategy to promote incorporation of its Central and Eastern European neighbors into the EU and NATO has helped to put those countries at greater ease without completely erasing mistrust toward Germany. The euro made German unification more palatable to other members of the EU, in particular, France; however grudgingly, Germans now seem to have accepted the potential benefits of EMU, but the 2010 Greek debt crisis rekindled the skeptical attitude. The lack of interest in and knowledge of the EU in Germany and elsewhere becomes more critical when the stakes are higher and latent anti-EU sentiments more pronounced. Voter turnout in elections to the European Parliament has been declining from 62.3 percent in 1989 to 43 percent in 2004. On the eve of the June 2009 elections to the European Parliament, almost 70 percent proclaimed indifference; in the end, 43.3 percent went to the polls. The peace and economic benefits resulting from European integration are now taken for granted, but additional forms of legitimization must emphasize a Europe "from below."

A REWORKED CIVILIAN POWER: FROM DOMESTIC TO INTERNATIONAL SECURITY

A culture of restraint in military matters has infiltrated the attitudes and values of German elites and citizens, and life on the front line of the Cold War left its imprint. In the 1980s, approximately 340,000 Soviet soldiers were stationed in East Germany; in the western part, more than 400,000 foreign soldiers, of whom about 245,000 belonged to the U.S. armed forces, did their duty. Today, no foreign troops are stationed on the territory that used to be the GDR, and in the west, only about 100,000 foreign soldiers, all part of NATO, remain. The U.S. contingent has been reduced to roughly 64,000.

The capability gap between European and U.S. forces is real, but the German army is not inconsiderable. It is an established part of NATO and EU forces and, despite budget cuts, ranks among the top ten defense spenders in the world. Down from an enrollment of 495,000 at the height of the Cold War, the Two-Plus-Four Treaty that paved the way to unification limited the German army to 370,000 soldiers; in 2009, the size of the armed forces stood at 256,500. The changing security environment and new demands have sparked modernization of the German military. Against consistent budgetary restraint, it has been restructured to emphasize expeditionary forces. Organized as response, stabilization, and support forces, these forces are geared almost solely toward deployment abroad and incorporation into multilateral units. For example, the response forces consist of 35,000 soldiers, with 18,000 earmarked to the EU Rapid Reaction Force and 15,000 to the NATO Rapid Response Force.

Germany still conscripts its army, but the voices advocating a professional army, like those of other major NATO partners, such as the United States, France, and the United Kingdom, are becoming louder. Conscription has a long history and is vital to the concept of "citizens in uniform," who are said to put a brake on military interventionism and to integrate with society at large. Others point to the changed role of the Federal Armed Forces from the domestic to the international theater of operations in arguing for specialized, professional troops and note that, at this time, only a relatively small proportion of young men are recruited. Indeed, the term *conscription* is increasingly a misnomer. In April 2009, slightly fewer than 44,000 of the approximately 256,000 total were conscripts serving the prescribed nine-month military duty. Twice as many young men serve in kindergartens, hospitals, assisted living for the elderly, or the developing world than in the army, exercising their right to conscientious objection on religious, moral, or ethical grounds. While conscription is limited to men, since 2001, women can serve in all functions in the professional military.

The wars in Bosnia-Herzegovina and Kosovo in the 1990s catalyzed the emergence of the ESDP by glaringly revealing the divisions in and military powerlessness of the EU and its reliance on the United States. Development of a new German security policy that had started with the first Gulf War took off. Financial assistance for international military efforts was no longer sufficient. International pressure mounted for more involvement, and, in retrospect, the step-by-step approach aimed to demonstrate international solidarity, albeit always in noncombat roles, for example, in Somalia and Cambodia.

Two moments in the evolution from humanitarian to military engagement stand out. First, the 1994 ruling of the Federal Constitutional Court settled the hitherto unresolved question of whether the German constitution allows military operations outside the NATO area. The court ruled in favor but with conditions: approval from the Federal Parliament and a clear international mandate from the United Nations, limited in time and part of multilateral involvement are essential. The second moment permeated important psychological barriers. It started with the massacre in Srebenica (Bosnia and Herzegovina) in the summer of 1995 and ended with the Kosovo War in 1999. Although a clear UN Security Council mandate was missing, German forces took part in combat missions against Serbia. It took a reframing of the discourse and the unlikely intervention of a coalition government that united the SPD with the pacifist Greens. In particular, Foreign Minister Fischer (Alliance 90/The Greens) successfully linked the concept of "never again" (Auschwitz) with the ethnic cleansing massacres in Kosovo against fierce resistance in the ranks of the Green Party. In a dramatic improvised speech at the May 1999 Party Congress of his party, Alliance 90/The Greens, in Bielefeld, he refused to be silenced and challenged his party's view of pacifism: "A prerequisite for peace is that people are not murdered, people are not expelled, women are not raped. That is a prerequisite for peace!"[11]

Since 1990, Germany has been involved in more than forty multilateral operations around the world. More than 160,000 soldiers have served, but the exact number stationed in trouble spots remains small. Currently deployed on three continents, the largest contingents are in Afghanistan (about 4,300 with an upper limit of 4,500) and Kosovo (2,000) as of December 2009. Military operations include antipiracy duties in the sea off Somalia, securing the Lebanese coastline to prevent arms smuggling, monitoring the development of security structures in Kosovo, and combating international terrorism. The policy of civilian power has evolved from no engagement to limited humanitarian engagement to limited military operations, demonstrating that historical memory can be applied to a range of policy options: "military engagement to avoid genocide (Kosovo), military involvement on the side of the United States on the grounds of loyalty and the avoidance of a German *Sonderweg* (Afghanistan) as well as a rejection of military support for a pre-emptive strike and regime change (Iraq)."[12] Germany's military engagement has evolved "almost with the speed of light," claims former U.S. ambassador to Germany John Kornblum. "The trouble is," he says, "the world is changing faster."[13]

A strong preference for nonmilitary options and budgetary constraints curtail international military involvement. The military is an established and respected institution in Germany with a low public profile; President Horst Köhler aptly described the relationship between the German public and its military as "friendly indifference." The public is very reluctant to send German troops overseas and tolerates it only in pursuit of democratic and humanitarian goals, envisioning soldiers as "development aid workers who do good works for the people, but do not harm or get harmed."[14] Discourse has been reshaped to emphasize a comprehensive security approach that combines civilian and military instruments. Diplomatic efforts, development assistance, and humanitarian and social measures have to be part of conflict prevention and management. These sentiments keep budgetary outlays under tight control and armed forces capabilities stretched to their limits.

FROM DEPENDENCY TO PARTNER IN LEADERSHIP?

Germany is firmly committed to a policy of multilateralism based on strong bilateral relations. Two countries form a policy triangle with Germany: France and the United States. With the end of the Cold War, the United States was no longer needed as Germany's special protector, crucial to its defense, but, at the same time, Europe as a whole lost some of its eminence in U.S. foreign policy. Balancing relations with its main alliance partners has become more complicated for Germany, as Europe has assumed a more prominent role and support for the United States has become more conditional.

German attitudes toward the United States often waver between solidarity and criticism but reached a low point during the first administration of President George W. Bush. While in the aftermath of the terrorist bombing of the World Trade Center in New York City on September 11, 2001, Chancellor Gerhard Schröder ensured Germany's "unconditional solidarity" with the United States and secured German troop involvement in Afghanistan, the impending U.S. war in Iraq soured relations quickly. Together with France and Russia, Germany tried to forge an international alliance against the U.S. invasion and occupation. Blunt antiwar rhetoric in a successful appeal to his constituents during the election campaign of 2002 drew the ire of the U.S. administration. Relations between the United States and Germany entered a crisis, and President Bush refused to talk to Schröder for several months.

Damage control started almost immediately, and the new grand coalition government under Merkel that came to power in 2005 stepped them up. The Bush administration reciprocated, signaling its willingness to return to a better relationship. The transatlantic crisis over the Iraq War was laid to rest, but the election of President Barack Obama has nurtured hopes for a reinvigorated alliance. More than 200,000 people gathered in Berlin in the summer of 2008 to hear then–presidential candidate Obama deliver a speech in which he asked Europe and the United States to join in confronting global challenges. His campaign was followed with intense interest and extensive media coverage. Germany experienced its own Obamamania. The outcome of the 2008 presidential election was greeted with undisguised hope and joy; according to surveys, between 70 and 80 percent of Germans would have voted for the Democratic candidate. During the Bush presidency, favorable opinion of the United States in Germany declined from 78 to 31 percent; 86 percent had little or no confidence in his leadership. After Barack Obama took power, the image of the United States improved markedly: by mid-2009, favorable opinion of the United States reached 64 percent, and more than 90 percent of those surveyed professed confidence in his leadership.[15] These numbers indicate broad consensus across party lines.

Obama's first trip to Europe in spring 2009 raised high expectations, and he was credited with restoring trust in U.S. leadership. His administration has been praised for changes in policies—for example, signing an order to close the Guantanamo Bay detention camp at a U.S. naval base in Cuba, where the Bush administration had authorized indefinite imprisonment of any noncitizen believed to be involved in international terrorism without trial or the protections of the Geneva conventions—and its willingness to listen and learn before taking action. Caution remains: a United States open to dialogue with other international powers also demands more burden sharing, particularly in Afghanistan. Obama's 2009 call on NATO partners to step up their troop commitments met a skeptical audience in Germany. Chancellor Angela Merkel is under pressure to support the United States and NATO, yet her government increasingly has difficulty convincing a reluctant public that German security interests are at stake in Afghanistan.

While policy style and personal relationships are important, recent ruptures in U.S.–German relations have left lasting legacies. On the one hand, they confirmed that the dense political, economic, and civic networks between the two countries can not only withstand a crisis but also remediate it to develop a more productive footing. Transatlantic economic relations, for example, are deep and wide. The United States is Germany's most important trading partner after France. Much of the trade is intrafirm, that is, between parent companies and affiliates on either side of the Atlantic, indicating the high level of direct foreign investment. Tourism and exchanges in business, education, and research have fostered a societal infrastructure that is independent of political ties. On the other hand, Europe and Germany have changed; the unilateralism of the Bush administration fostered greater European resolve and the importance of the CFSP. German leaders have shown that they no longer automatically say yes to U.S. actions.

Challenges became visible sooner than expected when the global economic and financial crisis hit in 2008–2009. While German and U.S. politicians agreed on the need to mend ailing systems, they disagreed on the role of government spending and regulation of agencies, among other things. Not surprisingly, those responses were conditioned by national economic and political cultures and experiences. In economic and financial matters, Germany places utmost importance on security, stability, and the avoidance of potentially inflationary pressures. The German government explained its actions, dubbed slow and uncooperative by U.S. media, by noting that the German stimulus package rivaled others in percentage of gross domestic product spent (4.7 percent for 2009 and 2010). Its fiscal restraint can be explained by other factors. The real estate market did not collapse—almost half of home owners have paid off their mortgages—nor were Germans burdened by huge credit card debts. Bank savings are guaranteed by the federal government, and a wide social safety net is in place. Germany felt the brunt of the economic recession in late 2008 and early 2009, when its export-oriented industries were hard hit by the worldwide decline in demand, but its economy rebounded earlier than expected. At the end of 2009, cautionary appeals about continued challenges mingled with optimism, spurred by predictions about positive economic growth rates in 2010.

At the time of unification, President George H. W. Bush invited Germany to become a partner in leadership. Since then, the relationship with the United States has evolved in unanticipated ways. German leaders were slow to respond to the new international environment; they were also preoccupied with the challenges of unification. Since then, Germany has drawn closer to Europe. Conflicts around the world have revealed the differences in European and U.S. strategic cultures and global aspirations. While the wounds from disagreements about Iraq have healed, scars remain, and the balance of power between the United States and Germany is still asymmetrical. Germany has taken steps toward greater leadership, its engagement is growing gradually, and President Obama and Chancellor Merkel foster close partnership.

RUSSIA AND GERMANY: A STRATEGIC PARTNERSHIP

Germany is no longer at the dividing line between East and West but rather is the central power in middle Europe. It played a major role in setting the agenda and mediating the inclusion of Central and Eastern European countries in the EU and NATO. Russia has also changed dramatically in the past two decades: after the Soviet Union collapsed in 1991, it went through a period of near anarchy. With the rise of Vladimir Putin as the leading political figure, stability and institutionalization of politics returned, albeit with authoritarian features. Once again, Russia started to wield power on the international stage; many important problems, such as the fight against terrorism and the nonproliferation of nuclear weapons, can be solved only with its cooperation.

Germany's relations with Russia are crucial and interdependent. Politicians have preferred to pursue a policy of strategic partnership, not rivalry. In this view, dealing with Russia is difficult but essential. Slightly more than half of Russia's trade is with the EU, and Germany is its most important trading partner. Germany, in turn, along with many other European countries, heavily depends on Russia's energy sources, importing more than a third of its oil and about 45 percent of its natural gas from Russia.

More is at stake than economic interactions. Russia has been reluctant to recognize the EU as a major negotiating partner and exploited divisions between eastern and western members to gain the upper hand. It prefers bilateral relations. For its part, Germany wants and needs to draw Russia closer to Europe. It has been asked to step up its policy presence while forging a cohesive Western strategy toward Russia. In the eyes of some observers, success or failure in this endeavor will be a litmus test of its "legitimacy as a leader in Europe and as a partner for the United States."[16] Germany is uniquely positioned to assume this role as bridge builder. A dense network of political, economic, and cultural ties links the two countries and includes regular political dialogue among top officials. Mutual economic interests bind them together. But challenges are palpable since Germany's leaders have to consider divergent attitudes toward Russia. Some close alliance partners, among them the United States, the eastern newcomers to the EU, and, to some extent, the United Kingdom, view Russia primarily as a strategic rival and favor a policy of containment. France and other allies in Western Europe tend toward engagement and partnership. These challenges are compounded by divisions in Germany about how to deal with Russia. The government has to deal with interests that emphasize business and a widening circle of politicians and activists who demand a more critical approach toward the Russian government's increasingly authoritarian manner. Merkel has been credited with walking a fine line, accommodating both camps. The recent global financial and economic crisis has hit Russia particularly hard; consequences for the conduct of its foreign policy are not yet determined. However, interdependence between Russia and the West is likely to grow, not diminish.

WHEN THE DOMESTIC BECOMES THE INTERNATIONAL

For many, Merkel is Germany's international voice. In 2009, for the fourth time in a row, she was ranked first on the *Forbes* list of the 100 most powerful women in the world. Her diplomatic style has generally been seen as a welcome departure from her predecessor, the more assertive and media-savvy Schröder. The press has dubbed her Miss World for successfully chairing the EU presidency that led to the Treaty of Lisbon and the G-8 summit that brought the United States under George W. Bush on board to advance climate change measures in spring 2007. The environment and climate change have long been important to her; she was environmental minister under the last Kohl administration. In her address to the U.S. Congress in November 2009, the second only by a German chancellor, she thanked the United States for its support for Germany and German unification. But she also used the occasion to appeal to U.S. lawmakers "to tear down today's walls" in cooperation with Europe. Among the most pressing challenges of the twenty-first century, she ranked peace and security first, prosperity second, and "protecting our planet" third.[17] After the disappointing outcome of the UN Climate Change conference in Copenhagen in December 2009, the fight for internationally binding climate protection targets remains high on her agenda. Her outreach to smaller neighboring countries in Central and Eastern Europe has quieted concerns about a newly powerful Germany.

To some, she also contrasts positively with flamboyant French president Sarkozy and benefits from British prime minister Gordon Brown's lack of international profile. Composure under pressure and competency are her strong suits; her approval ratings among the German public remain high, although her low-key style and wait-and-see approach at times arouses criticism of her management of crises. According to one German journalist, her mastery may inhere in her ability to wait. "For her, governing is not to complete projects but to keep possibilities open."[18]

Foreign policy is shared among the executive domain; the chancellor is responsible for the general direction of foreign and security policy, leaving the details to the federal foreign and defense ministries. Only in European matters, the *Länder*, or states, have achieved important influence. The parliament has expanded its role from debate theater to ultimate veto power and co–decision maker in matters of security policy, in particular for out-of-area operations. The Federal Constitutional Court has been asked to address particularly sensitive policy issues: in doing so, it defined, among others, the framework of inner-German relations and military deployment abroad. It has been crucial in delineating the role of the EU.

In electoral campaigns and in party programs, foreign and security policy is routinely relegated to secondary importance; domestic issues dominate as political profiles can be more clearly delineated—and elections won—by addressing social and economic concerns. Executive dominance and broad consensus on the major principles of foreign and security policy among the major parties and the German people reinforce this trend. Disagreements emerge in achieving desired goals but not in the goals themselves. Recurring topics involve, among others, the modalities of out-of-area deployment and the future of the EU, in particular further enlargement. Intraparty discourse is often as controversial as debates across party lines.

Among the political parties represented in the national parliament, only the Left Party—a merger between the postcommunist Party of Democratic Socialism and a splinter group of dissatisfied Social Democrats and trade unionists—does not fit the consensual mold. It claims the space left vacant by Alliance 90/The Greens when most of their members succumbed to support out-of-area operations by the German military. Representatives of the Left Party routinely call for a withdrawal of Germany from NATO and vote against German troop employment abroad. But the Left Party is divided among its various ideological wings, making it difficult to delineate a clear foreign policy position. Neither CDU/CSU nor SPD consider it a viable coalition partner at the national level, citing, among others, its foreign policy positions that would isolate Germany internationally.

Public opinion matters, prompting and restraining leadership actions. Media reporting on international affairs is comprehensive but does not automatically elevate foreign policy to a priority. In survey after survey, domestic policy, especially economic concerns, takes precedence. With the exception of terrorism, on matters of internal security, Germans feel safe but also endorse NATO as a warrant for the country's external security. They share with the elite a consensus on foreign policy, emphasizing the core tenets of multilateralism and soft power. When they are threatened—for example, by the U.S. policy toward Iraq—public opinion can be used effectively for domestic gain, as demonstrated by Chancellor Schröder in the 2002 national elections. This flare-up of emotions has remained an episode. The experiences of two world wars and political socialization have made the German populace see war as the last resort; the lives of soldiers should not be put in jeopardy. Security policy no longer relies on traditional military means. The deeply rooted aversion to military involvement by the citizenry at large ties the hands of the executive and frustrates Germany's NATO partners, particularly in Afghanistan, where German soldiers are stationed in the safer northern part of the country. While the elite has accepted the notion that engagement in out-of-area operations is the price Germany has to pay for increased international exposure, the public has been reluctant.

FROM RESTRAINED PASSIVITY TO RESTRAINED ACTIVITY: CHALLENGES AHEAD

Interpretations of Germany's international role vary, and observers will write about the puzzles and paradoxes of its foreign policy for some time. Some call for greater international engagement, and others argue that it was achieved in the past decade. Despite lingering ambiguity, some findings are unmistakable. Although foreign policy is the domain of the executive, in one important aspect it does not differ from other policy areas: the Berlin republic is characterized by persistent transition. Thus, continuity is a hallmark of foreign policy but within a framework of pragmatic change. Germany's leadership role in the EU is firmly embedded; its international engagement has widened, and policy actions have diversified since the end of the Cold War. A stronger role of the EU in international affairs enhances Germany's influence. Its leaders persistently and with success champion the benefits of multilateralism and soft power. Helmut Kohl made unification of the two German states acceptable to its alliance partners and neighbors. His successor, Gerhard Schröder, together with Foreign Minister Joschka Fischer, can claim to have moved Germany from importer to exporter of security through participation in multilateral missions around the globe. Under the leadership of Merkel, Germany can take credit for deepening its international involvement in an amenable style but one that displays growing self-confidence. Germany has earned the respect of international alliance partners, but occasionally trust still mingles with suspicion, as the legacies of the Third Reich are complex, lasting, and resurface with some regularity.

Challenges lie ahead: the wider range and complexity of international problems make it more difficult for policymakers to maintain the traditional balancing act between Europe and the United States. If Germany wants to be a player in shaping the future international order, political elites have to engage citizens in a public discourse that delineates the country's international responsibilities. Calls for leadership and greater international engagement will persist.

SUGGESTIONS FOR FURTHER READING

Banchoff, Thomas. *The German Problem Transformed: Institutions, Politics, and Foreign Policy, 1945–1995*. Ann Arbor: University of Michigan Press, 1999.

Crawford, Beverly. *Power and German Foreign Policy: Embedded Hegemony in Europe*. Houndsmill: Palgrave Macmillan, 2007.

Dalgaard-Nielsen, Anja. *Germany, Pacifism and Peace Enforcement*. Manchester: Manchester University Press, 2006.

Dyson, Kenneth, and Klaus H. Goetz, eds. *Germany, Europe and the Politics of Constraint*. Oxford: Oxford University Press, 2003.

Erb, Scott. *German Foreign Policy: Navigating a New Era*. Boulder, CO: Lynne Rienner, 2003.

Fulbrook, Mary. *The Divided Nation: A History of Germany, 1918–1990*. Oxford: Oxford University Press, 1992.

Haftendorn, Helga. *Coming of Age: German Foreign Policy since 1945*. Lanham, MD: Rowman & Littlefield, 2006.

Leithner, Anika. *Shaping German Foreign Policy: History, Memory and National Interest*. Boulder, CO: FirstForumPress, 2009.

Maull, Hanns W., ed. *Germany's Uncertain Power: Foreign Policy of the Berlin Republic*. Houndsmill: Palgrave Macmillan, 2006.

Miskimmon, Alister. *Germany and the Common Foreign and Security Policy of the European Union*. Houndsmill: Palgrave Macmillan, 2007.

Sarotte, Mary Elise. *1989: The Struggle to Create Post-War Europe*. Princeton, NJ: Princeton University Press, 2009.

11

Italy

The Astuteness and Anxieties of a Second-Rank Power

Mark Gilbert

Since unification, Italy has never been in the front rank of Europe's powers. Its sacrifices in blood and treasure during World War I entitled it to a place at the top table in Paris in 1919, but its then premier, Vittorio Emmanuele Orlando, was only a nominal member of the so-called Big Four (Clemenceau, Lloyd George, and Wilson being the members who counted), and his diplomatic skills proved less than statesmanlike. Mussolini's colonial adventures and allegiance to Adolf Hitler's Nazi regime managed to get Italy taken seriously between 1936 and 1940, but entry into the war in June 1940 exposed his regime's pretensions in pitiless detail. Otherwise, however, Italy was notoriously the "least of the great powers."

The civilization that produced Machiavelli does not want for good diplomats, though it has conspicuously lacked a Prince. A leading historian of Italian foreign policy, commenting on the choices facing the newly constituted Italian Republic in the late 1940s, made this assessment of the pragmatic strategy Italy's leaders followed:

> Both [Prime Minister Alcide] De Gasperi and [Foreign Minister Carlo] Sforza considered that Italy, for all its military defeat, economic weakness, political uncertainty and social instability, should attempt to reassert herself as a middle-ranking, regional power fully inserted into the broader international context and well able to make its voice heard in the two spheres of traditional interest for Italian foreign policy: Europe and the Mediterranean.[1]

It should be underlined that Italy has achieved the sensible goals that De Gasperi and Sforza set for her since 1945. Although Italy has not punched at the same weight either in the North Atlantic Treaty Organization (NATO) or in the European Union (EU) as France, Germany, or Great Britain, post-war Italian foreign policy is a success story in minor key, especially when one takes into account the unstable nature of domestic Italian politics. Post–Cold War Italian foreign policy is showing signs of becoming rather more than a minor success story.

Foreign observers, however, have tended to focus more on the actors than the script and to depict Italian politics as a world of intrigues, corruption, collapsing governments, and plotting by obscure bosses skilled in the corridor politics of Rome but who count for nothing on the world stage. This tendency has become even more marked since Italy's current premier, the billionaire media entrepreneur Silvio Berlusconi, took over the government for the second time in 2001.

Berlusconi has kept Italy on the world's front pages for all the wrong reasons. Greeting a British prime minister while wearing holiday clothes and a piratelike bandanna was more sartorial misjudgment than foreign policy disaster. Comparing a senior (German) member of the European Parliament (EP) to a concentration-camp guard during a speech in July 2003 made all Europe cringe. Italy's presidency of the EU in the second half of 2003 became, thanks largely to Berlusconi's awkwardness, a textbook case in how not to run a major international organization. His friendship with Vladimir Putin has led him to defend Russian actions in Chechnya and even to ventilate Russian membership of the EU. During the recent U.S. presidential election campaign, Berlusconi joked offensively about President Barack Obama's *"bella abbronzatura."*

Berlusconi's numerous brushes with the law have tarnished his reputation too, although, to keep things in perspective, he has not yet risked impeachment for perjury (Clinton), sunk a Greenpeace ship in a foreign harbor (Mitterrand), or misled the United Nations about the presence of weapons of mass destruction in Iraq (Bush and Blair). Had he not been premier between 2001 and 2006 and again since May 2008, Berlusconi would surely, even in a court system as slow and inefficient as Italy's, have risked jail.

The fact that Berlusconi is out of his depth in questions of protocol and good manners, however, should not distract readers from the fact that Italy has followed a shrewd foreign policy in recent years and has enhanced its position as an interlocutor for the United States. As an acute student of contemporary Italian foreign policy has pointed out, much early scholarly analysis of fascist foreign policy concentrated on Mussolini's buffooneries and intemperate decision making. It is not analysis that has stood the test of time. Italy's foreign policy should not be "reduced to the prime minister's whims or mannerisms, eccentric or extravagant as they might be."[2]

FOREIGN POLICY DURING THE COLD WAR

Choosing the West, 1945–1958

Italy regained its freedom at the end of April 1945, when German resistance finally collapsed and Mussolini's Nazi-backed Salò Republic fell. Italy in 1945 was a bankrupt nation rent with violent hatreds. Blood feuds continued for months after the end of the conflict, with former fascists, priests, and industrialists facing rough justice at the hands of partisan bands. Thousands died, adding to the tens of thousands killed in massacres by fascist death squads and German troops during the latter stages of the war. The military power of the Communist Party (PCI), with its hundreds of thousands of party members, pro-Moscow orientation, and caches of hidden arms, was a looming presence in the immediate postwar period.

Neighboring states were eyeing weak Italy hungrily. France tried to seize the Aosta valley but was warned off by the British and the Americans; Austria claimed German-speaking Süd Tirol. In both cases, Italy managed to hold on to its territory, negotiating, in the case of Austria, the innovative September 1946 De Gasperi–Gruber accords that guaranteed linguistic and other rights for the German community. Communist Yugoslavia invaded northeastern Italy in the spring of 1945, occupied Trieste for more than a month, and carried out what would today be called "ethnic cleansing" against the Italian population. Thousands were murdered, their bodies being dumped in the *foibe*, underground fissures that are a geological feature of the area. Tens of thousands fled their homes. Only the intervention of allied troops compelled the Yugoslavs to withdraw from the city of Trieste, though Yugoslavia retained control over most of Trieste's hinterland.

Italy's international status was somewhat ambiguous. At the end of the war, Italy was a "cobelligerent" power whose provisional government in Rome regarded itself as an ally, not a defeated enemy. The first postwar government, which was constituted in June 1945 and headed by the resistance hero Ferruccio Parri of the small, left-wing Action Party, was adamant about this point. Northern Italy's big cities had been liberated not primarily by allied military action but by the bravery of the partisans and the industrial working class. Italy's leaders of all stripes regarded the country as a *victim*, not as an *accomplice* of the fascist dictators. Its status was comparable, in Italian eyes, to France's rather than, say, Romania's or Hungary's. Such arguments found some sympathetic ears among U.S. policymakers but cut no ice whatever among the British, the French, the Ethiopians, the Greeks, the Soviets, or the Yugoslavs, all of whom had been victims of aggression (and, in the case of Ethiopia, Greece, and Yugoslavia, of brutal military occupation) by fascist Italy.

The peace treaty with Italy, signed in Paris in February 1947, was depicted as a Versailles-style *diktat* by the Italian press. Italy had to pay large indemnities to the countries it had attacked, lost control of Trieste (which became an international zone administered by the United Nations), and lost the colonies seized under fascism. The fate of Italy's other colonies (Libya, Somalia, and Eritrea) were to be determined by the United Nations: Libya, the most important from Italy's point of view because of the large number of Italian settlers, was recommended for independence in 1949 and became an independent country in 1951. The loss of Trieste, in particular, was a huge psychological blow.

While it would be an exaggeration to say that Italy was a pariah state in 1947, it was certainly a despised nation whose fortunes were at a low ebb. Crucially, it was particularly discredited with the British policymaking elite, who admired some individuals, notably Parri and De Gasperi, prime minister and leader of the *Democrazia cristiana* (Christian Democracy: DC), the largest party in the constituent assembly elected on June 2, 1946, but who trusted Italy's new politicians scarcely more than their predecessors. Italian historiography is very conscious of the almost racialist air of superiority exuded by British diplomats in their dealings with Italians.

It was under these circumstances that Italy made its decisive postwar choice in foreign affairs and chose the West rather than take a neutral stance between the Soviet Union and the United States. De Gasperi formed a new government in May 1947 without the PCI and its Socialist (PSI) allies. This government, with a wafer-thin parliamentary majority, negotiated Italy's constitutional settlement with the PCI (the constitution was promulgated on January 1, 1948) and adhered to the Marshall Plan. Italy received over $1.3 billion from the Marshall Plan in its first two years of operation: an important reason for choosing the West. Cold War elections in April 1948 were a huge success for the DC, which, assisted by generous aid from the United States and by an Anglo-American declaration during the electoral campaign in favor of restoring Trieste and its surrounding territory to Italy, obtained 48 percent of the vote, the highest figure any party has obtained in a democratic election in Italy. Even so, the Communist-Socialist opposition "front," which was openly pro-Moscow, won 40 percent of the vote. Italy's postwar leaders had to contend in their foreign policy with the fact that the loyalties of a large body of public opinion lay on the other side of the Cold War divide: inevitably, this fact conditioned their freedom of maneuver.

Despite the PCI's threat, Italy's leaders nevertheless pressed to join NATO. This decision originated within the foreign ministry, where a set of able ambassadors in Washington, London, and Paris alerted De Gasperi in late 1948 to the danger that Italy would be excluded from what was bound to become the core structure of the democratic West. Objectively, a Mediterranean nation was a strange signatory of the North *Atlantic* Treaty. Italy owed its membership to France, whose foreign minister, Robert Schuman, persuaded Italy to apply in December 1948 (France, as a Latin country, risked being marginal within the new alliance) and backed Italy's case with vigor. France actually threatened to walk out of the negotiations if Norway was included but Italy was not. Italy's diplomats meanwhile skillfully played up the damage that would be done to De Gasperi's credibility and prestige if Italy were not admitted. Here, as so often in postwar Italian history, the country's foreign policy establishment was able to use the internal political divisions of the country as a bargaining chip.

Italy's adhesion to the pact was still a close run thing. As late as March 1949, U.S. policymakers doubted the wisdom of admitting Italy. There was, moreover, considerable opposition within the country itself, both from the PCI, which opposed the treaty with a huge "peace" campaign, and from politically progressive Catholics within the DC that wanted Italy to reject the logic of the Cold War and find a third way between the blocs. Italy nevertheless became a founder signatory of the North Atlantic Treaty on April 4, 1949, and hence benefited from a U.S. security guarantee. The country had taken an important step back toward international respectability: it was part of what would become the West's most important club.

Being part of the West also meant, at any rate for Italy, supporting the idea of European unity. The Americans wanted European federation, and so did important domestic constituencies within the DC and within the small centrist parties (Liberals, Republicans, and Social Democrats) that backed the De Gasperi government. Italian politicians from all the major parties of government participated in the Hague Congress of Europe in May 1948, at which delegates advocated the creation of a federal European state, boasting a charter of human rights, a single market and currency, progressive social policies, and an enlightened policy of cultural exchanges between workers and students across Europe. De Gasperi became an honorary president of the new European Movement born from the Congress.

Institutionally, the main result of the Congress was the Council of Europe, created by the Treaty of Saint James on May 5, 1949. Italy was a founder member of the new organization, a place at the table won in the face of British hostility. When the council proved a delusion, the Italian government responded positively to Robert Schuman's May 1950 call to construct a European Coal and Steel Community (ECSC) despite the opposition of many industrialists who feared the eruption of foreign competition. The government shrugged off such concerns and became a founder member of the ECSC in August 1952, along with France, West Germany, Belgium, Luxembourg, and the Netherlands.

Italy was also a protagonist in the negotiations for the European Defense Community (EDC). Initially a French plan to "Europeanize" West German rearmament, the EDC was transformed into an ambitious plan to subordinate the military forces of the ECSC "Six" to NATO military control while permitting West Germany to rearm and regain full sovereignty. The EDC plan was unpopular inside Italy, where the PCI whipped up the threat of German revanchism and where the Soviet counterproposal for a neutral Germany was thought even by noncommunists to be a workable alternative, and yet it was also the apple of the Eisenhower administration's eye. The De Gasperi government managed to enthuse domestic opinion *and* the United States by inserting into the EDC Treaty the idea of a European Political Community (EPC)—in effect, a set of supranational institutions—to coordinate the whole process of integration in the defense as well as the economic field. As Tommaso Padoa-Schioppa has reminded us, "Italy has never lost sight of the final goal" of European integration: the "creation of a politically united Europe based upon supranational powers."[3] The proposal to establish the EPC was a foretaste of this characteristic in postwar Italian foreign policy. There is no doubt that the Mussolini period purged Italy of the virus of nationalism, at any rate in its more virulent strains, more completely than any other Western European nation with the possible exception of Germany.

This does not mean that Italy is unaware of its national interests. The EDC (and with it the EPC) failed spectacularly on August 30, 1954, when the French National Assembly refused to ratify it amid an orgy of heated rhetoric. Italy itself had dragged out ratification of the treaty as a way of getting the United States and Britain to transfer de jure authority over the western zone of Trieste to Italy (a step that was eventually taken in November 1954; Italy also entered the United Nations in 1955 after the Soviet Union dropped its opposition to Italian membership).

Italy also managed to secure its national interests in negotiations for the creation of the European Economic Community (EEC) between June 1955 and March 1957. Italy was intent on ensuring that the EEC treaty contained commitments to the free movement of people and capital and a social dimension. It was successful in these goals. The Italian role in negotiating the EEC treaty is sometimes forgotten by commentators intent on celebrating the political attitudes of France and Germany. The *relance* of European integration after the disaster of the EDC vote was, after all, begun at Messina (Sicily) in June 1955 and pushed ahead in May 1956 at a Venice summit of the Six's foreign ministers, and the Euratom and Economic Community treaties were signed in Rome in March 1957. There is a case for saying that Italy's foreign minister in this period, Gaetano Martino, is one of the founding fathers of the present-day EU, although his name remains little known outside Italy.

Clinging to the West, 1958–1992

If post-*Risorgimento* foreign policy had been taken as a guide, Italy might have been expected to play off Moscow against Washington for the sake of short-term gains. Before 1914, Italy had played precisely such a game with the Triple Alliance and the *Entente Cordiale* while Italy's cynical diplomacy between 1933 and 1940 was of course a byword. The DC, to its credit, picked its side in the Cold War conflict and stuck to it. Paradoxically, the reputation Italy won in the 1960s for being "NATO's Bulgaria" was in reality a testimony to the tenacity with which Italy's leaders pursued their original choice. In the late 1950s, Italy permitted the United States to build and maintain several large military bases on Italian soil and stock them with nuclear weapons. Such loyalty did not go unrewarded. In the early 1960s, the DC, under the leadership of Aldo Moro and Amintore Fanfani, wished to enlarge the party's perpetually shaky parliamentary majority by "opening to the left" and including the still-Marxist PSI in the governing coalition. This policy was contested within the DC itself and was the object of "protracted sparring" between supporters and opponents in Washington, but the Kennedy and Johnson administrations did not ultimately interfere.[4] Atlantic obsequiousness, in short, had paid domestic political dividends.

Such a foreign policy might seem unheroic. Yet what was Italy to do? The grandstanding of a Charles de Gaulle was not an option for Italy in the 1960s: Italy possessed neither *gloire*, nor nuclear weapons, nor a stable political system, nor politicians of world-historical rank. Her leaders had the good sense to realize this. De Gasperi's successors were *not* all negligible, moreover. Fanfani, despite his diminutive height, might have cut a bigger figure on the world stage had he been the product of a politically more confident and enabled country. In his memoirs, de Gaulle goes out of his way to praise Fanfani with a warmth he showed for few others among his postwar peers. Each of his meetings with Fanfani, de Gaulle says, "made me appreciate his wide-ranging intellect, his prudent judgment and his urbanity. Through him I saw an Italy anxious to keep in touch with everything that was afoot, willing to join in on condition that she was treated with the consideration due to a nation with a very great past and a very important future, ready to subscribe to declarations of principle which expressed good intentions, but careful not to commit herself too deeply."[5]

De Gaulle's words ring true as a judgment on subsequent Italian foreign policy until the 1990s. Italian foreign policy continued pro-Atlanticist and pro-European, but when these twin pillars of Italian foreign policy rubbed against one another, Italy tended to follow the U.S. line. But Italy almost never "committed herself too deeply." Unlike West Germany or even Sweden, Italy did not take a high profile on the international stage. Italy was a follower, not a leader, a consumer of security, not a provider.

To have taken a higher profile, Italy would have had to have the self-confidence that comes with being a model for other nations to follow. Despite its rising prosperity, Italy was anything but a model during the 1960s and 1970s. Rampant inflation, terrorism by both the far left and the ultraright, chaos in the factories and universities, and political corruption at the highest levels combined to propel the PCI to electoral parity with the DC by 1974 and caused international alarm for the country's stability. Henry Kissinger, for one, feared that the "Eurocommunism" propagated by democratic communist leaders such as Santiago Carrillo of Spain and Italy's Enrico Berlinguer might generate enough support among the Italian electorate to sweep the DC from office. But Berlinguer was a man with a "sense of the state," as Italians say, and the PCI, which gave parliamentary support to a DC "government of national solidarity" headed by the resolutely pro-American Giulio Andreotti between 1976 and 1979, was careful to assert its adherence to Italy's choice of Cold War camp by endorsing membership of NATO.

The point is that domestic constraints prevented Italy from using its courageous postwar foreign policy choices as a springboard to launch the country's role in the world and seek greater prestige and influence. Rather, the country clung to the institutions of the Western world, treating membership as a symbol of belonging, not as an opportunity for shaping the policy of others. One natural consequence of this state of mind was that Italy became extremely sensitive to any hint that it was being "left out" by the other most important nations of the West. When, in 1975, French president Valery Giscard D'Estaing invited the United States, Great Britain, West Germany, and Japan to a French government chateau at Rambouillet to discuss world economic affairs, Rome's diplomacy moved into overdrive and secured permanent Italian inclusion in what, following Canada's adhesion, became the G-7 summit of highly industrialized nations.

Something similar occurred in 1979. In January 1979, Presidents Carter and Giscard, Prime Minister James Callaghan, and Chancellor Helmut Schmidt met in Guadaloupe to decide on the installation of cruise and Pershing missiles in Western Europe. The Italians were not invited. As a leading scholar of Italian foreign and defense policy has written, "[The meeting in Guadaloupe] was experienced by the diplomatic corps and by most of the political élite as a real slap in the face, an uncalled-for humiliation that seemed to underline Italy's growing international marginalization."[6] As far as Italy was concerned, NATO had nuclear strategy planning groups to deal with issues related to missile deployment, and the decision should have been taken there. In general, Italy was (and is) deeply critical of the creation of any kind of policymaking "directory" in either NATO or the EC/EU since it would always be the biggest state to be excluded under such arrangements.

Yet mark the sequel. Despite the fact that Italy's leaders knew that the new American missiles would be deeply unpopular with many of its own voters (Italy has thousands of Catholic voluntary groups whose activists tend to be pacifists) and with the PCI and despite the fact that the internal political situation in 1979 was a shambles even by Italian standards, Italy's minority government, thanks also to discreet lobbying by Richard Gardner, the U.S. ambassador, committed itself by December 1979 to accepting its share of the missiles at NATO bases in Italy. This bold decision would have been impossible had the PSI, under the leadership of the reformist Bettino Craxi, not decided to make acceptance of the missiles a symbol of its ongoing shift from neo-Marxism to the political center and had the leaders of the DC, especially Premier Francesco Cossiga and Foreign Minister Arnaldo Forlani, not been prepared to put their government's survival on the line. The cruise missile decision, Leopoldo Nuti argues, served the "dual purpose of testifying to the country's willingness to play a more ambitious international role and placing the PCI in a difficult situation."[7]

The Italian decision was crucial, indeed, for the broader deployment of the missiles in Europe. Helmut Schmidt, despite the fact that he had been the first to make the intellectual case for new American theater nuclear weapons in Western Europe in a London speech in October 1977, insisted that West Germany could not be the only continental European NATO power to accept deployment of the missiles on its territory. Italy's resolution prompted other NATO countries to brave public opinion and made deployment on a large scale possible: Italy authorized actual deployment in 1983, when Craxi had become premier. For all the problems posed for its foreign policy by its dysfunctional political system (the 1980s were a decade of tense political infighting between the DC and the PSI, nominally allies in government), when its national interests and prestige were genuinely at stake, NATO's Bulgaria could and did make itself count.

The same is true of Italy's record within the EU. It is easy to look at the slowness with which Italy has transposed European directives into national law, to look at how France and Germany (but even Britain, the Netherlands, and Spain) have consistently taken a more active role than Italy in making new policy, or to judge the dismal record of some Italian politicians in Brussels and come to the conclusion that Italy has played only a small role in the construction of the EC after 1958. Easy but mistaken. Italy "has played a consistently positive role in the construction of the EU," says Padoa-Schioppa, a leading Italian academic economist who has also held a senior post in the European Central Bank and has been Italian finance minister.[8]

Padoa-Schioppa argues that Italy's contribution to European unity has been both intellectual and practical. Italy has acted as the conscience of European integration. Italy "did not refrain" at any moment from reminding its partners that the "ultimate benchmark" of any given decision was to be the contribution it made to building a supranational state. Italian political thinkers (one major reason for Italy's enthusiasm for the European cause is that liberal intellectuals regard European unity as the completion of the

Risorgimento, while Catholic thinkers see it as a way of dethroning the false god of nationalism) have played an important part in conceptualizing the form a united Europe should take. Luigi Einaudi, the first constitutionally elected postwar president; Altiero Spinelli, a liberal-socialist thinker who was also a cold warrior; and Mario Albertini, a political philosopher who headed the European Movement, all exercised a profound intellectual influence on the formulation of the ideology of European integration and on the beliefs of the chief Italian politicians of the past thirty years: the debt, for instance, of Carlo Azeglio Ciampi, president of Italy from 1999 to 2006, and before that the finance minister who somehow got Italy into the euro, to these three thinkers is very considerable.

Padoa-Schioppa argues that Italian diplomacy has made contributions in four areas to the European project. First, it has broken the "vise of unanimity." Italy's willingness to accept majority votes has brought about notable evolutions in the institutions of the EC/EU on several occasions, perhaps most notably in June 1985, when Italian diplomats engineered a majority vote of the European Council to hold an intergovernmental conference to amend the EEC treaty. This skillful move led directly to the signature of the Single European Act, an act of defining importance for the subsequent history of European integration. Second, if one believes that the EP is a democratic body, one must concede Italy has made a point of "strengthening democratic control" within the EC/EU. Italy has been the strongest exponent of the powers of the EP and has intervened decisively to increase its weight in the process of decision making in Brussels. Third, Italy, like Germany, has rarely demanded *juste retour* for its contributions to the integration process. Italian governments have always argued that treating Europe as a ledger, in which incoming funds must balance outgoings, is a false concept that in the long run must undermine the European ideal. It is also true that Italy has never been called on to make great financial sacrifices, as Britain was in the 1970s and early 1980s, and that Italy has never volunteered, as Germany or the Netherlands consistently have, to bear a disproportionate share of the EC's costs.

Last but certainly not least, Italy has been one of the most enthusiastic proponents of EC enlargement. Italy supported British entry against de Gaulle and Greek, Spanish, and Portuguese entry despite the fact that all three nations would become direct competitors in sectors (agriculture and textiles) where Italy was strongly placed; took a consistently positive position on eastern enlargement in the 1990s; and is one of Turkey's few allies today. The contrast between Italy's position and France's on this issue is stark.[9] The EU might today be more of an inward-looking, Western European club had Italy really been the passive, uninfluential nation it often is reputed to be.

FOREIGN POLICY AFTER THE COLD WAR:
THE CHANGING MILIEU, 1991–2001

New Challenges

Arnold Wolfers's famous essay "The Goals of Foreign Policy" introduced the concept of "possession goals" and "milieu goals" to the study of international relations. When a nation directs its foreign policy to the attainment of "possession goals," its objective is to secure the "enhancement or the preservation of one or more of the things to which it attaches value." This is abstract, but what Wolfers means is that nations direct all their efforts to gaining a particular tract of territory, to obtaining greater power within an international organization, or to keeping tariff barriers that benefit its commerce disproportionately. "Possession goals" are essentially competitive: nations demand that their share of something generally regarded as being valuable is increased or left intact. When a nation directs its foreign policy toward the attainment of "milieu goals" by contrast, it is seeking to improve the environment in which it has to live. It is looking at the broader context of national interest rather than immediate gains in just the same way that a wealthy citizen, if he or she is public spirited, will strive to achieve safe streets, good public welfare, and fair life chances for the less wealthy and not just retreat behind the walls of a gated community.[10]

If one applies this distinction, which clearly has conceptual merit, to Italian foreign policy, one sees that in the postwar period Italy was exceptionally committed to the construction of a better milieu. This does not mean that Italy did not battle hard for its immediate interests in any given negotiation, but both in its relations with NATO and in its role in the EC, it normally made the preservation and strengthening of these institutions its priority rather than concentrating all its efforts on the securing of specific goals. It was only in relatively rare instances—dragging out ratification of the EDC to bolster its case on Trieste or remonstrating with France over the G-7—that Italy deviated from this rule. The contrast, say, with Britain, which begins every European negotiation with a narrowly defined set of "red lines" beyond which the other member states may not cross, or with France, whose *gloire* is not negotiable, is very striking.

The end of the Cold War posed a new set of challenges. Italy bordered on disintegrating Yugoslavia and was a beacon of hope and prosperity for the huddled masses of postcommunist Albania: thousands of Albanian refugees began arriving in Italy in 1990–1991, presaging the even greater influx of 1997 when the Albanian state imploded. Potentially, Italy was "on the frontier of a new arc of crisis."[11] The end of the Cold War also accelerated the pace of European integration as West Germany, anxious to ensure that German reunification did not jeopardize relations with France, emphasized that it would take place beneath the roof of a strengthened European house. The ambitious objectives of the 1992 Treaty of Maastricht, with their promise of a single European currency, a European Central Bank, a much-empowered European Parliament, and greater cohesion in foreign and defense policy, were of course supported by Italy (whose diplomats were instrumental in organizing the so-called ambush in Rome in October 1990, whereby the EC states, except Great Britain, committed themselves in principle to the essential features of what ultimately became the Maastricht treaty).

These new circumstances initiated a debate over whether Italy needed to rethink the basic principles of its foreign policy. Broadly speaking, this debate revolved around the "milieu-possession goals" distinction. On the one hand, there were some foreign policy professionals, the most vocal of whom was the strategist General Carlo Jean, who argued that Italy had to promote its immediate national interests in the Balkans and the Mediterranean and generally take a more assertive approach toward its national interests, especially in the Balkans region. The influential magazine *Limes*, the approximate Italian equivalent of *The National Interest*, gave a high profile to views of this kind. On the other hand, defenders of the status quo, of whom the Bologna-professor-turned-politician Beniamino Andreatta was perhaps the best known, insisted that there was no reason to change the basic thrust of Italy's stance, with its commitment to working through the established institutions of the West.[12] Andreatta was a great influence on another Bologna professor turned statesman, Romano Prodi, who would become prime minister in 1996 and then, in 1999, president of the European Commission.

The position was complicated by the fact that the end of the Cold War had a direct impact on Italy's political system, which imploded spectacularly between 1991 and 1993. The collapse of Soviet communism naturally had repercussions for the PCI, which split into a diehard communist party, Communist Refoundation (which itself split in 1998) and the Democratic Party of the Left (PDS), which would gradually inch its way into the political center by the late 1990s, changing its name to the Left Democrats on the way. This disintegration of the main opposition party did not mean a peace dividend for the ruling DC and the PSI, however. The criminal justice system, after being kept under the politicians' thumb for a generation, got its own back with a vengeance as soon as it became clear that the collapse of the PCI would not reinforce the DC and the PSI. Both parties were swept away by the huge "Clean Hands" corruption investigations (1992–1995), during which literally hundreds of leading politicians and officials (and thousands of minor ones) were charged with soliciting bribes, taking illegal payments, fixing public contracts, and other serious crimes.

New political forces soon filled the political vacuum. The Northern League (LN), an unorthodox right-wing movement headed by the gifted demagogue Umberto Bossi, briefly looked in 1992 as if it might succeed in splitting off the wealthy north of the country from Rome and the south. Millions of small businessmen, skilled workers, and artisans gave their votes to a party that promised to end Roman domination. The former neofascist party, the Italian Social Movement, under the shrewd leadership of Gianfranco Fini, renamed itself the National Alliance (AN) and began a decade-long shift away from fascist ideology and Mussolini worship. It is only in the past five years or so that the AN has become accepted as a bona fide conservative party by the rest of Europe.

Above all, wealthy media entrepreneur and longtime Craxi confidant Silvio Berlusconi formed a political movement called *Forza Italia* (Come On, Italy!) from scratch, allied it with the LN and the AN, and managed in a few short months of intense political campaigning/marketing to defeat the left and to win elections held in March 1994. Berlusconi himself was soon under investigation, and his government, based as it was on a "virtual" party of his own employees and hangers-on, an ultranationalist party of fascist sympathizers, and a party committed to dismantling the Italian state, collapsed amid angry rhetoric in January 1995. The lira fell off a cliff, briefly reaching over 1,250 to the German mark. Italy's international credibility sank to its lowest level since the 1970s in these months. The LN knew nothing about foreign policy but knew that it did not like foreigners, especially nonwhite ones; the AN, still a fascist party in all but name, took advantage of newly independent Slovenia's wish to join the EU to reopen the Trieste question; Berlusconi was soon hit by corruption investigations.

This loss of international standing is almost certainly one reason why President Oscar Luigi Scalfaro did not call fresh elections after the collapse of Berlusconi's government but relied until April 1996 on a committee of unelected technocrats (professors, soldiers, lawyers, and economists) chaired by a former central banker Lamberto Dini. This government was sustained in parliament by a motley majority of the PDS, Communist Refoundation, various uncompromised remnants of the DC, and the LN, whose withdrawal from the Berlusconi government had precipitated its collapse, but the ministers themselves were figures of high professional reputation that the rest of Europe could take seriously.

The Dini administration governed long enough to let the center-left coalesce behind the portly figure of Romano Prodi, a progressive Christian Democrat from a prominent academic family who had nevertheless had executive experience running a major nationalized corporation. Prodi, as an independent, was a necessary frontman. The PDS had still not been fully *sdoganato* ("passed through customs," i.e., had not overcome its communist past), yet the PDS did not want the coalition to be headed by a member

of the Italian Popular Party, the largest surviving fragment of the old DC.
Prodi had the bright idea of calling his coalition the *Ulivo* (Olive Tree), sym-
bolizing Italy's age-old values and contrasting with the somewhat meretri-
cious values espoused by Berlusconi, and successfully won a narrow victory
over Berlusconi in the April 1996 elections. He nevertheless depended for
a majority on Communist Refoundation and owed his victory to the fact
that the LN, which obtained an astonishing 10 percent of the national vote
for a program explicitly advocating the country's dissolution and the establishment of a new northern Italian state called *Padania*, had not allied itself
with Berlusconi's "House of Freedoms" (*Casa delle libertà*) coalition.

The Ulivo somehow stayed in power for five years, although Prodi
himself survived only until October 1998. The Ulivo government was in
perpetual danger of collapse as the dozen or so parties of which it was
composed, whose political identities ranged from conservatives through to
apologists for Castro, warred constantly. Prodi's two successors aged visibly
while they were in office.

Well-Tried Responses

The point of this brief discussion of Italian party politics in the 1990s is
to underline that Italy was not a normal European country after the end of
the Cold War. Its domestic politics more resembled those of Latin America
than they did the more staid world of northern Europe. Italy was a major source of alarm for its EU partners, who had wrinkled their collective
nose when the AN entered government in 1994 and who feared, perfectly
reasonably, that the country might enter into an Argentina-like economic
nosedive with unpredictable political consequences. Under these circumstances, it is unsurprising to discover that Italy's foreign policy in the 1990s
was anything but assertive. Italy, far from innovating in its foreign policy,
found itself struggling simply to retain its hard-won place in the EU and
NATO. Once more, it was clinging to the West as if to a lifeline.

Becoming a member of the euro at its launch in 1999 became a national
obsession. It was simply unthinkable for Italy to take the attitude of Britain
and Denmark and opt to stay out. Being excluded, as Greece and Sweden
were, would have been worse. Such a slap in the face would have created a
crisis of national confidence, at any rate among the political elite, similar in
intensity to that evoked by the 1956 Suez crisis in Britain or by the Vietnam
debacle in the United States. From 1996 on, therefore, Italy made considerable sacrifices to retain its place in this most crucial institution for its regional milieu. The shaky Ulivo government levied a massive one-off "Euro
tax" in 1996–1997, froze public spending, and accelerated its privatization
program. By the spring of 1998, when the entry decision was taken, Italy,
discounting interest payments on its debt, was running a budget surplus of

about 3 percent of gross domestic product (GDP). Although sacrifices were made, entry still took a good deal of astute diplomacy. Letting Italy into the euro zone tore up the Maastricht rule book. Italy's accumulated national debt of 125 percent of GDP was more than double the amount permitted by the treaty. By quietly pointing out the certain calamitous consequences of Italy's being excluded, Italy's diplomats were able to use the threat of national meltdown as a negotiating tactic. Nobody wanted an Argentina on their back doorstep.

The other key guarantor of Italy's milieu, the U.S. alliance and NATO, also required Italy to subordinate immediate possession goals for the broader good of maintaining its position within the alliance. Italy, despite doubts over the decision's constitutionality, made a contribution of three warships and a squadron of fighter bombers to Operation Desert Storm against Saddam Hussein in February 1991 despite vocal public opposition from the Catholic Church and from the PDS, whose leadership used militant pacifism (and anti-Americanism) as a temporary substitute for communist ideology. Italy also keenly supported plans for NATO enlargement, particularly pressing the claims of Slovenia and Romania for membership, while urging the maximum engagement with Russia. Above all, Italy took a relatively high profile role in NATO's war in the spring of 1999 against Yugoslavia over the Kosovo question.

There is little doubt that Italy was drawn into the conflict against its wishes. Italy knows a lot about the Balkans; possessed small but significant trade links with Belgrade and good relations with Russia, the Serbs' main backer; and had very little sympathy for the Kosovo Liberation Army (KLA), the guerilla group leading the fight for Kosovar independence. Had Italy been left to itself, it would certainly have cultivated links with the Belgrade regime, which, apart from anything else, was seen as a bulwark against German influence in the Balkans. In 1997, acting in the face of strong opposition from Germany and the United States, Italy had led a UN-sanctioned peacekeeping mission to Albania: *Operazione Alba*. In April–May 1997, together with France, Greece, and Turkey, Italy led the deployment of more than 7,000 soldiers from the four countries.

The intervention, which was compelled by the collapse of the regime of Sali Ram Berisha in March 1997 and the subsequent surge in the numbers of boat people fleeing Albania in the hope of a better life in Italy, was a big deal for Italy: Italian troops basically headed into a situation of low-grade civil war in which power was often exercised locally by armed gangs. Since an earlier commitment of more than 2,000 men to Somalia in 1992–1993 had ended in a fiasco, Italy could not afford to get it wrong a second time.

The mission, which carried out humanitarian relief activities and had no brief to intervene in domestic politics, "helped stop the security emergency and indirectly offered an important contribution to the process of national reconciliation."[13] Relatively free elections, unthinkable a few months previously, were held in June 1997. *Operazione Alba*, aside from proving that the Italian army is competent at humanitarian missions, taught Italy many lessons about the instability of Albania and about the complex historical causes of the conflict in the area. Italy's diplomats were accordingly less disposed than almost any other Western country simply to see the Serbs as the bad guys.

The Kosovo crisis began to worsen, moreover, with a flood of refugees pouring into neighboring states to escape Serbian military actions against the KLA. This took place in October 1998 at a moment of great political sensitivity. Prodi was defenestrated by his majority at the end of that month, and the new premier, Massimo D'Alema, was a highly intelligent but internationally inexperienced former communist, the first to hold the job. D'Alema was keen to prove that he could be more Catholic than the pope on security questions and throughout the crisis defended NATO's actions with aplomb. Foreign Minister Lamberto Dini, a conservative, could afford to be more critical since his "Western" credentials were not suspected by anyone. D'Alema's majority was nonetheless dependent for its survival during the bombing phase of the crisis (March 23–June 9, 1999) on hardline former communists—the "Communists of Italy"—who regarded NATO's intervention as an act of imperialist aggression.

In these circumstances, the fact that Italy stuck to the official NATO line throughout the military action showed a certain political courage, though it would also have shown courage to distance the country, as Greece did, from a policy that ultimately led, via an unplanned escalation of force, to the U.S. Air Force bombing Belgrade. Dini had said in June 1998 that NATO intervention without a UN mandate was "impossible." Italy nevertheless went along with the bombing, which was begun, without a UN mandate, after the Serbs rejected a U.S.-sponsored plan to hand Kosovo over to a NATO-appointed "Civilian Implementation Force" that would supervise Serbian withdrawal from the disputed territory and then hold a plebiscite on independence. As Italy well knew, the U.S. plan was tantamount to promising a gradual transition to independence since Albanians constituted a large majority of the local population and the KLA, in the absence of the Serbian police, was well capable of enforcing its will on the local community. Italy would have preferred further talks aiming at persuading Belgrade to restore the degree of local autonomy enjoyed by Kosovo between 1974 and 1989, with guarantees for the human rights of the Serbian minority. Throughout the bombing phase of the crisis, Italy kept its embassy in Belgrade open, the only NATO country to do so.

Italy's motivation was to show that it was a good NATO citizen and to ensure that it continued to play a leading role within the organization. Diplomatic historians will doubtless dig deeper in future years, but the public comments of Italy's policymakers leave little room for doubt. Dini said, "Italy is part of the Alliance and cannot therefore renege on its responsibilities. Fifteen members were in favor of intervention: to disassociate ourselves would have been a pretty dramatic gesture." In the Chamber of Deputies on March 26, 1999, D'Alema said that "by isolating itself from its allies in NATO . . . Italy would have no chance of contributing to a peaceful solution to this conflict." D'Alema added in an interview/book, published together with the journalist Federico Rampini, that Italy was compelled "to fulfil properly the task that the new NATO had assigned to it, namely to project stability in the Mediterranean and the Balkans." Italy would also have seemed a "second division country" had it not participated.[14]

It should be noted that the Italian contribution was not negligible: many of the air strikes took off from Aviano in northeastern Italy and NATO combat operations would have been definitely hampered if Italy had refused its airspace to the U.S. jets. But simply to state that phrase is to grasp how impossible such a course of action would have been. Refusing airspace to U.S. bombers meant renouncing forty years of foreign policy. Letting discretion take the better part of valor and genuinely convinced that NATO was an essential feature of the post–Cold War security architecture, Italy contented itself instead with "doing the dishes," taking charge of "Operation Rainbow," the distribution of humanitarian aid to the tens of thousands of Albanian refugees who had fled into neighboring Macedonia and Greece to escape from the fighting and Serbian ethnic cleansers.

Underlying this somewhat passive attitude was military weakness. Despite the increased threats to Italian territory and interests posed by the post–Cold War period, the political-economic crisis meant that Italy's already low spending on defense and foreign affairs eroded still further. Of the big four Western European states, France and Great Britain spent the most on defense in 1992–1994; both spent an average of $37 billion per year. Germany invested almost $35 billion. Italy spent half as much: $17.5 billion, about 2 percent of GDP.[15]

This figure is cited not because it is low but because it is relatively high. Italian defense spending stayed low for the remainder of the 1990s and has broadly declined, with occasional spikes, as a percentage of GDP ever since. Italy today spends only 1.1 percent of GDP on defense and in cash terms spends little more than it did fifteen years ago.[16] Lack of spending is one big reason why the Italian contribution to the NATO mission in Afghanistan, agreed in the aftermath of the 9/11 attacks, has been so low key. Italy does not have the equipment to take a high-profile role in a situation like that of Afghanistan. Nevertheless, in response to President Obama's policy of a "surge" in troop deployments, Italy promised in December 2009 that it will raise its overall commitment of troops by 1,000 by October 2010. Italy will then have approximately 3,700 troops serving in Afghanistan. Even so, Italy will not be perceived as an equal member of the alliance, unless its leaders invest in defense more heavily.

To use management jargon, Italy has outsourced its security function. Unlike an outsourcing company, however, it cannot change its contractor according to results. Italy has to accept whatever the contractor decides is best practice, even when it is convinced that the Americans are wrong. During the Kosovo crisis, it is fair to say that this is what happened. It is small wonder that Italy is a keen supporter of the EU's taking a higher-profile role in defense questions. In addition to strengthening European identity, it would also give the Italians extra options.

Foreign Policy in the Age of Berlusconi: Continuity and Change, 2001–2008

Since May 2001, the dominant political force in Italy has been the right-wing coalition led by Silvio Berlusconi. In that month, Berlusconi's House of Freedoms coalition, consisting of, in addition to *Forza Italia*, the AN, the LN, and a center-right Christian Democrat Party, the Union of Christian Democrats, beat the Ulivo and took power. Berlusconi's cabinet not surprisingly proved to be very unstable, and several times it fell apart amid futile bickering.

It nevertheless hung on for a full parliament, when it was beaten in a Florida-style election thriller by Romano Prodi, returned from exile in Brussels and once again at the head of the Ulivo (itself a multiparty coalition) and a ragbag of far-left parties, including Communist Refoundation and the Communists of Italy, all of which had to be accommodated in the new government. Only a few thousand votes separated the two opposing blocs, and Prodi often had to rely on a handful of life senators for a Senate majority.

Prodi's government unsurprisingly survived less than two years. In April 2008, Berlusconi was back in Palazzo Chigi, the prime minister's official residence, this time at the head of what has hitherto proved to be one of the most stable governments of contemporary Italian history. The core of the government is the new "People for Freedom" party (*Popolo della libertà*) formed of the fusion between *Forza Italia* and the AN. This party is allied with the LN, which has moderated its more extreme positions, taken a strong stance against immigration, and returned to the same levels of national popularity that it enjoyed in 1996. It is not an exaggeration now to compare the LN to the Bavarian Christian Social Union: a right-wing party that promotes traditional bourgeois values and represents a particular region of the country only but that is intent becoming a party of government and exercising long-term power.

Breaking with Europe?

Berlusconi often has been accused, both in the 2001–2006 government and now, again, in his latest administration of having radically changed the direction of Italian foreign policy. It is widely alleged in the more liberal Italian newspapers that he and his ministers are anti-European, neoconservative, and frankly an international embarrassment. Berlusconi himself, who understands the black arts of image building as well as any politician living and whose popularity rests on his undeniable capacity to communicate a sense of leadership to the Italian people, is quite happy to go along with the media fiction that he is an innovator in foreign affairs (and in domestic policy) who is shaking up the traditional establishment.

In fact, in both areas, he has been more of a perpetuator of traditional policy than a radical. The root of the accusation of foreign policy radicalism was the equivocal—some alleged Euroskeptic—attitude to the EU taken by Berlusconi and some of his chief ministers, notably the finance minister Giulio Tremonti and the defense minister Antonio Martino, during the early stages of his 2001–2006 administration. These attitudes led in the first week of January 2002 to the resignation of Berlusconi's foreign minister, Renato Ruggiero, an international civil servant of great experience who had been director of the World Trade Organization between 1995 and 1999 (and who would become Romano Prodi's special adviser on foreign affairs between 2006 and 2008). Berlusconi was forced to combine the portfolio of foreign minister with the premiership for several months before he handed the job over to the current incumbent, Franco Frattini.

With hindsight, the furious polemics aroused by this affair seem somewhat infantile. Berlusconi described them at the time as typical *teatrino politico*, and he was, in this at least, quite right. "What remains of Europeanism without Ruggiero?" wailed an op-ed in the left-leaning *La Repubblica* before insinuating that Berlusconi's main motive was sheer vainglory, a desire to hog the limelight by doubling his appearances on the world stage.[17] Ruggiero was a highly respected figure. But he was not Jean Monnet. Nevertheless, for most of 2002, the chattering classes in Rome talked of little else except Italy's lost credibility in Europe and of the Berlusconi government's new Euroskeptic direction. As Osvaldo Croci has sensibly argued, that the Berlusconi government of 2001–2006 was "more outspoken and assertive in its dealings with Brussels and its European partners than any of its predecessors" is a fact but not one that should not necessarily be equated with Euroskepticism, still less outright anti-Europeanism.[18]

The Berlusconi government was simply sometimes guilty of pressing its immediate national priorities rather than espousing lofty European objectives. Tremonti and Berlusconi, who wished to launch a more expansionary economic policy, made an authentic possession goal out of relaxing the

EU's Stability and Growth Pact in order to allow themselves some budgetary room for maneuver. Italy, which had been allowed into the euro zone despite its swollen national debt and which had benefited greatly from the convergence of interest rates on its government bonds to within a few basic points of German levels, had been supposed, in return, to squeeze its indebtedness down to under 100 percent of GDP by 2010.

In the fall of 2003, Italy took advantage of the fact that both France and Germany risked being sanctioned by the EU under the terms of the pact, and the fact that the Intergovernmental Conference negotiating amendments to the draft of the would-be European Constitution was taking place during the Italian presidency of the EU, to lead an all-out rhetorical assault on the supposed "inflexibility" of the pact, which restricts euro zone members' deficit spending and even, theoretically, envisages member states' being fined for breaches of the limits. At the end of November 2003, a majority of EU finance ministers, with Tremonti at the fore, voted not to sanction France and Germany despite the fact that their deficits, at more than 4 percent of GDP, were well beyond the levels permitted. National governments thus reacquired, de facto, the sovereign right to make future generations pay for the self-indulgence of the present. For the rest of Berlusconi's first administration, the ratio of debt to GDP began creeping up again. At the cost of deeply unpopular fiscal policies, Prodi's 2006–2008 ministry briefly slowed the rot, but under the impact of the global recession, the ratio has since begun to climb again and is expected to reach or even surpass 120 percent of GDP by the 2013 election.

Italy is not, of course, the only offender in the fiscal field within the EU. As recession bites, many other euro zone countries are allowing their national debts to mount almost to Italian levels. Nevertheless, in the Berlusconi era, it is fair to say that the goal of contributing to the overall macroeconomic stability of the EU has been subordinated to the immediate need of the Italian government not to inflict too many sacrifices on the voters.

Nevertheless, it would be an error to think that under Berlusconi, Italy ceased placing lofty European objectives at the core of its foreign policy. The Italian presidency of the EU in the second semester of 2003, which began with Berlusconi's humiliating "concentration camp guard" speech to the European Parliament, faced the task of getting the fifteen member states' approval for the text of the draft EU Constitution produced by the "convention" chaired by former French president Giscard D'Estaing. Several leading Italian politicians, including two former premiers, Giuliano Amato and Lamberto Dini, and the leader of AN, Gianfranco Fini, had taken a prominent role in the convention's activities, and the EU Constitution enjoyed bipartisan support within the Italian political elite.

The Italian presidency failed to get the assent of the other nations by December 2003. It is convenient to blame Berlusconi's ineptitude during the negotiations for this flop, and certainly the subsequent Irish presidency did a more professional job. Nevertheless, the cause of the failure was the flat refusal by Spain and Poland to sign until they got an agreement that did not diminish their voting power in the EU's central legislative organ, the Council of Ministers. Had Italy been in a similar position to Spain and Poland, it would almost certainly have made—Berlusconi or no Berlusconi—a compromise deal for the sake of European unity.

During the Irish presidency in the first semester of 2004, in fact, Foreign Minister Frattini tried talking tough over certain amendments to the text that Italy regarded as highly desirable. Frattini told the Italian Parliament in April that he would not accept any "lowest-common-denominator solution" that preserved national vetoes in areas such as foreign affairs, the process of amending the constitution, and taxation. Under pressure from the Vatican, Italy also wanted the constitution's preamble to begin with a reference to Europe's "Christian roots." But on the eve of the decisive EU summit in mid-June 2004, Frattini and Berlusconi backed away from making these preferences "redline" issues. Frattini said—and the phrase sums up Italy's attitude to European unity—"Our red line is to say no to the prevalence of outright vetoes, to say yes to values and principles." They did not threaten to block the treaty as a whole until they had gotten their way. Unlike almost every other country in Europe, Italy is still playing from Europeanist sheet music. Every now and then, Italy sounds discordant notes, but such slips are the exception rather than the rule.

In fact, it may be legitimate to argue that the real weakness of Italy's position in Europe is not Berlusconi's alleged Euroskepticism but rather Italy's own attachment to an outmoded conception of what the EU is all about: "A vision of Europe conceived in the 1940s is not necessarily the most appropriate one for a Europe of almost 30 states."[19]

The Iraq Conflict and Its Ramifications

The "biggest piece of evidence" generally advanced to suggest that Berlusconi's 2001–2006 administration was less Europeanist than its predecessors is its partisan support for the United States of George W. Bush during the Iraq crisis.[20] Berlusconi, like Tony Blair in Great Britain, took a great deal of domestic flak both for his evident personal liking for the U.S. president and for his government's willingness to give moral (and some material) support for the U.S. adventure in Iraq, which was deeply unpopular with European (and Italian) public opinion. Italy was one of the "group of eight" EU nations that signed the January 30, 2003, letter to the *Wall Street Journal* backing the U.S. position on Iraq (and hence distancing themselves from Franco–German opposition within the United Nations to the Americans). Italy did not take part in the conquest of Iraq but contributed a "humanitarian" force of *carabinieri* in the aftermath of the invasion and persisted with its contribution even after a suicide bomb in November 2003 killed nineteen Italian soldiers in Nassiriya in southern Iraq, where the Italian contingent was based.

No one should be surprised at Berlusconi's stance on Iraq. It is, in fact, possible that the moderates within the center-left opposition, which made hay with the accusation that the Berlusconi administration was servile toward the United States and was damaging European unity, would have followed an essentially similar policy had they been office. One of the objectives of this chapter has been to underline that historically Italy has not seen its commitments to European unity and Atlantic partnership as being mutually exclusive. Quite the opposite. Whenever, as in this case, France has tried to mobilize Europe against the United States, Italy has invariably sided with the Americans. To this extent, Berlusconi's Iraq policy was anything but a radical change of direction in Italian foreign policy.

It was indicative of continuity for a second reason. Italy feared the emergence of a "directory" in European foreign policy. Franco–German policy in the months prior to the U.S. invasion in March 2003 had the potential to split NATO in two, but Italy was concerned that such a policy would leave her—to translate the expressive Italian phrase—with a "fistful of flies." Italy is keenly aware that Berlin and Paris would love to speak in Europe's name on foreign policy issues, perhaps bringing in London on certain key issues. In this regard, her interests are closer to "new Europe's" than "old Europe's." In fact, in the first semester of 2004, when the Blair government organized the first of what was intended to be regular meetings between Britain, France, and Germany, Italy led a whirlwind campaign of the EU's second-rank powers, notably Poland, to stop the plan from taking off.[21] Just as she was determined not to be excluded from the G-5 in 1975, so Italy remains prickly about any attempt by the more presumptuous EU nations to suggest that "all EU states are equal, but some states are more equal than others."

Italy's Place in the World

This prickliness reflects the fact that Italy's standing in the world is not so evidently inferior to that of France and Germany. One of the possession goals most tenaciously pursued by Italian diplomacy over the past two decades has been that of ensuring that no reform of the United Nations Security Council (UNSC) takes place that raises Germany to the rank of permanent member along with France and Great Britain. Italy does not agree that Britain and France, merely because they happened to be among the victors of World War II, should possess permanent membership and a veto; it is resolutely opposed to Germany's acquiring the prestige that a permanent seat would bring. Italy's preference, naturally, is for the EU to have a single seat from which it can espouse a single foreign policy. Since, short of divine intervention, this is not likely to happen any time soon, Italy has kept itself busy since the mid-1990s sabotaging various attempts by Germany, Japan, India, and Brazil to acquire permanent membership and promoting alternative schemes to broaden access to the UNSC. Italy was the most active member of a group of influential nations (the "coffee club") that includes Spain, Canada, Mexico, Argentina, Turkey, Pakistan, Egypt, and South Korea and that shares Italy's doubts—for obvious reasons—about elevating the four previously mentioned states to the UNSC. The issue is not just about jealously and prestige. Italy has been in recent years a much more significant contributor to UN peacekeeping missions than either France or Germany, is the sixth-largest contributor to the UN budget, and provides a striking number of top officials to the organization. In July 2006, in the aftermath of the border conflict between Hezbollah and Israel, Italy took the lead role in organizing UNIFIL, the UN peace mission monitoring the territory between Lebanon and Israel. This decision, which was taken by the Prodi government and hailed, prematurely, as evidence of a new course in Italian foreign policy, has been appropriated by the Berlusconi government. Italy wants its significant contributions in expertise and treasure to be recognized by the United Nations.

In 2005, then secretary-general Kofi Annan proposed two alternative schemes for reform to the membership of the United Nations. Model A proposed increasing the number of permanent members from five to eleven. Of the six new seats, two would go to Asia, two to Africa, one to Europe, and one to Latin America. Model B borrowed from earlier plans suggested by Italy to propose an increase in the size of the UNSC "through the creation of a new category of non-permanent members that would sit for four years instead of two and be re-elected."[22] Such states would have to meet various criteria (respect for human rights, contributions to the activities of the United Nations, and so on). Under model A, the UNSC would have consisted of eleven permanent members (five with veto) and thirteen non-permanent members. Model B foresaw five permanent members with veto; eight four-year renewable seats and eleven two-year rotating members.

Neither of Annan's models was acceptable. The Germans, Japanese, Brazilians, and Indians have formed a "G-4" to press their case for permanent membership; Italy took the lead in forming a group called "United for Consensus" along with other members of the coffee club to coordinate opposition to any increase in the number of permanent seats. So far, the efforts of Italy to frustrate the G-4's proposals have succeeded. UNSC reform gives a good indication of what Italy can do when it decides to fight its corner. It is perhaps the most striking instance in recent years of Italy's identifying a "possession goal," albeit a negative one, and mobilizing all its diplomatic efforts in order to obtain it. It is worth emphasizing that this policy has united both the two right-wing governments headed by Berlusconi and the center-left coalition headed by Prodi.

The fight over the UNSC is arguably a sign that Italy is chafing at second-rank status: in effect, Italy is saying, "Why *should* we count for less than Germany?" Italy's leaders are equally clearly chafing at being seen as inferior to France. In recent years and with greater intensity since the Berlusconi government was elected in the spring of 2008, Italy has been pursuing a much more active policy in the Mediterranean—a policy that incidentally puts it into competition with France, whose own Mediterranean policy has benefited from a raised profile since the election of President Nicolas Sarkozy.

There are several reasons for this policy. One is concern about migration. In the space of less than twenty years, Italy has gone from being a monocultural to a multicultural society. About 7 percent of Italy's residents now come from abroad, with the Maghreb countries being the largest single source. Migration from North Africa has caused a great many human tragedies, when small boats carrying huge numbers of desperate would-be migrants capsized and drowned and created a fillip to illegality as human traffickers exploited the misery and hopes of Africans wanting to migrate to Europe. A second reason is oil. ENI, the Italian multinational, is playing a large role in developing Libya's oil and gas reserves and is also a big investor in the Caspian Sea region, a fact that goes far to explain Italy's prolonged and attentive courtship of Turkey, whose EU application Italy strongly supports—in contradistinction to France. In June 2008, Italy signed a "reinforced strategic partnership" with Egypt by which the two nations agreed to hold annual summit meetings, presided over by the two countries' respective heads of government, on matters of mutual concern.[23]

Despite this attentiveness to the Muslim world, Italy has been careful to not take sides against Israel. Indeed, during the recent Israeli action against the Gaza Strip, Italy's leadership, including several former fascists, made a point of supporting Israel's right to take action against Palestinian terrorism. Massimo D'Alema, who was foreign minister during the 2006–2008 Prodi government, was almost the only high-profile Italian politician to condemn Israel for abusing its military supremacy. In the Mediterranean, Italy is trying hard to stay friendly with all parties and gradually extend its influence in the region. On the whole, it is succeeding. Italy counts for far more than it did even a dozen years ago in this most sensitive of geographical areas.

The Berlusconi government, in short, far from being the maverick of international repute, can be said to be following in the footsteps of previous Italian governments. Italy has typically pursued its interests indirectly, promoting the international and regional institutions that guarantee its welfare and security. Italy is more prepared than most countries to pay a price in prestige and sovereignty in order to keep those institutions intact. At the same time, the country does not like to be excluded and is capable of asserting itself with surprising determination when it feels slighted. Italy's foreign policy is a study in the astuteness and anxieties of a second-rank power.

SUGGESTIONS FOR FURTHER READING

In English

The best source in English for articles giving the Italian perspective on world politics is the *International Spectator*, a quarterly journal published by the Istituto Affari Internazionali (Rome). Some recent books or collections dealing with aspects of Italian foreign policy are the following:

Carboni, Maurizio, ed. *Journal of Modern Italian Studies* 13, no. 1 (2008). Special edition: "Beyond the Three Circles: Italy and the Rest of the World."
Daedalus 130, no. 2 (spring 2001). Special edition: Italy: Resilient and Vulnerable, vol. 1, "The European Challenge."
Fabbrini, Sergio, and Simona Piattoni, eds. *Italy in the European Union: Redefining National Interest in a Compound Policy*. Lanham MD: Rowman & Littlefield, 2008.
Gardner, Richard N. *Mission Italy: On the Front Lines of the Cold War*. Lanham, MD: Rowman & Littlefield, 2005.
Smith, Timothy E. *The United States, Italy and NATO, 1947–1952*. New York: St. Martin's Press, 1991.

In Italian

Craveri, Piero, and Antonio Varsori, eds. *L'Italia nella costruzione europea: Un bilancio storico (1957–2007)*. Milan: Franco Angeli, 2009.
Nuti, Leopoldo. *La sfida nucleare: La politica estera italiana e le armi atomiche*. Bologna: Il Mulino, 2007.
Varsori, Antonio. *L'Italia nelle relazioni internazionali dal 1943 al 1992*. Rome: Laterza, 1998.

12

Poland and Eastern Europe

Historical Narratives and the Return to Europe

Krzysztof Bobinski

When the Berlin Wall came down in 1989, marking the end of the Cold War, Sir Peter Inge, the commander in chief of the British Army on the Rhine, remembers that his spies came to see him. They gathered around and asked, "Now that it's all over who do want us to keep an eye on?"[1] General Inge remembers he told them to dust off post–World War I maps and try and work out which of the national conflicts then simmering in Europe were likely to burst out all over again. It turned out, however, that he was wrong about Eastern Europe. The potential for conflict was certainly there, but the transition from being part of the Soviet Empire to a hodgepodge of independent states went off peacefully and smoothly. Indeed, in 1993, Czechoslovakia peacefully broke into two countries—the Czech Republic and Slovakia—in what came to be called the "velvet" divorce. But it was farther to the south that the tragedy that General Inge feared in Eastern Europe actually happened. That was when communist Yugoslavia broke up, after 1989, into its constituent republics, and many of these went into a brutal war with each other two years later. This war, tragically, replayed age-old hatreds, feuds, and rivalries.

Miraculously, the situation in Eastern Europe turned out differently. The year 1989 initiated the breakup of the Soviet Empire. Russia reemerged as the successor state to the Soviet Union, with a minimal loss of life and none of the civil strife that had accompanied, say, the retreat of the British from India in 1947. Indeed, the Soviet Union went out, as T. S. Eliot had it, "not with a bang but a whimper." Russia found itself, after four centuries of westward expansion, back behind its sixteenth-century western frontier with a bankrupt economy, a nuclear arsenal, and a profound failure to understand how all this had come to pass. Meanwhile, on its western flank, a trio of minute states on the Baltic—Estonia, Latvia, and Lithuania—which had been incorporated into the Soviet Union in 1940, energetically set about establishing their credentials as independent states. Belarus and Ukraine, which had been part of the Soviet Union since 1920, moved less assuredly in the same direction. Others that had not been part of the Soviet Union but that had been colonized and became part of the Soviet bloc after 1945 reaffirmed their sovereignty in the second half of 1989. Then they looked expectantly to the West to help them break, once and for all, with the Soviet Union and to take them in as members of purely Western institutions—the North Atlantic Treaty Organization (NATO) and the European Union (EU). These were Poland, Czechoslovakia, Hungary, Romania, and Bulgaria, which in the post–World War II period had retained their status as separate countries but enjoyed a sovereignty that was severely limited by *diktats* flowing from Moscow.

The maps that General Inge's spies dusted off showed a completely different Eastern Europe than the one we see in pre–World War I atlases. Before 1914, the area had been divided between Prussian Germany to the west, tsarist Russia to the east, and the Austro-Hungarian Empire stretching down to the Balkans in the south. World War I saw the collapse of all these three European empires and the emergence from the debris of a series of smaller states: Poland, the three Baltic countries (Estonia, Latvia, and Lithuania), Czechoslovakia, Hungary, Romania, Bulgaria, and Yugoslavia and, farther to the east, Soviet Russia after the Russian Revolution in 1917. It was a settlement that owed much to U.S. president Woodrow Wilson, who in a speech to the U.S. Congress in January 1918 had set out his Fourteen Points, which established national self-determination as the organizing principle of post–World War I Europe. It was the 1919 Treaty of Versailles that put this Wilsonian principle into action. The treaty sanctioned the birth of a fragmented Eastern Europe, full of newly minted states that were defined by a set of nationalisms that gave them a fiery self-confidence. That mood was matched by Germany and Austria, which were beaten in World War I but remained determined to recoup their losses. And despite the massive casualties suffered during the war, this revanchist mood set the stage for a renewal of hostilities in Europe a mere twenty years later.

The war that broke out in 1939 demolished the order established by the Treaty of Versailles and President Wilson. But the 1930s had also seen the steady emergence of increasingly authoritarian regimes in the region, most strongly in Nazi Germany and Stalinist Russia but also in Poland, the Baltic states, Romania, Hungary, and Bulgaria. Indeed, it was only Czechoslovakia that managed to preserve a functioning democracy during the entire interwar period. These political developments presaged the great clash in Europe between the two totalitarian powers—Soviet Russia and Germany—during World War II. Most of the Eastern European states sided with the Germans during the war. Only the Poles, attacked by the Germans on September 1, 1939, saw an active resistance at home and had military units in the field throughout Europe and the Middle East from the beginning to the end of the war. They and the Czechs, occupied before the war started, were allied with the Western powers. The war ended in 1945 with the total defeat of Nazi Germany and the advance of Soviet Russia deep into Central Europe at the beginning of the Cold War. This was farther west than either the Soviet Union or Russia had ever been before.

In 1945, with the Soviet Red Army firmly entrenched eighty miles west of Berlin, the Soviets proceeded to establish regimes pliant to their commands in the countries that had fallen to them as a result of their westward advance. The ruthless clampdown did not seem to differentiate between wartime allies and foes. Between 1945 and 1948, communists loyal to Moscow took control of governments in Eastern Europe. Representatives of democratic parties were either imprisoned or cowed into silence. After 1948, even communists whom Joseph Stalin deemed disloyal were either shot or imprisoned. A command economy was installed and a policy of rapid industrialization set in train that provided the promise of social advance for the rural masses in most of these hitherto underdeveloped countries. The Western powers—the United States and Great Britain—showed no inclination to challenge the Soviet takeover that had been presaged by a wartime agreement at Yalta in 1945 between the Soviet, British, and U.S. leaders, Stalin, Winston Churchill, and Franklin Roosevelt. Yalta divided Europe into two spheres of influence—the Soviet sphere and the Western sphere. As a consequence of both the Soviet terror and a realization that they had been abandoned by the West to the Soviets, people in Eastern Europe set about making the best of their situation. Infrastructure destroyed by war had to be repaired, education and careers disrupted by the hostilities had to be restarted, families had to be reunited, and a semblance of normal life had to be reestablished. In Western Europe, economic recovery came with the U.S.-funded Marshall Plan. The establishment of NATO in 1949 organized the defenses of the West against a Soviet Union deemed to be bent on aggression. In 1952, the European Coal and Steel Community was founded. This set in train a process of European integration that ultimately resulted in today's EU. The Community provided a way of rearming Germany to face the Soviet threat without provoking fears throughout Europe that Germany would once again go to war against its neighbors. The two parts of Europe divided by an "iron curtain" began to grow apart, and for forty-five years an uneasy peace, enforced by the threat of nuclear weapons, ensued.

The power sharing bargain struck in Yalta between the Soviets and the Western leaders held firm for more than four decades. Periodic crises in various Eastern European states, such as the Hungarian uprising against the Soviets in 1956 and the Czechoslovak movement for liberal reforms in 1968, were crushed by invasions of the Warsaw Pact armies with the Western powers doing nothing to intervene. Poland's Solidarity revolution in 1980, led by Lech Wałęsa, a shipyard worker from Gdańsk, was put down in 1981 by Poland's own military forces. Little more than symbolic protests came from the West.

The events of 1980 in Poland were a turning point. They showed that the communist system was no longer in a position to satisfy the economic demands of a working class that up to then had been the main beneficiaries and the backbone of the Soviet regime. It became clear then that modernizing changes were needed throughout the Soviet bloc, and in 1985 Mikhail Gorbachev, a young reformer, came to power in the Kremlin. It was he who set in train new policies that he hoped would make Soviet communism more efficient. Gorbachev's reforms failed to save the system. Instead, they led to the dismantling of the command economy and the destruction of the power of the ruling Communist Party. The changes led to the fall of the Berlin Wall and the dissolution of the Soviet Union in 1991.

The events of 1989 caught EU officials in Brussels unprepared. If General Inge's army spies were busy digging out post-1914 maps, so in Brussels the bureaucrats had to dust off atlases of present-day Eastern Europe and statistical yearbooks from the region. They needed to learn something about the newly liberated countries in the east that they knew would soon come knocking at their doors. In 1957, the Treaty of Rome, which established the European Economic Community, the forerunner of today's EU, had promised that all European countries would be eligible to join. That included those that were now stumbling into the sunlight from the ruins of the Soviet bloc. The first step the EU took was to put into place an aid program for Poland and Hungary called PHARE. This program recognized that it was these two states that had made progress in introducing market reforms in the last stages of communist rule. Brussels was at the time in accession negotiations with Sweden, Finland, and Austria. (Norway also negotiated accession, but a referendum decided against membership.) These states joined in 1995. Consequently, the EU had little stomach for a new set of accessions, especially from former communist states whose economies were weak and whose laws and institutions needed a major overhaul if they were to be compatible with the EU's legal and institutional framework. As Brussels negotiated association agreements with Poland and the others, EU officials fought a rearguard action to exclude from the agreement a clause explicitly stating that these agreements were a step toward membership. In 1993, the EU outlined the Copenhagen criteria, which set out the conditions a candidate had to fulfill to be able to join. These included a functioning market economy strong enough to compete in the EU's single market and a viable democracy that respected human rights.

Meanwhile, the Eastern Europeans were determined to join and continued to implement the major reforms that were expected of them. Hungary and Poland applied in 1994; Romania, Bulgaria, Estonia, Latvia, Lithuania, and Slovakia in 1995; and the Czech Republic and Slovenia in the following year. The EU had little choice but to finally open membership negotiations. It was caught in a "rhetorical trap." The Western countries had said for so long during the Cold War that they would accept these states if the situation changed in Europe that they had little choice, in the end, but to accept them when the situation had changed. In addition, Germany strongly supported the principle of enlargement. It wanted to have Poland as an EU member state on its eastern frontier rather than a potentially weak and unstable state in a borderland between Germany and Russia. Indeed, the Germans played a crucial role in pushing through enlargement of the EU to the east, in contrast to France, which had its doubts and delayed the process as much as possible.

The Eastern Europeans wanted to join the EU so that they could anchor their economic and political reforms in Western Europe. They were also equally fixed on joining NATO to insure against any possible resurgence of a threat from Russia. Western officials were less convinced. Timothy Garton Ash, then a British reporter, recalls hearing senior officials from France, Germany, and Great Britain tell him in 1990 that it "was a mad idea" that these countries join the EU and NATO. "The Soviets would never stand for it," he was told.[2] The leaders of the Czech Republic, Hungary, and Poland pressed on, however. Vaclav Klaus, an author and former dissident; Arpad Goncz, a lawyer and insurgent in 1956; and Lech Wałęsa, a shipyard worker and former leader of Solidarity, lobbied President Bill Clinton on the issue of NATO enlargement at the opening of the Holocaust Museum in Washington, D.C., in April 1993.

The decision to say yes did not come easily. NATO had begun to wonder what its future would be given that the Cold War was over. It was less convinced of the merits of enlargement than these three anticommunist veterans from Eastern Europe. The military equipment of the former Soviet bloc states was thought to be out of date. The soldiers themselves were deemed to have little battle value. American generals were afraid that once security guarantees were granted to the Eastern Europeans, NATO would get "sucked into some godforsaken Eurasian quagmire." And even though President Wałęsa of Poland got Boris Yeltsin to declare in August 1993 that Polish membership of NATO would not conflict with Russia's interests, the Russian military and foreign policy establishment was deeply opposed to NATO's eastward expansion. This was important to Clinton, as the United States was locked in a delicate negotiation with Russia on a new post–Cold War settlement in Europe that could be derailed by any sign of radical expansion of NATO to the east. In addition, important voices in the U.S.

foreign policy establishment, such as that of George Kennan, were also very skeptical. Kennan called the planned NATO expansion "the greatest mistake of western policy in the entire post-cold-war era."[3] He argued that "it would inflame the existing nationalistic, anti-Western and militaristic tendencies in Russian opinion, restore the atmosphere of the cold war to East-West relations, and impel Russian foreign policy in directions decidedly not to our liking." Strobe Talbott, then deputy secretary of state, told Clinton that as Kennan had originally opposed the formation of NATO, his doubts as to its expansion were not surprising. At that point, however, the question for Clinton was no longer whether but when the Eastern Europeans would be asked to join NATO. In a holding action, NATO proposed the "Partnership for Peace," an innocent-sounding program consisting of joint planning, exercises, and peacekeeping missions with Eastern European participants (including Russia), which signed up to the program in 1994.

The moment for expansion came in 1999 when the Czech Republic, Hungary, and Poland joined NATO on the very eve of the alliance's first shooting war with Serbia over that country's refusal to relinquish control over Kosovo, a province that was overwhelmingly populated by Muslim non-Serbs. The missing country was Slovakia, which had been slated to join at the same time but was put off because of the nondemocratic practices employed by Vladimir Meciar, the country's elected leader. He ceased to be prime minister toward the end of 1998. A further enlargement came five years later, when the three Baltic states—Estonia, Latvia, and Lithuania—joined, along with Slovenia, Slovakia, Romania, and Bulgaria.

The expansion of NATO to former Soviet bloc countries marked a major step in extending Western security guarantees eastward. It was a move that Russia grudgingly accepted. Russia also accepted the expansion of the EU when in 2004 four countries that had been Soviet bloc satellites (the Czech Republic, Slovakia, Hungary, and Poland), three former constituent states of the Soviet Union (Estonia, Latvia, and Lithuania), and Slovenia (formerly part of Yugoslavia) all joined the EU. Romania and Bulgaria became members in 2007. By the time these countries had joined the EU, all were also members of NATO.

The eastward expansion of NATO and the EU had been a major operation. These two Western institutions provided a stable framework that not only stabilized the region but also delivered a road map for the transition from one-party rule and a command economy to a multiparty democracy and a free market system. In contrast to the previous forty years when the Cold War division of Europe had stabilized the free and the unfree sides of the continent, the map of the region in the 1990s bore a remarkable similarity to the map of the interwar period. But the post-Versailles European settlement had been inherently unstable. It had been left to a weak League of Nations, another of Wilson's initiatives, to try to provide a framework for the resolution of territorial and other disputes. The League of Nations, unfortunately, had failed to prevent the onset of war in 1939.

As the countries that had been subjugated by the Soviet Union regained their independence in 1989, conflicts powered by nationalisms frozen for four decades might well have reemerged, as General Inge feared. But this time, happily, in contrast to the post–World War I era, the EU and NATO were in existence, and these newly sovereign states could be slotted into these organizations. They provided a democratic and free market institutional framework and a promise of security against any future attempt by the Russians to reestablish their power in the region. This was what the post-Soviet Europeans were most interested in. Both NATO and the EU also gave a seal of approval for these countries that had for so long been isolated from the West. Now they wanted, once again, to be recognized as part of the cultural and political family to which they had once belonged. "The return to Europe" or, more simply, "coming home" was a slogan often heard in those years throughout the region. There was a price, however. This was that the countries that wanted to join had to adhere to certain standards— to press ahead with market reforms, establish working democratic systems, and establish (and maintain) good relations with their neighbors. These were strict conditions, as Slovakia found to its cost. The nationalistic and authoritarian policies of its leader, Vladimir Meciar, caused that country's drive toward NATO and the EU to be delayed by several years. If there was anything that ensured the Eastern Europeans' smooth transition from the communist regime, it was the conditionality that the Western institutions imposed as the price for membership. Indeed, with foresight, it is clear that these countries would never have implemented the complex reforms that were expected of them if the "carrot" of membership had not been dangled before their eyes.

The Eastern Europeans had little space in which to build a creative foreign policy in those years. They had nowhere else to go. The retention of a close relationship with Russia was emotionally, politically, and economically out of the question. The only alternative was to stay in a "gray" area between Russia and the West. But this was not a real alternative. The initiative in foreign policy was with the NATO and EU member states. It was they who set the conditions for accession, and there was very little that the applicants could do to modify those conditions. Their overriding aim was to join NATO and the EU. Their entire diplomatic and administrative effort was focused on this goal. Foreign policy came down to individual countries presenting the best possible case for membership and working on their image in the West. Applicant countries also did everything to conceal their policy preferences on issues that divided the existing members, especially within the EU. These included the ongoing debate on whether to press ahead with integration or to retain the present level of cooperation

within the EU between member states. Discretion was essential, as each
member state would have to sanction the accession of each candidate at
the end of the negotiations. None of the aspirants wanted to make enemies
within the EU who might block their entry. In addition, individual applicant countries sought, at times, to overtake their other Eastern European
partners in making progress in the negotiations with the EU on various
parts of the accession treaty that each country had to sign. The Hungarians, for example, complained bitterly that they were in the same group of
applicants as Poland, a country larger than Hungary and thus with bigger
problems to resolve before becoming a member than their smaller Eastern
European partner. But this factor turned out to be of minimal significance
as it became clear that, especially in the case of the EU, all the applicants,
bar Romania and Bulgaria, would join together. Thus, any country that
completed its negotiations before the others would simply have to wait for
the others to catch up before joining.

There was room, however, for bilateral negotiations. Because of their
wartime experience, Poland and Germany made a special effort in the early
1990s to establish a good relationship, and they succeeded. In addition,
Germany was, first and foremost, interested in having Poland, the largest
and most strategically located of the applicant states, join the EU. At the
same time, France was noticeably less enthusiastic about enlargement. Paris
was happy to pounce on real or imagined shortcomings in Poland's state
of preparations in order to slow down the process. Initially, France had
been worried that after absorbing East Germany (the German Democratic
Republic) following the fall of the Berlin Wall in 1989, Germany would
become even more influential inside the EU if its close ally, Poland, were
also to join. The Germans and the Poles proposed the establishment of a
three-way group with the French that would discuss accession policy and
ease relations within the triangle. The idea was to allay France's suspicions
that its traditional leading role together with Germany at the center of
decision making in the EU was about to be whittled away. Thus, the three
foreign ministers of France, Germany, and Poland, Roland Dumas, Hans
Dietrich Genscher, and Krzysztof Skubiszewski, met in Weimar in 1991 to
set in train a process of consultations that came to be known as the Weimar
Triangle.

It was also in 1991, that the Czechs, then still with the Slovaks, and the
Hungarians as well as the Poles established a forum for cooperation—the
Visegrad group. This aimed to smooth their entry into NATO and the EU
and recognized that the common experience of being in the Soviet bloc
gave them grounds for working together. But individual ambitions to join
the Western organizations as quickly as possible and national rivalries
meant that the four countries never really worked together as a group in
talks with the EU and NATO. Each preferred to go its own way with the

smaller countries, the Czechs, the Slovaks, and the Hungarians, resentful of Poland's demographic weight, while Warsaw showed little skill in building constructive relations with its Eastern European partners.

It was only in 2004 when the countries of the region were safely inside the EU and NATO that they began to have a foreign policy of their own. In a sense that was also true of the Western Europeans, who until 1989 had been forced by the Cold War divide to toe the Western line in the confrontation with the Soviets. After the fall of the Berlin Wall, it turned out that General Inge's intuition about looking at the present and the future through the perspective of the past was correct. Central Europe is a fascinating example of this. Memories stretching back hundreds of years play an important role in shaping the way governments and societies think about foreign policy. Past grandeur and past traumas are as important as countries' present-day geographic location, size, economic strength, and political clout. Literature and the visual arts, history taught in school, and even architecture and landscapes determine the way people think about the role their countries have played and are destined to play in the greater scheme of things. Anyone who has been inside the British Foreign Office, designed in the second half of the nineteenth century at the height of the British Empire, will understand why, despite their country's diminished stature, British diplomats still look at the world as a whole and are ready to involve Britain in far-flung foreign projects. Dutch diplomats and think tankers discuss issues in seventeenth-century merchant townhouses in The Hague, the country's capital, surrounded by portraits of the original owners who traded across the globe and built Holland's wealth. Those pictures remind them that they owe it to their ancestors to play a role in the world. The parliament building in Vienna, completed in 1883, has the coats of arms of the seventeen former provinces of the Austro-Hungarian Empire on the gable on the front of the building. The motif is repeated in the reception room used by the parliament's present-day budget committee. Any deputy whose attention momentarily wanders from the minutiae of the Austrian budget and looks up at the ceiling sees how far the empire reached before 1918, especially into the Balkans. For Poles, architecturally, the limits of their eastward influence is marked out by Catholic baroque churches that still can be found deep into Belarus and as far east as in today's Ukraine.

It is, of course, a gross oversimplification to suggest that the policies that member states pursue within the EU and toward NATO are determined by their memory and traumas of the past. There is a vast amount of everyday business that is conducted within the EU that deals with the regulation of the single market and that touches on internal arrangements in each of the twenty-seven member states. Coalitions between member states are formed on particular issues where countries have a specific interest to defend or pursue. But memory does play a role in how the various member states view the EU's role in the world and in their attitude to other member states and to the EU's neighborhood to the south and east. The new member states in Eastern Europe function here at two levels. Their common experience within the Soviet bloc is a trauma that defines their attitude toward Russia. Membership of the EU and NATO is seen as a safe haven for these recent escapees from the Soviet Union. For these countries, the 1990s was merely an interlude when Russia was weak.

But they are convinced it is a situation that will not last. President Lennart Meri of Estonia summed up the view typical for other Eastern Europeans such as Václav Havel, the playwright president of the Czech Republic, or Lech Wałęsa, the Polish Solidarity leader, in a conversation with Strobe Talbott in 1993. "Russia was a malignancy in remission; the Yeltsin era was at best a fleeting opportunity to be seized before Russia relapsed into authoritarianism at home and expansionism abroad," the U.S. deputy secretary of state remembers being told.[4] This feeling of distrust was reinforced by memories of Stalinist repression after World War II, mass deportations of Eastern Europeans to the Russian hinterland, and military crackdowns in Hungary in 1956, Czechoslovakia in 1968, and Poland in 1981. For the Poles, the massacre of around 22,000 Polish officers interned by the Soviets in 1939 and murdered by the Soviet security police, the NKVD, in the spring of 1940 and then buried in mass graves in Katyń and other places has become a symbol of past relations.

The wounds of Katyń were rubbed raw again when a plane crash in Smolensk in western Russia on April 10, 2010, killed Polish president Lech Kaczyński, his wife Maria, and ninety-four others, including senior members of the president's staff, the entire high command of the armed forces, and the head of Poland's central bank. The presidential party was traveling to Katyń to commemorate the seventieth anniversary of the 1940 massacre. The tragic irony of the time and place of the crash escaped no one in Poland.

The Russian leadership responded swiftly with condolences and promises of help for the victims as well as a full and transparent inquiry into the causes of the crash. President Dimitriy Medvedev attended President Kaczyński's funeral in Kraków, generating goodwill that augured well for the future of Polish–Russian relations.

For its part, the Polish government made it clear that it wanted an end to the hesitation the Russian side has sometimes shown about accepting full responsibility for the wartime massacre. The Poles also requested all the archives on the case to be opened, a sine qua non for any lasting improvement in bilateral relations. The Russian leaders appeared to accept this condition and promised to do what they could.

Yet the Soviet legacy, which is strongly felt in Eastern Europe, remains, a source of some confusion in the West and of misunderstanding in relations between the new and the old member states. Since joining the Western institutions, the Eastern Europeans have sought to get their Western partners to recognize and commemorate their tragic postwar experiences. Representatives of the new member states want to establish that the twentieth-century crimes of the Soviets were as foul as or even more so than those perpetrated by the Nazis. This attempt to put an equals sign between the two totalitarian regimes of the past century has, however, met with resistance. This controversy can be followed most easily in the European Parliament in the 2004–2009 term, where deputies from the Eastern European new member states arrived for the first time. There they saw their motions commemorating Soviet-era crimes and antitotalitarian resistance heroes contested by deputies from left-wing parties. The reasons for this are rooted in the controversy not only over the past but also toward present-day Russia under Vladimir Putin, which remains ambivalent about the Soviet past.

While the political left in Europe has condemned the excesses of Stalin's rule, it is still sensitive about outright censure of the Soviet system and any wholesale comparisons with fascism, as these would undermine its basic left-wing ideals and its criticism of the European right. At the same time, the memory in Western Europe of World War II is that the Soviet Union was an ally in the fight against Hitler. The war is seen by many as a just war. Thus, the picture would be blurred if Stalin, the ally of the Western democracies, were to be arrayed in the same dock of history as Adolf Hitler. The comparison being made by the Eastern Europeans also reminds the Western Europeans of the uncomfortable fact that after 1945 the easterners were abandoned by the Western democracies on the wrong side of the iron curtain and left in the clutches of a brutal Soviet regime. In the West, this is a sign of amnesia, not of memory.

On top of this comes the contemporary controversy over attitudes to present-day Russia. When Eastern Europeans warn, as did the late Meri, that Russia is returning to the authoritarian and expansionist traits of its Soviet past, they are told that they are being paranoid. The mainstream Western European approach represented by Germany is that an accommodation with Russia has to be sought on the assumption that the country is slowly changing but that it will indeed revert to its old traits if it is criticized and isolated by the Europeans as the new member states appear to be demanding.

But there is another level in the foreign policy debate in the EU that goes beyond the traumas of the past century. The attitudes of states and nations are shaped by long-term memories, and this is also true of the policy preferences of EU member states. Thanks to the worldwide role they have played in the past, France and Great Britain opt for an active role for the EU abroad, be it in aid policies or an appetite for military involvement in conflicts in other continents. France is especially interested in North Africa, and its troops made up the largest contingent of an EU mission in Chad, a former colony. The Austrians have a keen memory of the Austro-Hungarian Empire, and they have not only taken an interest in the expansion of the EU to the Balkans but also invested heavily in banking and other industries throughout their pre–World War I territories. The Hungarians have a memory of a glorious past but also of interminable fights with the Ottoman Empire to the south. But in the final analysis, the Hungarian memory is of being left with a truncated state after the Treaty of Trianon in 1920. Then the country lost 72 percent of its territory and 64 percent of its inhabitants. Its population shrank from 21 million to 8 million with much of its population finding itself a national minority in neighboring states. The proponents of the Czechoslovak state that was restored in 1918 were motivated by the memory of a history that had ended at the battle of the White Mountain in 1621 when Protestant Bohemia was crushed by the Catholic Habsburgs. As with the Hungarians, the main aim of the Czechoslovaks was to survive. Their instinct now within the EU is to keep their heads below the parapet and avoid challenging the policy preferences of the great powers.

The memory of the Poles differed from that of their southern neighbors. Their country, which in the seventeenth century had been one of the largest in Europe, had been partitioned by three neighboring powers in 1795 and literally wiped from the map. But Poland's elites retained a sense of loss and struggled throughout the nineteenth century for the reestablishment of their state. That struggle, however, had not been just about the restoration of the state as such but for the restoration of the state within its prepartition frontiers. This meant that in the east, the Poles, hopelessly it might seem, were struggling to push back the Russian Empire to in effect its sixteenth-century limits. That tradition carried over into the twentieth century when, in 1920, in the aftermath of World War I, the Polish leader Józef Pilsudski launched an eastern offensive to forestall a planned attack by the Red Army. The attack was also designed to bolster an independent Ukrainian state allied to Poland. The offensive failed, and a Red Army counterattack faltered at the gates of Warsaw. The newly independent Poland survived. The bid to establish an independent Ukraine also failed, but the Poles kept up their efforts throughout the 1920s to support a Ukrainian national movement within the Soviet Union. Agents also were sent to the Caucasus and elsewhere in the Soviet Union in a project called the Promethean initiative.[5]

This secret war between Polish agents and the Soviet NKVD, the forerunner of the KGB, surely remains embedded in the collective memory of the Soviet secret services. The Russian authorities, subconsciously, acknowledged this rivalry when they instituted November 4 as "Unity Day" in 2005 as one of the more important of the Russian national holidays. This was the anniversary of a popular uprising in Moscow in 1612 that drove out a pro-Polish ruler from the Kremlin and ended a Polish occupation of the Russian capital that had lasted two years.

That eastward drive that had taken the Poles to the Kremlin had come after an act of union with the Grand Duchy of Lithuania in 1569, which created one of the largest states in Europe of the time. The Lithuanians also have a memory of a glorious past. This helps to explain the fact that they, too, are ready to play an active role in EU eastern policy. It may seem far-fetched to suggest that, subconsciously, a contest rooted in the past continues between Poland and Lithuania on one side and Russia on the other. But it also has to be said that today's Polish foreign policy in the east concentrates to a great extent on attempting to secure Ukraine's independence and entry into the EU and NATO while Poland and Lithuania are the most active EU member states working for the democratization of Belarus. The eastern frontier of these two countries that made up the Polish-Lithuanian Commonwealth in 1569 is, by and large, today's western frontier of Russia, and the Eastern Europeans want to keep it that way.

A Polish historical memory that comes down to one of rivalry with Russia runs very much counter to the German tradition, which is that of cooperation with Russia—despite the punishing wars the two countries waged against each other twice in the twentieth century. Indeed, Germany was finally forged into a nation-state by Otto von Bismarck only in 1871 and has a short historical memory as such. And much of that consciousness is dominated by the nightmare years of the 1930s when Adolf Hitler's criminal, Nazi regime led to the destruction of the country and its division and the occupation of the eastern part by the Soviet Union in 1945. Germany has no colonial tradition to speak of. But it does have a strong positive memory of cooperation between the two countries dating back to the reign in Russia of Catherine the Great.

It was Catherine, the daughter of the German prince of Anhalt-Zerbst, who ruled the Russian empire from 1762 to 1796 and extended its frontier westward to incorporate large parts of Poland as a result of the partitions. That tradition of German involvement in Russian affairs also includes the domination by a German aristocracy of the territories of Estonia and Latvia in tsarist times and their role in the Russian administration. After World War I, Germany looked to the newly established Soviet Russia as an attractive market. In the 1920s and early 1930s, the Soviet Union helped to train German airmen and develop and produce armaments for the German state that was suffering from restrictions on expanding its military potential imposed by the Treaty of Versailles. This cooperation was broken off in 1933 when Hitler and the Nazis came to power but revived with the Molotov–Ribbentrop pact on August 23, 1939. This was a de facto alliance between the Soviet Union and Nazi Germany and opened the way to the invasion of Poland by the Germans a week later and the start of World War II. The alliance was broken only when Hitler invaded the Soviet Union in June 1941.

These are only part of the remembered historical narratives in the old and new member states that help to shape their policy within the EU and with which the EU as a whole has had to cope since 2004 when the new member states joined. A year before that, however, the United States led a "coalition of the willing" to war against Iraq, which President George W. Bush accused of stockpiling weapons of mass destruction and harboring al-Qaeda. The call for support from the United States split the European member states. France and Germany refused to join in, while the United Kingdom, Italy, and Spain, as well as a number of the Eastern European candidates to the EU, backed President Bush. The Czech Republic, Hungary, and Poland even signed a letter of support for the United States that dismayed Gerhard Schröder, the German leader who was in the process of persuading the other EU member states to expedite membership negotiations for the candidates, including and especially Poland. To Schröder's chagrin, Leszek Miller, the Polish prime minister of the time and a Social Democrat like the German chancellor, failed to give forewarning to his colleague that Poland was about to make this move.

This support for the United States in Iraq revealed a number of things about the prospective new member states, including the fact that they looked for their security not to the EU and not even to NATO, of which they had recently become members, but to the United States. In a nutshell, a country like Poland went into Iraq because it felt that by fighting in Baghdad, it was taking out an insurance policy for any future threat to Białystok on its eastern border. The reasoning of the then Polish administration went further. Poland had joined the EU because this was the organization in its immediate neighborhood that it could not afford to ignore. But it was the United States that was the power in the world, not only in military but also in economic terms. Miller felt that it was by strengthening links with the United States that his country could infuse dynamism into its economy. The EU, he thought, was all very well, but it still labored under various restrictive practices. Efforts to make it the most competitive economy in the world were faltering. Thus, in 2003, instead of purchasing the Swedish–British Gripen fighter for its air force, Poland went for the U.S. F-16 made by Lockheed Martin. The deal was worth US$3.5 billion, and the cost was to be offset by $6 billion worth of inward investments in Poland. It was to this and to expected lucrative contracts in Iraq for Polish companies after the allied victory over Saddam Hussein that the Polish government was looking to provide a boost to the economy. Meanwhile, the Czechs and the Hungarians went for the "European option" and purchased the Gripen fighter.

In the end, all the Eastern European countries went into Iraq to support the United States. They won praise from Donald Rumsfeld, the U.S. defense secretary, who called them "new Europe" in contrast to the Germans and the French who had refused to get involved. The term was not strictly accurate, as the Spaniards, the British, and the Italians, who were very "old Europe," also supported the United States, but the description stuck. More worrying was the fact that the hopes that the Polish prime minister had entertained of a strong and profitable relationship with the United States failed to be fulfilled. Even though the Polish military involvement in Iraq at around a thousand fighting personnel was considerable, the effort failed to produce tangible economic benefits. The F-16 deal that was also designed to produce U.S. direct investment in Poland remained fraught by controversy as to the exact level of implementation. Public opinion came away with the impression that the contract had not been very beneficial. In what appears to be a small issue but one that had enormous significance for Polish public opinion, the United States adamantly refused to waive the visa requirement for Poles coming to the United States. This was because the proportion of Poles illegally outstaying the length of their visas remained and remains too high. But in the public eye, this was an unwarranted indignity imposed on the citizens of a country that thought of itself as a valued ally of the United States. Initially, the issue remained a perennial item on the bilateral agenda. But domestic pressure on the Polish government eased when Poles found that they could go to Great Britain and Ireland to work legally and no longer needed to travel and find illegal work in the United States.

These were the factors that soured what had traditionally been a good relationship between the United States and Poland thanks to the massive immigration to the United States in the past century and the lasting links between Polish Americans and Poles at home. But another, more important security issue clouded relations between the two countries. This was the fact that when, in the 1990s, the United States negotiated NATO's eastward expansion with Boris Yeltsin, the Russian leader, unwritten promises were made that the change in status of the Eastern Europeans would not lead to a change in the military balance of power in the region. The Russians took this to mean not only that nuclear weapons would not be located on the territory of the new NATO states but also that no significant modernization of the new members' armed forces would be undertaken, nor would NATO forces be stationed in these countries. This is a commitment that the Russians take very seriously and that NATO and the United States by and large have met. For the Eastern Europeans, though, this is a matter of much concern because it implies that there is one set of NATO members who can do what they see fit to secure their defenses and another set of members over whose military status the Russians have a say.

That concern was deepened by a close reading of the NATO treaty dating back to 1949 that to all intents and purposes contains the "one for all and all for one" mutual defense clause that has never been tested. Article 5, the relevant clause, shows that the mutual defense commitment is not as tight as appears at first glance. The article says that "an armed attack against one or more of (the members) . . . shall be considered an attack against them all and consequently . . . they agree that each of them . . . will assist the Party or Parties so attacked by taking forthwith individually and in concert with the other parties, *such actions as it deems necessary*, including the use of armed force to restore and maintain the security of the North Atlantic Area." The key phrase that has caught the eye of the new member states is "such actions as it deems necessary." This in their mind suggests that NATO member states have a great deal of leeway in deciding what their response would be if there were, for example, a limited armed attack against one of the NATO states.

To make things worse, the post-1989 NATO alliance has been unwilling to identify Russia as a potential aggressor in public or, for all intents and purposes, in private. This contrasts with the pre-1989 situation when the Soviet threat was the sole reason for NATO's existence. But it fails to match up to the present situation as defined by the new member states. For them, a potential if distant threat from Russia still remains the most important reason why they wanted to join NATO in the first place. An exact reading of article 5 of the NATO treaty would be less worrying for the new member states if NATO were to have contingency plans for their defense if such an eventuality were to arise. However, such plans do not exist, and work on them is not proceeding. Admittedly, a NATO air squadron does patrol the eastern borders of the Baltic states, but that is about all. Indeed, insistent suggestions made inside NATO by new member states such as Poland and the Estonia that work on such plans might be initiated are set aside by, among others, Germany, which is ever careful not to upset Russian sensibilities.

These concerns explain why a country like Poland, which does not believe that the EU's fledgling military capacity will in the foreseeable future become a serious force and has its doubts about NATO, looks to a special relationship with the United States to ensure its security. But given the commitments made by Washington to Moscow in the 1990s, this has not been easy. Indeed, it was seen by Warsaw as a godsend when the Bush administration stepped up plans for its antimissile defense system and expressed a desire to locate a military installation in northern Poland with a massive tracking and listening radar facility in the Czech Republic. This was exactly the opportunity the Poles needed to try and break the moratorium on new Western military projects on their territory. Not only did they agree to the missile defense project, but they also demanded that the Americans install a battery of Patriot missiles in Poland to defend the installation. In its dying days, the Bush administration agreed. Of course, the military significance of the battery was negligible but the symbolic significance huge. The Russians, angry about the missile defense facility itself, were furious about the battery and reacted immediately. They threatened to install Iskander medium-range missiles in Kaliningrad, a Russian enclave on the Baltic, and to aim them at Poland and the Czech Republic.

The heat came off the issue with the election of President Barack Obama. The new Democratic administration decided to reconfigure the missile defense project but keep the Patriot missile battery plan in place. But there remained a number of worrying questions for the Poles and the other Eastern Europeans raised by the new administration. Would the Democrats seek a new relationship with Moscow that would aim at arms control agreements? How far would they seek to enlist the Russians in helping with achieving an accommodation with Iran? And would the price be recognition by the United States of a specific Russian sphere of influence in the countries that had once belonged to the Soviet Union or had been Soviet allies in the Warsaw Pact? Another question for the Poles and other Eastern Europeans who had been pushing, along with the Bush administration, for NATO membership for Georgia and Ukraine was whether these two countries would be left outside the alliance to drift closer to Russia.

For the Poles as well as the Baltic countries and for the Czechs, Slovaks, and Hungarians, the principle that the Soviet successor states were independent entities that had the right to chose to link up with Western organizations such as NATO and the EU became a foreign policy axiom. But they went further and actively supported the Western aspirations of countries such as Georgia and Ukraine. This invariably raised hackles in Moscow. If the aim of drawing more and more former Soviet states into the Western community had met with Bush's approval and remained to be tested with Obama, it had always been greeted with mixed feelings in the EU. Here, Germany steadfastly stuck to the line that Russian concerns had to be taken into account. Berlin argued that access to Russian energy resources was crucial to the EU and that, because of their experiences under Soviet domination, the Eastern Europeans were unable to take a realistic and levelheaded approach to present-day Russia and would by their stance jeopardize that aim.

Energy supply and security of those supplies especially from Russia was the issue that lay at the very heart of the dispute inside the EU between, in effect, the new and the old member states. Germany, as in the 1920s, saw Russia as a major present and future export market as well as a supplier of natural gas. Italy took a similar approach. In the 1990s, many Western energy companies had entertained hopes of obtaining a significant stake in Russia's energy industry. After all, Russian gas and oil fields and transport systems needed Western capital and technology to maintain output. But a decade later under Putin, many Western companies were squeezed out of the Russian market, while the Germans retained an important role in Russia. The point of view of the Eastern European new member states was different. As past members of the Soviet bloc, their energy supply systems were tied into the infrastructure of the former Soviet energy industry, and in some cases they were 100 percent reliant on Russian energy supplies. This was seen as a dangerous level of dependence that, at the threat of the turn of a gas switch, could be translated into Russian political leverage. Accordingly, the Eastern Europeans looked to the EU to devise schemes to guarantee their energy security. The most ambitious and least successful plan came from Poland, which in 2006 proposed a NATO-style "one for all and all for one" plan. This would, in case of energy supply cuts from Russia or elsewhere to any state, oblige other states to come to its aid with emergency supplies.

At the same time, a planned joint Russo–German gas pipeline under the Baltic from Russia to Germany called Nord Stream came to symbolize for Poland at least an agreement between the two countries to cooperate without regard for the interests of other EU partners. For the Russians, this project was designed to avoid the necessity of having its gas deliveries to Germany travel across other states—in this case, Poland and Belarus. This marked a shift of policy compared to the 1990s. Then the Russians had built the "Yamal" land pipeline across these two countries to Germany and had planned to construct a second, parallel pipe along the same route. This was a cheaper option than the pipe under the Baltic, and its advantage for the Poles was that it would have made it more difficult for the Russians to cut off supplies solely to their country, to say nothing of the fact that, thanks to the pipeline, Poland and Belarus earned transit fees. At the same time, the Russians were toying with the idea of closing down the "Friendship" pipeline that had been built in the 1960s and since then had supplied oil to refineries in Poland and eastern Germany. The closure would force these customers to buy their oil at a port in the Gulf of Finland and bring it by sea to their refineries. Inside the EU, the Poles have campaigned against the Baltic pipeline. Indeed, the argument that at some point the Russians would be tempted to use their strong position as an energy supplier to gain political advantage was strengthened by periodic cutoffs of gas supplies to Ukraine and to Europe as a result of tussles between Ukraine and Russia over the terms of gas supplies. But the implementation of an energy policy enabling the EU to speak to Russia with one voice continued to elude the organization.

The foreign policy of the new Polish government elected in 2007 and led by the center-right Platforma Obywatelska (PO, Civic Platform) contrasted with that of its predecessors, the Prawo and Sprawiedliwość Party (PiS, Law and Justice), a more nationalistic party that had adopted a confrontational approach to Russia. PO was committed to establishing a rapprochement with Moscow and thus to enter the mainstream of EU policy toward Russia. At the same time, PO developed a pragmatic attitude toward Belarus, where President Aleksander Lukashenko's authoritarian regime had led the EU to impose mild political sanctions on the country. Poland maintained its support for Ukraine's aspirations to join NATO and the EU, but the tone of policy became less strident, especially compared to that of the preceding administration. The problem with this new policy was that although the elections brought a new government to power, the president, Lech Kaczyński, a supporter of a tough line on Russia and the twin brother of the PiS leader Jaroslaw Kaczyński, still had three years in office.

In Poland, the president is elected on a universal ballot but has limited powers, including in foreign policy, where he is mandated merely to represent Poland abroad. The constitution, which is not entirely clear on this point, obliges the government to shape and conduct foreign policy. However, President Kaczyński used the formula of "representation abroad" to extend his powers and to conduct a foreign policy of his own. Lech Kaczyński's policies underscored the dangers that, in his view, Russia posed, and he eagerly supported those former Soviet states such as Georgia whose position he felt was threatened by Moscow. Thus, when the short war broke out between Russia and Georgia in August 2008 and the Russian army came to within striking distance of Tbilisi, the president flew to the Georgian capital with other Eastern European leaders, notably Ukrainian president Viktor Yushchenko, and offered Poland's support for Mikheil Saakashvili, their Georgian colleague. The Polish government, with whom the move had not been cleared, preferred to rely on the EU to bring the conflict to a halt and salvage Georgia's independence.

The contrast between the two approaches is worth dwelling on, as it shows the dilemma that a country like Poland now faces in its policy toward Russia. The confrontational approach adopted by PiS and supported by President Kaczyński won Poland few plaudits in Berlin and in Brussels, where Germany's voice carries weight. But it is popular in Baltic states, such as Estonia, where Western-born, U.S.-educated president Hendrik Ilves sees the value of the Polish president's role in helping to keep up Europe's guard against Russia. Many people throughout the former Soviet bloc greeted the demise of the PiS government in Poland in 2007 with dismay and saw it as a sign that Russia would be able to extend more easily its sphere of influence throughout the region. But at the same time, Poland's influence within the EU and its ability to secure its interests in internal EU matters is limited by a confrontational approach on Russia that tends to push the country to the margins of EU policymaking. Indeed, Ukraine was thankful to the PiS government for its support in trying to help the country come closer to NATO and EU membership. But Ukrainian diplomats were also well aware that Polish support could be counterproductive given the country's approach to Russia and its frayed relations with Germany. In a word, Kiev knew that it needed to get the support of Germany itself if its chances of EU membership were to improve.

The PO-led administration sought to resolve this contradiction between confrontation and accommodation with Russia by proposing to the EU an "Eastern partnership" policy that was modeled on the Mediterranean Union propagated by President Nicolas Sarkozy of France and intended to bring the countries on the southern side of the Mediterranean closer to the EU. Accordingly, in 2008 Donald Tusk, the Polish prime minister, suggested that the EU conclude a new agreement with six eastern states: Armenia, Azerbaijan, Belarus, Georgia, Moldova, and Ukraine. The plan, which won the support of Sweden, envisaged the establishment of a free trade area with these countries as well as an easing of visa restrictions and a number of joint projects that would enable them to approximate their legal systems, institutions, and democratic practices to those in the EU. These reforms meant that at some time in the future, they would be able to seek to join the EU. The Eastern Partnership won the grudging approval of the EU member states, but the lack of enthusiasm was evident not only in the paucity of the €600 million budget for the project but also in the fact that the leaders of the "southern states" of the EU—Italy, France, and Spain—stayed away from the summit in Prague in May 2009 that was supposed to unveil the partnership.

To make things worse, just as Russia is adamantly opposed to further NATO enlargements, before the Prague summit Moscow signaled that it saw the Eastern Partnership as an encroachment by the EU on its sphere of influence. Another danger was that engagement with the six states by the EU led it dangerously close to a set of leaders whose commitment to democratic values and practices left much to be desired. Only in Ukraine has democracy, albeit in a fairly chaotic form, taken root after the "Orange Revolution" in 2004. In Georgia, a vociferous opposition accuses President Saakashvili of autocratic practices. In Armenia, Azerbaijan, and Belarus, democracy appears to be "managed" by these countries' rulers. In Moldova, an election in April 2009 led to demonstrations by young people who accused the authorities of fixing the result. These demonstrations were crushed by Soviet-style methods designed to put an end to public criticism of the country's rulers. These included restrictions on the media, expulsion of foreign journalists, and harassment of nongovernmental organizations. In a word, the Eastern Partnership, which was designed to involve the EU in an active drive for democratic change in the east, began to look like a dangerous flirtation with a group of inherently unstable states led by autocratic rulers who, when their power was challenged, were willing to brutally crack down on dissenters. Poland, even though it sought to position itself in the mainstream of EU thinking on eastern policy, once again, thanks to the Eastern Partnership, risked being seen as an irresponsible force dragging the EU into adventures in the east.

Since entering the EU, Poland has tried to cajole the organization into taking account of its security concerns as well as the concerns of the other Eastern European countries. But Poland's position might have been stronger if the country had not adopted a confrontational position on the attempts of the EU to streamline decision making exactly in response to enlargement of the EU. Almost from the very day that Poland came in to the EU, the country sought to block the introduction of a new constitutional treaty that would have changed the voting system inside the EU in a way that Warsaw charged was detrimental to its interests. The dispute set Poland, working together with Spain, against the rest of the EU member states. A compromise was finally reached, but the treaty was rejected by voters in France and Holland, and an attempt to resuscitate it was once again contested by Poland's former PiS government. Attempts to get the treaty ratified were blocked by voters in Ireland but also by President Kaczyński, who refused to sign the treaty for many months. This record of confrontation with the EU has given Poland a reputation inside the organization of being an awkward country, and its image among Brussels policymakers has suffered as a result. Consequently, Poles have suffered in the sharing out of posts inside the EU institutions. Candidates from other new member states have been awarded jobs over the heads of Poles, who are thought to be not strongly enough imbued with the EU spirit. This means that Polish interests may not be defended as well in the future when today's young recruits reach influential positions that will be held by representatives of other countries from the region.

For the Eastern Europeans, the process of adapting to and finding a place inside the two Western organizations, NATO and the EU, will continue in the coming years. The EU is important because it provides a secure economic and political anchor for the post-1989 changes. NATO is important because, for all its failings, it remains a major military organization with the crucial element of U.S. support. While Poland withdrew from Iraq in the autumn of 2008, it stepped up its commitment to the NATO contingent fighting the war against the Taliban in Afghanistan the following year. Poland also promptly agreed to send further troops to the country in response to Obama's request for reinforcements in late 2009. Once again, Poland was looking to defend Bialystok at some time in the future by fighting in Ghazni province now.

And while the urgency of the missile defense project declined with the arrival of the Obama administration, the Poles and their neighbors will continue to look to the United States for special arrangements that could secure their future. The question will always remain as to what extent the United States will pay attention to the security concerns of the Eastern Europeans. The problems of the Eastern Europeans look very regional indeed from Washington, which has so many other places and issues on its agenda, including seeking a rapprochement with Iran, trying to solve Middle East problems, looking for ways to bring down arms levels and stop nuclear proliferation throughout the world, and establishing relations with China and other rising powers.

The challenge for the Eastern Europeans is to continue to work for a foreign policy consensus within the EU on a policy toward the east, including Russia, that would secure the new members' interests as well as those of the older member states. It seems unlikely that the Eastern Europeans will allow countries such as Ukraine to sink into a gray area between Russia and the EU and thus into greater dependence on Moscow. Were that to happen, it would mean the betrayal of hopes of independence engendered after 1989 in these countries and the abandonment of a young generation born after that year that has traveled and studied in the West and that wants to see their countries become "normal" places. This is the ambition of the young people who streamed out onto the streets of Chisinau, the capital of Moldova, in April 2009 to demonstrate against the results of an election there that returned the communist-style old guard to power. If hopes such as these are dashed and they are forced to conform to old-style political regimes, then in the longer term this will create a new source of instability in the region.

Zbigniew Brzezinski has remarked that the struggle for the independence of post-Soviet states such as Ukraine is also the struggle for the reform of Russia. That is a major prize. If the Eastern Europeans who are now members of the EU and NATO are looking for a relevant role in the world, then the modernization of their own countries and the modernization of the countries to the east is task enough. The jury is still out on whether they will succeed.

SUGGESTIONS FOR FURTHER READING

Bush, George, and Brent Scowcroft. *A World Transformed*. New York: Vintage, 1998.
Epstein, Rachel. *In Pursuit of Liberalism*. Baltimore: Johns Hopkins University Press, 2008.
Lieven, Anatol, and Dmitri Trenin, eds. *Ambivalent Neighbours*. Washington, DC: Carnegie Endowment, 2003.
Macmillan, Margaret. *Paris 1919*. New York: Random House, 2003.
Mayhew, Alan. *Recreating Europe*. Cambridge: Cambridge University Press, 1998.

Pond, Elizabeth. *The Rebirth of Europe*. Washington, DC: Brookings Institution, 1999.

Snyder, Timothy. *The Reconstruction of Nations: Poland, Ukraine, Lithuania, Belarus, 1569–1999*. New Haven, CT: Yale University Press, 2003.

———. *Sketches from a Secret War*. New Haven, CT: Yale University Press, 2005.

Talbott, Strobe. *The Russia Hand*. New York: Random House, 2002.

Zamoyski, Adam. *Warsaw 1920*. New York: Harper Press, 2008.

Notes

CHAPTER 1: INTRODUCTION:
EUROPE AND THE GEOPOLITICAL ORDER

1. A remarkable exposition of the importance of geography in the constitution of Europe is Alexander B. Murphy, Terry G. Jordan-Bychkov, and Bella Bychkova Jordan, *The European Culture Area: A Systematic Geography* (Lanham, MD: Rowman & Littlefield, 2009).

2. Political scientist Joseph Nye originated the concept of soft power as fundamental in international relations. See his *Bound to Lead: The Changing Nature of American Power* (New York: Basic Books, 1990) and *Soft Power: The Means to Success in World Politics* (New York: Public Affairs, 2004).

3. Robert Kagan, *Of Paradise and Power: America and Europe in the New World Order* (New York: Alfred A. Knopf, 2003), 5.

4. See Mark Leonard, "Europe's Transformative Power," *CER Bulletin*, February/March 2005, Issue 40, and *Why Europe Will Run the 21st Century* (New York: Public Affairs Books, 2005), xiii. Political scientist and former government official Richard Haass makes a similar point about U.S. foreign policy. "Realists" believe that U.S. power should be directed at the external actions of other countries that affect important U.S. interests; it should focus on what countries do rather than what they are. "What goes on inside states is not irrelevant, but it is secondary." A Wilsonian approach, however, "believes the principal purpose of what the United States does in the world is to influence the nature of states and conditions within them." The first Iraq War, to roll back Saddam Hussein's invasion and "annexation" of Kuwait (including its immense oil reserves), epitomized the realist principle, the second Iraq War was an example (a bad one) of what others have called "Wilsonianism in boots." See Haass, *War of Necessity, War of Choice: A Memoir of Two Iraq Wars* (New York: Simon and Schuster, 2009), 12.

5. These are the famous second and third "images" of the sources of war and peace formulated in Kenneth Waltz's classic book *Man, the State, and War*, 3rd ed. (New York: Columbia University Press, 2001). Henry Kissinger's essay "Domestic Structure and Foreign Policy" in *American Foreign Policy*, 2nd ed. (New York: Norton, 1979), is an example of a second image analysis. The basic idea in the second image goes back to Kant's essay *Perpetual Peace: A Philosophical Sketch* (1795) and is the foundation of the "democratic peace" theory today.

6. A good analysis of this is Jeremy Shapiro and Nick Witney, *Towards a Post-American Europe: A Power Audit of EU-US Relations* (Berlin: European Council on Foreign Relations, 2009). See also Alvaro de Vasconcelos and Marcin Zaborowski, *The Obama Moment: European and American Perspectives* (Paris: European Union Institute for Security Studies, 2009), and Mark Leonard and Nicu Popescu, *A Power Audit of EU-Russia Relations* (Berlin: European Council on Foreign Relations, 2009). These reports can be downloaded at the European Council website at http://www.ecfr.eu and the European Union Institute website http://www.iss.europa.eu.

7. Hubert Védrine, interview, *Le Monde*, May 30, 2009. See also Gideon Rachman, "Is Irrelevance Europe's Logical Choice?," *Financial Times*, May 20, 2008.

CHAPTER 2: THE EUROPEAN UNION AS A FOREIGN POLICY ACTOR: TOWARD A NEW REALISM

1. European Council, "A Secure Europe in a Better World: European Security Strategy, December 12, 2003," in *From Copenhagen to Brussels: European Defence: Core Documents*, ed. Antonio Missiroli (Paris: EU Institute for Security Studies, 2003), 324–33.

2. "Article J.4, Treaty on European Union (TEU)," in *European Union: Selected Instruments Taken from the Treaties* (Luxembourg: Office for Official Publications of the European Communities, 1995), vol. I, bk. I, 38.

3. "Declaration on European Defense," December 3–4, 1998, UK–French summit, St. Malo, http://www.fco.gov.uk.

4. "Article J.5, TEU," in *European Union*, 40.

5. Mark Leonard, *Why Europe Will Run the 21st Century* (New York: Public Affairs Books, 2005).

6. Edouard Balladur, *Pour une Union occidentale entre l'Europe et les Etats-Unis* (Paris: Fayard, 2007).

7. Andrew Rettman, "US Blames Lisbon Treaty for EU Summit Fiasco," *EU Observer*, February 3, 2010, http://euobserver.com/9/29398.

CHAPTER 3: EUROPE AND THE UNITED STATES: THE OBAMA ERA AND THE WEIGHT OF HISTORY

1. Remarks by President Obama at Strasbourg Town Hall, April 3, 2009, http://www.whitehouse.gov/the_press_office/Remarks-by-President-Obama-at-Strasbourg-Town-Hall.

2. See Chris Patten, *Cousins and Strangers: America, Britain, and Europe in a New Century* (New York: Times Books, 2006).

3. Francis Fukuyama, *The End of History and the Last Man* (New York: Free Press, 1992).

4. Remarks by British prime minister Tony Blair, Economic Club of Chicago, Chicago, April 22, 1999.

5. Dean Acheson, *Present at the Creation: My Years in the State Department* (New York: Norton, 1969).

6. Robert Kagan, *Of Paradise and Power: America and Europe in the New World Order* (New York: Knopf, 2003).

CHAPTER 4: EUROPE AND RUSSIA: STRATEGIC PARTNERSHIP AND STRATEGIC MISTRUST

1. *Official Journal of the European Communities*, L 157, June 24, 1999, 2.

2. "EU-Russia Summit Joint Statement," Helsinki, October 22, 1999.

3. Dmitri Trenin, "Russia and the European Union: Redefining Strategic Partnership," in *Partnerships for Effective Multilateralism: EU Relations with Brazil, China, India and Russia*, ed. Giovanni Grevi and Álvaro de Vasconcelos (Paris: EU Institute for Security Studies, May 2008), 133.

4. Compare Nina Bachkatov, "EU-Russia Relations Worsen," *Le Monde Diplomatique* (English ed.), June 1, 2006, http://mondediplo.com/2007/01/06russia. "If Europe wants to play the role to which it aspires in tomorrow's world, which will be dominated by China and the US, cooperation with the Russia-CIS bloc is essential."

5. Álvaro de Vasconcelos, "'Multilateralising' Multipolarity," in Grevi and Vasconcelos, *Partnerships for Effective Multilateralism*, 27.

6. *Wider Europe-Neighbourhood: A New Framework for Relations with Our Eastern and Southern Neighbours*, COM(2003), 104 final, March 11, 2003, 4.

7. For an analysis of the Mediterranean aspects of this policy, see chapter 6.

8. Dmitry Medvedev interview with Russian TV channels, August 31, 2008, http://www.kremlin.ru/eng/speeches/2008/08/31/1850_type82912type82916_206003.shtml.

9. *Eastern Partnership: Communication from the European Commission to the European Parliament and the Council*, COM(2008), 823, December 3, 2008.

10. Council of the European Union, Joint Declaration of the Prague Eastern Partnership Summit, May 7, 2009.

11. U.S. Energy Information Administration data, cited in Jeffrey Mankoff, *Eurasian Energy* (New York: Council on Foreign Relations, 2009), 13.

12. Nikolai Zlobin of the Center for Strategic Studies in Washington, D.C., as quoted in the *Wall Street Journal*, June 11, 2009.

13. In the most notorious case since the killing by poisoning of Alexander Litvinenko, the investigative journalist and human rights activist Anna Politkovskaya was assassinated in the elevator of her apartment building in October 2006. As of the date of writing, the most recent killing was that in March 2009 of Medet Sadyrkulov, a former high official of the government of Kyrgyzstan, who had become a critic

of President Murtanbek Bakiyev's steering of the country back into Moscow's orbit after its own color revolution in 2005. *Wall Street Journal*, June 11, 2009.

14. Andrew E. Kramer, "Criticized, Putin Says Europe Has Rights Abuses of Its Own," *New York Times*, February 9, 2009.

15. Andrew Rettman, "EU-Russia Summit Ends with Prickly Exchange over Energy," May 23, 2009, http://euobserver.com.

16. Dmitry Medvedev, "Speech at the Meeting with Russian Ambassadors and Permanent Representatives to International Organisations," July 15, 2008, http://www.kremlin.ru.

17. President of Russia, Official Web Portal, "European Security Treaty," November 29, 2009, http://eng.kremlin.ru/text/docs/2009/11/223072.shtml.

18. See Celeste A. Wallander, "Russian Transimperialism and Its Implications," *Washington Quarterly*, Spring 2007, 107–21.

19. Andrew E. Kramer, "Russia Says Dollar Makes a Poor Reserve Currency," *New York Times*, June 6, 2009.

CHAPTER 5: EUROPE–CHINA RELATIONS: A DELICATE DANCE

1. See Michael Yahuda, "The Sino-European Encounter: Historical Influences on Contemporary Relations," in *China-Europe Relations: Perceptions, Policies, and Prospects*, ed. David Shambaugh, Eberhard Sandschneider, and Zhou Hong (London: Routledge, 2008).

2. For further details on these years, see David Shambaugh, *China and Europe, 1949–1995* (London: SOAS Contemporary China Institute, 1996).

3. For a discussion of China's reaction to and analysis of the collapse of the Soviet Union, see David Shambaugh, *China's Communist Party: Atrophy and Adaptation* (Berkeley: University of California Press, 2008), chap. 4.

4. Zhao Junjie, "An Uneasy Balance," *Beijing Review* 50, no. 2 (January 11, 2007): 10.

5. See Dan Levin, "Chinese Wrestle with Europe in Space," *International Herald Tribune*, March 23, 2009.

6. See David Shambaugh, "China's Quiet Diplomacy: The International Department of the Chinese Communist Party," *China: An International Journal* 5, no. 1 (March 2007): 26–54.

7. Song Zhe [China's ambassador to the EU], "The Current State and Prospect of China-EU Relations," *Foreign Affairs Journal*, Spring 2009, 15.

8. For a list of these dialogues, see http://ec.europa.eu/comm/external_relations/china/intro/sect.htm.

9. These monies were expended in three program areas: economic and social reform (50 percent), sustainable development (30 percent), and good governance (20 percent). See http://www.delchn.cec.eu.int/en/Co-operation/General_Information.htm.

10. "China and EU Begin Renegotiating Commercial Treaty," *International Herald Tribune*, January 18, 2007. This is also known as the "Framework Agreement." Negotiations are anticipated to last at least two years before final conclusion of the new pact.

11. European Commission, *A Long-Term Policy for China-Europe Relations*, COM (95), 279 final, Brussels, July 1995.

12. European Commission, *China-Europe: Closer Partners, Growing Responsibilities*, and *Competition and Partnership: A Policy for EU-China Trade and Investment*. See, respectively, http://ec.europa.eu/comm/external_relations/china/docs/06-10 -24_final_com.pdf and http://ec.europa.eu/trade/issues/bilateral/countries/china/ pr241006_en.htm.

13. All of these are selected direct quotations from European Commission, *China-Europe*.

14. "EU-China Strategic Partnership: Council Conclusions," 2771st Council Meeting, December 11–12, 2006, 16291/06 (Press 353), http://register.consilium .europa.eu/pdf/en/06/st16/st16291.en06.pdf.

15. See François Godement and John Fox, *A Power Audit of EU-China Relations* (London: European Council on Foreign Relations, 2009).

CHAPTER 6: EUROPE, THE MEDITERRANEAN, AND THE MIDDLE EAST: A STORY OF CONCENTRIC CIRCLES

1. M. Comelli, E. Greco, and N. Tocci, "From Boundary to Borderland: Transforming the Meaning of Borders in Europe through the European Neighbourhood Policy," *European Foreign Affairs Review* 12 (2007): 203–18; R. Dannreuther, "Developing the Alternative to Enlargement: The European Neighbourhood Policy," *European Foreign Affairs Review* 11, no. 2 (2006): 183–201; J. Kelley, "Promoting Political Reforms through the ENP," *Journal of Common Market Studies* 44, no. 1 (2006): 29–56; Karen Smith, "The Outsiders: The European Neighbourhood Policy," *International Affairs* 81, no. 4 (2005): 757–73.

2. N. Tocci, ed., *Talking Turkey in Europe: Towards A Differentiated Communication Strategy* (Rome: IAI Quaderni, 2008).

3. J. Joseph, ed., *Turkey and the European Union: Internal Dynamics and External Challenges* (New York: Palgrave, 2006).

4. K. Derviş, M. Emerson, D. Gros, and S. Ülgen, eds., *The European Transformation of Modern Turkey* (Brussels: CEPS, 2004); S. Verney and K. Ifantis, eds., *Turkey's Road to European Union Membership* (London: Routledge, 2009).

5. N. Tocci, ed., *Conditionality, Impact and Prejudice in EU-Turkey Relations* (Rome: IAI Quaderni, 2007).

6. F. S. Larrabee and I. O. Lesser, *Turkish Foreign Policy in an Age of Uncertainty* (Washington, DC: Rand, 2003).

7. S. Krauss, "The European Parliament in EU External Relations: The Customs Union with Turkey," *European Foreign Affairs Review* 5 (2000): 215–37.

8. N. Tocci, "The Europeanization of Turkey's Kurdish Question," and "The Glaring Gap between Rhetoric and Reality in the Israeli-Palestinian Conflict," in N. Tocci, ed., *The EU and Conflict Resolution* (London: Routledge, 2007).

9. Ergenekon is the name of an alleged clandestine, secular, and ultranationalist organization in Turkey, including members from wide sectors of society (academia, media, politics, administration, judiciary, and military) with ties to members of the

country's military and security forces. The group is accused of terrorism in Turkey and the aim of toppling the AKP government and derailing Turkey's accession process. More than 100 people, including generals, party officials, lawyers, and a former secretary-general of the National Security Council, have been detained or questioned since July 2008. Hearings began on October 20, 2008, and are expected to last for more than a year.

10. On EU policy toward the Mediterranean, see F. Bicchi, *European Foreign Policy Making toward the Mediterranean* (New York: Palgrave Macmillan, 2007).

11. EU Council of Ministers, *Report on the Implementation of the European Security Strategy*, Brussels, December 2008; EU Council of Ministers, *A Secure Europe in a Better World: European Security Strategy*, Brussels, December 12, 2003.

12. Elena Aoun, "European Foreign Policy and the Arab-Israeli Dispute: Much Ado about Nothing?," *European Foreign Affairs Review* 8 (2003): 289–312.

13. A. Le More, *International Assistance to the Palestinians after Oslo: Political Guilt; Wasted Money* (London: Routledge, 2008).

14. W. Douma, "Israel and the Palestinian Authority," in *The European Union and its Neighbours: A Legal Appraisal of the EU's Policies of Stabilisation, Partnership and Integration*, ed. S. Blockmans and A. Lazowski (The Hague: Asser Press, 2006), 437–39.

15. K. Karam, D. Pioppi, and N. Tocci, "Domestic Politics and Conflict in the Cases of Israel, Palestine and Lebanon," *Euromesco Report*, no. 53/2006, 2006.

16. W. Posch, "The EU and Iran: A Tangled Web of Negotiations," in *Iranian Challenges*, ed. W. Posch, Chaillot Paper, no. 89 (Paris: EUISS, 2006), 100.

17. The Mykonos case refers to the verdict of the Berlin Court of Appeals in 1997 condemning Iranian officials for having ordered the assassination of four Kurdish dissidents in a Greek restaurant in Berlin in 1992.

18. J. Reissner, "EU-Iran Relations: Options for Future Dialogue," in Posch, *Iranian Challenges*, 115–25.

19. The most relevant resolutions are UNSC Resolution 661 of August 6, 1990 (sanctions regime); UNSC Resolution 687 of April 3, 1991 (UNSCOM inspection and monitoring instruments); and UNSC Resolution 1284 of December 17, 1999 (suspending economic sanctions on condition that Iraq complies with the new monitoring system, UNMOVIC).

20. The Oil-for-Food Program was set up by UNSC Resolution 986 in 1995. It allowed Iraq to sell oil for food, medicine, and other humanitarian products for the benefit of the Iraqi population. An obvious consequence of this program was an increase in trade: from nonexistent trade relations up until 1995, by 1999 EU imports from Iraq amounted to almost €3.7 billion, whereas exports approximated €600 million.

21. P. Van Ham, "The EU's War over Iraq: The Last Wake-Up Call," in *European Foreign Policy: From Rhetoric to Reality?*, ed. D. Mahncke, A. Ambos, and C. Reynolds (Brussels: P.I.E., 2004), 209–26.

22. On January 22, 2003, Rumsfeld spoke about an "old Europe" and a "new Europe," which soon became a clichéd yet inaccurate label to describe the division among EU member states. In Rumsfeld's definition, the former included old member states such as France and Germany, which opposed U.S. policy toward Iraq, while the latter comprised new member states, which had signed statements of

solidarity with the United States on Iraq, which became known as the Declarations of the "Gang of Eight" and the "Vilnius Ten." The definitions are inaccurate insofar as "old" member states, such as Italy, Spain, and the United Kingdom, championed the U.S. line, while other soon-to-be "new" member states, such as Cyprus and Malta, opposed it.

23. R. Dover, "The Iraq War—The Problem of National Interests for Europeanization," in *Europeanization of British Defence Policy*, ed. R. Dover (Aldershot: Ashgate, 2007), 95–116.

24. M. Overhaus and A. K. Meyer, *Chronological Overview: The European Involvement in the Conflict over Iran's Nuclear Program from 2003 until Present*, 2007, http://www.deutsche-aussenpolitik.de/resources/dossiers/iran06/Dossier-Iran-Chrono.pdf.

25. R. Linden, *Die Initiative der EU-3 im Iran: Ein Testfall für die europäische Sicherheitspolitik nach der Irak-Krise?*, 2006, http://www.deutsche-aussenpolitik.de/resources/monographies/Linden.pdf.

26. This enlarged diplomatic format, known as E3+3, or the "Contact Group," includes the five permanent members of the UNSC plus Germany. In January 2006, the E3—the United States, Russia, and China—issued the "London Declaration." Since then, these six countries have collectively addressed the diplomatic approach to Iran.

27. European Commission, *The European Union and Iraq: A Framework for Engagement*, Brussels, June 9, 2004, 2.

28. E. Burke, *The Case for a New European Engagement in Iraq*, FRIDE Working Paper, no. 74, Madrid, 2009; R. Youngs, *Europe and Iraq: From Stand-Off to Engagement?*, FRIDE Policy Paper, Madrid, November 2004.

29. Dover, "The Iraq War," 95–116; J. Lewis, *EU Policy on Iraq: The Collapse and Reconstruction of Consensus-Based Foreign Policy*, UDC Dublin European Institute Working Paper 08-9, July 2008.

30. S. N. Kile, "Final Thoughts on the EU, Iran, and the Limits of Conditionality," in *Europe and Iran: Perspectives on Non-Proliferation*, ed. S. N. Kile, SIPRI Research Report, no. 21, 2006, 122–35.

31. S. K. Sajjadpour, "The Evolution of Iran's National Security Doctrine," in Kile, *Europe and Iran*, 22–26.

32. W. Posch, *E pluribus unum: Decision-Makers and Decision-Making in Iran*, ISS Policy Brief (Paris: EUISS, 2008); Posch, "The EU and Iran," 102.

33. S. Sabet-Saeidi, "Iranian-European Relations: A Strategic Partnership?," in *Iran's Foreign Policy: From Khatami to Ahmadinejad*, ed. A. Ehteshami and M. Zweiri (Reading, MA: Ithaca Press, 2008), 55–87.

CHAPTER 7: EUROPE AND GLOBALIZATION: INTERNAL AND EXTERNAL POLICY RESPONSES

1. Visit by the author and other Brussels-based EU correspondents to London (July 1, 2005).

2. Joseph Stiglitz, *Making Globalization Work* (New York: Norton, 2006).

3. Daniel S. Hamilton and Joseph P. Quinlan, "Globalization and Europe: Prospering in the New Whirled Order," Center for Transatlantic Relations, Washington, D.C., and Johns Hopkins University, 2008.

4. Conversation with the author. The executive spoke on condition of anonymity because of the political sensitivity of his comment (November 2008).

5. http://globalization.kof.ethz.ch.

6. "Staying Competitive in the Global Economy: Compendium of Studies on Global Value Chains," 2008, http://www.oecd.org/document/62/0,3343,en_2649 _34443_40815102_1_1_1_1,00.html.

7. For a comprehensive survey of European public opinion on globalization, see "Perceptions of Globalization: Attitudes and Responses in the EU," compiled by the European Foundation for the Improvement of Living and Working Conditions, Dublin, 2008, http://www.eurofound.europa.eu/docs/erm/tn0708016s/ tn0708016s.pdf.

8. Kevin O'Rourke, "Politics and Trade: Lessons from Past Globalisations," Bruegel Essay and Lecture Series, 2009.

9. "Community preference" was a principle applied to agriculture in the 1950s and 1960s, but the European Court of Justice ruled in 1994 that it had not basis in EU treaty law.

10. Speech by Peter Mandelson, European Trade Commissioner, to The Work Foundation, London, March 6, 2008, http://ec.europa.eu/trade.

11. Speech by Gordon Brown, British prime minister, to the "Business Priorities for a Global Europe" conference, January, 14, 2008, http://www.number10.gov .uk/Page14251.

12. Key source documents on the original 2000 Lisbon Agenda and the revised 2005 strategy for growth and jobs can be found at http://ec.europa.eu/growthand jobs/faqs/background/index_en.htm#maincontent.

13. For a critical assessment of the EU's implementation of the Lisbon Agenda, see the series of annual pamphlets by the London-based Center for European Reform at http://www.cer.org.uk/lisbon_comp_new/index_lisbon_comp_new.html.

14. Interview with the author (May 2008).

15. Author's interview with a senior EU foreign policy official (February 2008).

16. Ronald Findlay and Kevin H. O'Rourke, *Power and Plenty: Trade, War and the World Economy in the Second Millennium* (Princeton, NJ: Princeton University Press, 2007).

CHAPTER 8: FRANCE: NOSTALGIA, NARCISSISM, AND REALISM

1. In the Fifth Republic's fifty-year history, there have been three periods of cohabitation government: the left/right version in 1986–1988 (the socialist president François Mitterrand with the Gaullist prime minister Jacques Chirac), the left/right version in 1992–1995 (Mitterrand and conservative prime minister Edouard Balladur), and the right/left version in 1997–2002 (President Jacques Chirac with the socialist prime minister Lionel Jospin).

2. Charles de Gaulle, *The Complete War Memoirs of Charles de Gaulle* (New York: Simon and Schuster, 1964), 761, 763.

3. Stanley Hoffmann, *Decline or Renewal? France since the 1930s* (New York: Viking Press, 1974), 288. Hoffmann's is still by far the best work on de Gaulle and de Gaulle's foreign policy. Another excellent book is Daniel J. Mahoney, *De Gaulle:*

Statesmanship, Grandeur and Modern Democracy (New Brunswick, NJ: Transaction, 2000).

4. See Michael Mannin's book on Britain and Europe in this series.

5. Quotations in the following section are from Charles de Gaulle, *Memoirs of Hope: Endeavor and Renewal* (New York: Simon and Schuster, 1971), 201–15.

6. See Ronald Tiersky, *François Mitterrand: A Very French President*, 2nd rev. ed. (Lanham, MD: Rowman & Littlefield, 2000), and David S. Bell, *François Mitterrand: A Political Biography* (New York: Polity Press, 2005).

7. Two best-selling books warned against Mitterrand's risky experiment: Raymond Aron, *In Defense of Decadent Europe*, trans. Stephen Cox (South Bend, IN: Regnery/Gateway, 1979), and Jean-François Revel, *The Totalitarian Temptation*, trans. David Hapgood (New York: Penguin, 1978).

8. The best account of the Euro-missile crisis is Josef Joffe, *The Limited Partnership: Europe, the United States and the Burdens of Alliance* (New York: Ballinger, 1987).

9. Joffe, *The Limited Partnership*, 93.

10. Tiersky, *François Mitterrand*, 173.

11. Tiersky, *François Mitterrand*, 174.

12. On these events see Tiersky, *François Mitterrand*, chap. 6. On Bush's and Scowcroft's views, see their joint effort in George H. W. Bush and Brent Scowcroft, *A World Transformed* (New York: Knopf, 1998).

13. One devastating account of French policy is Andrew Wallis, *Silent Accomplice: The Untold Story of France's Role in the Rwandan Genocide* (London: I. B. Tauris, 2006).

14. Jolyon Howorth, *Security and Defense Policy in the European Union* (New York: Palgrave Macmillan, 2007), 36.

15. Philip Stephens, "A Transatlantic Opportunity for Britain," *Financial Times*, May 19, 2008.

16. *The Economist*, April 11, 2009, 11.

17. On past trends, see Daniel S. Hamilton and Joseph P. Quinlan, *Partners in Prosperity: The Changing Geography of the Transatlantic Economy* (Washington, DC: Center for Transatlantic Relations, 2004), and Daniel S. Hamilton and Joseph P. Quinlan, *Globalization and Europe: Prospering in the New Whirled Order* (Baltimore: Center for Transatlantic Relations, Johns Hopkins University, 2008).

18. In 2009, approximately 36,000 French troops were deployed abroad, with 13,000 in military operations in five theaters, 37 percent of which were serving under a NATO flag. NATO Parliamentary Assembly report, April 27–29, 2009, 1.

19. Hubert Védrine, "L'intégration à l'Alliance atlantique ne nous donnera pas plus d'influence," *Le Monde*, March 6, 2009.

20. See Jeremy Shapiro and Benedicte Suzan, "The French Experience of Counter-Terrorism," *Survival* 45, no. 1 (spring 2003): 67–98.

CHAPTER 9: THE UNITED KINGDOM: OLD DILEMMAS AND NEW REALITIES

1. "Britain Snubbed as Bermuda Takes in Uighurs after Deal with US," *The Times* (online edition), June 12, 2009.

2. Speech at Columbia University, New York, January 11, 1952, quoted in Richard Mayne, *The Recovery of Europe: From Devastation to Unity* (New York: Harper and Row, 1970), 204.

3. Speech to the College of Europe, September 20, 1988, http://www.margaret thatcher.org/speeches.

4. Protocol No. 11 (on certain provisions relating to the United Kingdom of Great Britain and Northern Ireland) in *European Union: Selected Instruments Taken from the Treaties* (Luxembourg: Office for Official Publications of the European Communities, 1995), bk. I, vol. I, 609, 610.

5. David Owen, *Balkan Odyssey* (New York: Harcourt Brace, 1995).

6. See the Presidency Conclusions of the Birmingham European Council, October 16, 1992, and the Edinburgh European Council, December 11–12, 1992, in *The European Councils: Conclusions of the Presidency, 1992–1994* (Brussels: European Commission, Directorate-General for Information, 1995).

7. For a firsthand account, see Alastair Campbell and Richard Stott, eds., *The Blair Years: Extracts from the Alastair Campbell Diaries* (London: Arrow Books, 2007).

8. James Dobbins et al., *Europe's Role in Nation-Building* (Santa Monica, CA: Rand, 2008), 25–48.

9. Cabinet Office, *The National Security Strategy of the United Kingdom: Security in an Interdependent World*, Cmd. 7291, March 2008, 4.

10. Samuel Brittan, "How the Budget Hole Developed," *Financial Times*, July 24, 2009.

11. Max Hastings, "What Britain Must Give Up for the Soldiers in Need," *Financial Times*, July 15, 2009.

12. *The National Security Strategy of the United Kingdom*, 7.

13. According to the EU's founding treaties, "Member States which are also members of the United Nations Security Council will concert and keep the other Member States and the High Representative [the EU's top foreign policy official] fully informed. Member States which are members of the Security Council will, in the execution of their functions, defend the positions and interests of the Union." Moreover, when "the Union has defined a position on a subject which is on the United Nations Security Council agenda, those Member States which sit on the Security Council shall request that the High Representative be invited to present the Union's position." Article 34 of the (ex Article 19 TEU) of the consolidated version of the Treaty on European Union (as amended by the Treaty of Lisbon), *Official Journal of the European Union*, C 115, May 9, 2008, 35.

CHAPTER 10: GERMANY: ASCENT TO MIDDLE POWER

1. See, for example, Walter Isaacson et al., "Is One Germany Better Than Two?," November 20, 1989, http://www.time.com/time/time/magazine/article/ 0,9171,959068,00.html.

2. Wolf Lepenies, *Folgen einer unerhörten Begebenheit: Die Deutschen nach der Vereinigung* (Berlin: Siedler, 1996).

3. For a detailed account, see Mary Elise Sarotte, *1989: The Struggle to Create Post-War Europe* (Princeton, NJ: Princeton University Press, 2009).

4. James Sheehan, *Where Have All the Soldiers Gone? The Transformation of Modern Europe* (Boston: Houghton Mifflin, 2008).

5. Jürgen Habermas, *The Past as Future*, trans. Max Pensky (Lincoln: University of Nebraska Press, 1994).

6. Beverly Crawford, *Power and German Foreign Policy: Embedded Hegemony in Europe* (Houndsmill: Palgrave Macmillan, 2007), 176.

7. Dimag Gruppe and Deutsche Gesellschaft für Auswärtige Politik e.V., eds., Trends der deutschen Außenpolitik: Erste außenpolitische Elitestudie (February 2009), 4.

8. Hanns W. Maull, "Germany and the Art of Coalition Building," *European Integration* 30, no. 1 (March 2008): 131–52.

9. Crawford, *Power and German Foreign Policy*, 175.

10. Eurobarometer 70, "Public Opinion in the European Union (Autumn 2008)," http://ec.europa.eu/public_opinion/archives/eb/eb70/eb70_first_en.pdf.

11. Reprinted in Eberhard Rathgeb, *Die engagierte Nation: Deutsche Debatten, 1945–2005* (Munich: Hanser, 2005), 415–16.

12. Ruth Wittlinger and Martin Larose, "No Future for Germany's Past? Collective Memory and German Foreign Policy," *German Politics* 16, no. 4 (December 2007): 492–93.

13. John Kornblum, "The Berlin Stonewall," *The Economist*, October 30, 2008.

14. Franz-Josef Meiers, "Crossing the Red Lines? The Grand Coalition and the Paradox of Foreign Policy," *AICGS Policy Report* 32 (2008): 25.

15. Pew Global Attitudes Project, "Confidence in Obama Lifts U.S. Image around the World," July 23, 2009, http://pewglobal.org/reports/display.php?ReportID=264; Pew Global Attitudes Project, "Key Indicators Database: Confidence in the U.S. President," http://pewglobal.org/database/?indicator=6&country=81&response=Confidence.

16. These views are forcefully articulated by Constanze Stelzenmüller in "Germany's Russia Question: A New *Ostpolitik* for Europe," *Foreign Affairs* 88, no. 2 (March/April 2009): 91–100.

17. "Speech by Federal Chancellor Angela Merkel before the United States Congress," November 3, 2009, http://www.bundesregierung.de/nn_6516/Content/EN/Reden/2009/2009-11-03-merkel-usa-kongress.html.

18. Patrik Schwarz, "Die wahre Angela," *Die Zeit*, March 5, 2009, http://www.zeit.de/2009/11/Buecher-machen-Politik (author's translation).

CHAPTER 11: ITALY: THE ASTUTENESS AND ANXIETIES OF A SECOND-RANK POWER

1. Antonio Varsori, *L'Italia nelle relazioni internazionali dal 1943 al 1992* (Bari: Laterza, 1998), 48.

2. Elisabetta Brighi, "One Man Alone? A *Longue Durée* Approach to Italy's Foreign Policy under Berlusconi," *Government and Opposition* 41, no. 2 (2006): 280.

3. Tommaso Padoa-Schioppa, "Italy and Europe: A Fruitful Interaction," *Daedalus* 130, no. 2 (spring 2001): 24.

4. Leopoldo Nuti, "Commitment to NATO and Domestic Politics: The Italian Case and Some Comparative Remarks," *Contemporary European History* 7, no. 3 (November 1998): 370.

5. Charles de Gaulle, *Memoirs of Hope* (New York: Simon and Schuster, 1971), 191

6. Leopoldo Nuti, *La sfida nucleare: La politica estera italiana e le armi atomiche 1945–1991* (Bologna, Il Mulino, 2008), 362, author's translation.

7. Nuti, "Commitment to NATO and Domestic Politics," 373.

8. Padoa-Schioppa, "Italy and Europe," 24.

9. Padoa-Schioppa, "Italy and Europe," 26–30.

10. Arnold Wolfers, *Discord and Collaboration: Essays in International Politics* (Baltimore: Johns Hopkins University Press, 1962), 74–75.

11. Filippo Andreatta and Christopher Hill, "Italy," in *National Policy Making and the European Community: National Defence and European Security Integration*, ed. Jolyon Howorth and Anand Menon (London: Routledge, 1997), 67.

12. Beniamino Andreatta, "Una politica estera per l'Italia," *Il Mulino*, no. 349 (September/October 1993): 881–91. See also, in English, Roberto Aliboni and Ettore Greco, "Foreign Policy Renationalization and Internationalism in the Italian Debate," *International Affairs* 72, no. 1 (1996): 43–51.

13. Paolo Tripodi, "Operation Alba: A Necessary and Successful Preventative Deployment," *International Peacekeeping* 9, no, 4 (2002): 98.

14. Quotations from an essay by Osvaldo Croci, "Forced Ally? Italy and Operation Allied Force," in *Italian Politics: The Faltering Transition*, ed. Mark Gilbert and Gianfranco Pasquino (Oxford: Berghahn, 2000), 33–50 at 39 and 42.

15. Andreatta and Hill, "Italy," 78.

16. NATO press release PR/CP(2009)009, February 19, 2009.

17. Filippo di Robilant, "Quale europeismo senza più Ruggiero?," *La Repubblica*, January 9, 2002.

18. Osvaldo Croci, "Much Ado about Little: The Foreign Policy of the Second Berlusconi Government," *Modern Italy* 10, no. 1 (2005): 63.

19. Mark Gilbert, "Playing the Wrong Tunes? Italy and the European Union in 2004," in *Italian Politics: Quo Vadis?*, ed. Carlo Guarnieri and James L. Newell (Oxford: Berghahn, 2005), 114. The quotations in the previous paragraph are from this source.

20. Croci, "Much Ado about Little," 66.

21. Franco Frattini, "Exclusive Summits Will Deepen Europe's Divisions," *Financial Times*, February 18, 2004.

22. Ferdinando Salleo and Nicoletta Pirozzi, "Italy and the United Nations Security Council," *The International Spectator* 43, no. 2 (2008): 100.

23. See the essays in the symposium "Italy's Foreign Policy in the Mediterranean," *Modern Italy* 13, no. 2 (2008).

CHAPTER 12: POLAND AND EASTERN EUROPE: HISTORICAL NARRATIVES AND THE RETURN TO EUROPE

1. Conversation with the author.
2. Lecture at the Jagiellonian University, Polish-British Round Table Meeting, May 9, 2009.
3. Letter quoted by Strobe Talbott in *The Russia Hand* (New York: Random House, 2002), 231.
4. Letter quoted by Talbott in *The Russia Hand*, 94.
5. See Timothy Snyder, *Sketches from a Secret War* (New Haven, CT: Yale University Press, 2005).

Index

About the Contributors

Krzysztof Bobinski is head of Unia & Polska, a pro-European organization in Poland. Born in the United Kingdom, he read modern history at Magdalen College, Oxford. He was for many years the Warsaw correspondent of the *Financial Times*. Later he published *Unia & Polska*, a magazine devoted to European integration issues. He contributes to publications such as *Open Democracy* and the *European Voice* and comments on current affairs for Polish electronic media.

Mark Gilbert is associate professor of contemporary history at the University of Trento and adjunct professor of European studies at Johns Hopkins SAIS, Bologna. His books include *The Italian Revolution: The End of Politics, Italian Style?* (1995) and *Surpassing Realism? The Politics of European Integration since 1945* (2003). He currently is writing a political history of Europe since the 1960s.

David Shambaugh is professor of political science and international affairs and director of the China Policy Program in the Elliott School of International Affairs at George Washington University. He is also a nonresident senior fellow in the Foreign Policy Studies Program at the Brookings Institution. He is a leading international authority on contemporary China.

Philip Stephens is associate editor and chief political commentator of the *Financial Times*. He is author of *Politics and the Pound* (1996) and *Tony Blair: A Biography* (2004). He is a member of the *Financial Times* editorial board, a director of the Ditchley Foundation, and an adviser to the Institute for Strategic Dialogue and the Franco-British Colloque.

Paul Taylor is associate editor of Reuters, based in Paris, specializing in European affairs. He has been a foreign correspondent with the international news agency for thirty-two years, working in Paris, Brussels, Berlin, Bonn, London, and the Middle East. He contributed to Ronald Tiersky, ed., *Europe Today* (1999) and Elie Barnavi et al., *Les frontières de l'Europe* (2001).

Ronald Tiersky is Joseph B. Eastman '04 Professor of Political Science at Amherst College. He is general editor of the Europe Today series and writes on France, Europe, transatlantic relations, and just war doctrines. Among his books are *François Mitterrand: A Very French President*, 2nd ed. (2003); with Alex Tiersky, *Europe: A Year of Living Dangerously* (2004); and *Euro-Skepticism: A Reader* (2001). With Erik Jones he edits the Europe Today series textbook, *Europe Today: A Twenty-First Century Introduction*.

Nathalie Tocci is senior fellow at the Istituto Affari Internazionali, Rome, and at the Transatlantic Academy, Washington, D.C. Her books include *The EU and Conflict Resolution* (2007) and *EU Accession Dynamics and Conflict Resolution in Cyprus* (2004). Tocci is the winner of the 2008 Anna Lindh award for the study of European foreign policy.

John Van Oudenaren directs the World Digital Library (http://www.wdl .org) project at the Library of Congress. Previously, he was chief of the European Division at the Library of Congress; a senior researcher at RAND; director of RAND's European office in Delft, the Netherlands; and a member of the policy planning staff of the U.S. Department of State. He is the author of several books and numerous articles on European politics, international relations, and U.S. foreign policy, including *Uniting Europe: An Introduction to the European Union* (2004).

Benedetta Voltolini is a PhD candidate at the London School of Economics and Political Science. She writes on the impact of nonstate actors on EU foreign policymaking and the Israeli–Palestinian conflict. She is a research associate of the Istituto Affari Internazionali in Rome.

Helga A. Welsh is professor of political science at Wake Forest University. Her recent publications on German politics have focused on transitional justice, German unification, and higher-education reform. She is one of the editors of "German History in Documents and Images," a Web-based project administered by the German Historical Institute (Washington, D.C.).